ECO-INQUIRY

A guide to ecological learning experiences for
the upper elementary/middle grades

Kathleen Hogan
Institute of Ecosystem Studies

KENDALL/HUNT PUBLISHING COMPANY
4050 Westmark Drive   Dubuque, Iowa 52002

Eco-Inquiry Project Team

Author and Project Director:	Kathleen Hogan
Project Co-Director:	Alan Berkowitz
Project Coordinator:	Lisa Morganstern
Evaluation Research Assistant:	JoEllen Fisherkeller
Ecology Research Assistant:	Erik Lillescov

Eco-Inquiry Production Team

Editor:	Susan Carnahan Vodrey
Designers:	Jan Milstead
	Richard Deon
Illustrators:	Eric Angeloch
	Lisa Morganstern
	Carol Morley
	Christian Angeloch
	Sharon Okada
Cover Illustration:	Gina Palmer, Speckled Bird Graphics
Cover Design:	Ed Atkeson, Berg Design
Page Layout:	Deborah Sottile
	Susan Napack
	Judith Moran
	Terri Sileno

TO PLACE AN ORDER
1-800-228-0810
CALL

Copyright © 1994 by Institute of Ecosystem Studies, Box AB, Millbrook, NY 12545

ISBN 0-8403-9584-1

Printed in the United States of America
10 9 8 7 6

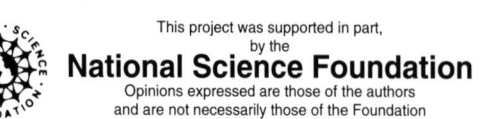

This project was supported in part,
by the
National Science Foundation
Opinions expressed are those of the authors
and are not necessarily those of the Foundation

ACKNOWLEDGEMENTS

Since its inception as a pilot program in 1985, Eco-Inquiry has grown into its current form with the help of many people.

First, thanks go to the staff members of the Institute of Ecosystem Studies who created the positive context within which Eco-Inquiry was born and nurtured. Particular thanks to Alan Berkowitz whose input and dedication to the project have been invaluable, and to Gene Likens and Joe Warner, whose unwavering support has helped bring Eco-Inquiry to fruition.

Thank you to members of the Eco-Inquiry Project Advisory Board for their perspectives and support: Michelle Cambier, New York City Board of Education, New York, NY; Paul Connolly, Institute for Writing and Thinking, Bard College, Annandale-on-Hudson, NY; Olive Covington, formerly at National Science Resources Center, Washingon, D.C.; Willard Jacobson, Teachers College, Columbia University, New York, NY; Gary Kreamer, Delaware Division of Fish and Wildlife, Smyrna, DE; Sally McCraken, Matthew Paterson Elementary School, Patterson, NY; Steward Pickett, Institute of Ecosystem Studies, Millbrook, NY; Pat Price, National Center for Improving Science Education, Washington, D.C.; and Karen Worth, Education Development Center and Wheelock College, Boston, MA.

The Evaluation Steering Committee—Joan Boykoff Baron, Ted Chittenden, and Grant Wiggins—helped shape the evaluation strategies that provided crucial information which fed the development of the curriculum and its embedded assessments.

Sincere thanks to the following scientists and naturalists who reviewed portions of Eco-Inquiry for content accuracy: David Andow, Alan Berkowitz, Joseph Boyer, Bryon Brown, Charles Canham, Margaret Carreiro, Jeff Cherry, Jon Cole, Peter Feinsinger, Geoff Hammerson, Karen Hollweg, Elaine Ingham, Gary Lovett, Joseph Mcauliffe, Lee Metzgar, Richard Ostfeld, Rob Parmalee, Jon Piper, Michael Plagens, Richard Pouyat, Mary Price, Catherine Reed, Louis Sorkin, Linda Wallace, Jim Wernz, and Janet Wright.

Other reviewers who provided valuable feedback on pilot versions of Eco-Inquiry include: Craig Altobell, Shirley Campbell, Meg Clark, Ellen Doris, Marianne Krasny, Shari Tishman, and Julie Winterbottom.

Gratitude also goes to staff members from the following institutions who have served as the Eco-Inquiry National Dissemination Team by offering workshops and teacher support in their regions: Cranbrook Institute of Science, Bloomfield Hills, MI; Desert Botanical Garden, Phoenix, AZ; Fernbank Science Center, Atlanta, GA; Missouri Botanical Garden, St. Louis, MO; and Oregon Museum of Science and Industry, Portland, OR.

Eco-Inquiry has been piloted in several hundred classrooms in fifteen states. Many thanks to the following teachers and school administrators for helping to shape Eco-Inquiry during its formative pilot stages: Adelaide Adams, Craig Altobell, Carol Barman, Pam Bendyk, Fran Bodnar, Kay Carr, Walter Cehanowicz, John Clemente, Sarah Coppersmith, Frank Day, Jane Donahue, Doug Edebohls, Vicky Evans, Mariane Geraghty, Roberta Green, Lisa Gustafson, Joyce Harris, Judy Joyner, John Kemnitzer, Carol Kolb, Gary Kreamer, John Kroha, Susan

Lewis, Katina Lotakas, Diane Lusier, Christina McCalla, Joan McEllhatten, Karen McIntyre, Stephanie Mathews, Evangeline Mercado, Jayne Meschter, JoAnn Miles, Cathy Moore, Trishia Murphy, Elaine Noe, Linda Olsen, Guantella Palmer, Effie Panagiotopoulos, Barb Pepper, Dolores Pepple, Elisabeth Petersen, Mary Pezzo, Joe Phaneuf, Sally Pittman-Smith, Felicia Pomarico, Suzanne Posner, Gary Post, Charlie Powers, Ruth Ransom, Frank San Felice, Charles Sandusky, Tracy Schmidt, Carol Seem, Suzanne Slankard, Steve Spiegel, Mary Stevens, Ann Stewart, Al Tate, Darlene Taylor, Mary Valentino, Rose Villani, Wendy Vishnesky, Mikki Weiss, Tim White, Larry Wilson, Bill Yaeger, and John Yarachowicz.

Thanks to the National Science Foundation, the New York State Council on the Arts, and the Mary Flager Cary Charitable Trust for the funding that helped make Eco-Inquiry possible.

Final appreciation goes to the multitudes and diversity of students who have experienced and shaped Eco-Inquiry, and whose minds and spirits have been, and continue to be, its inspiration.

The Institute of Ecosystem Studies (IES) is a research and education facility located in Millbrook, New York. IES is dedicated to creating, disseminating, and applying knowledge about ecological systems. This knowledge is created through scientific research, disseminated through teaching, writing, and exhibits, and applied through participating in making decisions about the ecological management of natural resources. Through these avenues, IES promotes a broader awareness of the importance of ecological relationships to human welfare.

TABLE OF CONTENTS

OPENING

Introduction

Assessment Tools

MODULES

Module 1: Who Eats What?

Module 2: Decomposer Dynamics

Module 3: Cycles—From Rot to Radishes

Appendices

Appendix A

Appendix B

Appendix C

INTRODUCTION

Picture your classroom as a "collaboratory." The room is buzzing with investigations and interactions. Lists of ideas and questions hang on the walls. Students are asking each other: *How could we figure that out? What does the evidence say?*

In your collaboratory there is as much reflection as action. Through writing and dialogue, your students are building scientific understandings and awareness of their own growth as inquirers. They're comfortable discovering gaps in their reasoning and searching for better explanations.

Eco-Inquiry provides in-depth learning experiences to help you create this kind of learning environment in your classroom. As an Eco-Inquiry teacher, you'll be an experimenter, guide, challenger, encourager, innovator, analyst, consultant, and mediator. Most importantly, you'll be an inquirer along with your students.

Eco-Inquiry modules contain investigations that build students' understanding of ecological processes in their local environment. The modules present real-world projects and challenges that unfold over time. After experiencing one, two, or all three Eco-Inquiry modules, your students will be more reflective, creative, and self-confident thinkers. They'll know more about the ecological processes in their everyday environment, and will understand how their actions can have positive and negative effects on ecosystems.

You and your students are about to embark on a wondrous journey of ecological exploration and inquiry. Enjoy!

USING THE ECO-INQUIRY MODULES

This guide contains three modules that can stand alone or be used in sequence. They can be used at one grade level or across several grades. The modules have been shaped and tested primarily in fifth and sixth grade classrooms, but have also proven successful with seventh and eighth graders. Many school districts favor using Module 1 with fifth graders, and Modules 2 and 3 with sixth graders.

Instructional Sequence

Over the course of several weeks, each module moves through a four-part instructional sequence:

■ **Activating Ideas.** Topics are introduced and students are given opportunities to share prior ideas, as well as to generate new ideas and questions to investigate.

■ **Investigating.** Students explore the ecology of the local environment through hands-on experiments.

■ **Processing for Understanding.** Students formalize their conceptual understanding by processing the findings of their investigations and learning new terminology.

■ **Applying and Assessing.** Students reflect on their learning by communicating and using information and skills they acquired during the module in meaningful contexts.

Module Overviews

Module 1

Who Eats What? (4–5 weeks)

Topic: Food Webs

Students fulfill a request from the local community to survey what's living on a plot of land, such as the schoolyard or a neighborhood park. Investigations of animals' feeding habits help students make a food web of their study site. They also write environmental impact statements to trace how one change in the site could affect the entire food web.

Module 3

Cycles—From Rot to Radishes (6–7 weeks)

Topic: Nutrient Cycling

Students do research for a firm called Green Resources of the World Unlimited (GROW) to test the effects of compost tea on radish growth. They also explore plant and soil nutrient connections in the schoolyard.

Module 2

Decomposer Dynamics (4–5 weeks)

Topic: Decomposition

Students explore decomposition outdoors and in the classroom to become familiar with microbes, then do research to determine the best conditions for making plants decompose in a classroom decomposition chamber.

Lesson Format

Each Eco-Inquiry module contains from seven to ten lessons. The detailed lesson plans communicate strategies that have worked successfully in a range of classrooms. However, your students bring different prior experiences, interests, social maturity, developmental levels, and personal needs to science class. Eco-Inquiry lessons come to life in a different way for each teacher, and differently each year for new groups of students.

The descriptions below highlight the type of information you'll find in each lesson.

Action Synopsis

A one-sentence summary of the lesson is followed by a list of activity steps for each session. Many lessons span more than one day and thus have several sessions. The estimated time needed for each session is given. When a session occurs outdoors, this is specified next to the time.

Each activity step is followed by an icon and a descriptor. The icons symbolize four types of learning processes, and the descriptors further specify those processes:

 Building a Framework

 Developing Knowledge

 Inquiring

 Applying

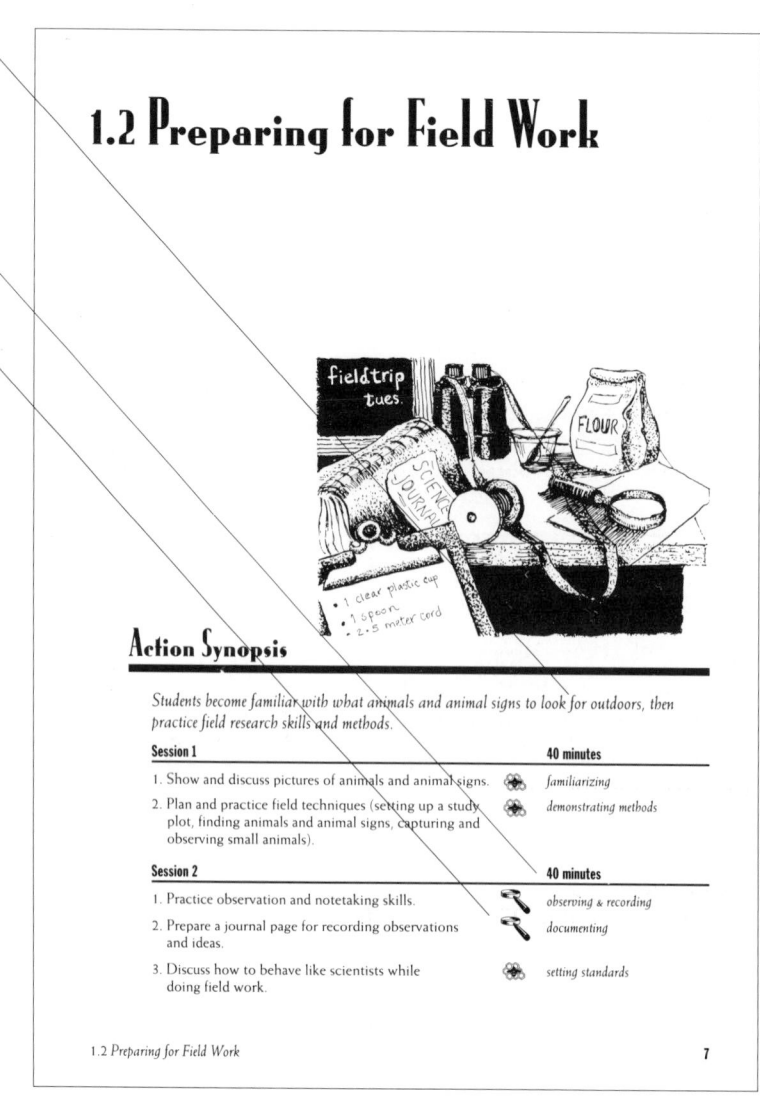

1.2 Preparing for Field Work

Action Synopsis

Students become familiar with what animals and animal signs to look for outdoors, then practice field research skills and methods.

Session 1		40 minutes
1. Show and discuss pictures of animals and animal signs.		*familiarizing*
2. Plan and practice field techniques (setting up a study plot, finding animals and animal signs, capturing and observing small animals).		*demonstrating methods*

Session 2		40 minutes
1. Practice observation and notetaking skills.		*observing & recording*
2. Prepare a journal page for recording observations and ideas.		*documenting*
3. Discuss how to behave like scientists while doing field work.		*setting standards*

1.2 Preparing for Field Work   7

Desired Outcomes

This section lists the lesson's main learning objectives to help you focus your teaching of the lesson, as well as help you take stock of your students' learning at the end of the lesson.

What You'll Need

Lists of the materials you'll need for the lesson are organized by sessions, and indicate whether you'll need them for the whole class, groups, pairs, or individual students. A complete list of materials used in each module, and suggestions for where to obtain them, appear in the Appendix (pages 383–389).

Vocabulary

This feature lists definitions of science terms introduced in the lesson. The vocabulary words appear in capital letters the first time they're used within a lesson. They are not listed or defined again when they appear in subsequent lessons or modules. The Appendix contains a complete list of vocabulary words used in all of the modules (pages 390–392).

Desired Outcomes

Throughout the lesson, check that students:

✓ Are familiar with some of the animals and animal signs they might see outdoors.

✓ Know how to gather evidence of what animals eat.

✓ Know how to set up a study plot and where to look for animals within the plot.

✓ Are able to use humane techniques for capturing and observing small animals.

✓ Have sharper observation skills, and understand the difference between an observation and an idea.

✓ Are ready to behave like scientists outdoors.

What You'll Need

Session 1

For the class:
- ❑ overhead transparencies of animals and animal signs (see "Getting Ready")
- ❑ set of field equipment:
  - pointed metal or wooden stake, about 60 cm long
  - 2.5 meter cord tied to a metal ring that fits over the stake
  - clear plastic cup
  - plastic spoon
  - cotton swab
  - index card
  - small eraser or piece of chalk

Session 2

For each student:
- ❑ hand lens
- ❑ item to observe (see "Getting Ready")

Vocabulary

FIELD - Scientists' name for the outdoors.

STUDY PLOT - A small piece of land used for observations.

Module 1: *Who Eats What?*

Action Narrative

This is the heart of each Eco-Inquiry lesson. The bold text represents the teacher's words, and the plain text suggests how to facilitate students' learning. The bold text is intended to communicate the flow of the lesson in a friendly, narrative style. It is not intended to put actual words in your mouth, or to limit your creativity or spontaneous adaptations to students' needs and interests.

Several subsections, highlighted with decorative borders, occur within the Action Narrative:

 helpful teaching hints

 supplementary background information

 open-ended questions

 children's ideas about ecological concepts

 caution statements

Also, two icons appear in the margins:

 when students are writing;

 when students are working outdoors

Getting Ready

This section outlines the preparations you'll need to make before each session of the lesson.

Getting Ready

Session 1

♦ Make overhead transparencies using pictures from the *Who Eats What* guide (pages xx-xx). First find the habitat description that most closely resembles your study site. Then choose pictures of a few signs of animals from pages xx-xx, and several animal pictures from pages xx-xx. Animals students are most likely to see include squirrels, sow bugs, millipedes, beetles, and spiders. You might want to enlarge the pictures on a copier so that you have just one image per overhead.

Session 2

♦ Gather enough objects so that each student (or every two students) has something to use to practice observation skills. Small stones, dead leaves, pine cones, twigs, or pieces of fruit are appropriate materials. Using items that are similar to one another will allow you to extend the activity by mixing them and challenging students to find the object they observed.

Action Narrative

Session 1

Let's look at some pictures of animal signs we might see on our study site.

Show and discuss the animal signs overheads you've made, pointing out that looking on or among plants provides many clues about animals. Also emphasize that finding animals and animal signs takes careful observation and patience.

Ongoing Assessment

This section encourages assessment as a daily process by providing ideas to help both students and teachers reflect on what was learned during the lesson. **Student Reflections** offers optional writing prompts to motivate students to record their thoughts about the lesson in their journals. It also suggests that students send messages to their peers using a form called C-Mail. (For more information about C-Mail, see page 10.) **Teacher Reflections** lists questions to help you assess the status of your students' skills and understandings.

Extensions

These suggestions of additional optional activities related to the lesson's theme can be done by the whole class, or as group or individual special projects. The activities extend students' learning across the curriculum.

Ongoing Assessment

Student Reflections

Have students send a C-Mail message or record thoughts in their journals. Optional writing prompts include:

The most interesting, amazing, or surprising discovery I made was...

Something I figured out was...

Some things I did that are like what a scientist does are...

Is the site a good place for animals to live? Why or why not?

Teacher Reflections

❑ Were students able to use their observations to generate ideas about what animals live on the site and what they eat?

❑ Were they able to compile their findings in a logical and useful way?

❑ Can they define an ecosystem and explain what makes their study site an ecosystem?

Extensions

Concept Map. Introduce concept mapping to students (see pages xx-xx). Select all or some of the concept map cards on pages xx-xx, then copy one set of cards for each group of 3–4 students. Help students construct concept maps that display their prior ideas about ecosystems. Have them save their concept maps so that they can compare them to maps they'll make as an extension to Lesson 1.8, to see how their knowledge grows.

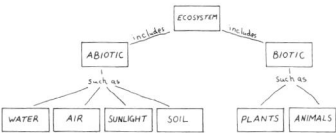

Mini-Ecosystem. Help students plan and make a terrarium that functions like a mini-ecosystem. They can start by writing a list of ingredients and what each needs to stay alive. Gallon jars, old aquaria, and 2-liter plastic bottles are good containers. Suggest that they plant some seeds in the terrarium as well as whole plants. Post an observations chart next to the terrarium for students to fill in. Keep the terrarium partly covered and out of direct sun. It should not need frequent watering.

Building A Community of Inquiring Minds

Scientific knowledge building is a collaborative process. Scientists develop ideas by expressing and refining them with other scientists. In a classroom, students can also construct knowledge and skills within a community of peers. Tackling questions together, communicating ideas and results, and convincing others of the validity of conclusions leads to meaningful science learning.

Encouraging Dialogue about Students' Ideas

Students come to science class knowing everyday meanings for words that scientists use in specialized ways. They also have personal explanations for scientific principles that they've encountered in daily life. These thoughts and experiences provide a starting point for science learning. When students' existing conceptions are sought out and valued, the whole community of learners is enriched by a range of perspectives.

Eco-Inquiry lessons encourage students to express, explain, and reshape their ideas by interacting with their peers as much as with the natural phenomena they're studying. When you ask students to explain what they're doing, observing, and thinking, you create an environment that supports this kind of sharing. It will take time for students to get used to engaging in exploratory, rather than presentational dialogue. Many students are accustomed to interpreting a request to elaborate on something they've said as a sign that they've given a wrong answer. You'll need to explain that you and other class members appreciate, and want to understand, each person's thinking, so that together you can create new knowledge. Many heads are better than one, but only when each head understands and can build on what's in the other heads!

Eco-Inquiry lessons suggest open-ended questions that will help your students process their experiences. You can probe students' responses to these questions by asking, *Could you explain that so I'm sure that I understand what you're saying? That's interesting—can you say more? Would anyone like to build on her line of thinking?* The purpose of these interchanges is to help students refine and expand their ideas by thinking aloud, and to withhold your own knowledge about the topic being discussed until students are ready for input.

Using Writing to Promote Interaction and Reflection

In a community of inquiry, writing can flow from, or initiate, conversations about ideas. Writing in science class need not be limited to lab reports.

JOURNALS Help your students make science journals before beginning Eco-Inquiry. A 3-ring binder makes an ideal journal because it allows students to create sections, such as for daily reflections and data charts. Students can easily add handouts and field notes to binders, as well as remove journal pages to add to portfolios. Clipboards, which can be made from cardboard and a clothespin or rubber band, are convenient to have so that students don't have to take their binders outdoors.

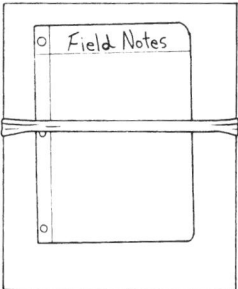

Whether you suggest a focus for students' journal entries, or just give them time to write their thoughts after a lesson, it is important to establish journal writing as a regular habit. When students get used to writing in journals, writing will become a way for them to make connections between familiar and new experiences, and to generate, as well as document ideas.

In order to maintain an interest in journal writing, students need to see that their writing has a purpose. Have volunteers share journal passages aloud as a way to initiate class meetings. Also, read and write comments on their journals occasionally, and encourage students to include a variety of forms of writing in their journals:

♦ *Reflections.* Optional writing prompts are provided at the end of each Eco-Inquiry lesson to help students generate and record thoughts about their learning experiences.

♦ *Quick Writes.* Taking a minute or two to have students write at the beginning, middle, or end of a lesson can help focus their thoughts. Prompts for quick writes include: *What are we learning? What questions do you have? What are your thoughts about this? How do you feel about . . . ?*

♦ *Learning Logs.* Students can keep track of their learning in tables with categories such as:

   What I know
   What I wonder
   What I found out
   What I want to try
   What I'm good at

♦ *Problem Solving and Planning Logs.* Writing out the steps they took, or plan to take, to solve a problem or accomplish a task can make students more aware of how they tend to do things, and help them realize new possible approaches for the future.

♦ *Double Entries.* When students are reading science books, they can jot down notes about the text on one page, and on the facing page write their own response to what the author has said.

WALL CHARTS Down-loading the ideas and questions that emerge during a class discussion onto a poster, provides a tangible record of the group's thoughts at different points in time. This helps students compare their thinking at the beginning and end of a unit of study. They might revisit lists of questions to decide which can and can't be answered through science investigations. The lists can also express evolving perspectives on topics such as "Being a Good Observer" and "Being a Team Player."

STORIES Science experiences can stimulate students' imaginations and creativity. Stories are a comfortable form of writing for students, so they're an ideal way for them to process and share aspects of science experiences that they've found interesting or meaningful.

PERSUASIVE WRITING Several Eco-Inquiry assessment tasks ask students to create written pieces that will convince an audience to adopt their point of view. This provides a fun way for students to organize their thoughts and connect ideas.

C-MAIL C-Mail can stand for community, classroom, or company mail. The C-Mail form (page 17) takes advantage of students' attraction to sending notes to their friends. Exchanging C-Mail messages gives students' writing immediate purpose and relevance. A variety of sentence starters are provided on the C-Mail form to help students focus their messages.

Some Eco-Inquiry teachers have set up C-Mail mailboxes that are exciting hubs for community interchange. After students have received a response to their C-Mail messages, they can add the sheet to their journals, and later choose significant ones to go in their portfolios.

Supporting Diverse Strengths, Styles, and Perspectives

Science lessons that seek out and value students' ideas and prior experiences send a strong message that each individual has something important to contribute. However, you'll need to take extra steps to counteract prevalent images of science as largely an endeavor for white males with similar personalities and thinking styles. These images may limit many of your students' science aspirations. Here are some ways to make sure that all of your students reach their science potential:

◆ Challenge and respond to girls in the same ways that you respond to boys. Let girls solve their own problems, rather than coming to their aid too quickly. Draw them out during discussions, and call on them as frequently as you call on boys. Encourage reluctant girls to manipulate materials, instead of just observing.

◆ Reinforce creative and divergent thinking styles, which are as valuable in science as logical thinking. Also acknowledge that emotions such as elation and disappointment are part of doing science.

◆ Encourage students from different cultures to share their perspectives about the topics you're studying. They may have different ways of viewing ecological processes, environments, and organisms based on their family's cultural heritage.

◆ Invite professional scientists to visit your class. Try to find people who reflect the diversity of your students—women and men from different ethnic groups, as well as people with physical disabilities. If you're not able to have such people visit in person, work with your librarian to collect books and articles about a variety of scientists.

◆ Have high expectations for the science achievement of all your students.

You might want to begin Eco-Inquiry with the following activity developed to help students confront their stereotypes of scientists.

Dress the Scientist

(40 minutes)

Preparations

◆ Put a variety of clothing (e.g., skirt, shirt, blazer, rain slicker, pants) into a duffle bag or suitcase. Add a white lab coat and a variety of science props (e.g., plastic gloves, test tube, graduated cylinder, forceps, laboratory flask).

◆ Make three necklaces by cutting three circles from oak tag or cardboard. Decorate them with doilies or wrapping paper. Write three labels: "Knowledge," "Skills," and "Attitudes." Glue one label to each circle. Punch a hole in the top of each circle and insert a loop of yarn large enough to fit over a student's head. Put the finished necklaces in a manilla envelope.

Activity Sequence

① *Imagining a Scientist*

• Ask students to get out their journals and a pencil, then close their eyes and listen.

• Dim the lights. Help students imagine a scientist by saying the following, pausing to give them time to develop mental pictures: *Make your mind a blank screen. Now, on that screen, call up a picture of a scientist. Take a good look at this person. What does the person look like? What is the person wearing? What is the person doing? Where is the scientist?*

• Once students have developed their images, have them open their eyes and write and/or draw a description of their scientist.

② *Sharing Images*

• Ask students to describe their images of scientists. Make a class list of the features they mention.

• After several students have shared their images, read the items on the list and tally how many students raise their hands to indicate that their image also included that feature.

- Summarize by having students name the features that were most common. Most likely, they will have pictured a white male scientist who wears a white coat, has wild hair and eyes, and is holding a frothing test tube. It is important also to point out the characteristics mentioned least often, such as a female scientist, a person of color, a person in regular clothing, or someone making observations outdoors.

③ Dress the Scientist

- Choose one student to come to the front of the room to be dressed as a scientist. Choose another to select clothing and props for the scientist.

- Instruct the dresser to choose from the suitcase whatever would be appropriate for a scientist to wear and use. The dresser can hold up each item to solicit opinions from the rest of the class.

- When the scientist is fully dressed, ask the class what else the scientist would need.

④ Beneath the Surface

- Tell students that you have symbols of three things that the model scientist is missing. Have them suggest what these could be.

- Take the necklaces from the envelope one at a time, and put them on the scientist. Ask students for examples of knowledge, skills, and attitudes that scientists need.

⑤ Getting Down to Essentials

- Have students name which items the model scientist should remove that are not essential for doing good science. Usually they decide to take away everything they've added but the three necklaces.

⑥ The Scientific Self

- Lead a discussion about stereotypes of scientists. Ask students where they get their images of scientists. Often they can easily separate their images of fictitious scientists from those they have of real scientists. But even if they realize that most scientists do not look and behave like mad scientists, students might have other stereotypes about the kinds of people or personalities that are best suited for science. Have them consider how these ideas influence their own attitudes toward doing science and pursuing scientific careers.

- Have students brainstorm positive scientific characteristics that they already have. You might also want to have students write journal entries recounting events when they've used their own scientific qualities. Encourage them to share their writings with partners.

Facilitating Collaborative Learning

The majority of Eco-Inquiry activities are designed for small group work. Although collaboration in science classrooms models the practices of the professional scientific community, this is only one reason for its use in Eco-Inquiry. Most importantly, collaborative learning uses to advantage the social interests and inclinations of students in the upper elementary/middle grades. When students work together they learn and retain more, are more motivated, develop social skills and confidence, and take responsibility for their own learning.

Working in collaborative groups will take time to get used to, both for you and your students. A good way to begin is by acknowledging that collaboration is an explicit goal that takes work to achieve. Students need to understand that collaborative learning goes beyond sitting in groups—its purpose is to enable them to do and talk about science together. They should also realize that they'll need to focus on their group process as well as on their science tasks, especially while beginning to develop habits of productive interactions.

Much of the vision and responsibility for collaborative learning can come from your students. They already have sensibilities about what behaviors encourage and squelch positive interactions. Before beginning Eco-Inquiry, have students brainstorm two lists: one of the responsibilities of individual group members, and the other of responsibilities of the group as a whole. These lists can stay posted in the room, and be enhanced as the year progresses.

Each person in the group is responsible for:

doing a fair share of the work
encouraging and helping each other
not using put-downs
sharing ideas and questions
listening when someone talks
trying to understand other points of view
being positive, even when saying that
    you disagree with an idea
being a leader, not a boss

Each group is responsible for:

getting organized quickly and quietly
staying together - no wandering off
taking turns at different jobs
trying to solve our own problems
trying to answer our own questions
not disturbing other groups by being loud
having fun, but getting our work done, too

Another option is to have the class develop its own *Guidelines for Groupwork Manual*. Start by brainstorming different topics the manual should cover, such as:

Part 1. *Being Supportive Group Members*
- How do we encourage everyone to participate?

Part 2. *Sharing Responsibilities*
- How do we make sure everyone does equal work, and gets a chance to do different jobs?

Part 3. *Making Group Decisions*
- What are ways to make sure everyone agrees with a decision?

Part 4. *Making Sure Everyone Understands*
- How can we help each other learn?

Part 5. *Dealing with Difficulties*

- What if someone won't participate?

- What if one or two people do all the talking?

- What if someone always takes over all the time?

- What if some people can't get along, or can't agree on anything?

- What if someone is absent a lot?

Students can develop ideas for each section of the manual as a class, or different groups can prepare drafts of different sections. Students could also role-play what the positive and negative interactions they're documenting look and sound like (e.g., smiling and nodding when someone shares an idea and saying *I like your idea, but what if we . . .;* versus rolling your eyes and saying *That's so stupid—how could we ever do that?*).

Getting Started with Collaborative Learning

Who should be in which groups? Create groups that are heterogeneous as often as possible, so that students learn to appreciate and tolerate perspectives and styles that differ from their own. Keep the groups together for several weeks so that students have time to adjust to one another.

Should each group member have a specific job? It is important that students share leadership within their groups. One way to accomplish this is by having each person be in charge of a different task. A popular way to manage group learning is to define a variety of roles, such as Recorder, Materials Retriever, Coach, and Reporter, and have students take turns fulfilling each of them. However, the primary role for each student should be Explorer, so make sure that special roles don't preclude anyone from having a piece of the hands-on science action. Also, if you want all group members to work as often as possible on skills such as notetaking and encouraging their peers, you can make these everyone's roles.

How can I help each student be accountable for the group's work? If you randomly choose one student to speak on behalf of the group, or one person's papers to represent the group's work, students will quickly realize that the quality of each individual's work should be up to the group's standards. These random checks help students monitor how well they're meeting the goals of collaborative learning. Also, having students do self-evaluations of their group process helps them take responsibility for group work (see the "Group Work Evaluation" form, page 42).

What is my role during group work? Think of yourself as a consultant to student groups. Having students rely on themselves to solve problems helps them grow as independent learners, and helps you maintain your sanity as a teacher of hands-on science. When students ask for your input, start by asking them questions to see if they're able to arrive at their own solutions. You can also use questions to suggest new approaches (*Have you tried . . .?*), or to remind them of a technique they're neglecting to use (*Are you making sure each person's ideas are being heard?*).

What if some groups finish earlier than others? Anticipate that groups will work at different rates. When a group finishes early, first check to make sure they've done everything thoroughly. Have in mind other things they can do if they've gone as far as they can with their task, such as looking through your collection of ecology books, writing in their journals, or working on "Extensions" activities that are provided at the end of each lesson.

How should the students and I deal with conflicts? When conflicts arise, you may need to remind students that the ground rule for group work is that everyone is respected and included. But it is also important to acknowledge that working together is not always easy. Often students who create difficulties for their group need opportunities to prove to themselves that they can make valuable contributions. Finding these opportunities is preferable to removing students from their groups, since their troubles are likely to follow them to a new group. Recognizing a group's efforts at trying different strategies to improve cooperation will help them feel that their struggles are worthwhile and valued.

THE COMPANY OPTION

Many teachers begin Eco-Inquiry by transforming their class into an ecological research company. A classroom company provides a context for emphasizing the collaborative nature of science. Students (particularly fifth and sixth graders) enjoy the sense of excitement, autonomy, and professionalism of running their own company.

The company can be modeled after scientific institutes that do basic research and publish their findings primarily for other scientists. Or your class can become an ecological consulting firm that produces results for clients. The Eco-Inquiry modules fit either of these contexts.

The following activity will help you launch the company theme. Students form and name a company, create a motto, logo, and I.D. badges, and write "Company Codes" that define standards for employees.

CREATING A COMPANY

(40 minutes)

PREPARATIONS

◆ If you think that your students will enjoy wearing company I.D. badges, figure out a way to make them look professional—students are unlikely to wear badges made out of construction paper and safety pins! Check with your school or district office to see if they have any plastic badge holders left over from conferences. If not, badge holders can be purchased at stationery stores or through office supply catalogs.

ACTIVITY SEQUENCE

① *Becoming a Company*

- Tell students that they're going to form a company to do ecological research. Make sure they're familiar with the word *ecology*.

- Have them work in pairs to brainstorm possible names and mottos for their company. Explain that these should reflect the mission of their company, and communicate the company's focus to other scientists and potential clients.

- Create a class list of ideas, then let students choose one of the names and mottos by vote or consensus.

- Ask interested students to submit a logo design for the company. Once the class settles on a logo, you or a student can design an I.D. card for company members.

② *Standards of Excellence*

- Have students create a "Company Codes" wall chart called that lists the characteristics they'd like their company's scientists to have. It works well to have students work with a partner to brainstorm characteristics, and then share their ideas with the whole class. They can compile their ideas on a sheet of newsprint which can be posted in the classroom. Encourage students to update the chart periodically as they gain experience doing scientific research.

Introduction

C-MAIL

Try some of these ways to start your message:

Something I think is neat is…   Now I understand that…

What I'd really like to know is…   I'm confused about…

I discovered…   I'd like to investigate…

An idea I have is…   I'm frustrated about…

SENDER'S THOUGHTS

To:_____ From: _____ Date: _____

_____

_____

_____

_____

_____

_____

_____

_____

RECEIVER'S COMMENTS

To:_____ From: _____ Date: _____

_____

_____

_____

_____

_____

_____

_____

_____

Resource List for Collaborative Learning

Circles of Learning: Cooperation in the Classroom

by D. Johnson, R. Johnson, E. Holubec, and P. Roy (Association for Supervision and Curriculum Development, 1984)

A concise introduction to cooperative learning by two of its pioneers and their associates. Provides a rationale for cooperative learning, and methods for implementing it in the classroom.

The Cooperative Classroom: Social and Academic Activities

by J. Rhoades and M. McCabe (National Education Service, 1992)

Provides a wealth of activities for developing social and communication skills, as well as techniques for encouraging thinking and problem-solving skills.

Cooperative Learning

by S. Kagan (Resources for Teachers, 1992)

Provides a diversity of strategies for implementing the author's model of cooperative learning.

Cooperative Learning in Middle-Level Schools

by J. Rottier and B. Ogan (National Education Association, 1991)

Explains how cooperative learning fits the emotional, social, intellectual, and physical needs of middle-level students. Contains several sample lesson plans, staff development workshop materials, and a project planning form.

Designing Groupwork

by E. Cohen (Teachers College Press, 1986)

How to plan, implement, and evaluate groupwork, with a chapter on groupwork in bilingual classrooms.

The Friendly Classroom for a Small Planet

by P. Prutzman, L. Stern, L. Burger, and G. Bodenhammer (New Society Publishers, 1988)

A handbook on creative approaches to living and problem solving for children.

Guidebook for Cooperative Learning

by D. Dishon and P. O'Leary (Learning Publications, 1984)

Practical cooperative learning techniques, activities, and planning forms from two experienced educators. Includes chapters on getting started with cooperative learning, processing social skills, and the teacher's role.

Kids Can Cooperate: A Practical Guide to Teaching Problem-Solving

by E. Crary (Parenting Press, 1983)

This book looks at why children quarrel and offers a step-by-step negotiation process for children.

The Second Cooperative Sports and Game Book

by T. Orlick (Pantheon, 1982)

A source of cooperative games, presented by age group. Includes a chapter on games from other cultures.

Silver Bullets: A Guide to Initiative Problems, Adventure Games and Trust Activities

by K. Rohnke (Kendall/Hunt, 1984)

A collection of outdoor and indoor trust and leadership building activities from Project Adventure.

Structuring Cooperative Learning: Lesson Plans for Teachers

by D. Johnson, R. Johnson, and E. Holubec (Interaction Book Company, 1987)

Contains sample lesson plans for primary, intermediate, and secondary grade levels.

Student Team Learning: An Overview and Practical Guide

by R. Slavin (National Education Association, 1986)

Presents the effects of cooperative learning on academic achievement, inter-group relations, mainstreaming, and self-esteem. Includes several approaches for implementing student teams.

ASSESSMENT TOOLS

Throughout Eco-Inquiry your students will do investigations, solve problems, interpret data, formulate explanations, modify their ideas, and apply and communicate their new knowledge and skills. The depth and breadth of the learning that results from these activities are difficult to assess with traditional tests.

This section describes a variety of assessment methods that will help you develop a system for monitoring and documenting your students' growth as active thinkers and learners. Expanding your assessment repertoire will take time and effort, so start by getting comfortable with one new method at a time. Your students will also need to adjust to new ways of demonstrating and reflecting on their learning. The satisfaction of knowing that your assessments reflect the richness of your teaching and your students' learning will make your extra efforts worthwhile.

PROFICIENCY STANDARDS

Assessment of student learning needs to be rooted in standards that define what students should know and be able to do. Pages 28–34 present Eco-Inquiry "Proficiency Standards" for science Knowledge, Skills, and Habits of Mind.

Each standard defines achievement along a continuum of student growth from Novice (N) to Proficient (P) to Advanced (A) levels. These frameworks communicate how you can expect your students to develop as scientific thinkers and investigators. Since the knowledge and behaviors defined for each stage of development are generalizations, they don't represent the exact course of growth every student will follow. You can enhance the "Proficiency Standards" with additional indicators of achievement levels that you discover.

General characterizations of the Novice, Proficient, and Advanced levels are:

Novice (N) Within the Knowledge standards, students at the Novice level have naive ideas about the nature of science and ecological concepts. They may have elaborate alternative explanations that are coherent and functional, but which are based on everyday logic rather than scientific understanding. These are firm beliefs and ideas that could be barriers to learning scientific ideas, so they need to be addressed in order for learning to progress. In some cases, students at the Novice level may have erroneous ideas that are more sketchy. Although these ideas are still incompatible with scientific viewpoints, they are often easier for students to abandon when they discover alternative explanations.

Within the Skills and Habits of Mind standards, students at the Novice level are lacking the desired behaviors. In some cases, they may demonstrate well-developed contrary or negative behaviors, but most often they simply have not yet gained experience using the particular skills or habits of mind.

Novice+ (N+) Students at the Novice+ level are beginning to abandon the knowledge and behaviors they showed at the Novice level, but they sometimes revert to their former stage. They are trying out new understandings, skills, and habits, but have not internalized them enough to use them as a regular matter of course.

Proficient (P) The Proficient level characterizes students who have solid scientific knowledge, skills, and habits of mind. They may require prompting or occasional guidance to use them.

Proficient+ (P+) At the Proficient+ level students demonstrate the desired knowledge and behaviors more consistently and independently. They may also occasionally show some pieces of the understandings and skills that characterize the Advanced level.

Advanced (A) Students at the Advanced level have mastered the knowledge and skills specified at the Proficient level, plus the more sophisticated knowledge and skills specified as Advanced. Within the Habits of Mind standards, the Advanced level characterizes students who consistently demonstrate the range of desired behaviors specified within each category.

Keeping Records

You can use the "Proficiency Standards" for grading students' work products by assigning scores to each proficiency level, such as N = 0, N+ = 1, P = 2, P+ = 3, and A = 4. But since the standards define stages of growth, you may prefer to use them to help keep track of your students' development over time. The two record-keeping sheets described below provide possible formats for recording your students' growth.

CLASS OBSERVATIONS Students demonstrate their knowledge, skills, and habits of mind while they're engaged in activities. Observing their behaviors and listening to their reasoning often gives a better sense of their performance levels than reviewing their written work. Try to get in the habit of roaming the classroom with a clipboard to observe students in action. The "Class Observations" sheet on page 35 provides a format for noting the proficiency level of each student you observe, and to make brief comments that will help you remember why you chose the level you did.

You might find it helpful to make a copy of the "Proficiency Standards" to keep on your clipboard. Decide before an activity which particular knowledge, skill, or habit of mind students are most likely to be using. Then you can keep that page of the standards behind the "Class Observations" sheet to refer to as you make notes.

You don't need to observe every student each time you use the "Class Observations" sheet. However, try to get information on all of the relevant standards for each student at some point during a grading period.

LEARNING PROFILE The "Learning Profile" on page 36 lets you create an individual portrait of each student's learning in all of the standards. You can fill it in periodically, using your observations and student work products to help you make proficiency level designations.

The more often you make entries on the "Learning Profile," the better picture you'll have of the stages students go through and how long it takes them to progress. However, you may find it more convenient to complete a "Learning Profile" once at the end of each grading period as a summary portrait of each student's proficiency levels.

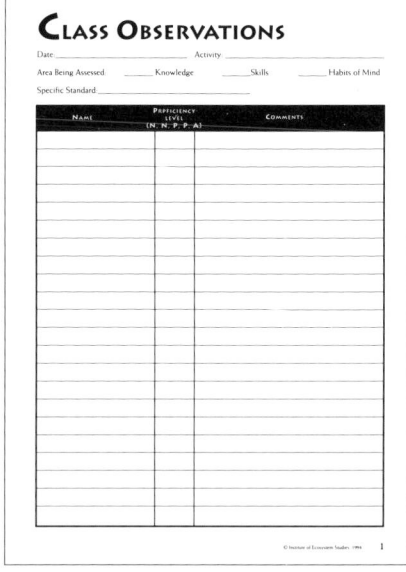

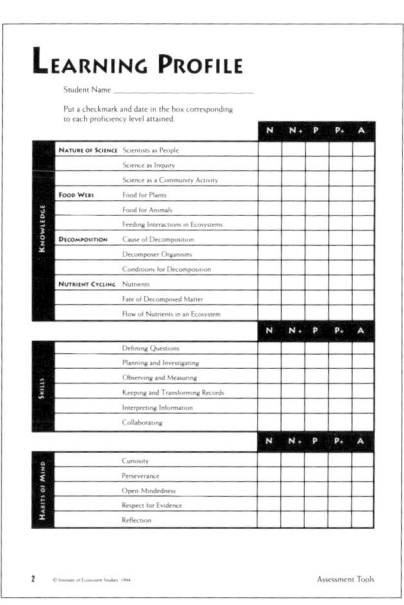

ECO-INQUIRY'S MULTIPLE FORMS OF ASSESSMENT

Eco-Inquiry provides a variety of assessment strategies designed to help you evaluate the learning you value. These include embedded assessment challenges, ongoing assessment suggestions for each lesson, portfolios, students self-evaluations, and concept mapping.

Embedded Assessment Challenges

Three authentic assessment challenges are embedded within each Eco-Inquiry module. One occurs mid-way through each module, and two are culminating challenges. Some are Performance Assessments for which students create products and exhibitions, while others are Written Assessments that require students to analyze written problems or challenges, then write responses.

All of the embedded assessments are a natural outgrowth of students' learning, and are written as lesson plans. They require students to use and demonstrate their knowledge, skills, and habits of mind in situations that are relevant to their immediate lives, and/or that simulate challenges that adults face.

Each assessment challenge is defined on a "Challenge Sheet." The "Scoring Sheet" provided for each assessment will help you evaluate students' work, as well as communicate to students the criteria by which their work will be judged.

Ongoing Assessment

An "Ongoing Assessment" section occurs near the end of each Eco-Inquiry lesson (see page 7). Making assessment part of your daily routine will help you take stock of your students' learning and plan future instruction. Daily assessment can be as simple as taking a few minutes to reflect on how your students responded to activities and questions, doing quick, focused check-ins with small groups, or taking notes when you have time to stand back and observe your students engaged in tasks. Be sure to record ordinary as well as outstanding indicators of your students' learning.

Portfolios

Portfolios are your students' autobiographies of themselves as learners. Portfolios contain collections of work samples that students select and organize to show their achievement of milestones, as well as their growth over time. Gathering portfolios is suggested near the end of each Eco-Inquiry module (Lessons 1.9, 2.6, and 3.7).

Establishing a portfolio culture in your classroom makes you, your students, and their families partners in monitoring and assessing student growth. Through participating in the portfolio process, students learn to set standards that help them distinguish between high quality and mediocre work. Portfolios also cultivate excitement and respect for learning as a process of individual growth and change.

SETTING STANDARDS The portfolio process should begin with the class deciding what constitutes good work in science. Before students can gather evidence of their science achievement, they need to have a clear sense of what they should aim to achieve.

Two activities that are suggested in the Introduction—"Dress the Scientist" (pages 11–12) and "Creating a Company" (page 16)—ask students to think about what knowledge, skills, and attitudes are desirable for doing science. Another option for beginning a discussion of science standards is to ask an open-ended question such as *What behaviors are important for doing a good job in science?* Yet another possibility is to tell students the titles of the Eco-Inquiry "Proficiency Standards" categories for Skills and Habits of Mind, then have them specify behaviors for each. Specific Knowledge standards will be difficult for students to generate, so a single standard such as "understands important ecological concepts" can suffice.

A Good Scientist:

is curious
knows how to experiment
works well with others
is a careful observer
asks questions
can explain and predict things
keeps good records
has self-control
has respect for living things
is patient
is honest
tries to stay positive
can give and take suggestions
knows a lot about nature

The class can make a wall chart of its science standards, and/or each student can make a personal list of standards using "The Ladder of Growth" on page 37. "The Ladder of Growth" can also serve as a self-evaluation prompt. Each time students submit a portfolio, they can decide whether they are at the Trainee, Apprentice, or Scientist level—kid-friendly terms for the Novice, Proficient, and Advanced levels of the "Proficiency Standards." Some teachers use "The Ladder of Growth" as part of the company theme by having "employees" submit portfolios to move up the company career ladder.

Have your students take stock of their lists of science standards each time they are ready to submit portfolios—probably two to four times a year. Their ideas of what's important for doing science will grow and change as they gain science experience.

WHAT GOES INTO PORTFOLIOS

◆ *Work Samples.* A presentation portfolio contains pieces of work that a student selects from a folder or notebook of all the work s/he completed during a given time frame. The work should provide evidence of the student's science abilities. The following types of work could go into an Eco-Inquiry portfolio:

- journal entries
- C-Mail forms
- concept maps
- peer reviews
- drawings
- data sheets
- completed projects and assignments
- "Scoring Sheet" forms
- "Group Work Evaluation" sheets
- "Reflections" sheets

Each piece of work should be dated, and could also indicate if the work was done independently, as a group, or with teacher assistance.

◆ *Student Comments.* A crucial element of portfolios is students' explanations of why they selected each piece of work. You can copy and cut a supply of the "Portfolio Work Sample Comments" sheet on page 38 so that students can attach one to each work sample in their portfolios. As students comment on each work sample, they personalize, reflect on, and communicate their learning process and achievements.

◆ *Summary Statement.* The "Portfolio Cover Sheet" on page 39 provides a chance for students to summarize their abilities as science learners. This gives them practice in presenting their strengths and qualifications, as they would do in a letter of application for a job.

◆ *Teacher Feedback.* There is a space on the "Portfolio Cover Sheet" for you to add your insights on each student's growth and achievement in science.

◆ *Family Feedback.* The letter to parents on page 40 involves the students' families in reflecting on the work presented in portfolios. Sending portfolios and letters home a week or so before parent conferences can help to focus such meetings.

MANAGING A PORTFOLIO SYSTEM

◆ *Choose a Portfolio Container.* Experimenting with a variety of portfolio containers is the best way to decide which works best for you and your students. Manilla file folders are one option, but it helps to adapt them to prevent papers from falling out. Adding a spine binder clip to each, or taping the sides to make them into a pocket works well. Three-ring binders fitted with plastic sleeves for work samples that students do not want to hole-punch are another portfolio option. Pocket folders or accordion file folders also work well.

A convenient filing system will help you streamline the portfolio process. Many teachers set up boxes where students can keep their ongoing work portfolios, as well as their presentation portfolios.

◆ *When to Gather Portfolios.* One option is to have your students assemble portfolios near the end of each Eco-Inquiry module. Portfolios can also be assembled at the end of a longer time frame, such as at the close of each grading period. In this case, Eco-Inquiry work samples might be just some of the items representing students' growth during that period.

A year-end portfolio that contains work from all subject areas is a powerful way to reflect on growth during an entire school year. Consider having students create a culminating portfolio, and then write a cover letter to the teacher they'll have next year to present who they are, what they are interested in and good at, and what they want to work on.

◆ *Reporting Portfolio Results.* Some teachers use portfolios as a percentage of students' grades, whereas others use them for their narrative assessment value alone. Since individual pieces within a portfolio often have already been graded, a portfolio grade can be based on the quality and thoughtfulness of the portfolio's composition and reflections.

Student Self-Evaluations

Each of the assessment techniques described thus far in this section provide opportunities for students to be active participants in assessing their learning. Two additional self-evaluation tools are "Reflections" on page 41 and "Group Work Evaluation" on page 42.

Suggestions for when to have students complete these sheets are provided within Eco-Inquiry lesson plans, but they can be used whenever you want to raise students' awareness of their progress, efforts, and need for improvement. In addition to being beneficial for students, these self-evaluation tools will give you insight into students' reflective thinking abilities.

Concept Mapping

Creating concept maps is a powerful way to help students organize, display, examine, and assess what they're learning. Concept maps are diagrams that show how subconcepts are related to a main concept and to each other. The maps are usually arranged hierarchically, with the broadest, most inclusive concept on top or in the center. Subconcepts then appear below or around the main concept. Linkage words can be added to the lines that join the concepts to clarify relationships.

Introduce concept mapping to students by showing them a simple concept map, such as this one on plants.

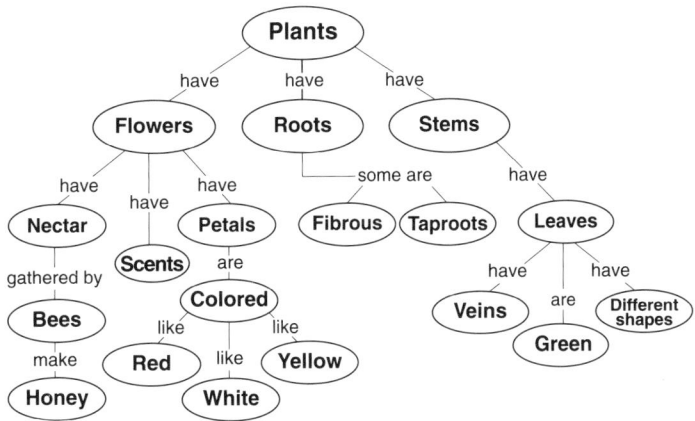

Next, encourage students to think about a familiar topic, such as sports, pets, music, fashion, food, or television. Ask them to generate a list of words that they associate with the topic. Then have someone find two words in the list that are related. Write these side-by-side with a line between them. Ask for a word that could go on the line to explain how the two words are related. Students often have trouble generating words that specify how concepts are related, so it helps to create and post a list of possible linkage words.

Concept Map Linkage Words:

becomes	includes
make	for
is/are	need
has/have	which are
some are	with
release	take up
uses	go between
used by	contain/are in
such as	cause
can be	from
like	shows

Finally, students can work in groups or as a class to organize their list of ideas into a concept map.

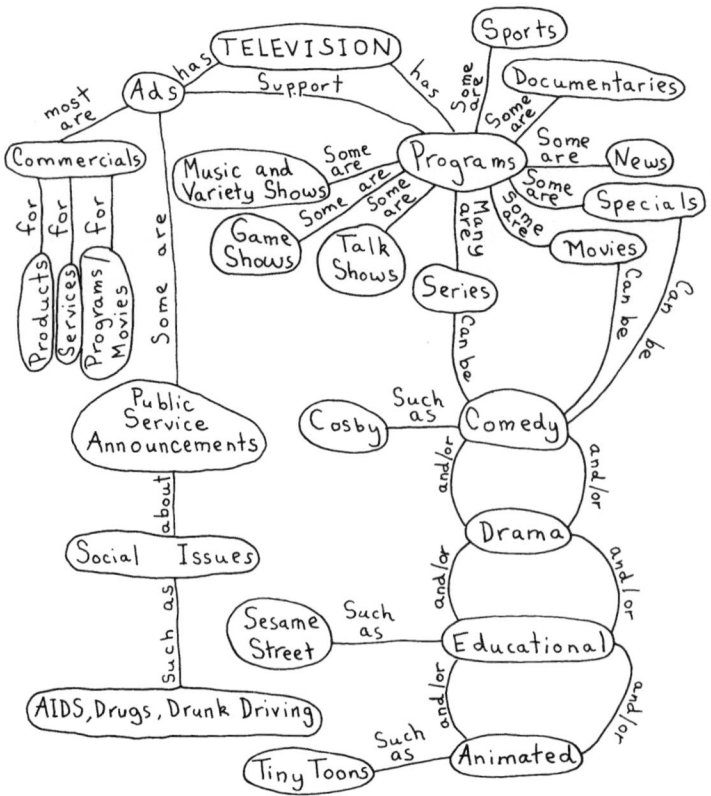

Concept mapping is suggested in the "Extensions" of lessons near the beginning and end of each module (see Lessons 1.3, 1.8, 2.1, 2.5, 3.1, and 3.6). A set of ecology concept map cards is provided on pages 43–44 for use during these activities. You can give a set of some or all of the cards to small groups of students so that they can easily play with a variety of arrangements. When they've settled on layouts, they can copy them onto large sheets of paper and add linkage words.

Making a group concept map is not easy because individuals think about relationships among ideas differently, all of which can be correct. However, the process is valuable because it forces students to explain, defend, and change or solidify their understandings.

Concept maps will also help you assess your students' thinking at a glance. Imagine seeing a map in which a group of students has shown microbes as part of the abiotic environment. You could ask students to explain their map so that you understand their reasoning. Then you could target subsequent discussions and instruction at helping them understand that microbes are living things.

In addition to assisting in the process of learning, concept maps are a tangible learning product. Concept maps can provide visible evidence of what students already know as they begin a new study, and can show how their thinking has grown and changed by the end. This makes concept maps ideal for portfolios, for sharing with parents, and most importantly for fostering students' pride in, and awareness of their learning.

PROFICIENCY STANDARDS

Knowledge—Nature of Science

SCIENTISTS AS PEOPLE

N • Scientists are geniuses, or strange, unusual people.
• A typical scientist is a mad-looking white male who wears a lab coat and works with chemicals, and/or someone who is antisocial and nerdy.
• Science is best suited as a career for men.

N+ • Shows some ideas from Novice level and some from Proficient level.

P • Scientists are regular people who are intelligent, educated, and hard-working.
• Scientists show a wide range of human characteristics (emotion, fallibility, diversity of lifestyles and personality) just like any other group of people.
• Scientists' knowledge, skills, and attitudes are more fundamental to their work than the clothes they wear, how they look, or what equipment they use.
• Careers in science are open to a wide range of people.

P+ • Shows some ideas from Proficient level, and some from Advanced level.

A • Characteristics helpful for doing science include being: curious, open-minded, able to give and take criticism, cooperative, creative, logical, observant, methodical, patient, diligent, good at communicating, and able to learn from mistakes.

SCIENCE AS INQUIRY

N • Predictions should be proven correct. If not, scientists have to keep repeating an experiment until it comes out right.
• Most scientific investigations are dangerous and/or thrilling, and are done in laboratories.
• A single scientist investigates a range of topics in a given week—from bombs to butterflies.
• Experiments, verifications, and application of results happen in a matter of days.
• Scientific knowledge is unchanging.
• The main purpose of science is to make the world better, such as by finding cures for diseases.

N+ • Shows some ideas from Novice level and some from Proficient level.

P • Experimental science requires asking questions, making predictions, controlling variables, and doing replicates.
• Scientific inquiry is done in many different places, not just in laboratories.
• Most scientists have a specialty in the biological, physical, earth, or social sciences, that they study in depth over many years.
• It is important to gather data carefully and systematically, and to keep good records of experiment procedures and results.
• Scientists have to rely on evidence to draw conclusions and support their claims.

P+ • Shows some ideas from Proficient level, and some from Advanced level.

A • Outcomes of scientific inquiries are uncertain, and experiments sometimes fail.
• Scientists can learn as much from negative results as from results that support their predictions.
• Results of scientific investigations usually lead to new questions.
• Scientific knowledge builds over a long time period.
• All scientific knowledge is subject to revision, so conclusions are temporary.

SCIENCE AS A COMMUNITY ACTIVITY

N • Scientists work in isolation.
• Most scientific work is "top secret" so scientists keep results to themselves.

N+ • Shows some ideas from Novice level and some from Proficient level.

P • Many scientists often work in collaboration with other scientists.
• Scientists use peer review to get helpful criticism and ideas from other scientists.

P+ • Shows some ideas from Proficient level, and some from Advanced level.

A • Scientists spend a lot of time communicating with other scientists by writing papers, giving presentations, and having discussions.
• The checks, balances, and sharing within the scientific community are essential to the process of building valid scientific knowledge.

 Assessment Tools

Knowledge — Food Webs

FOOD FOR PLANTS

N • Soil, water, and air are food for plants.
• Plants take in food and make their own food.

N+ • Shows some ideas from Novice level and some from Proficient level.

P • Plants need soil, nutrients, water, and air to live, but these are not food.
• Plants meet their food needs differently than animals do because they cannot eat or take in food.
• Plants use soil, water, carbon dioxide, and energy from sunlight to make their own food (sugars), using the process of photosynthesis.
• Plants use the food they produce to grow and stay healthy.

P+ • Shows some ideas from Proficient level, and some from Advanced level.

A • Some food energy is stored inside plants, and some is released as heat when plants use the food to grow and function.

FOOD FOR ANIMALS

N • Anything an animal takes in is food.

N+ • Shows some ideas from Novice level and some from Proficient level.

P • Animals need food, water, and air to live.
• Animals get food from eating plants or other animals.
• Animals get both nutrients and energy from food.

P+ • Shows some ideas from Proficient level, and some from Advanced level.

A • Unlike plants, animals take in food and break it into small particles in their guts.
• Some food energy is stored inside animals, and some is released as heat when animals use the food to grow and function.

FEEDING INTERACTIONS IN ECOSYSTEMS

N • Big things eat smaller things.
• An ecosystem is where plants and animals live.

N+ • Shows some ideas from Novice level and some from Proficient level.

P • An ecosystem is an area where living things interact with each other and their physical environment.
• Plants are called producers in an ecosystem because they produce food.
• Animals and microbes are called consumers in an ecosystem because they consume plants and/or animals for food.
• Consumers include: herbivores that eat plants; carnivores that eat animals; omnivores that eat plants and animals; and decomposers that eat dead plants, dead animals, and animal wastes.
• The flow of food from producers to all types of consumers is called a food chain.
• No matter what an animal eats, it depends on the green plants that are at the base of its food chain.

P+ • Shows some ideas from Proficient level, and some from Advanced level.

A • Most organisms and microbes eat and are eaten by more than one thing.
• A food web is the connections among everything animals and microbes in a location eat and are eaten by.
• If a population of plants, animals, or microbes in a food web increases or decreases significantly, the sizes of the populations of other organisms in the web may also change.

Knowledge — Decomposition

CAUSE OF DECOMPOSITION

N • Dead things disappear on their own as time passes.
• Physical conditions, such as wind, rain, battering, and trampling, cause dead things to break down and disappear.

N+ • Shows some ideas from Novice level and some from Proficient level.

P • Some dead things get eaten by bugs, but dead things also decompose because of physical conditions.

P+ • Shows some ideas from Proficient level, and some from Advanced level.

A • Dead things decompose because decomposer organisms use them for food.
• Dead things do not decompose without the action of decomposers.

DECOMPOSER ORGANISMS

N • The only organisms that eat dead plants and animals are things like insects, earthworms, and vultures.
• All microbes are germs that cause diseases.
• Microbes are not living things.

N+ • Shows some ideas from Novice level and some from Proficient level.

P • Decomposers are animals and microbes that use dead plants and animals and their wastes as food.
• Microbes are everywhere, but are usually invisible to the naked eye.
• Microbes are living things.
• Decomposer microbes get nutrients and energy by consuming food.
• Some bacteria and fungi are decomposer microbes that use dead plants and animals as food.

P+ • Shows some ideas from Proficient level, and some from Advanced level.

A • Bacteria and fungi consume dead material by being inside or beside it, releasing chemicals to break the material down, then absorbing the tiny particles of nutrients and food energy.

CONDITIONS FOR DECOMPOSITION

N • Things decompose better in certain conditions, like where it is wet, because the condition itself (e.g., the water) makes them decompose.

N+ • Shows some ideas from Novice level and some from Proficient level.

P • Most microbes grow best in warm, moist conditions.
• Microbes grow best on dead material that is high in nutrients and energy, and is easy to digest.

P+ • Shows some ideas from Proficient level, and some from Advanced level.

A • When more decomposers grow on dead material, it decomposes more quickly.
• When people change environmental conditions, decomposition may speed up or slow down.

          Assessment Tools

Knowledge — Nutrient Cycling

NUTRIENTS

N • Nutrients are like good food.
• Nutrients provide energy.

N+ • Shows some ideas from Novice level and some from Proficient level.

P • Nutrients are tiny particles of matter, not energy.
• Nutrients are the building blocks of all living things.
• Nutrients are in food, living things, and the physical environment.
• Living things grow and stay healthy by taking nutrients into their bodies.

P+ • Shows some ideas from Proficient level, and some from Advanced level.

A • Living things that aren't getting the right kinds or amounts of nutrients often show physical symptoms of stress, such as discolored leaves on plants.

FATE OF DECOMPOSED MATTER

N • When things decompose, the matter they were made of disappears.
• When things decompose, some of the matter they were made of goes into the ground, but much of it vanishes from existence.

N+ • Shows some ideas from Novice level and some from Proficient level.

P • Decomposed matter goes into the ground as tiny particles.
• Decomposed matter might disappear from sight, but the material it was made of does not disappear from existence.

P+ • Shows some ideas from Proficient level, and some from Advanced level.

A • Decomposed matter becomes part of the organisms that consume it, or it is released into the soil, water, or air.
• Matter is not created or destroyed, but is recycled into new forms.

FLOW OF NUTRIENTS IN AN ECOSYSTEM

N • Nutrients float in the air, not necessarily driven by any particular biological or physical processes.
• Nutrients go from one thing to another like a disease travels from person to person.

N+ • Shows some ideas from Novice level and some from Proficient level.

P • Nutrients are passed along food chains from plants to animals, from animals to animals, and from dead plants and animals to decomposers.
• Decomposers release nutrients from dead material into the physical environment.

P+ • Shows some ideas from Proficient level, and some from Advanced level.

A • A nutrient cycle is the flow of nutrients back and forth between living things and the physical environment.
• Nutrient cycles are driven partly by biological processes such as the uptake of materials from the physical environment by plants, and the consumption of food and the release of wastes by animals.

Skills

DEFINING QUESTIONS

N • Doesn't form questions when encountering new experiences or ideas

N+ • Asks mostly general or superficial questions

P • Forms focused questions based on experiences

P+ • Forms questions about ideas and interpretations, as well as about concrete experiences
• Distinguishes between testable and non-testable questions

A • Refines testable questions to guide inquiry
• Forms new questions based on findings

PLANNING AND INVESTIGATING

N • Doesn't make an investigation plan
• Tries things out unsystematically
• Can't determine what could be important to watch or measure

N+ • Outlines a general plan for answering a question, but doesn't specify details
• Doesn't plan to control all variables
• Relies heavily on defining an investigation while doing it

P • Understands rationale for the procedures of a fair test (controlled experiment)
• Makes (with guidance) a sequenced and detailed plan for what variables to change and control, and what indicators to observe, measure, and compare
• Can explain how the planned experiment will help answer the research question
• Predicts possible outcomes
• Doesn't always carry out details of plans, such as controlling variables

P+ • Plans a controlled experiment without guidance
• Works through the steps of the plan systematically, accurately, and thoroughly
• Makes reasonable adjustments to the plan while going along

A • Does a sufficient number of tests to get reliable results
• Uses supplemental experiments to feed into the main experiment
• Critiques and refines experimental design in retrospect
• Uses experiment results to devise new investigation plans

OBSERVING AND MEASURING

N • Sees only obvious things Notices few details or changes; poor discrimination ability
• Doesn't use all senses

N+ • Makes somewhat focused and active observations, but their quality, depth, breadth, and accuracy is inconsistent

P • Uses all senses to notice details, patterns, similarities, and differences
• Can quantify observations using appropriate measurements

P+ • Follows a regular program of observation and measurement
• Makes objective and accurate observations and measurements consistently

A • Judges how frequent and accurate observations and measurements need to be for an experiment, and makes them accordingly
• Uses discerned patterns and relationships to focus further observations

      Assessment Tools

Skills — Continued

KEEPING AND TRANSFORMING RECORDS

N • Keeps no records, or sloppy, indecipherable records

N+ • Keeps records sporadically
• Records information on some, but not all, important indicators

P • Makes a chart or other organized system for keeping records
• Records all important indicators, but not regularly enough to document changes or trends

P+ • Transforms (with guidance) quantitative records into graphs or tables, but these might lack appropriate labels
• Uses clear, accurate, descriptive, and objective language and drawings to present qualitative results

A • Keeps accurate, comprehensive, systematic, and frequent records
• Transforms records (without guidance) into a form that communicates results clearly
• Labels graphs and charts appropriately

INTERPRETING INFORMATION

N • Makes little attempt to look for patterns in data and draw conclusions
• Clings to original ideas despite contradictory evidence
• Doesn't use new information to enrich prior ideas

N+ • Takes some, but not all data into account when drawing conclusions
• Uses evidence selectively to support predictions

P • Recognizes patterns in data and relationships among variables
• Uses results to draw conclusions, even when contrary to expected results
• Draws appropriate conclusions, but may be unable to explain the supporting evidence

P+ • Relates results back to research question—doesn't just report what happened
• Integrates and interprets results from several replicates
• Draws conclusions that are supported by data
• Can explain the supporting evidence
• Doesn't overstate evidence or make unsubstantiated inferences

A • Identifies and explains errors or weaknesses in experiment, and the impact these have on conclusions
• Changes and/or enriches prior ideas with new information

COLLABORATING

N • Works in isolation; withdrawn and/or untrusting
• Tends to be domineering and/or hostile, to the detriment of group goals and enrichment

N+ • Cooperates passively
• Doesn't initiate plans and activities
• Doesn't volunteer to take on responsibilities
• Tends to stray off task

P • Pulls own weight as an active and positive group member
• Communicates well with group members
• Performs a variety of jobs willingly

P+ • Helps manage group process by doing one or more of the following: sets goals, makes plans, allocates responsibilities, involves all members, resolves disputes, and keeps group on task
• Listens to, respects, and builds on ideas of others

A • Balances personal and group needs effectively and consistently to maximize the learning of all and the quality of the final product

Habits of Mind

Proficiency Levels

N
- Uses few of the listed traits
- Has some awareness or understanding of the traits
- Shows glimmers of the listed traits in action, or a desire to develop them

N+
- Shows a few of the listed traits sporadically

P
- Shows many of the listed traits, but may require prompting to use them.

P+
- Shows more of the listed traits more often

A
- Has internalized the habit of mind
- Uses the habit spontaneously, without reminders
- Applies the habit when appropriate to achieve goals and produce high quality work

CURIOSITY

- Notices and is inquisitive about things
- Desires to know what things are, and how and why they work as they do
- Shows discomfort with incomprehension
- Works to understand by asking questions and pursuing answers
- Values learning new things

PERSEVERANCE

- Stays on task to reach a goal
- Puzzles over a problem to gain clarity, get a solution, or devise a better approach
- Relies on own mind as a resource for problem solving
- Controls impulsiveness that would be detrimental to achieving goals
- Tolerates and works through frustration, confusion, and ambiguity to achieve goals

OPEN-MINDEDNESS

- Considers multiple possibilities and approaches
- Seeks out different points of view
- Can reason from alternative perspectives
- Reconsiders own ideas in light of input from others
- Uses input to improve work
- Shifts gears when a strategy isn't working

RESPECT FOR EVIDENCE

- Generates accurate and reliable evidence by watching patiently, measuring carefully, and revising or repeating procedures
- Presents evidence in an honest, unbiased, objective fashion, even when it contradicts expectations
- Recognizes how prior ideas and perspectives can influence interpretation of evidence
- Uses evidence to make appropriate claims and build arguments
- Suspends judgments and conclusions until has sufficient and convincing evidence
- Carefully evaluates the evidence behind claims and the credibility of sources
- Shows appropriate and productive skepticism for claims that don't make sense

REFLECTION

- Monitors own thinking and progress toward goals
- Uses personal standards for evaluating success and effectiveness of own actions
- Identifies own strengths, limitations, and ways to improve
- Can provide and explain evidence of growth
- Evaluates the ideas of others to give useful feedback

                     Assessment Tools

CLASS OBSERVATIONS

Date:_____ Activity: _____

Area Being Assessed: _____ Knowledge _____ Skills _____ Habits of Mind

Specific Standard:_____

NAME	PROFICIENCY LEVEL (N, N+, P, P+, A)	COMMENTS

LEARNING PROFILE

Student Name _____

Put a checkmark and date in the box corresponding
to each proficiency level attained.

			N	N+	P	P+	A
KNOWLEDGE	**NATURE OF SCIENCE**	Scientists as People					
		Science as Inquiry					
		Science as a Community Activity					
	FOOD WEBS	Food for Plants					
		Food for Animals					
		Feeding Interactions in Ecosystems					
	DECOMPOSITION	Cause of Decomposition					
		Decomposer Organisms					
		Conditions for Decomposition					
	NUTRIENT CYCLING	Nutrients					
		Fate of Decomposed Matter					
		Flow of Nutrients in an Ecosystem					

		N	N+	P	P+	A
SKILLS	Defining Questions					
	Planning and Investigating					
	Observing and Measuring					
	Keeping and Transforming Records					
	Interpreting Information					
	Collaborating					

		N	N+	P	P+	A
HABITS OF MIND	Curiosity					
	Perseverance					
	Open-Mindedness					
	Respect for Evidence					
	Reflection					

THE LADDER OF GROWTH

DESIRED CHARACTERISTICS

What knowledge, skills, and attitudes are important for doing science?

- ☐ _____
- ☐ _____
- ☐ _____
- ☐ _____
- ☐ _____
- ☐ _____
- ☐ _____
- ☐ _____
- ☐ _____
- ☐ _____
- ☐ _____
- ☐ _____
- ☐ _____
- ☐ _____
- ☐ _____

SCIENTIST

Shows all of the desired characteristics.
Uses them regularly.

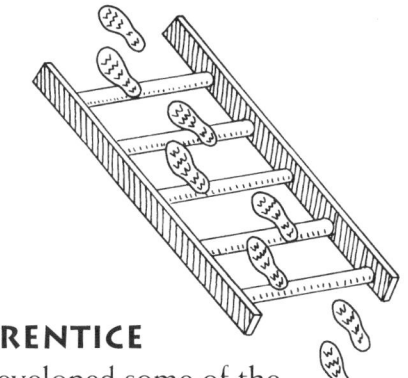

APPRENTICE

Has developed some of the desired characteristics. Needs to be reminded to use them.

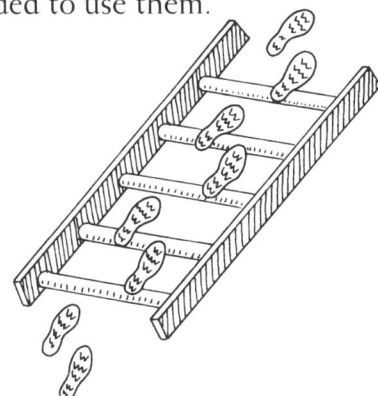

TRAINEE

Is able to develop the desired characteristics, but doesn't use them very much yet.

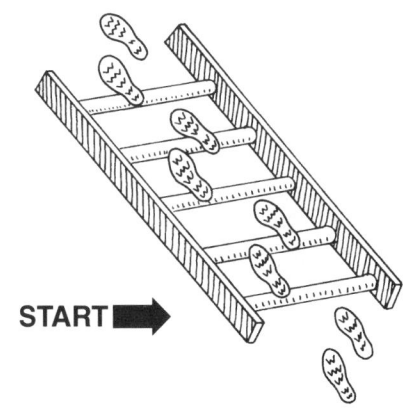

START ➡

PORTFOLIO WORK SAMPLE COMMENTS
◆◆

NAME _____ DATE _____

I chose this item for my portfolio because it shows _____

_____

_____

From this work I learned _____

_____

I could improve it by _____

_____

Reviewer's Initials: _____

◆◆

NAME _____ DATE _____

I chose this item for my portfolio because it shows _____

_____

_____

From this work I learned _____

_____

I could improve it by _____

_____

Reviewer's Initials: _____

                    Assessment Tools

PORTFOLIO COVER SHEET
◆◆◆

What are your science qualifications? Describe what your work in this portfolio and during class demonstrates about your knowledge, skills, and attitudes:

_____

_____

_____

_____

_____

Outline your future goals and learning plan:

_____

_____

_____

_____

_____

◆◆

Comments:

Signed: _____ Date: _____

DEAR PARENT,

Your child has created a portfolio of work that demonstrates growth and accomplishments. You might want to look over the portfolio on your own, then go through it with your child, asking questions such as:

What sample are you most proud of? Why?

How did you do this?

What was most challenging?

What are your goals for future work? How will you achieve them?

After you've reviewed and discussed the portfolio, please sign below and have your child return this letter to me. I'd also be interested in your responses to the questions at the bottom of this sheet.

Thank you for taking the time to reflect on your child's growth as a learner.

Sincerely,

---

1. What did looking at and discussing the portfolio samples tell you about your child as a learner?

2. Were you drawn to any particular piece of work, and/or were you surprised by anything? What and why?

3. What needs to be addressed to improve your child's learning?

4. Other comments and suggestions:

Signed: _____ Date:_____

REFLECTIONS

(1) Rate each item as ✔+ (high), ✔ (medium), or ✔- (low).

My effort	
My participation in class	
The quality of my work	
My satisfaction with my work	

(2) Often in class I feel _____ because _____

_____

(3) Something hard or confusing has been _____

_____

(4) Something interesting or fun has been _____

_____

(5) Ways I could improve my performance are_____

_____

(6) Describe in detail something you've done in class that shows how you are a

learner, thinker, and/or problem solver:_____

_____

_____

_____

_____

GROUP WORK EVALUATION

(1) What did your group accomplish? _____

_____

(2) Rate your contributions in the ME column as ✔+ (a lot), ✔ (a fair amount), or ✔- (not much).

Then rate your group as a whole in the GROUP column, using ✔+ (all members), ✔ (most members), or ✔- (few or no members).

	ME	GROUP
Helped plan and organize		
Shared information and ideas		
Respected different opinions and suggestions		
Helped others learn and get involved		
Helped get the work done and done well		
Took responsibility to work out difficulties		

(3) What helped your group succeed? _____

_____

(4) What held your group back? _____

_____

(5) How could your group do better in the future? _____

_____

 Assessment Tools

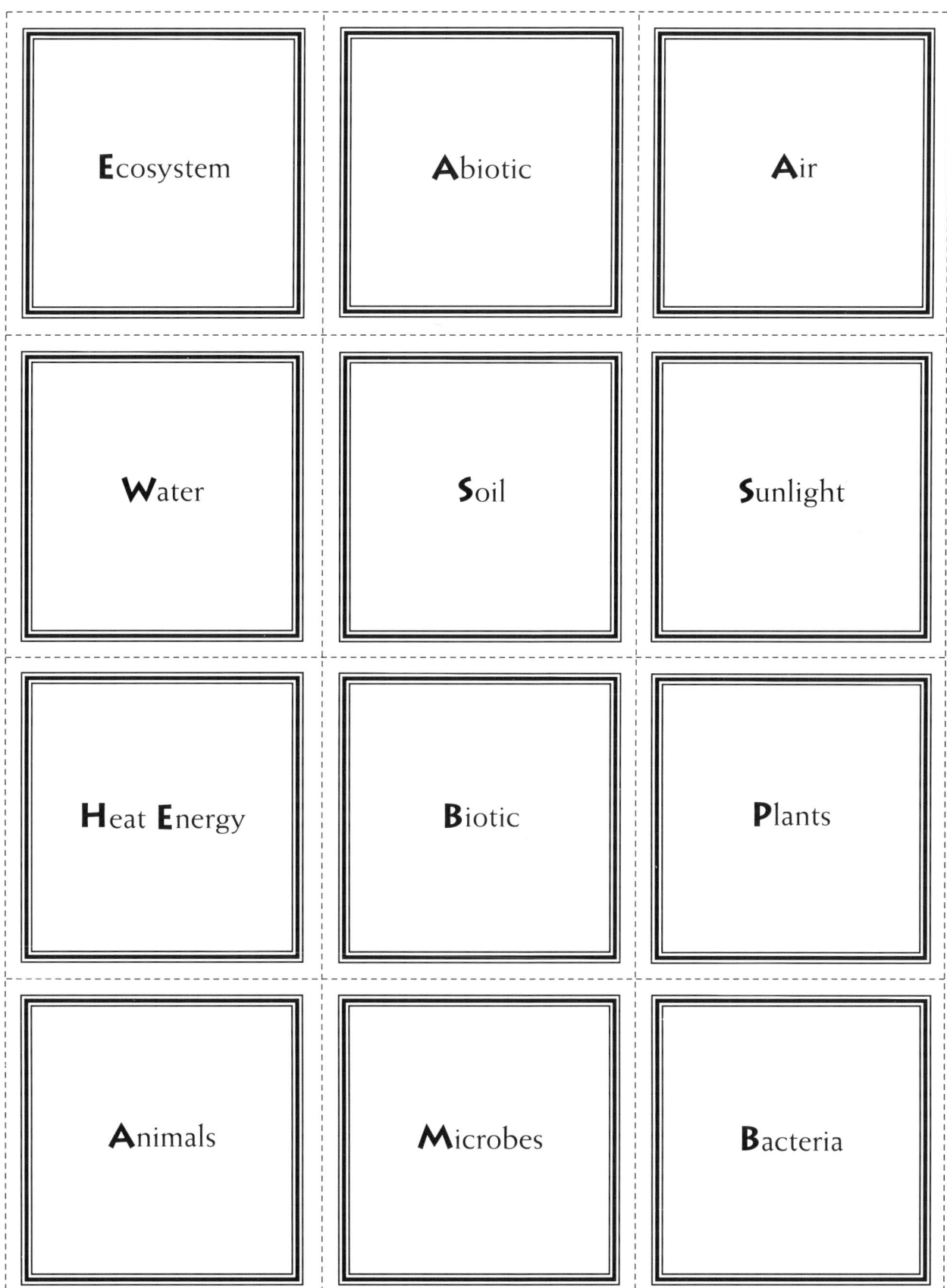

Ecosystem	Abiotic	Air
Water	Soil	Sunlight
Heat Energy	Biotic	Plants
Animals	Microbes	Bacteria

43

Fungi	**P**roducers	**C**onsumers
Herbivores	**C**arnivores	**D**ecomposers
Decomposition	**W**armth	**M**oisture
Food	**N**utrients	**N**utrient **C**ycles

WHO EATS WHAT?

Module 1

WHO EATS WHAT?

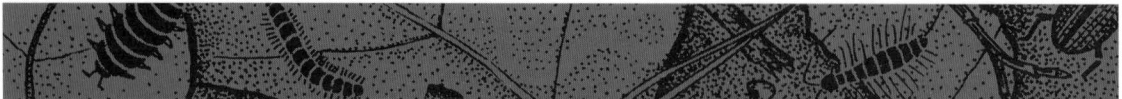

You are There

Imagine a full moon night in the desert, sunrise in a forest, or high noon in a field. You sit unnoticed, watching. Life pulses around you as animals forage for the food they need to survive.

We don't often witness feeding interactions in nature. They begin as sunlight strikes green leaves that convert solar energy to chemical energy, the sustenance of all life. An aphid sucks plant juices, a mouse nibbles grass seeds, a coyote kills a rabbit, a snake swallows a mouse. In each of these interchanges, nutrients and energy flow from one part of an ecosystem to another.

Humans are part of this interplay, also. Like all animals, we depend on the chemical energy that plants make during photosynthesis. Whether we eat fruit, vegetables, grains, dairy products, or meat, we consume energy whose source was sunlight.

Beyond our dietary link to other species through food chains, our daily actions also make us important players in how food relationships in ecosystems function. We have tremendous power to change landscapes or to introduce chemicals into food chains, which in turn affect animals and their food resources. As students get familiar with the ecological interactions within a local piece of land during this module, they become aware of the earth's life support system, and the impact they can have on it.

Overview of Students' Learning Experiences

Students' central challenge in this module is to determine the food web of a local site. They receive a request for this information from a school or community group, which establishes a real-world context for their studies. By investigating a familiar area, such as the schoolyard or a neighborhood park, students see their everyday environment as an ecosystem of which they are part.

As they tackle their challenge, students are at the center of their learning, solving problems, making decisions, and organizing their own work. After exploring outdoor study plots, students design investigations to answer their questions about animal feeding behaviors. Whereas in Modules 2 and 3 students learn and practice the disciplined procedures of controlled experiments, during this module they devise their own methods which may be more descriptive than experimental.

Once students find and interpret clues of feeding interactions, they are introduced to the language and frameworks ecologists use to organize this information. Fundamental ecological terms and concepts, such as *ecosystem*, *food chain*, *food web*, *food*, *nutrient*, and *energy*, take on meanings rooted in direct experience.

This module also develops students' communication and application skills through assessment activities. Students set up outdoor study stations to teach others about food web clues, and create an exhibition to share their findings. They also take on the role of professional ecologists by writing environmental impact statements to help people make land management decisions based on sound ecological knowledge.

Module 1 Overview Chart

		WHO EATS WHAT?
Mode	**Lesson Title**	**Activities**
Activating Ideas	**1.1** A Research Request	**Day 1:** Students receive and discuss an invitation to investigate animals and their food resources on a local site. They talk about what they already know and how they could find out more.
Investigating	**1.2** Preparing for Field Work	**Days 2–3:** Students become familiar with what animals and animal signs to look for outdoors, then practice field research skills and methods.
	1.3 Outdoor Research Excursion	**Days 4–5:** Students work in groups to investigate outdoor study plots for animals and clues to their food resources. The next day they process their findings.
	1.4 Feeding Habits Investigations	**Days 6–10:** Students hear a story about a scientist who studies animals and their food resources, then design and carry out indoor or outdoor studies to learn more about animals' feeding interactions.
	1.5 Outdoor Study Stations — Performance Assessment	**Day 11:** Students create stations at their outdoor site by making interpretive labels that teach others about signs of animals and what they eat.
Processing for Understanding	**1.6** Making Food Chains	**Days 12–13:** Students make food chains for their study site organisms, and learn food chain terminology.
	1.7 Food for Thought	**Days 14–15:** Students sort items into food and non-food categories, then play a game to get enough food — nutrients and energy — to support six ecosystem organisms.
	1.8 Making Food Webs	**Days 16–17:** Students make food webs of their study site, propose an event that affects one population in the web, then trace how that change might affect other populations within the web.
Applying and Assessing	**1.9** Environmental Impact Statements — Written Assessment	**Day 18:** Students judge a proposal for altering their study site by predicting how the change might affect the organisms that live there.
	1.10 Who Eats What Exhibition — Performance Assessment	**Days 19–21:** Students plan, prepare, and present an exhibition of their work to an audience.

Planning Ahead

CHOOSE A PROJECT FOCUS This module is designed to inspire and motivate students because it has relevance in the world beyond the classroom, and relies on them to become experts in ecology. Creating a real-world project requires finding a local community group or landowner who is genuinely interested in using information that students gather about the ecology of a local piece of land. This could be an environmental group, park commission, town committee, or the school board if you use the schoolyard as your study site.

Tell possible project sponsors that your goal is for students to learn how to study a piece of land to determine food web interactions. They might have additional goals, such as an inventory of the plants and animals on the site, that your students could help them fulfill. They might also be interested in making the project a long-term study of landscape changes by having new classes study the same site each school year.

In addition to inviting the project sponsor to present the study request in person (see Lesson 1.1), suggest that they write a letter to students. The letter could define the products that students produce during assessment activities described in Lessons 1.5, 1.9, and 1.10.

Dear Students,

The San Pedro Conservation Commission would like to know more about the property surrounding your schoolyard. We are particularly interested in what plants and animals are on the property, and how they interact. To help the school manage this property, we need to know what the animals living there eat, so that we can make sure their food sources don't disappear.

To increase people's enjoyment of the property, we would also appreciate it if you could create signs that point out animal signs and feeding interactions. Also, once you become experts about this piece of land, we'll ask your advice about any changes people want to make to it.

We hope that you will accept our request. Please let us know when you are ready to make a presentation of your findings.

Thank you, and good luck with the project!

Sincerely,

Michelle Rodriguez

Michelle Rodriguez, Chairperson
San Pedro Conservation Commission

SCOPE OUT A STUDY SITE If at all possible, use your schoolyard as the study site. The advantages are:

1) it avoids the need for buses and long travel times;

2) it makes revisiting the site for follow-up observations feasible;

3) it helps students realize that nature is everywhere;

4) it helps students develop pride and stewardship for their everyday environment; and

5) it lets students focus on using new field research skills without being distracted by the need to get comfortable and familiar with a new environment.

After you read the criteria below, take a walk along the perimeter of your schoolyard to see if it's suitable. If it is not, visit other nearby sites to assess their conditions:

◆ *Natural Features.* Look for sites that have healthy plants, a layer of dead plant material on the ground, and non-compacted soil. These will be areas that are not constantly subjected to heavy disturbance by people, such as patches of unmown grass and weeds, a hedgerow of shrubs, a patch of undisturbed desert scrub, or a small patch of woods. If you teach in an urban setting, try to locate a small park within walking distance to use as your study site. Where there is a thriving plant community there will be animals seeking food, moisture, and cover. Sites where leaf litter, branches, and logs cover the ground will have microhabitats and food sources for small organisms that are the easiest animals for students to find and observe.

In general, the more mature the plant community you choose (i.e., the longer it's been left undisturbed), the more likely it will have an abundance of life forms to discover. Alternatively, choosing an area where there are small patches of different types of vegetation (e.g., weeds, shrubs, trees) will also provide enough variety to make your study interesting. Remember that your students will find twice as much as you do! For more specific information on possible study site habitats see the *Who Eats What* guide in the Appendix.

◆ *Size.* Select a site that:

1) can comfortably accommodate your class;

2) allows each group of 3–4 students to make a circular study plot with a 5-meter diameter (a technique for making circular plots is described in Lesson 1.2);

3) has clear landmarks you can use to establish definite boundaries; and

4) allows you to keep the entire group in sight.

The exact size of the entire site and group plots can be flexible depending on the features of the area. If you choose a site that has small patches or rows of vegetation, such as along the perimeter of your playground, then the size and shape of each group's study area might be rectangular instead of circular. During your preliminary visit, decide where you will locate each student group so that you won't have to make those decisions with a class of energetic researchers at your side. If possible, mark each plot location (e.g., the center point of each circular plot) with flagging tape or ribbon.

◆ *Safety*. Avoid sites such as garbage-strewn vacant lots that have broken glass and other potentially hazardous refuse. If you'll be working on your schoolyard, try to enlist the help of the maintenance crew in picking up broken glass, nails, and other hazardous materials that might be in the far reaches of the property. If the site you choose has a pond or stream nearby, and especially if these aquatic environments have steep, sloping banks, either make sure you can enforce these areas as off-limits, or establish safety procedures for working near them.

Become familiar with drawings and information about poisonous plants and animals in your region. If you live in an area where ticks and Lyme disease are prevalent, familiarize yourself with precautions students can take to prevent tick bites and make sure parents know what actions to take if a tick is found on a child.

BRING BACK ARTIFACTS AND A MAP When scoping out the site, gather materials that will give students a preview of the area. You might want to take photographs or collect some natural artifacts, such as a pine cone, a leaf, fallen twigs, or a soil sample.

Also, you might want to make an outline of the study site to transfer to larger paper once back in the classroom. (In an optional activity, students add their plot maps to your master map in Lesson 1.3.) Orient a sheet of paper to the north and along its edges draw the landmarks (e.g., road, path, parking lot, tall tree, stream, school building) that designate the site boundaries. Next draw circles to indicate the study plots in their approximate relative locations. Finally, sketch and label any notable features, such as grassy or bare spots, large trees or rocks, brushy areas, fallen trees, or ditches.

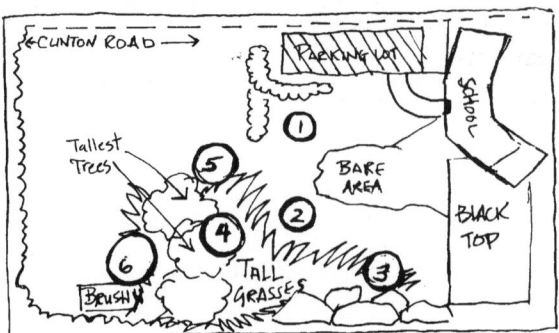

MAKE ARRANGEMENTS WITH THE LANDOWNER If you are using land not owned by the school district, you might need to get permission to go off paths, turn over rocks and logs, dig in the soil, and collect leaf litter and organisms for classroom study.

If your site is a park or nature area, ask for guidance from park officials on how and what to collect to minimize impact. Take full advantage of the expertise of rangers or park naturalists in helping plan your trip. They might be able to co-lead or supplement the excursion, visit your class beforehand, or provide brochures to give students a preview of the site.

GET FAMILIAR WITH THE *WHO EATS WHAT* GUIDE The information in this guide (see the Appendix) will give you a good overview of different habitats and what you can expect to see in each, as well as specific information on animal signs and what different animals eat.

GATHER MATERIALS A list of materials used in this module is provided in the Appendix. The materials for Lesson 1.4 vary depending on which feeding habits investigations your students do. You might want to read over that lesson to anticipate what materials you'll need. If you decide to order live animals such as earthworms for the investigations, instead of using local organisms, order them in advance so they'll be there when you need them.

COLLECT RESOURCE BOOKS Enlist the help of your librarian in gathering books for a reference corner in your classroom or a reserve shelf in the library. Three types of books will be useful to have on hand throughout the module: 1) stories that describe common plants and animals; 2) science books written as succinct references; and 3) field guides to local plants and animals. See the following resource list for suggested titles. A list of organisms common in your region of the country would also be especially useful.

RESOURCE LIST

For Teachers ▪ ▪ ▪ ▪ ▪ ▪ ▪ ▪ ▪ ▪ ▪ ▪

REFERENCES AND BACKGROUND READING

Animals in the Classroom
by D. Kramer (Addison-Wesley, 1989)

An indispensable reference on caring for critters in the classroom. Includes background information and detailed instructions on collecting, housing, and feeding over thirty organisms.

A Field Guide to Your Own Back Yard
by J. Mitchell (Norton, 1985)

Arranged by seasons, this book helps the reader become familiar with the many plants and animals found in a suburban backyard habitat.

The Power Plant: Teacher's Guide to Photosynthesis
by K. Roth and C. Anderson (Michigan State University, 1987) [Order Occasional Paper 112, Michigan State University, 252 Erickson Hall, East Lansing, Michigan 48824, $11.50]

An excellent collection of activities, readings, and worksheets that help students confront and change their misunderstandings about how plants get food.

The Urban Naturalist
by S. Garber (Wiley, 1987)

Each chapter features a different organism in this introduction to the wealth of animals and plants beyond urban doorsteps. Tells how to find wild creatures in the city, and includes fascinating facts about how they make a living.

The View from the Oak: The Private Worlds of Other Creatures
by H. and J. Kohl (Sierra Club, 1977)

Encourages observation and discovery of how environments are influenced by different animals. Portrays the human view as only one of many, and entices the reader to move away from familiar worlds in order to understand the experience of other animals. Lengthy, but thoughtful and interesting.

Wild Green Things in the City
by A. Dowden (Crowell, 1972)

This illustrated guide provides a multitude of natural history facts about weeds and wild plants found in the urban environment. Includes plant species lists for New York, Denver, and Los Angeles.

FIELD GUIDES

American Wildlife and Plants: A Guide to Wildlife Food Habits
by A. Martin, H. Zim and A. Nelson (Dover, 1989)

What's in a bluebird's stomach? This book will tell you the answer, plus the food habits of over 300 other common species of American birds, mammals, reptiles, and amphibians. Entries for each animal include range maps, habitat descriptions, and foods (including percentages of different plants comprising the animal's diet).

The Audubon Society Field Guides

North American Insects and Spiders
by L. and M. Milne (Knopf, 1980)

Reptiles and Amphibians
by J. Behler (Knopf, 1979)

Birds of the Eastern U.S.
by J. Bull and J. Farrand, Jr. (Knopf, 1977)

Birds of the Western U.S.
by M. Udvardy (Knopf, 1977)

Mammals
by J. Whitaker (Knopf, 1980)

Easy-to-use guides with color photos of hundreds of species, referenced to family and species descriptions, habitat, range, food, and life cycle.

The Audubon Society Nature Guides

Deserts
by J. McMahon (Knopf, 1992)

Eastern Forests
by A. and M. Sutton (Knopf, 1993)

Grasslands
by L. Brown (Knopf, 1989)

Western Forests
by S. Whitney (Knopf, 1986)

Comprehensive guides that describe trees, shrubs, wildflowers, birds, mammals, insects, reptiles, and amphibians found in each habitat. Include color photographs of each animal species, plus a range map, description, typical sounds, habitat, range, and a few interesting facts.

The Field Guide to Wildlife Habitats of the Eastern United States
by J. Benyus (Fireside/Simon & Schuster, 1989)

The Field Guide to Wildlife Habitats of the Western United States
by J. Benyus (Fireside/Simon & Schuster, 1989)

A detailed look at twenty eastern or western U.S. habitats including nine different forest types. Each habitat section contains a list of typical plant species, a wildlife locator chart, and detailed natural histories of three organisms commonly found there.

A Guide to Animal Tracking and Behavior
by D. Stokes (Little, Brown, 1986)

Life-size illustrations of tracks and scats, plus over 200 drawings of animals signs provide references for becoming a wildlife tracker. Also includes chapters on individual animals with information on locomotion, food and feeding habits, family life, habitat, range, and typical signs.

For Students ∎ ∎ ∎ ∎ ∎ ∎ ∎ ∎ ∎ ∎ ∎

SCIENCE BOOKS

Beastly Neighbors: All About Wild Things in the City, or Why Earwigs Make Good Mothers
by M. Rights (Little, Brown, 1981)

Readers take a journey from a supermarket to a wastewater treatment plant, and make an expedition to an old board along the way. This book makes it clear that kids can study nature wherever they are, and includes many enticing and unusual activity ideas.

Being a Plant
by L. Pringle (Crowell, 1983)

Portrays the interrelationships among flowers, birds, insects, and other animals. Includes clear illustrations of plant structure, reproduction, and adaptation.

The City Kid's Field Guide
by E. Herberman (Simon & Schuster, 1989)

Based on the Nova television series, this book features color photographs that inspire kids to understand that cities are crammed with wildlife, and offers tips for finding and observing animals in the city.

Ecosystems and Food Chains
by F. Sabin (Troll, 1985)

A brief and simple book that explains the interdependence of plants, animals, and their environment. It emphasizes the effects of human actions on ecosystems.

Keeping Minibeasts
by B. Watts (Franklin Watts, 1991)

Uses close-up color photographs and very simple text to show how to find, house, feed, care for, and observe small creatures that are found in gardens, parks, and open spaces.

Looking at Insects
by D. Suzuki (Warner, 1986)

Sharing his fascination with the strange world of insects, the author includes illustrated chapters on common orders of insects and spiders, as well as easy activities and experiments.

Nature Detective: How to Solve Outdoor Mysteries
by E. Docekal (Sterling, 1989)

For kids who want to figure out what is living, eating, and sleeping right in their everyday environment. Provides sixteen "cases" and over 200 illustrated "clues" to nature mysteries that take young detectives from fields, to forests, ponds, and even into outer space.

A Night and Day in the Desert
by J. Dewey (Little, Brown, 1991)

Vivid images of many desert life forms, interactions, and cycles are presented through rich illustrations and clear descriptions of a flurry of daily and nightly activities.

One Small Square Backyard
by D. Silver (W.H. Freeman, 1993)

Highlights the exciting discoveries that are possible to make in plant and animal communities contained in a square foot of backyard. Includes a multitude of detailed illustrations and activities, and an in-depth look at life in the soil.

Secrets in the Meadow
by L. Hess (Scribner's, 1986)

Riveting black and white photographs come together with text to capture the fascinating story of the interdependent inhabitants of the meadow.

24 Hours in a Forest
by B. Watts (Franklin Watts, 1990)

An outstanding photographic study with informative text that reveals the changes that take place, from the microscopic to the largest life forms in a forest habitat.

Urban Roosts
by B. Bash (Little, Brown, 1990)

Examines the inventive places that pigeons, barn owls, nighthawks, and peregrine falcons make their homes in the heart of the city. Useful to encourage observation of wildlife in odd places such as traffic lights, tile roofs, and train trestles.

Wonders of the Desert
by L. Sabin (Troll, 1982)

Although written for the lower elementary level, this colorfully illustrated book is a good resource for learning about many of the animals of the American deserts, and their special adaptations to their habitat.

FIELD GUIDES

Animal Tracks
by G. Mason (Linnet, 1988)

A simple, well-organized tracking guide that provides an introduction to animals—their families, habitats, behaviors, and foods. Short, anecdotal descriptions of common North American animals accompany illustrations of animals and their footprints. Emphasizes the location of tracks as a clue to identifying animals.

The Audubon Society Pocket Guides

Familiar Insects and Spiders of North America
edited by J. Farrand, Jr. (Knopf, 1988)

Familiar Mammals of North America
edited by J. Farrand, Jr. (Knopf, 1988)

Familiar Birds of North America - Eastern
edited by A. Whitman (Knopf, 1986)

Familiar Birds of North America - Western
edited by A. Whitman (Knopf, 1986)

These compact guides are illustrated with color plates, and contain information on each of the familiar organisms, such as identification tips, habitat, range, and life cycle.

Crinkleroot's Guide to Knowing the Trees
by J. Arnosky (Bradbury, 1992)

On a walk through his forest, Crinkleroot introduces broadleaf and evergreen trees. Includes a three-page field guide to identifying trees by their leaves.

No Bones: A Key to Bugs and Slugs, Worms and Ticks, Spiders and Centipedes and Other Creepy Crawlies
by E. Shepherd (Macmillan, 1988)

A simple key leads to short, fascinating, and simply-written chapters on soil invertebrates. Also includes chapters on various flying and non-flying insects, and a comprehensive chapter on spiders with drawings of their different webs.

STORIES

All Upon a Sidewalk
by J. George (Dutton, 1974)

This book presents an ant's eye view of ecology. The story of *Lasius flavius*, a yellow ant who has an important mission to perform for her queen. We follow her adventures as she searches the sidewalk for the "wondrous treasure."

The Cactus Hotel
by B. Guiberson (Holt, 1991)

This story dramatizes the life cycle of the saguaro cactus and its role as a haven for desert animals. Also highlights the beneficial interactions between plants and animals, such as a pack rat drinking water dripping off of a tree, while birds, bees, and bats drink nectar from the cactus flower.

The Day They Parachuted Cats on Borneo: A Drama of Ecology
by C. Pomerantz (Young Scott Books/Addison-Wesley, 1971)

Based on a true story of how Borneo was affected when sprayed with DDT to wipe out mosquito populations. This book explores the ecological reverberations for the entire food web, from cockroaches, rats, cats, and geckos, to the river and the farmer. The powerful, humorous text is recommended for reading aloud or performing as a play.

The Empty Lot
by D. Fife (Sierra Club/Little, Brown, 1991)

Is a vacant lot truly vacant? Vacant lot owner, Harry Hale wants to sell his lot, but when he takes a last look he is astonished to find that the lot is far from empty. From birds and their nests to frogs and dragonflies, the lot is full of living things in a variety of different habitats. He changes his "FOR SALE" sign to read "OCCUPIED LOT— EVERY SQUARE INCH IN USE."

Forest Log

by J. Newton (Crowell, 1980)

Beautifully illustrated in black and white, this story reveals the ecological interactions that occur when a huge Douglas fir tree falls. Although written for the lower elementary level, teachers in the Pacific Northwest might find it useful for older students as an introduction to the flora and fauna of that region.

Incident at Hawk's Hill

by A. Eckert (Little, Brown, 1971)

A gripping novel based on the true story of Ben, a young boy on the prairie who has a special gift for understanding animal behavior. An amazing relationship begins when Ben, lost in a prairie rainstorm, is taken in by a female badger who cares for him for over two months. The novel portrays prairie badger ecology, and is good for reading aloud.

Nicky the Nature Detective

by U. Svedberg (R&S Books/Farrar, Straus & Giroux, 1988)

Exploring changes in nature is Nicky's specialty, and her discoveries allow the reader to join her in carefully examining the structure of a nesting place, the tracks left in the snow, and a zillion other fascinating creatures and plants.

The Old Ladies Who Liked Cats

by C. Greene (HarperCollins, 1991)

What happened when the old ladies stopped letting their cats out at night? Based on Charles Darwin's story about clover and cats, this ecological tale highlights island ecology, particularly the interrelationships of plants and animals.

One Day in the Prairie

by J. George (Crowell, 1986)

Spend an interesting day on the prairie observing nature through the eyes of a boy, a buffalo, and a prairie dog. The book is full of the interactions of over thirty-five animals, and also conveys how the prairie has changed and why. Other books in this series include *One Day in the Desert* and *One Day in the Woods*.

The Roadside

by D. Bellamy (Clarkson N. Potter/Crown, 1988)

A meticulously illustrated story about the construction of a six-lane highway in a wilderness area, and how this temporary devastation forces the resident animals into a struggle for existence. Although set in the English countryside, the general events are similar to those in the United States.

Secret Neighbors—Wildlife in a City Lot

by M. Adrian (Hastings House, 1972)

A dramatic story about the lives of urban animals. Chapters describe groups of animals that survive in old tires, under rocks, in garbage cans, and in alleys as the seasons and the lot change.

The Song in the Walnut Grove

by D. Kherdian (Knopf, 1982)

When a curious cricket meets up with a grasshopper, they learn about each other's day and nighttime habits in an herb garden. They come to appreciate their differences when the cricket saves the grasshopper's life. Combines accurate information on insect behavior with descriptions of how insects affect the ecology of Walnut Grove.

Wolf Island

by C. Godkin (W.H. Freeman, 1989)

Simple, direct language and vivid full-color drawings transport the reader to a beautiful island. The story traces how changes in the size of a wolf population affect the island's entire food web.

1.1 A Research Request

Action Synopsis

Students receive a request to survey animals and their food resources on a local site, then talk about what they already know and how they could find out more.

One Session	40 minutes

1. Present the challenge of becoming ecologists to study a nearby site.

    posing a challenge

2. Talk about why knowing what animals eat is important.

    linking to real world

3. Create a visual image of the study site.

    familiarizing

4. Share thoughts about what animals live on the study site, and what they eat.

    examining prior ideas

5. Brainstorm ideas of evidence that will give clues about animals that live on the site.

    generating ideas & questions

Desired Outcomes

Throughout the lesson, check that students:

✓ Realize that people can harm or protect the food resources animals need to survive.

✓ Have a mental image of the study site, and some ideas about what animals live there.

✓ Are curious and have questions about animals and their food.

✓ Have ideas of how to look for animals and animal signs.

What You'll Need

For the class:
❏ items to help students preview their study site (see "Getting Ready")

Vocabulary

ECOLOGIST- A scientist who studies how living things interact with each other and their physical environment.

ORGANISM - A living thing (plant, animal, or microbe).

PHYSICAL ENVIRONMENT - The non-living surroundings (air, water, rocks, soil) and conditions (light, heat, wind) that something lives in.

Getting Ready

◆ Choose a project focus (see page 48). Invite a project sponsor — a local landowner, a member of an environmental group, or a school representative — to present the research request to the class. Explain that you want students to develop an understanding of food webs, and discuss how the sponsor can infuse a need for knowing what animals eat into the study request. See page xx for a sample letter from a project sponsor.

◆ Gather materials that will give students a preview of their study site. If they'll be studying a park or nature preserve you might be able to get brochures that describe the area. Otherwise, take some photographs, or collect some natural artifacts, such as a pine cone, a leaf, a soil sample, dead leaves and twigs from the ground, or a piece of trash. If you've taught this module in past years, gather lists, reports, and maps previous classes have left in the school "archives."

◆ Plan pairs of students.

Action Narrative

Over the next few weeks, each person in this class will be a type of scientist called an ECOLOGIST. What does an ecologist study?

Students are likely to mention plants, animals, and the environment. Confirm that ecologists study all of these parts of nature, but most importantly they try to figure out how these things — both living and non-living — interact.

Sometimes people ask ecologists to study a place they want to learn more about or protect. Our guest is here to tell us about a study s/he would like us to do.

Introduce your project sponsor, who might present an invitation letter to students (optional) and talk about the goals of the requested study. Continue with the following discussion after this presentation, involving your guest in familiarizing students with their study site.

So your job as ecologists will be to figure out what animals live in an outdoor area, and then figure out what those animals eat to survive. Why is it important to know what animals in a certain location use as food?

One reason students might suggest is that if an animal's food disappears or becomes toxic, the animal might die or have to find someplace else to live.

Endangered Food, Endangered Species

There is a direct link between wild animals, their food, and human activities. Species can become endangered when their food source changes, often as the result of people's actions. The giant panda, who eats only bamboo, has come close to extinction because people developed and disturbed the land where the bamboo once grew.

The whooping crane is also endangered because people harmed its food source, but in quite a different way. Hunters in marshes used lead bullets. Lead from their discarded bullets leaked into the soil, where it was taken up by plants. When the whooping crane ate these plants, the lead got into their bodies, reducing their ability to reproduce.

In both of these cases, people did not understand the link between their actions and the livelihood of animals. Research that uncovers ecological linkages can help people evaluate the consequences of their actions, and when necessary modify their plans.

Scientists always begin an investigation by thinking about what they and other people already know about the subject they're going to study. What do we already know about (name of the study site)? **Has anyone ever been there? What is it like?**

If students are familiar with the site (e.g., the schoolyard) make a list of the characteristics they mention.

If the site is not familiar, describe what you saw when you visited it, or have your guest describe it. Show them brochures, photographs, natural artifacts, or information that previous classes have gathered about the site. If you have enough items, divide the class into small groups and give each an object. Then have groups report to the class what they learned about the site.

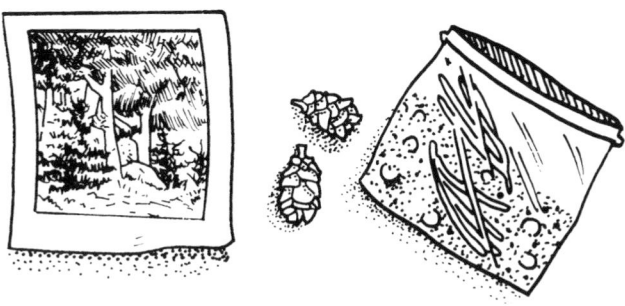

Scientists use the word ORGANISM for all living things — plants, animals, and other life forms such as bacteria and fungi. They use the term PHYSICAL ENVIRONMENT for non-living things such as rocks, soil, water, pavement, hills, and holes.

Reinforce the new vocabulary words by having students label the site characteristics they've mentioned as organisms or physical environment.

Now that we know a little bit about the site, what animals that we haven't mentioned do you think might live there?

Students will most likely think only of mammals and other vertebrates at first, so remind them that the term *animal* is used for all creatures, large and small, with and without backbones. This will help them consider common insects such as mosquitoes, flies, termites, and ants, as well as other familiar creatures such as snails, spiders, and earthworms.

What do you think those animals might eat?

Make a list of students' suggestions. Encourage them to talk about where their ideas came from — direct observations, books, television, other people. Ask them which sources of information they most trust to be accurate, and why.

 Invite students to record questions on a class chart. You might want to add some questions such as:

Do most animals eat just one thing or many different things?

Does more than one kind of animal eat the same thing?

Will we find more animals that eat plants, or more that eat other animals?

How are we going to figure out what animals live on our site? Then how will we figure out what they eat? Work with a partner for a few minutes to come up with some ideas of what we should look for outside to tell us what animals live there and what they eat. Remember that it's not always easy to see animals directly, so we'll also have to find evidence that they live there. Think about using all of your senses, not just sight.

Have pairs share some of their ideas with the whole class. Some animal evidence they might mention: seeing feathers, fur, bones, droppings, snakeskins, insect eggs, galls, nests, holes, tracks, trails, dens, burrows, woodpecker holes, chewed plants, scratchings, piles of pine cones; hearing bird calls, insects buzzing, dogs barking, squirrels and chipmunks scolding, scurrying sounds in bushes; smelling skunks and fox dens.

The idea of looking for animal signs outdoors might be foreign to some students, particularly if they live in a city. Using a human analogy might help. Ask students to imagine that they are visiting another country, and they want to figure out what the people there eat. Since they cannot speak or understand the language, they have to look for *evidence* of what the people eat. List students' ideas of where they would look to gather evidence. They might suggest cupboards, refrigerators, garbage cans, restaurants, grocery stores, and markets. They could go to dinner at someone's house, or watch people to see what food they buy or gather, observe if they have gardens or major crops, and if they raise and slaughter animals.

Once you have a list of suggestions, draw analogies:

Humans	Wildlife
Cupboards or refrigerator	Stashes of acorns, nuts, berries, etc.
Leftovers	Partially chewed or bored nuts, berries, leaves, etc.
Garbage	Piles of pine cone scales left by squirrels, chewed corncobs left by raccoons, etc.
Grocery shopping	Animals gathering food
Visit for dinner	Watch animals eat
Eating utensils	Animal mouthparts, claws, etc.

Ongoing Assessment

Student Reflections

 Have students send a C-Mail message or record thoughts in their journals. Optional writing prompts include:

What would it be like to have to find my own food in nature instead of going to a grocery store? What would I eat?

What animal signs have I seen before? What could have made them?

Teacher Reflections

❏ How rich is students' knowledge about what animals live in the local area?

❏ How familiar are they with different kinds of animal signs?

❏ Do they have realistic or imaginative notions about what wild animals eat?

Extension

Endangered Species. Challenge students to find out about an animal that is endangered and what circumstances led to its current situation. Encourage them to contact Congressional representatives for their perspectives on the federal Endangered Species Act.

1.2 Preparing for Field Work

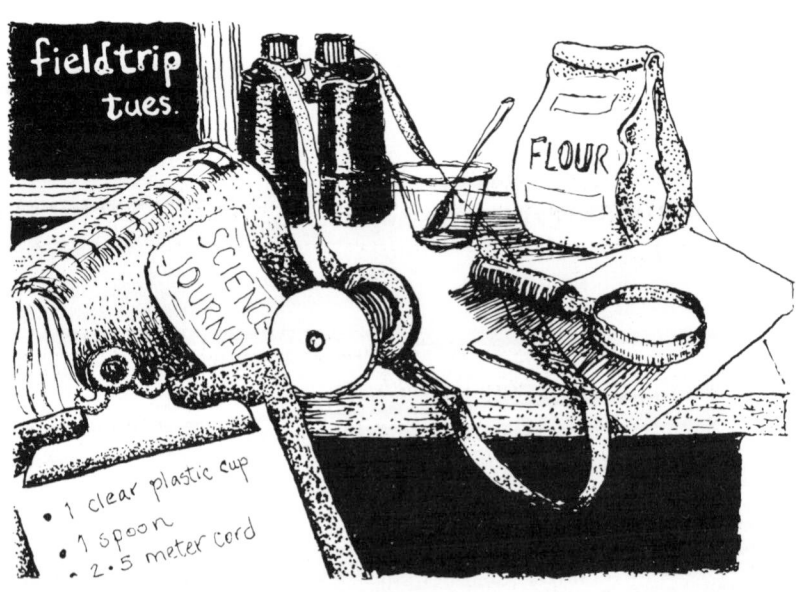

Action Synopsis

Students become familiar with what animals and animal signs to look for outdoors, then practice field research skills and methods.

Session 1   **40 minutes**

1. Show and discuss pictures of animals and animal signs.   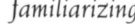 *familiarizing*

2. Plan and practice field techniques (setting up a study plot, finding animals and animal signs, capturing and observing small animals).    *demonstrating methods*

Session 2   **40 minutes**

1. Practice observation and notetaking skills.   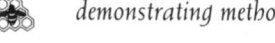 *observing & recording*

2. Prepare a journal page for recording observations and ideas.   *documenting*

3. Discuss how to behave like scientists while doing field work.    *setting standards*

Desired Outcomes

Throughout the lesson, check that students:

✓ Are familiar with some of the animals and animal signs they might see outdoors.

✓ Know how to gather evidence of what animals eat.

✓ Know how to set up a study plot and where to look for animals within the plot.

✓ Are able to use humane techniques for capturing and observing small animals.

✓ Have sharper observation skills, and understand the difference between an observation and an idea.

✓ Are ready to behave like scientists outdoors.

What You'll Need

Session 1

For the class:
- ❑ overhead transparencies of animals and animal signs (see "Getting Ready")
- ❑ set of field equipment:
  - pointed metal or wooden stake, about 60 cm long
  - 2.5 meter cord tied to a metal ring that fits over the stake
  - clear plastic cup
  - plastic spoon
  - cotton swab
  - index card
  - small eraser or piece of chalk

Session 2

For each student:
- ❑ hand lens
- ❑ item to observe (see "Getting Ready")

Vocabulary

FIELD - Scientists' name for the outdoors.

STUDY PLOT - A small piece of land used for observations.

Getting Ready

Session 1

♦ Make overhead transparencies using pictures from the *Who Eats What* guide (pages 355–382). First find the habitat description that most closely resembles your study site. Then choose pictures of a few signs of animals from pages 360–364, and several animal pictures from pages 367–381. Animals students are most likely to see include squirrels, sow bugs, millipedes, beetles, and spiders. You might want to enlarge the pictures on a copier so that you have just one image per overhead.

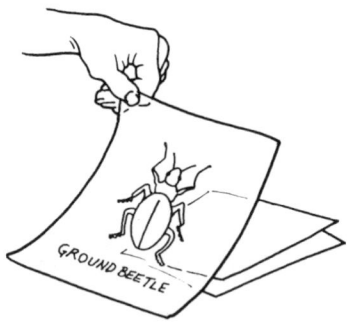

Session 2

♦ Gather enough objects so that each student (or every two students) has something to use to practice observation skills. Small stones, dead leaves, pine cones, twigs, or pieces of fruit are appropriate materials. Using items that are similar to one another will allow you to extend the activity by mixing them and challenging students to find the object they observed.

Action Narrative

Session 1

Let's look at some pictures of animal signs we might see on our study site.

Show and discuss the animal signs overheads you've made, pointing out that looking on or among plants provides many clues about animals. Also emphasize that finding animals and animal signs takes careful observation and patience.

One way to find animal signs is to think like Sherlock Holmes. When he walked onto the scene of a crime he looked for things that were out of place or different from usual. On the study site, green leaves and fresh twigs on the ground could mean that squirrels or insects are feeding overhead. Dirt and leaves scraped aside might indicate that an animal is burying or looking for food there. Leaves with holes or edges eaten away could mean that a caterpillar or other insects are eating the leaf. A white coating of droppings on leaves might be the result of a bird that flew over or perched above them. Keeping your eyes open for things that don't appear quite right is a good way to tune into animal activity outdoors.

Now let's look at some pictures of animals we might see at our study site. By thinking about the answers to three questions, we can figure out some information about what an animal eats:

1) Where is the animal located?

2) What sort of body (mouth, eyes, legs, and shape) does the animal have?

3) How does the animal behave?

If you show a picture of an earthworm, students might suggest that it is found in the soil near the surface, so there is a good chance it eats something that is in or on top of the soil. It doesn't seem to have eyes or legs. It does have a mouth opening, but no teeth or pincers, so it probably doesn't eat other animals. It stretches and contracts. This helps it get food in the soil, and to avoid becoming food for another animal by retreating quickly from the surface. Have students take this kind of reasoning as far as they can for each animal picture you show.

Scientists always make a plan of action before they start an investigation. What are some things we should plan before we go outside?

Students might mention that they need to decide what they should do, what equipment they'll need, what notes they should take, and how to split up the space and tasks. Give them as much responsibility for deciding how to run the study as possible, trying to strike a balance between encouraging them to develop their own plans and teaching them the field methods described below.

We're going to use some of the same methods ecologists use when they do studies like ours in the FIELD, their name for the outdoors. We'll work in small groups. Each group will have a set of field equipment to make a STUDY PLOT, a small piece of land used for observations.

Show students the field equipment. Ask a volunteer to hold the stake upright on the floor. Slip the ring and cord over the stake and have another student hold the end of the cord so that it is fully stretched.

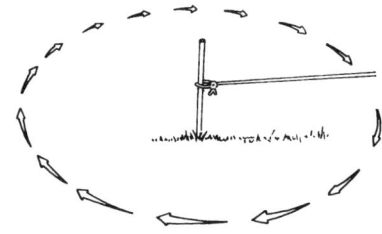

When you're outside, another team member will walk behind the person holding the cord to sprinkle a flour border in his or her footsteps.

Have the cord holder walk the circumference of the circle, acting like a human drawing compass, while a student follows pretending to sprinkle flour.

The area within your flour circle will be your study plot. Where will you look for animals and animal signs within your plot?

Students might suggest looking under leaves, sticks, rocks, and logs; on leaves, twigs, and trunks; in moist spots, crevices, and topsoil.

In order not to trample any plants, animals, or animal homes, remember to step lightly, touch gently, and move gracefully within your plot. Imagine yourselves "stalking" nature, acting like Native Americans did while hunting, being both aware and respectful.

Have a few students demonstrate stalking around the classroom.

Ecologists often capture small animals for closer observation. How would it feel to be an ant captured by a giant? How would you want to be treated?

Demonstrate three ways that a small animal can be gently captured, using a pencil eraser or a small piece of chalk to represent the animal:

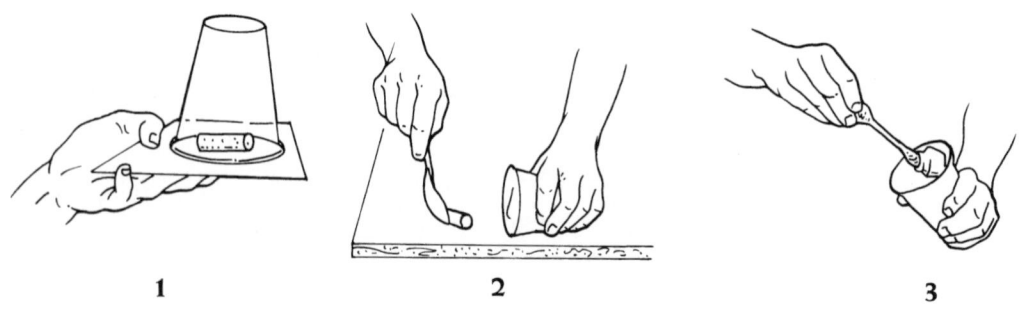

1

2

3

1) Put the open end of the cup over the object, then slide an index card beneath it. Once sealed, turn the cup right side up and keep the card on top.

2) Coax the animal into the cup using the spoon.

3) Put the cotton swab in the path of the animal so it will crawl up it, then put the swab and animal in the cup.

Demonstrate how to use the hand lens through the top, side, or bottom of the cup for closer viewing.

After you observe a small animal, it is important to return it back where you found it. Be sure not to touch animals with your bare hands — for your own safety and for the creature's protection.

Session 2

Scientists have to be careful observers. What does a good observer do?

As students list characteristics of good observers, encourage them to talk about times when they have watched something carefully or noticed something that nobody else did. Key qualities of observers include: looking closely and carefully, listening intently, noticing key features, watching something over time, being patient and aware, and practicing these skills often. You might want to record students' ideas on a poster to hang in the classroom, and encourage them to continue to add to or revise the list.

> To Be a Careful Observer
> Look at something for a long time.
> Look underneath stuff.
> Keep your eyes peeled when you're somewhere new.
> Close your eyes and see how much you remember about something.
>
> Tell someone else exactly what something looks like.
> Keep checking on a place to notice how things change.

Let's practice observation and recording skills using your science journal. On the left side of a page write "Observations." When I give you something to observe, look closely at it. Then, when you're ready, jot down some words that describe it.

Give each student or pair of students an object to observe (e.g., a twig, leaf, rock). Make your own observations of an object along with the students.

> Observations
> It is thick at one end and skinny at the other.
> The thick part is brown.
> The skinny tips are yellow.
> It's bendy.
> There are little white spots all over its bark.

After five or ten minutes, show students a hand lens and demonstrate how to use it. The best approach is to hold the hand lens up to your eye, resting your thumb on your cheek, then bring the object up to the lens, or move your head to the object, rather than moving the lens away from your eye toward the object. Give each student a lens so that they can practice this technique.

Have them record any additional observations of their object they make using the hand lens.

Now, on the top of the right side of the page write "Comments and Questions." As scientists make observations they get ideas and generate questions about what something is, how it works, what it is related to, how it survives, and so forth. Take a few minutes to note some comments and questions about your object.

You might want to share a few examples of ideas you have about the object you've been observing to get students started. Comments can be musings about what made the object look like it does (*Something ate a hole in it*), personal reactions to it (*This rock is pretty*), conjectures (*The twig probably came from a big tree because it is long and thick*), etc. Questions can arise from something puzzling (*Do those white spots have a purpose?*), a desire to know the item's origin (*What kind of tree did this come from?*), general queries (*Do plants have feelings?*), etc.

Observations	Comments and questions
It is thick at one end and skinny at the other.	An animal chewed off the tip.
The thick part is brown.	Why is the bark red?
The skinny tips are yellow.	
It's bendy.	
There are little white spots all over its bark.	

When students are done writing, have them share some of their observations, comments, and questions with a partner, or share them aloud as a class.

If you have used items that are only slightly different from one another, a fun additional activity is to mix them all together and challenge students to find the one they observed.

 Conclude the activity with questions such as:

How many new things did you notice after you used the hand lens?
Point out that scientists use tools like lenses to improve and extend their observations.

What happened the longer you looked at the object?
It is amazing how much it is possible to see in one small item just by taking the time to look carefully. This is a particularly useful way to learn to identify plants and animals.

What is the difference between an observation and a comment or idea?
An observation is a statement of fact that anyone who looks at the same item will probably agree with. A comment or idea is more personal, a hunch or an opinion that not everyone would share. Ideas and questions can lead to investigations.

 **You'll need a place to record notes while we're outside. Scientists always prepare a data sheet to remind them what information to record. Prepare a page in your journals for your notes by drawing a line down the center of an empty page. Write "Observations" on the left half, and "Comments and Questions" on the right side. What kinds of notes will you put in each of these sections?**

Students are likely to respond that in the "Observations" section they'll record whatever they see that gives them clues about what animals live on the site and what they eat: animals, plants that animals have been eating, and other signs of animals. In the "Comments and Questions" section they'll write ideas about what they think an animal they saw might eat, what animal might have made a sign they see, as well as questions relating to animals and their food. They might want to note some of these points in their journals to remind them what to record in each section when they're outside.

Observations	Comments and Questions
Reminders - Look for and describe: ☐ Animals ☐ Plants that animals have been eating ☐ Other animal signs	Reminders – Write ideas and questions about: ☐ What animals made signs ☐ What different animals eat.

What other information would be useful to record?

Encourage students to make additional sections for notes they think are important to take, such as: the date, notes about weather conditions, a list of non-living things, an overall description of the site, etc.

One last thing we need to talk about is how scientists behave while doing outdoor research. What are your ideas?

After students have shared their thoughts, add anything they haven't mentioned, such as:

- Outdoors is a place for work, like the classroom, so use time wisely.

- Handle living things and equipment with care.

- Don't damage plants by ripping leaves or bark off trees, etc.

- Stay inside the boundaries of the study area.

- Never put any leaves, berries, mushrooms, etc. in your mouth.

- Don't run, throw things, or chase animals.

- Work quietly so as not to scare away wildlife.

- Don't touch or collect any sort of dead animal, whether it's a bird, mammal, insect, worm, or whatever.

- Don't touch or pick mushrooms.

- Don't touch or collect animal droppings.

- Don't touch human artifacts that are a health hazard (e.g., needles, vials, band-aids, broken glass).

- Don't put anything, including your hands, in your mouth.

- Wash your hands as soon as you come indoors.

If exploring the outdoors is new to your students, talk through any anxieties or fears they have. Help them think of ways to get comfortable with being outdoors, so their emotions don't lead to behaviors that will distract them and others from their tasks.

Ongoing Assessment

Student Reflections

Have students send a C-Mail message or record thoughts in their journals. Optional journal writing prompts include:

Animals I'd like to see and learn more about are...

Times when I've been a good observer are...

Teacher Reflections

❑ Do students have ideas of where and how to look for animals and clues about what they eat?

❑ Are they prepared to set up study plots, use observation equipment, and take notes while outdoors?

Extensions

Mapmaking Preparation. Making a map of the study site is an optional part of the next lesson. A map of the site's natural features provides a compelling visual nucleus for students' reports, and is a common component of professional field ecologists' reports. Students will need some practice in map making techniques, however, before going outdoors.

Bring to class, and ask students to collect, examples of site maps, such as from nature center, zoo, and museum brochures. Also try to borrow a survey map of some local land from a realtor or the town or county planning department. Talk about how the scale and purpose of these maps differ from road and continent maps.

Place the map samples at stations that students can visit to observe the different techniques the map makers used. Discuss what they notice about the maps, such as how plants, paths, roads, and other features are represented, and whether or not symbols and a key are used.

You might want to enlist the help of the art teacher in providing instruction and practice drawing maps, perhaps by mapping the classroom. Precise scale is not so important for the study site map as is simply getting the prominent features of the plots drawn in a way that is easy for the viewer to interpret. The maps shown below use combinations of symbols and pictures from two viewpoints: a bird's eye view in which the artist imagines s/he is hovering over the plot looking down on what is there, and a ground level view in which the artist stands at one edge of the plot.

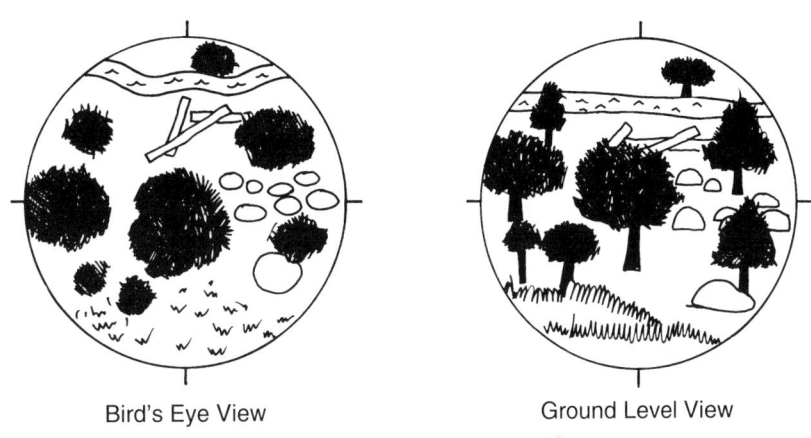

Bird's Eye View   Ground Level View

Before going outside, students might want to make a key of symbols for common objects such as dead logs, pine trees, other trees, shrubs, small plants, and rocks. They can refine and add to these symbols once they are outside.

Finally, help students make a map template by drawing a circle on a piece of unlined paper to represent their study plot This is best done with a compass (or a string tied to a pencil), or by tracing a circular object. Ask them to imagine the circle as a clock face and make short lines at 12, 3, 6, and 9 o'clock. At the top of the circle (12 o'clock), have them write a large N for north. When they are outside students can use flour to mark these same lines on their plot circle, to use as guides for placing features on their map.

More Observation Practice. Take the class outdoors. Set boundaries. Then give students about ten minutes to find a plant or non-living object and write a description of it. Have them exchange their descriptions with a partner, and try to find the object their partner has described. When they have found it (either on their own or with their partner's help), have them add as many new written details as they can to the original description. Once back indoors, discuss why it was easy or difficult to find the objects and how the activity helped them sharpen their observation and recording skills.

1.3 Outdoor Research Excursion

Action Synopsis

Students visit their study site to look for animals and clues about their food resources. The next day they process their findings.

Session 1		**1½–2 hours** **OUTDOORS**
1. Get oriented to the outdoor site.		*familiarizing*
2. Set up study plots, and record observations of animals, animal signs, and food clues.		*observing & recording*
3. Show and describe discoveries.		*processing findings*
4. Make maps of the study plots. (optional)		*documenting*

Session 2		**40 minutes**
1. Refine and compile field notes.		*processing findings*
2. Discuss the biodiversity of the study site.		*introducing new information*
3. Decide what makes the study site an ecosystem.		*introducing new information*

Desired Outcomes

Throughout the lesson, check that students:

✓ Are able to point out evidence of what animals live on the study site and what they eat.

✓ Know how to categorize things in nature, and use the terms biotic and abiotic.

✓ Are able to make some general statements about the biodiversity and food resources on their study plots, and on the site as a whole.

✓ Understand that their site is an ecosystem.

What You'll Need

Session 1

For the class:
- ❑ supplementary field equipment (optional)
  - trays (e.g., cookie sheets, foil pans, dishpans) lined with white paper
  - whistle
  - video or polaroid camera
  - several metal soupspoons
  - field guides (see "Resource List," pages 52, 54)
  - compass
  - sweep nets (see "Getting Ready")

For each group of 3-4 students:
- ❑ pointed metal or wooden stake, about 60 cm long
- ❑ 2.5 meter cord tied to a metal ring that fits over the stake
- ❑ cup of flour in a baggie
- ❑ shopping bag
- ❑ copy of the *Who Eats What* guide (pages 355–382)

For each student:
- ❑ clear plastic cup
- ❑ plastic spoon
- ❑ cotton swab
- ❑ index card
- ❑ hand lens
- ❑ map template (if created in Lesson 1.2)

Session 2

For the class:
- ❑ newsprint sheets for class lists
- ❑ 2 pieces of oak tag for master map (optional)

ABIOTIC - Something that was never alive (water, rocks); the physical environment.

BIODIVERSITY - The variety of different kinds of living things in an area.

BIOTIC - Something that is alive, or used to be alive.

ECOSYSTEM - An area where living things interact with each other and their physical environment.

LEAF LITTER - A layer of dead leaves on the ground.

Getting Ready

Session 1

◆ The most important preparation for this lesson is to visit the study site to decide on boundaries and placement of students' study plots, and to get familiar with it yourself (see "Scope out a study site," page 49).

◆ Send home a field trip permission slip along with a list of recommended clothing for the day (e.g., closed-toe footwear, socks, light-colored long pants and long-sleeved shirts, jackets, hats, and rain gear).

◆ Schedule a school bus if necessary, arranging to spend about two hours at the site. Also try to arrange for some chaperons to help out on the field trip.

◆ You might want to buy (from a science supply catalog) or make (using a broom handle, nylon stocking or cheesecloth, and a coat hanger) insect sweep nets, especially if your study site is a grassy or shrubby area.

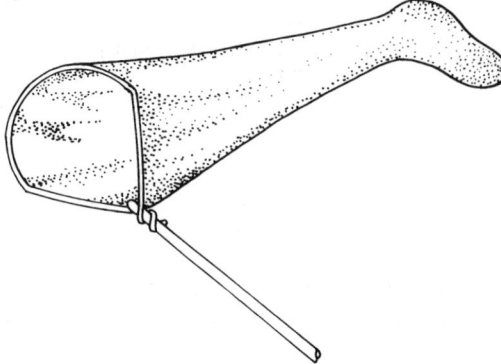

◆ Decide if you want to document the site with photographs or videotape, and if so gather the necessary equipment.

◆ Plan groups of three to four students.

◆ Divide the field equipment into a set for each group. A plastic or paper shopping bag works well as a carrying container for each group's equipment.

◆ If this field trip will be your only visit to the study site, read the information in Lesson 1.4

about collecting organisms for further study, and make preparations to do that during this trip.

◆ Read "Hidden Critters" (page 84) to decide if you want to make Berlese funnels as a follow-up to the field trip. If so, bring plastic bags outside to collect soil and leaf litter samples, and have students bring in 2-liter soda bottles.

◆ If students are going to make maps, prepare a large master map by taping together two pieces of oak tag. Transfer the sketch you made during a preliminary site visit (see page 50) of the site boundaries and prominent features to the oak tag, and mark the approximate locations of each study plot so students will know where to attach their plot maps.

Session 2

◆ Prepare a wall or bulletin board where class lists and a master map can stay posted for a while.

Action Narrative

Session 1

Before we go outside, let's review the purpose of our study trip.

Have students tell you their goals for the outdoor excursion — finding out what animals live on the site and what they use as food resources.

I'm going to bring out some books that might be useful for looking things up in the field.

Show students the field guides you've collected. Distribute a copy of the *Who Eats What* guide to each group. Tell them that they can use the "Where to Look" (page 359) and the "How to Figure Out What an Animal Eats" (page 366) sections to remind them of procedures they practiced during the last session.

Each group needs one set of field equipment, and each person needs to bring your journal and a pencil.

As students collect their materials and gather into groups, assign a number to each group so that you can refer to each study plot by the group's number.

Remember that we'll see more by being quiet and moving carefully within our study plots. And we should treat the environment with care.

 When you arrive at the study site, gather students in an open area.

This is our meeting spot. Leave your lunches and packs here so they don't clutter your study plots. When you hear this signal (demonstrate a whistle or some other attention-getting sound), **finish up what you're doing and gather back at this spot.**

While still gathered at the central meeting location, point out key landmarks that serve as site boundaries.

Show each group to its plot location, and oversee the setting up of study plots. If the ground is too hard for the stake to penetrate, one student can hold the stake upright while the others walk around it, holding the outstretched cord and marking a circular border with flour.

Once the plots are outlined, visit each group to remind everyone to look at all levels, from below their feet to above their heads.

Caution! In regions where there are venomous creatures such as snakes, scorpions, and spiders, caution students against reaching underneath anything before looking. They should stand behind rocks they are lifting to keep a barrier between themselves and anything poisonous, or use a stick to turn things over.

Let students explore freely for a while before reminding them to take notes. They'll want to feel they've done and seen things worth recording before they write.

Initially students might think there is nothing to see if animals are not jumping out at them within their study plots. Children vary in their inclination towards observation, and in what they find interesting. Some will get absorbed in one pursuit while others ricochet around their study plot. Invite these less-focused students to show you what they've found, and ask them questions about their findings. With focusing and encouragement, children soon tune in to the subtleties of nature, and end up finding more than most adults would!

As important as it is to set the atmosphere for focused field work right away, it's also important to respond to the students' level of excitement. If someone finds something right away that causes a lot of commotion, gather the group around to see it, then remind them that they have a lot to do, so they need to get back to their work. If students are too wound up to focus, lead a "silent nature walk" by having them follow you around the site without talking, collecting images to report at the end of the walk. Give students who are uncomfortable in the outdoors some individual attention and guidance. You might capture a small critter for them to observe to show them that there is nothing to be afraid of.

Provide groups with supplementary equipment such as trays, metal spoons, and field guides. If you have sweep nets, have students sweep different areas (e.g., a mown lawn and a tall patch of weeds) and compare how many different kinds of insects they find in each location.

If you have brought a camera or camcorder, involve each group in deciding what aspects of its study plot to document on film.

Help each group look for signs of animals eating plants and mushrooms, other animal signs, animals, and other notable features.

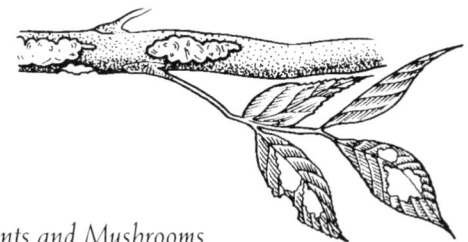

Signs of Animals Eating Plants and Mushrooms

Remind students to look for nibbles and holes on leaves, stems, trunks, fruits, seeds, and mushroom caps.

 Ask focusing questions such as:

What parts of the plant are being eaten? Are those parts tough, juicy, tender?

Do some kinds of plants have more evidence of being eaten than others?

Why would insects prefer certain types of plants?

Can you tell what kinds of mouthparts made the signs?

How big do you think the animal was that made the marks?

Did more than one kind of animal feed on this plant? How can you tell?

Other Animal Signs

Help students look for: burrows and holes in the ground, especially near tree roots; bird and mammal nests in branches and among grass; trails, tunnels, and runways in tall grass and rotten logs; scat on rocks or soil; bedding areas in grass; anthills and termite mounds in sandy soil; digging and scratching marks on the ground or on tree trunks; tracks on moist sand or mud; bones and feathers on the ground; galls on plant stems and leaves; and cocoons and webs on or between plants stems or hanging from branches. Remind students that trash and other human debris are also animal signs. Food wrappings and containers give direct evidence of what humans eat, and sometimes provide habitats for non-human animals.

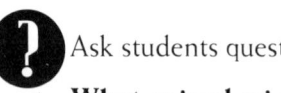 Ask students questions such as::

What animal might have made the sign?

Is it a recent or an old sign? How can you tell?

Was it made by one animal or several animals?

What was the animal doing or looking for when it made the sign? Was its activity related to getting food? If not, what other aspect of survival does the sign tell us about?

Animals

Help students look for insects on plants, especially on leaf and flower buds, on the tips of branches, in curled leaves, and on the underside of leaves. You might find other small animals among dead leaves on the ground. Shake leaves gently over a white tray or use the tray for sorting through the dead leaves, where small critters will stand out against the white background.

Tree stumps, dead logs, and the underside of fallen branches and rocks also provide dark, humid environments where students are likely to find small animals. Make sure that they treat these microhabitats with care — ripping bark off a fallen log, for instance, will ruin the covering and climate that the animals need — and replace anything they moved. Students should also look and listen for animals overhead, such as flying or perched birds, and squirrels leaping from limb to limb.

 When students see a small animal, encourage them to watch its behavior before capturing it. As they observe it, first within its context and then in a cup using a hand lens, ask:

Can you guess what it eats based on where your found it?

What behaviors help it get food?

What body parts help it get food?

Is its mouth like a straw, a needle, a scraper, a sponge, a chisel, or scissors?

Based on its shape, mouthparts, legs, and behaviors, do you think it eats other animals?

What helps it escape from becoming another animal's food?

Which area of the LEAF LITTER, the layer of dead leaves on the ground, has the most animals?
    Most animals stay in the inner, moist layer of a leaf stack.

Are different kinds or amounts of animals in different kinds of leaf litter?
There will most likely be a greater number and diversity of animals in moist, tender leaves.

Do the animals in dead leaves behave the same or differently from one another?
Some will "scram" and some will "freeze" when their leaf covering is removed.

How do these behaviors help them survive?
Escaping predators or blending into the background by being still are survival tactics.

Can you tell which animals eat the leaves, and which eat the animals that eat the leaves?
Sow bugs and millipedes eat dead leaves, whereas centipedes with their pincers, agile bodies, and quick movements, eat small animals among the leaves.

Pill Bugs and Sow Bugs

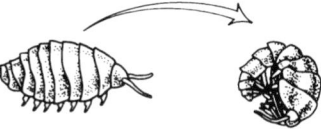

Pill Bug   Sow Bug

Two small critters that are common among dead leaves and wood are pill bugs and sow bugs. They are both members of a group of animals called isopods and look very much alike, but have a few noticeable differences. A pill bug (also called a roly poly) rolls into a ball when it is disturbed. Its back is round like a dome and it can't flip back over when it is turned upside-down. A sow bug has a flat body, two tail-like appendages, can quickly flip right side up, and scrams when disturbed.

Other Notable Features

Encourage students to record other interesting things. These could include topography and prominent features of their plot, names or descriptions of plants, and a list of non-living things.

Everyone come to our meeting spot to tell the other groups about one interesting thing you found.

Students will be ready to share some of their findings with the whole class after they've spent about an hour exploring. Have everyone think about what each group's discovery tells about potential feeding interactions on the study site. Even if every student made just two observations, such as a hole in a leaf and a millipede, the class will have enough information to begin to build food chains and webs. If they didn't see as many animals or animals signs as they expected, ask them to think about why.

Optional Mapping Activity

Hand out the map templates students prepared (see "Mapmaking Preparation," page 70). Show them which way is north (either use a compass or make your best guess), and make sure mapmakers stand in their plots and orient their papers so that the N is pointing to the north before they begin drawing.

If there is time, students can test their maps by inviting a neighboring group member to see if they can locate the features shown on the map, then make adjustments to make their maps more accurate.

Session 2

Take a few minutes to talk over your field notes in your groups. Complete any observations or ideas you didn't finish recording outside. Choose someone to be the group reporter, and make sure that person has a complete list of everything you found in your study plot.

Discussing and refining their notes helps students process their study trip findings. Especially encourage them to expand the "Comments and Questions" section of their notes, by sharing thoughts about what animals might have made what signs, and who eats what.

If students have made plot maps, this is a good time to have one person from each group cut out a circle map and attach it to the master map you've outlined on oak tag.

What would be the best way for us to pool our information to get a complete picture of the study site? We need a way to present our findings to (the group that requested the study).

Students are likely to decide to compile their results by listing findings by category or by listing findings by study plot:

Listing Findings by Category

Students decide on the major categories within which their observations fall (e.g., plants,

Module 1: *Who Eats What?*

insects, other animals, animal signs, non-living things) and assign a recorder to each category. Groups read their findings for the recorders to list. It is helpful for later analysis if the recorder puts the plot numbers where each item was found next to each listing.

ANIMAL SIGNS	Plot #									
	1	2	3	4	5	6	7	8	9	10
1. Chewed leaf	X		X		X	X				
2. hole in ground		X	X						X	

As groups read their findings, students will debate in which category some of the items belong. Encourage them to refine or expand their category titles as they encounter examples that are difficult to categorize, or as you see an opportunity to teach them how scientists group plants, animals, and fungi. For example "Plants" might become "Plants and Mushrooms"; "Insects" might be changed to "Insects and Spiders"; "Animals" might be divided into "Mammals" and "Other Small Animals"; "Animal Signs" might be elaborated to include the names of the animals they think made the sign; "Non-living" might become "Things that were never alive" (e.g., rocks, water, soil) and "Things that were once alive" (e.g., dead plants, animal bones). Students might decide to record the number of each item they found as well as its name. As they sort out where to list items and how to deal with the overlap between categories, students will be thinking like professional biologists and ecologists.

Listing Findings by Study Plot

Each group prepares, posts, and presents a large chart of its findings to the rest of the class. Categorization discussions go on in small groups as members figure how best to arrange their findings. With this method it is easy to see the character of each study plot, but more difficult to see the composition of the overall site at a glance. Students who choose this method might decide to create a whole class chart later, as well.

Plot #1

Animal Signs	Plants
1. Spider web	1. grass
2. Chewed leaves	2. dandelions

Scientists use the term BIOTIC for things that are alive or used to be alive. They call things that were never alive ABIOTIC.

Have students name examples of biotic and abiotic components of the study site.

Now that we have our findings all together, let's see what comparisons and general statements we can make.

 Help students process their findings with questions such as:

The term scientists use to describe how many different kinds of organisms live in a place is BIODIVERSITY. Which plots have high biodiversity (a lot of different kinds of living things)? Which have low biodiversity (only one or two kinds of living things)?

Did the physical conditions of plots with high biodiversity differ from plots with low biodiversity?

What organisms were found in many plots, or in other words were common on the study site?

Why do you think some organisms are more common than others?

Could how common something is have anything to do with the food it eats? How?

How well were you able to figure out what's eating what on your plots? What clues did you use? What are you still unsure about?

Where within each plot did you find the most evidence of feeding activity?

What signs of animals did you find that you aren't sure what made them?

On plots that had the same kind of animal sign, like a chewed leaf or a hole in the ground, how would you know if it was the same animal that made it in all the plots?

Have people had a high, medium, or low amount of impact on the site?

Does anyone know what an ECOSYSTEM is?
Students have usually heard the word *ecosystem*, but often aren't able to define it. You might want to break the word into its components, ECO and SYSTEM. Talk about ecology relating to the living and non-living environment, and systems having parts that work together, like stereo systems or the digestive system.

After students have shared their ideas, either write on the board or tell them the following definition: "An ecosystem is an area where living things interact with each other and their physical environment."

Can we call our study site an ecosystem?
Students should support their answers by stating if there are living things and a physical environment on their study site, and citing examples of interactions. They might mention animals interacting with the water they drink and the air they breathe; animals interacting with plants and animals they eat; animals interacting with the plants or soil where they make their homes; or plants interacting with the soil, air, water, and sunlight they use to make food.

Module 1: *Who Eats What?*

Ongoing Assessment

Student Reflections

Have students send a C-Mail message or record thoughts in their journals. Optional writing prompts include:

The most interesting, amazing, or surprising discovery I made was...

Something I figured out was...

Some things I did that are like what a scientist does are...

Is the site a good place for animals to live? Why or why not?

Teacher Reflections

❑ Were students able to use their observations to generate ideas about what animals live on the site and what they eat?

❑ Were they able to compile their findings in a logical and useful way?

❑ Can they define an ecosystem and explain what makes their study site an ecosystem?

Extensions

Concept Map. Introduce concept mapping to students (see pages 25–27). Select all or some of the concept map cards on pages 43–44, then copy one set of cards for each group of 3–4 students. Help students construct concept maps that display their prior ideas about ecosystems. Have them save their concept maps so that they can compare them to maps they'll make as an extension to Lesson 1.8, to see how their knowledge grows.

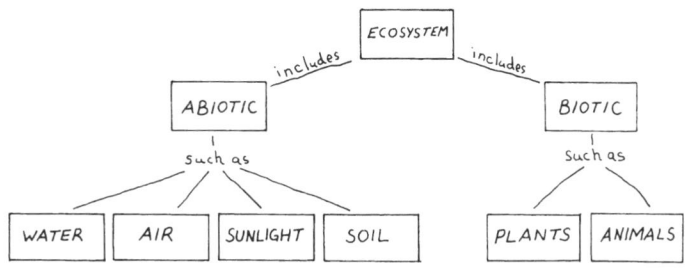

Mini-Ecosystem. Help students plan and make a terrarium that functions like a mini-ecosystem. They can start by writing a list of ingredients and what each needs to stay alive. Gallon jars, old aquaria, and 2-liter plastic bottles are good containers. Suggest that they plant some seeds in the terrarium as well as whole plants. Post an observations chart next to the terrarium for students to fill in. Keep the terrarium partly covered and out of direct sun. It should not need frequent watering.

Microclimates. Challenge students to collect and compare data on the air and soil temperature, moisture, and light intensity in different locations, such as under trees, out in the open, and on concrete. Try to correlate physical conditions with the types of plants and animals found in each place.

Adopt-a-Site. Return to the study site throughout the year to make observations of how things change over time, such as the life cycles of plants. A photo journal, field guide, or action projects (e.g., a clean-up or wildlife habitat improvements) could result.

Local History. Have students do library research and conduct interviews to find out what the study site looked like at different intervals in the past (e.g., 10, 50, 100, 500 years ago). Trace the causes of change. If the study site is a park, students can find out when it was established, by whom, and why.

Recreated Ecosystems. Visit a zoo and talk with its staff about how and why they try to recreate animals' ecosystems within their displays.

Hidden Critters. Scientists use an apparatus called a Berlese funnel to extract tiny organisms from soil samples. They put a sample of soil and leaf litter in the funnel, then put the funnel beneath a light for a day or two. As the soil gets warm and dry, critters crawl or fall into a container at the bottom of the funnel.

Guide students in collecting a small amount of topsoil, along with the dead leaves on top of the soil, from several locations. Put each sample in a separate plastic bag. Label and number each bag. Then make a Berlese funnel using a 2-liter soda bottles as follows:

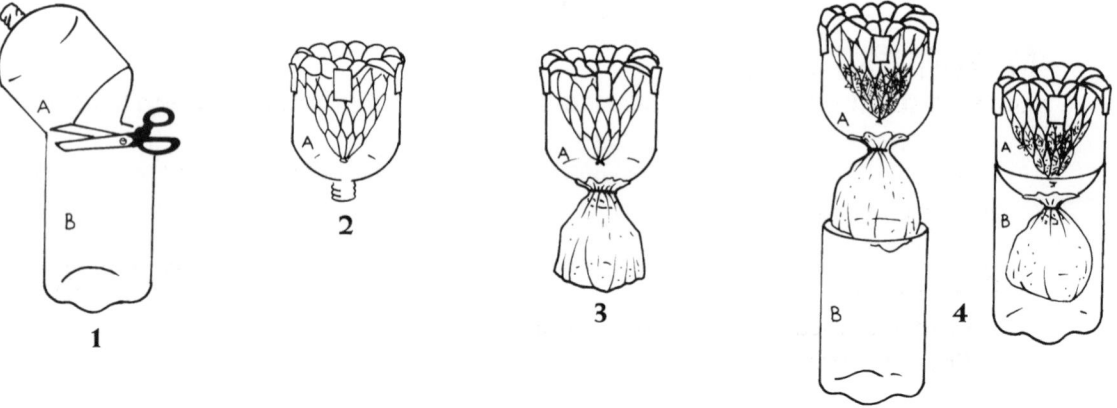

1. Cut the bottle in half to make two sections, A and B.

2. Tape a mesh bag to the inside of A so that it hangs suspended about two inches above the mouth of the bottle.

3. Attach a small plastic bag with a rubber band to the outside of the mouth of the bottle.

4. Invert A and rest it inside B. Fill the upper portion of A with soil and leaf litter, and place it under an incandescent light or in sunlight. When critters fall into the plastic bag, transfer them as soon as possible to a small dish or cup with a few drops of water. Also look for critters in the mesh bag among any material that is still moist. Look at the critters with a hand lens. Try to identify them and find out what they eat using the *Who Eats What* guide, especially the "Other Animals Without Backbones" section (pages 371–372). Springtails and mites are two organisms that might be in your sample.

1.4 Feeding Habits Investigations

Action Synopsis

Students design and carry out indoor or outdoor investigations to learn more about animals' feeding interactions.

Session 1		40–80 minutes
1. Read and discuss the story of Dr. Mary Price's research.		*linking to real world*
2. Brainstorm research questions and review a list of suggested questions.		*developing research questions*
3. Plan investigations.		*designing experiments*

Session 2		1–1½ hours IN & OUTDOORS
1. Discuss habitats.		*introducing new information*
2. Set up investigations.		*investigating*

Sessions 3 & 4		40 minutes IN or OUTDOORS
1. Take measurements, collect data, and refine investigation methods.		*investigating*
2. Record observations and ideas in journals.		*observing & recording*

Continued

3. Think about conclusions, and plan how to communicate methods and findings.

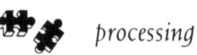 *processing findings*

Session 5	40 minutes

1. Share results of investigations.

 communicating

2. Discuss strengths and weaknesses of completed investigations.

 reflecting

Desired Outcomes

Throughout the lesson, check that students:

✓ Are familiar with the procedures of scientific research.

✓ Are able to shape a question into a form that can be answered through research.

✓ Are able to make a general plan of action for a research project, and refine it during and after the investigation.

✓ Realize that investigations don't always lead to clear conclusions, and that claims need to be backed by evidence.

What You'll Need

Session 1

For the class:
❏ overhead transparency of "Kangaroo Rat and Pocket Mouse" (page 98)

For each group of 3–4 students:
❏ copy of handout listing possible research topics (see "Getting Ready")

Session 2

For each group of 3–4 students:
For indoor studies:
❏ copy of "Classroom Critter Care Chart" (pages 105–106)
❏ copy of the *Who Eats What* guide (pages 355–382)
❏ habitat chamber (see "Classroom Critter Care Chart," pages 105–106)
❏ spoon or trowel
❏ various animal foods (see "Suggested Investigation Descriptions," pages 99–104)

For outdoor studies:
❏ various tools and animal foods (see "Suggested Investigation Descriptions," pages 99–104)

Sessions 3 & 4

For each student:
❏ hand lens

HABITAT - The place where an organism lives that provides all of its needs for survival.

HYPOTHESIS - A statement that can be tested. It often states an action as well as a predicted result (e.g., "If I do such-and-such, then such-and-such will happen").

Getting Ready

Session 1

♦ Read "Suggested Investigation Descriptions" (pages 99–104). Decide if you'll have students do indoor or outdoor studies. Prepare a handout that lists research topics, research questions, and/or possible methods. As you develop the handout, consider three levels of guidance you can provide, based on how much experience your students have had doing investigations:

Most Guided	**Somewhat Guided**	**Least Guided**
Provide a research question and a possible method.	Provide research questions, let students come up with methods.	Suggest a research topic, let students brainstorm questions and methods.

Research Question:	Possible Research Questions:	Possible Research Topics:
• How do two of the same kind of animal interact over a piece of food?	• Do earthworms prefer to eat newly fallen or partly decomposed leaves?	• Feeding behaviors
		• Food choices
	• Do different kinds of ants prefer different kinds of food?	• Foraging abilities
Possible Method:		• Amount of food consumed
• Put two sow bugs in a container with a particle of potato and watch how they interact.		

Try the Least or Somewhat Guided approach to start, using information provided in the Possible Methods sections of the "Suggested Investigation Descriptions" only as a larder for students to raid if they are hungry for ideas. The suggested investigations are observational studies rather than controlled experiments, but each can be adapted to become a "fair test" if students have done lots of simple investigating in the past and are ready to learn this more elaborate form of scientific investigation.

- Familiarize yourself with the "Classroom Critter Care Chart" (pages 105–106). For information about where organisms listed in the chart live, refer to the *Who Eats What* guide (pages 355–382).

- To attract soil organisms and scavengers/decomposers, such as sow bugs and millipedes, to an area, place damp cardboard or newspaper outside several days before students' collection.

- An alternative to collecting organisms for indoor study is to order them from a biological supply catalog. A worm farm with bedding material and redworms is a very convenient, commercially available system for investigating earthworm feeding habits.

- Plan to use either the same student groups as before, or decide on new groupings.

Session 2

- Make logistical arrangements for going outside, either to collect organisms or to set up outdoor studies.

Action Narrative

Session 1

When we were outside you gathered evidence about what different animals eat. This week you'll set up your own studies to find out more about animals and their food. First I have a story to share about a scientist named Dr. Mary Price who also does research on animals and their food.

Read aloud the story on pages 95–97. Summarize by asking students to list the steps of Dr. Price's research.

Dr. Prices's Research Steps
She...
1) saw something that made her curious
2) read what other scientists had already found out about the topic
3) asked a question
4) developed hypotheses
5) did investigations and experiments in the field and laboratory
6) came up with new questions
7) did more experiments
8) wrote up her results and gave them to other scientists to review
9) made changes to her papers and published her findings

Scientists start their research by asking a question about something that interests them. Then they develop a HYPOTHESIS — a statement that can be tested. What animals did you see, or see signs of, whose feeding behaviors you'd like to know more about?

Have students refer to the observations, comments, and questions they recorded while outdoors. Make a list of their suggestions and questions on the board. Most likely their questions will be simple to start with, such as *What do centipedes eat?*

Once you have written a list of questions in students' own words, work through one example of how to make a question specific enough to guide research. Some examples of action-oriented questions are: *Does a centipede eat dead leaves? If I put a millipede in a container with a centipede, would the centipede eat it? How much food does a centipede eat in a day?*

Scientists spend a lot of time coming up with a question because this is the first step towards finding answers. I've made a list of topics and research questions that you can investigate, or you can investigate your own question. You'll have one week to do the investigations from start to finish.

Explain whether students should plan to conduct their investigations outdoors or indoors. Hand out and go over your list of research topics and/or questions with students, then break them into groups to choose one research question, or to refine one of their own questions. Help students who are writing their own questions to put them into a form that is helpful for doing research. Use the questions you've listed on the handout as models.

If you will be doing indoor studies, discourage students from writing questions about small vertebrates such as lizards and salamanders, since it is difficult to assure their comfort and survival in the classroom.

Now that each group has settled on a research question, discuss how you could answer it. Jot down the steps your group will take, and make a list of the materials you'll need.

Show students the materials you have on hand so they know what is readily available. Touch base with groups as they develop their plans.

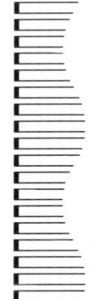 *Students can explain what they are thinking more easily by talking than writing, so help them bridge the gap between what they've said and what they've written if you want them to hand in formal plans. Or you might want to wait until the end of the experiment to have students hand in their methods. The best way for children of this age to figure out what they want to do is by doing it; their planning continues while they are experimenting. Planning doesn't need to be complete before students begin their investigations, but it does need to be a conscious part of their research process.*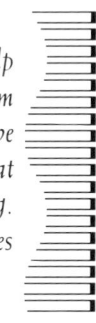

 As students are planning, ask them questions such as:

How will the actions you've outlined help you answer your question?

What will you measure or observe to find your answer?

What will you know if (X) happens? What will you know if (Y) happens?

How will you keep track of what you are finding out?

It is often more fruitful to wait until students have begun their investigation to help them see weaknesses in their design, and to figure out ways to do things better. Although the planning phase is important, there is no need to prolong it until everyone's plan is perfect.

Review each group's materials list before the next session. Discuss with them which materials you have on hand and which they'll need to bring from home.

Session 2

Today you'll set up your investigations according to the plans you made.

Unless you've ordered organisms from a biological supply company, this phase will begin with a trip outdoors, either to collect organisms for indoor study or to set up outdoor investigations. Continue with the narrative below if you will be collecting organisms for indoor studies.

If you'll be doing outdoor studies, make sure that students have all of the materials they need, and then head outside to spend the rest of the period setting up the investigations.

What are some of the pros and cons of collecting organisms that we should consider?

Help students weigh the benefits of collecting organisms for their scientific knowledge, against the possible risks it could pose to the site and the organisms. They need to understand that, like scientists, they should justify any collecting by stating how it will help them create new knowledge.

How can we minimize our impact on the site as we collect?

Ideas for minimizing impact include collecting only a few organisms that are in abundance, and being careful not to trample or uproot vegetation.

How can we do our best to assure the survival of the animals we collect, so that we can return them outdoors after our studies?

Students might suggest handling the animals gently and making sure they have food, water, and shelter.

Who knows what a HABITAT is?

A habitat is the place where something lives. An animal can meet all of its needs within its habitat — food, water, shelter, mating.

We can make habitat chambers to assure that the organisms we collect will survive once we get them back to the classroom.

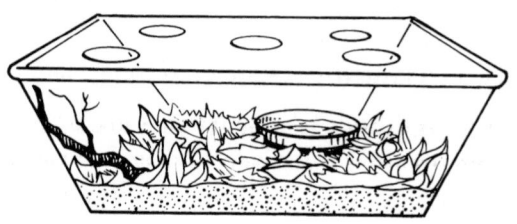

Show students an empty habitat chamber and tell them that they should put in it materials from the habitat where they find their organism. Hand out a "Classroom Critter Care Chart" to each group. Encourage them to find the food the animal eats in the chart, or in the *Who Eats What* guide, so that they can include a food source in the chambers as well.

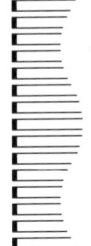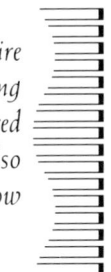

An alternative to having each group make its own habitat chamber is to bring in an entire micro-habitat such as a rotting log. This way you can be assured that everything living in the log has the food it needs. Keep it in a large plastic bag or a large aquarium covered with plastic wrap. Each group can find organisms within the log to observe. They can also observe the entire community within the log, considering what different residents eat, how long it will take them to use up their food, what are the different "housing sites," etc.

Before we go outside, each group needs a habitat chamber and a spoon or trowel for collecting.

Review outdoor study rules and safety guidelines if necessary (see page 69). Once outside, check on each group as they collect organisms, habitat materials, and food. If soil organisms such as sow bugs are plentiful, each group can include two or three of them in its chamber so each group member has an organism of his/her own to observe. Make sure that students don't collect anything that is not necessary, such as whole, living plants.

Back in the classroom, give students time to set up their feeding studies. Encourage them to refer to the "Classroom Critter Care Chart" for information on caring for the organisms.

Sessions 3 & 4

Check on your investigations, take measurements, and record your observations.

Either take the students outside to check on their investigations, or have them observe habitat chambers if they are doing indoor studies. They can continue to try different manipulations after they record the results of their first trials. Also, they might want to spend time refining the technical aspects of their experiments (e.g., *How can I see sow bugs eat when they scram from the light?*).

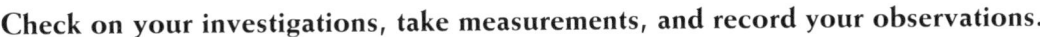

Facilitating Students' Investigating

Offering ideas. When students are working productively, it is best to wait to visit them until they have something to tell you, rather than interrupting them to check in. When they are having a problem, find out what ideas they already have about how to deal with it, then offer your suggestions as other possibilities to consider.

Questioning for reflection. You might want to use questions to call students' attention to potential improvements they could make in their methods. For instance, asking *Is there another way besides just looking at the leaf that you could tell how much of it the caterpillar ate since the last time you looked?* will help them consider the benefits of objective measurement over subjective observation.

Supporting notetaking. Encourage students to use their journals to write and draw what they see, measure, and think. Not everyone's notetaking schemes will or need to be the same. Students should think of their notes as information for themselves, rather than something they are producing for a grade from you. When you look over their notes with them, ask what they want to remember and help them find language or a format that expresses their thoughts and observations clearly.

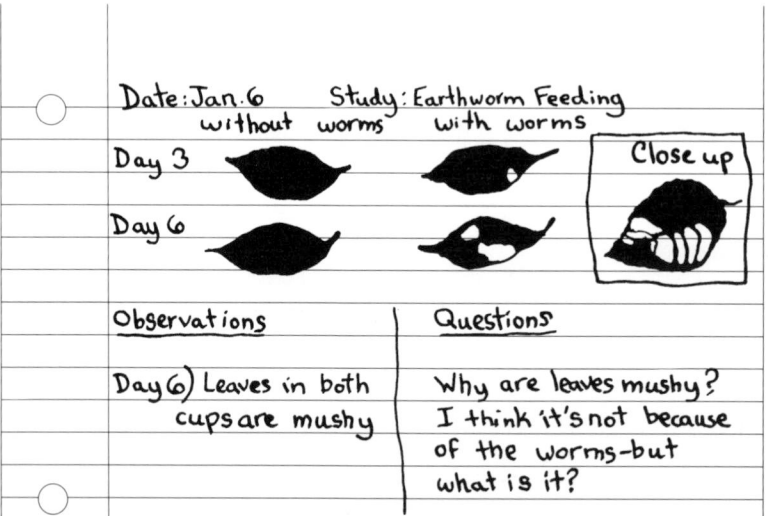

Encouraging sketching. Sketching is a good way to sharpen observation skills and document findings. When you suggest that students make sketches of their organisms and food sources, help them establish a purpose for the sketches — to help them observe details, to make a record for future comparisons, to share with other people when discussing results, etc.

During our next class you'll be sharing your results with one another, so work with your group members to summarize your findings.

Have students wrap up their investigations in time to think about conclusions. Most likely they will not have enough data to answer their research questions, so they could plan to share something new they discovered, rather than conclusions. They should also think about the best way to communicate their research methods and findings. This could involve showing charts of data and drawings, as well as giving a verbal summary. Encourage students to refer to their notes as the source of information for their reports.

Session 5

Scientists often touch base with one another to talk about their latest findings. We'll take some time now for each group to tell the others what you did and found out.

Encourage students to offer positive comments on one another's work and ideas, and to compare their findings to those of their classmates. At this stage in students' development as

Module 1: *Who Eats What?*

scientists, it is most important that they realize that scientists create knowledge by conducting and reflecting on research, just as they are doing. Getting definitive answers about animals' eating habits is of secondary importance.

Ask each group how they could improve their original plan if they were to continue their investigations. You might need to point out specific aspects of an investigation with questions such as *In how many different locations did you put the bait?* to call their attention to things that could be improved.

Thinking Like a Scientist

Some points about research and scientific thinking habits that you might want to stress through discussion are:

Science involves a lot of trial and error. Even if students have no results because "nothing worked" as they planned, they've learned a lot about the "how to" aspect of science. Discussing what methods worked, what didn't, and what could be done differently is an important part of doing science.

A conclusion is strong only to the extent that it is supported by evidence. The stronger the evidence, and the greater the number of people who find it convincing, the stronger the conclusion. A big part of science is convincing other people that your claims are justified by your evidence. When many different scientists finally agree about something, they become more sure that what they are saying is correct.

There can be more than one way to interpret a result. A lot of good ideas can emerge when different people point out other ways to interpret an observation. For instance, if a slug ate lettuce but not spinach, it could mean that: 1) it preferred the lettuce; 2) it had no preference, but just ate what it encountered first; or 3) it preferred spinach, but never found it. Becoming aware of alternative explanations spurs a scientist to refine an experimental design to try to rule out competing explanations.

Be sure to have students return any organisms they collected to the location where they were found.

Ongoing Assessment

Student Reflections

Have students send a C-Mail message or record thoughts in their journals. Optional writing prompts include:

What would be the absolute best way to figure out what an animal eats? What equipment would I need?

What new investigations of animals and their food could I do?

Teacher Reflections

❑ Were students able to make their general questions more specific for research purposes?

❑ Did they continue to refine their methods as they went along, and could they reflect on the strengths and weaknesses of their completed investigations?

❑ Did they keep helpful records of their observations and thoughts?

❑ Did they communicate their results clearly to their peers, and give feedback to one another?

❑ Did they realize when they did and didn't have enough evidence to draw conclusions?

Extensions

Natural History Stories. Help students prepare to write stories about animals' lifestyles by reading a variety of nature writing (see "Resource List," pages 52–55). Students might enjoy reading animal fables and folk tales, and talking about where, how, and why the truth was stretched. Ask each student to choose an animal and do background research to find out more about its interactions and life cycle. Use a writing workshop method (listing ideas, sharing thoughts, writing drafts, sharing and peer review, editing and revising) to create original stories. These can be modeled after the accurate natural history accounts of nature writers, or in alternative formats such as: an animal's diary entries; a radio news or sportscast; a newspaper article; a chapter from a biography; or cartoon drawings and captions. Share finished products and talk about which parts of each story are fact and which are fiction.

Habitat Resource Maps. Challenge students to depict the study site or habitat chamber from the point of view of one animal. Draw the important places to that animal, such as where it gets food, water, and shelter. Map out where the animal goes and what it does in a day or a week.

Scoping out Seed Eaters: The Work of Ecologist Dr. Mary Price

Dr. Mary Price, an ecologist and professor at the University of California, has been studying the feeding habits of pocket mice and kangaroo rats in the desert of Arizona for the past twenty years. These rodents eat seeds, feeding mainly at night. They have a pouch outside their cheeks where they hold the seeds they collect until they stash them or eat them.

When Dr. Price was in graduate school, she helped some other scientists who were studying desert rodents. They put bait in cages called live traps. These traps have a door that closes behind the animal when it goes in to eat the bait, so it is caught alive and unharmed in the cage. The scientists caught one kind of kangaroo rat called Merriam's kangaroo rat, and three kinds of pocket mice: Arizona pocket mouse, desert pocket mouse and Bailey pocket mouse.

Pause to show "Kangaroo Rat and Pocket Mouse" overhead.

This made Dr. Price very curious. She wondered how four different species of rodents that eat seeds could all survive in the same place, especially since seeds in the desert are in short supply. If more than one species eats the same kind of food, they often have to compete for food. If this happens, one species can win out, and the other species isn't able to live in the same place because it can't get enough food.

Imagine if you moved to a forest with only a few acorns, and had to gather enough of them to eat before the squirrels beat you to it. Who would be better and faster at getting acorns, you or the squirrels? Probably you would have to find something else to eat that another animal isn't already specialized at eating, or leave the forest to look somewhere else for food.

Dr. Price read papers that other scientists had written about animals competing for food, then formed her own research question: Do the kangaroo rat and the three kinds of pocket mice use seeds in a way that avoids having to compete for them?

She had two ideas, called HYPOTHESES, about how these different animals could survive in the same place even though they all eat seeds:

1. Maybe the different animals specialize in eating different kinds of seeds. For example, if some of the trees in the forest where you lived grew pizza-flavored nuts that only humans liked to eat, you could live on pizza nuts while the squirrels ate the acorns.

2. Maybe the animals stay far enough apart so that they don't compete for the same seeds. For instance, if you stayed in one part of the woods and the squirrels stayed in another part, you might be able to get enough acorns to eat without the squirrels getting them before you.

First Dr. Price tested her idea that the four different rodents preferred to eat different kinds of seeds. Can you think of an experiment to test this idea?

Pause for discussion.

Dr. Price put the different rodents in the lab and gave them a buffet of lots of different kinds of seeds — big and little seeds, oily and dry seeds, high and low protein seeds — and let the animals eat what they wanted. She counted how many of each kind of seed each animal ate. What do you think happened?

Pause for discussion.

Dr. Price found that the kangaroo rat and all three kinds of pocket mice preferred the same seeds — those that had the most energy and water in them! So this disproved her first hypothesis that the animals preferred to eat different kinds of seeds.

Next Dr. Price tested her second hypothesis — that the animals ate seeds in different areas of the desert. How do you think she tested this idea?

Pause for discussion.

Dr. Price put over 400 live traps with the same kinds of seeds in them, in two different parts of the desert: in open places and under shrubs. She had lots of assistants help her check the traps in the mornings before the sun got too hot for the animals inside them. What do you think she found when they checked the traps each morning?

Pause for discussion.

Dr. Price found that the kangaroo rats were in the cages out in the open. The pocket mice were all in cages under shrubs, but in different types of shrubby areas: the Arizona pocket mice were under small shrubs; the desert pocket mice were under large shrubs in sandy soil; and the Bailey pocket mice were under large shrubs in pebbly soil.

Now Dr. Price had evidence that the rodents avoided competing for food by eating seeds in different places. So she set up studies in her lab to gather more data.

She timed how long it took each rodent to find and eat seeds covered by sand, by pebbles, and by sticks and leaves. She also measured how much energy they lost and gained. She discovered that the kangaroo rats weren't good at finding seeds under sticks and leaves. But in sandy, open areas, the rats were faster at getting seeds than any of the three kinds of pocket mice. Dr. Price was well on her way to unraveling the mystery of how and why all these rodents could all eat seeds, but still live together in the same region.

Back in the desert, Dr. Price noticed another interesting thing. On nights when the moon was full, she always caught kangaroo rats under shrubs, even though they don't normally feed there. Can you imagine why?

Pause for discussion.

The desert rats and mice don't only have to worry about finding food, they have to make sure they don't *become* food for another animal! Dr. Price is now studying the rodents' risks of getting eaten. She is using techniques such as wearing night vision glasses to watch a Great Horned Owl hunt for the rodents in a huge outdoor cage.

When her experiments are finished, Dr. Price writes up her results. Other scientists review her papers, make suggestions for changes, and decide if they are good enough to be published. After she makes revisions, she publishes the papers so people can learn what she found out.

Dr. Price is still studying desert rodents and their food resources. She has seen how one big question she asked twenty years ago has led to many smaller questions. She hopes that what she is learning will help people understand and protect the natural conditions that allow many species to live in one area, and prevent extinctions. Improving conservation efforts is one long-term goal of Dr. Price's many late nights and early mornings under the desert moon and sun.

KANGAROO RAT AND POCKET MOUSE

Kangaroo Rat

Pocket Mouse

                     Module 1: *Who Eats What?*

SUGGESTED INVESTIGATION DESCRIPTIONS

INDOOR STUDIES

 Feeding Behaviors

The mouthparts and appendages of small animals are often not readily visible, so close observation is required to figure out how an animal eats its food.

Research Questions:

- Does the animal eat only some parts of its food?
- Does it eat its food in a systematic way (e.g., start at the edges and work in)?
- How does it get its food?
- What body parts and behaviors help it get food?

Possible Methods:

- Design different ways to view animals while they eat (e.g., a magnified feeding chamber, a narrow, double-walled container that keeps the animals near the edge, different kinds of lights or shades to see animals that shy away from light). Make careful observations.

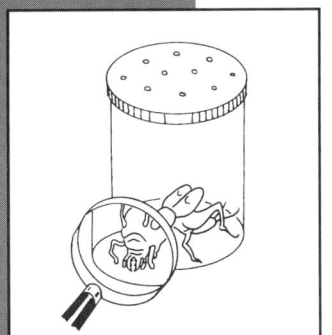

 Food Choices

Giving animals an assortment of foods reveals which foods they prefer and whether or not they will eat a variety of foods.

Research Questions:

- Does the animal prefer to eat (X) or (Y)?
- Does the animal eat one type of food more quickly or more slowly than another food?
- How many different kinds of food does the animal eat?

Possible Methods:

- Give earthworms (redworms purchased from a biological supply company will survive in classroom conditions better than local earthworms) and other decomposers: 1) a wet and dry sample of one type of leaf; 2) a green leaf, a newly fallen leaf, and a partly decomposed leaf, all of the same species; or 3) different species of newly fallen leaves. Trace leaf edges and interior holes on graph paper before giving them to the animals. Then retrace the leaves at different points after exposing them to the animals.
- Give earthworms identical size squares of fallen leaves from plants in a polluted and a less polluted environment (e.g., plants near and far from a busy road; or plants growing in the city and the country).

Make sure the leaves are from the same kind of plant. Either put the leaf squares on top of the worm's soil to see which disappear, or figure out a way to retrieve the leaves for periodic measurements (e.g., staple them to a pot marker; or put them in a mesh onion bag that can be pulled out of the soil).

◆ Foraging Abilities

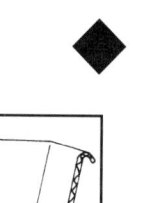

Foraging studies relate to Dr. Price's research on how desert rodents specialize in gathering seeds in open areas or under shrubs.

Research Questions:

- Can the animal find its food when the food is:
    - hidden under something?
    - mixed in with sand, pebbles, soil, or vermiculite?
    - artificially scented?
    - made into different sizes?
    - made a different color?

Possible Methods:

- Confirm that an animal eats a certain food by watching it eat or by measuring the food's disappearance. Then take a known amount of the food and vary its location (e.g., put it under something), its substrate (e.g., mix it with various materials), its scent, its size, or its color. See how long it takes the animal to find and eat the food. Compare amounts of altered and unaltered food it eats.

◆ Amount of Food Consumed

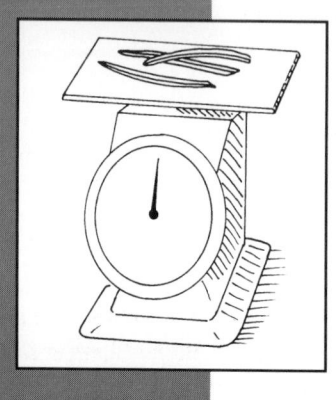

Animals not only have to get the right kind of food where they live, they also need to get enough food to survive. Weighing foods and animals will reveal how much food animals need to stay their same weight or grow bigger.

Research Questions:

- How much does the animal eat in a day or week?
- Does how much an animal eats relate to how big it is?
- Does the animal gain and lose weight as it eats food and releases wastes?

Possible Methods:

- Give a known weight of food to an animal, then weigh the leftover food daily to determine how much the animal eats per day.
- Measure and weigh different individuals of the same species and different species of animals, and compare their body sizes to how much food they consume.
- Weigh the animals on a regular schedule to determine if their body weight fluctuates up and down, steadily increases, or stays the same. Compare changes in body weight to the weight of the food consumed.

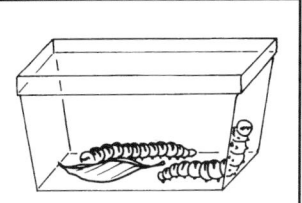

 Competition for Food

What happens when there is not enough food to go around? Temporarily putting several animals together with limited food will reveal whether they behave differently than they do when they are alone among plenty of food.

Research Questions:

- How do two of the same kind of animal interact over one piece of food?
- How do two different kinds of animals that eat the same food interact?

Possible Methods:

- Put several of the same kind of animals (e.g., sow bugs) in a container with a very small amount of food (e.g., a particle of potato) and watch how they interact.
- Put two different animals (e.g., a cricket and a grasshopper) in a container with a small amount of food (e.g., a dead mosquito) and watch how they interact.

OUTDOOR STUDIES

Caution!

- Use small quantities of baits so that animals don't become dependent on the food you're providing, and so you don't attract foreign animals into the site.
- Never feed any animal directly by hand.
- Never approach or touch an animal.

 Foods for Ants

Ants are just about everywhere. They'll come to food within 15 minutes to an hour in warm weather when they are active. This study will work well even in an urban setting or right outside the school building, if you can't get back to your study site.

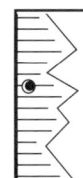

Caution!

- Keep your distance from red ants and fire ants to avoid getting stung!

Research Questions:

- Do different kinds of ants prefer different foods?
- Do ants that live in different habitats eat different things?
- Do ants differ in how they handle their food (e.g., suck out liquids vs. carry away chunks)?

Possible Methods:

- Put tiny amounts (1/8 tsp.) of foods such as peanut butter, honey, tiny grains or seeds, tuna fish, lettuce, diluted jelly, or cake crumbs on a laminated index card or jar lid, and note what kinds of ants are attracted to which foods, how quickly different foods disappear, etc. Try covering a set of bait stations (e.g., with an inverted paper cup with small holes cut into its rim and anchored with a rock on top) to exclude anything larger than an ant from the baits.
- Put the ant food buffet in different habitats to see if the types of ants attracted to the foods differ according to the habitat.
- Watch ants at the bait stations (using a hand lens, if possible) to see how different types of ants handle their food. Try to follow them to see where they take any food they carry away.

◆ *Plant-Eating Insects*

These studies extend the work students did during their previous field trips by requiring more systematic data collection to discover patterns in plant/insect feeding relationships.

Research Questions:

- Do different kinds of plants have different kinds of insects feeding on them?
- Do different insects eat different parts of plants (e.g., fruits, flowers, limbs, leaves, bark, buds, roots)?
- Which insects make which kinds of marks on leaves (e.g., holes, chewed edges, tunnels)?
- Which plants have the greatest number of the same kind of insect?
- Which plants have the most different kinds of insects?
- Are some insects eating the insects that are eating the plants?
- On which parts of plants do camouflaged insects feed?

Possible Methods:

- Survey the insect damage to leaves (e.g., holes, tunnels, scrapes). Compare the types of damage on different leaf types. Note whether some leaves have more than one type of damage.
- Look carefully for insects feeding on leaves. In the tips of leaf buds, in curled leaves, and along the veins of leaves are good places to look. Keep track of what insects are found on different parts of leaves on the same plant, on different plants, which insects are camouflaged, etc.

- Spread a white cloth on the ground below tree branches and shrubs. Gently but firmly shake branches to see what insects fall out. Note the types of insects associated with each plant type.
- Put different kinds of fruit collected from plants in the bottom of jars, then put a funnel into the jar. See what insects fly or crawl down the funnel to the fruit. Most will be trapped in the jar until you lift the funnel out.
- Soak strips of cotton in different sweet substances (e.g., plain or scented sugar water, molasses, honey, fruit juice). Hang strips in a variety of locations to see what insects visit them.

 ## Seed Stations

By covering or mixing seeds with different materials, students can find out physical limitations on local animals' abilities or inclinations to get food.

Research Questions:

- Do small or large seeds disappear more quickly in the open and under cover?
- Does the size and position of entry holes into a container with seeds inside determine how quickly the seeds disappear?
- Do seeds mixed with different materials disappear as fast as seeds under a box or out in the open?

Possible Methods:

- Put large and small seeds (e.g., millet, bulgur, shelled and unshelled sunflower seeds, grass seed heads, shelled and unshelled peanuts) in the open, under a shrub, and under a box with an entry hole. Check stations 2–6 days after set-up. Record the numbers and kinds of seeds in each location before and after animals have had time to visit. Look for clues, such as droppings or tracks, to determine whether mammals or birds are taking the seeds.
- Put equal numbers of the same kinds of seed in containers with different entry holes (e.g., big or small; covered by a flap of fabric or open; on the top, bottom, or side of containers) to compare how quickly the seeds disappear.
- Put a known number of seeds in piles of different materials (e.g., leaves, twigs, vermiculite, pebbles) to see how many disappear from each how quickly. Compare this with the disappearance of the same seeds when they're not buried.

◆ Tracking Stations

Setting out baits on a surface that will show tracks reveals what animals eat different types and sizes of foods, and how this varies in different habitats.

Research Questions:

- Do different animals eat different baits?
- Do different sizes of the same baits attract different animals?
- Do the same baits in different locations attract different animals?

Possible Methods:

- Make a surface where animal tracks will show by covering a large index card or square of oak tag with aluminum foil. Spread mineral oil on the foil then sprinkle it with talcum powder, or coat the foil with a thin layer of white vegetable shortening. (Alternative tracking substrates for an adult to make: hold a candle under a foil-coated card to get a black coating of carbon on the foil; spread a thin layer of lamp oil on a cookie sheet, then light it and let it burn off to leave a layer of carbon.)

- Put tiny amounts (1/8 tsp.) of baits (e.g., cat food, peanut butter, sugar, lettuce, liver, cheese, hot dogs, raisins, seeds, berries, nuts) in the center of the tracking cards and set them outside. Come back later and try to identify the tracks to see what visited each kind of bait (e.g., ants, roaches, mice).

- Use larger amounts of the baits to see if they are taken by animals that did not visit smaller amounts of the same baits.

- Put tracking cards with the same baits in different habitats to see if visitors vary according to habitat.

◆ Foods for Birds

This investigation will work best at an established bird feeder station, such as on a window ledge or pole outside the classroom, or in a park where pigeons gather.

Research Questions:

- Do different seed-eating birds prefer different kinds of seeds?
- Do birds choose among the same kinds of seeds that have been colored differently?
- Do birds react to flavorings (e.g., salt, sugar, vanilla or mint extract, garlic) in seeds, bread, suet, or popcorn?

Possible Methods:

- Feed pigeons in a park or the schoolyard, or other birds at a feeder, different kinds, shapes, artificially colored, or artificially flavored foods to discover their preferences.

Classroom Critter Care Chart — Herbivores and Scavengers *

Organism	Habitat Chamber	Food	Classroom Care
Snails and Slugs	Large, wide-mouthed glass jar or old aquarium with ventilated cover to maintain humidity and prevent escape. Add 2–3 cm of moist soil for burrowing, plants/branches for climbing, and a damp sponge.	Lettuce, carrots, apple, celery, or oats. Add some crushed chalk to provide calcium for their shells. Replace as needed or as food begins to rot. (Snails may go 2–3 days without eating.) *Wild Food Source: dead leaves*	• Habitat must be kept damp at all times. A sign of dryness is when snails crawl into shells for long periods. • Clean slug habitat often to prevent tiny white mites. • Roll slugs on paper towel to clean off mites.
Millipedes	Clear terrarium with ventilated lid or plastic salad take-out container with holes punched in lid. Add 2–3 cm of damp, forest, desert, or potting soil. Add plenty of bark and leaf litter from area where millipede was collected.	Plant material from forest or desert floor. Replace as needed. *Wild Food Source: dead leaves, cacti, and pine needles*	• Sprinkle soil with water to make sure it is damp at all times, but not saturated.
Sow Bugs and Pill Bugs	Clear terrarium with ventilated lid or plastic salad take-out container with holes punched in lid. Put 2–3 cm of damp woods soil, or potting soil on the bottom. Add decaying bark and leaf litter. Provide a darkened area by partially covering soil with cardboard placed on a few pebbles.	Slice of raw potato. Alternate with a raw carrot, lettuce, unsweetened cereal, or ripe fruit. Replace as needed or as food rots. *Wild Food Source: dead leaves and wood*	• Sprinkle soil with water to make sure it is damp at all times, but not saturated.
Earthworms	Styrofoam cooler or bucket with ventilated lid and 10 cm of bedding made of garden soil mixed with leaf litter, peat, sawdust, or cow manure.	Grass, dried leaves, lettuce, apple, potato, cornmeal, oatmeal, or coffee grounds. Chop all plants and fruits into ant-sized pieces. Replace as needed. *Wild Food Source: dead leaves and grass*	• Keep bedding moist (not wet) at all times with spray bottle and cover with a layer of damp newspaper. • Keep container in a cool spot in the classroom. • Replace bedding when it becomes blackish.
Ants	Clear plastic 2-liter soda bottle cut off at the neck, with a 1-liter soda bottle (cut 5 cm shorter than 2-liter bottle) set inside the larger bottle. Put a small piece of clay on the bottom of 1-liter bottle to keep it in place. Secure a piece of cardboard on top of the 1-liter bottle as a platform for food and a damp sponge. Fill the space in between the bottles with loose, sandy soil.	Bread, cracker crumbs, or bits of fruit and meat. Replace as needed. Remove rotting food. *Wild Food Source: seeds, fungus, and liquid from aphids (Some eat insects.)*	• Do not overfeed. • Cover sides with a dark paper or cloth to provide darkness. • Use artificial light to observe ants. • Dampen sponge when dry.
Crickets	Large wide-mouthed jar or terrarium with ventilated lid. Put 2–4 cm of sand on the bottom. Place a few layers of water-soaked paper towels in a saucer or place a piece of damp sponge in the jar.	Slices of apple, carrot, potato, celery, or lettuce along with dry dog food. Replace as needed or as food begins to rot. *Wild Food Source: roots, seeds, and berries*	• Keep crickets dry and habitat moist. • Keep at 30–35 degrees Celsius. • Remove accumulated droppings.
Caterpillars	Large, wide-mouthed glass jar with ventilated lid. Put 5 cm of moist soil on the bottom. Provide habitat with a large piece of bark and a twig leaning against the side of the jar for pupating substrates.	Provide a continuous supply of the plant you found the caterpillar feeding on. Put the plant's roots in a container of water covered with cardboard to keep caterpillar from falling in. *Note: Only keep those caterpillars that you found feeding on a plant.*	• Replace plant at first sign of wilting. • Keep container in a cool spot in the classroom.

* Note: All organisms should be released where captured after classroom study is over.

1.4 *Feeding Habits Investigations*

CLASSROOM CRITTER CARE CHART — CARNIVORES *

Organism	Habitat Chamber	Food	Classroom Care
LADYBUG BEETLES	Clear container with ventilated lid that is large enough for beetles to fly around in comfortably.	Requires live food: aphids. Set a plant stem covered with aphids in a small container of water and place it in the larger container with beetles.	• Replace with similar plant stem every 3 days. • Change the water when you replace the plant that the aphids are eating.
SPIDERS	Large, wide-mouthed glass jar with ventilated lid. Put 5 cm of damp soil on the bottom. Prop some twigs up in the jar. *Note: Spiders must be kept separate as they will prey on one another.*	Requires live food: houseflies, fruitflies, sow bugs, mealworms, or crickets. Needs to consume something its own size every 2 weeks.	• When soil begins to appear dry, moisten slightly with a water spray bottle.
CENTIPEDES	Clear terrarium with ventilated lid or plastic salad take-out container with holes punched in lid. Put 2–3 cm of damp, rich, woods soil or potting soil on the bottom. Add decaying bark and leaf litter. *Note: Centipedes must be kept separate as they will prey on one another.*	Requires live food: sow bugs. Set a slice of potato in the container for the sow bugs. Replace rotting food.	• Sprinkle soil with water to make sure it is damp at all times, but not saturated.
EARWIGS	Large, wide-mouthed glass jar with ventilated lid or plastic salad take-out container with holes punched in lid. Add 5 cm of damp soil, a few stones, plants, and a damp sponge.	Combined diet of bran cereal sweetened with molasses, plant leaves, apples, mealworms, and aphids. Replace rotting food. *Wild Food Source: rotting fruits, aphids, and fleas*	• Keep habitat moist with frequent soil spraying.
TIGER AND GROUND BEETLES	Clear container with ventilated lid or plastic salad take-out container with holes punched in lid. Put 5 cm of sandy soil on the bottom. Place a jar lid filled with water in a corner of the container. Ground beetles require leaf litter on the soil.	Requires live food: ants, caterpillars, earthworms, and slugs. Replace as needed.	• Refill water as needed.

Note: All organisms should be released where captured after classroom study is over.

© Institute of Ecosystem Studies, 1994

Module 1: *Who Eats What?*

1.5 Outdoor Study Stations—
Performance Assessment

Action Synopsis

Students create stations with interpretive labels that teach others about signs of animals and what they eat.

One Session		1½ hours	IN & OUTDOORS
1. Present a challenge to create study stations that show evidence of animals and what they eat.			*posing a challenge*
2. Discuss criteria for high quality work.			*setting standards*
3. Talk in groups about possible stations to create.			*planning*
4. Locate places to create study stations outdoors.			*applying knowledge*
5. Write station signs.			*communicating*
6. Tour stations, and (optional) have another class tour them.			*assessing*
7. Summarize and discuss experience.			*reflecting*

Desired Outcomes

By the end of this assessment activity, students should:

✓ Be able to point our evidence of what animals live on the study site and what they eat.

✓ Be able to communicate their knowledge.

What You'll Need

For the class:
❑ field guides (see "Resource List," pages 52, 54)

For each group of 3–4 students:
❑ copy of "Challenge Sheet" (page 111)
❑ 3–4 5" x 7" index cards or pieces of oak tag
❑ 3–4 pieces of string or yarn to hang cards
❑ magic marker
❑ copy of the *Who Eats What* guide (pages 355–382)

For each student:
❑ copy of "Scoring Sheet" (page 112)
❑ copy of "Group Work Evaluation" (page 42)
❑ copy of "Reflections" (page 41)

Getting Ready

♦ Make logistical arrangements to revisit your study site.

♦ If possible, make arrangements for another class or outside guests to tour the study stations that your students create. Teaching a real audience what they've learned will motivate students to solidify and apply their knowledge.

♦ Try to get some volunteers to accompany you outside. Brief the volunteers on how to keep students on task while letting them make their own decisions about their work.

♦ Plan to use the same student groups as before, or decide on new groupings.

Action Narrative

Now that you're familiar with how to find evidence of animals and what they eat, you should be able to teach what you know to someone else. Here is your challenge.

Give a copy of the "Challenge Sheet" to each group and talk it over.

Have any of you been to a museum, zoo, botanic garden, or nature center where there are signs next to exhibits or along trails?

Discuss the style and purpose of these signs.

What things would make good stations for teaching about feeding interactions?

Stations could focus on small animals, signs of animals eating plants, or other animal signs (e.g., spider webs, nests, burrows, scrapings, holes, anthills). Even if the animal sign does not give direct evidence of feeding activities, students should write on their station cards information about that animal's food interactions.

If you've arranged for another class or other guests to tour the stations, tell students who their audience will be.

Your study stations will be evaluated using several criteria. What would you look for to decide how successful each study station is?

After students have shared their ideas, either formalize their suggestions into a scoring checklist, or give a copy of the "Scoring Sheet" to each student and go over the criteria.

Take a few minutes to talk with your group members about three or four study stations you could create.

Give each group three or four index cards or pieces of oak tag, three or four pieces of string or yarn, and a magic marker. Remind students to bring their "Scoring Sheets" outside, as well.

When you arrive at the study site, gather students in a central meeting location and establish boundaries they are to stay within. Groups don't have to stay within their former study plots, but can wander throughout the area you designate.

Look for things you'd like to make into study stations, then make a sign for each one.

Students will need some time to explore and find small animals and food clues. After a while, help them to make a final decision on what to use as study stations, and to focus on creating signs. Remind students to include feeding information on their cards, since they sometimes get carried away with describing an animal sign and forget to mention how the sign gives clues about what the animal eats. Provide copies of the *Who Eats What* guide and other resources for students to use.

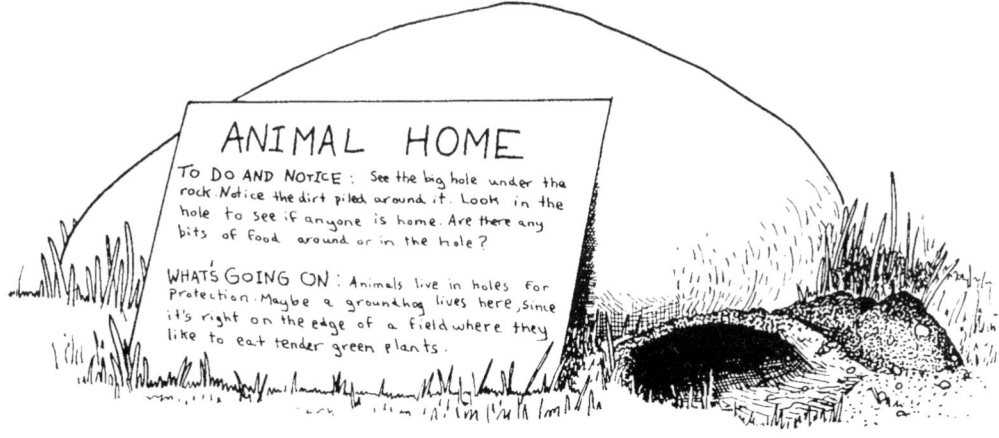

When all the signs are hanging or propped up in place, have students tour one another's study stations and/or show them to another class or invited guests. This is a good time for you to visit the stations and begin to fill out a "Scoring Sheet" for each group. Students can use their blank "Scoring Sheets" to evaluate their own and/or each other's stations. Collect the cards at the end of the session in order to complete the assessments later.

? Back indoors, wrap up the activity by talking over questions such as:

How challenging was it to find animals and food clues this time as compared to the first time we visited our study site?

Where are good places to find small animals? Why?

Where are good places to find animal signs? Why?

What are some of the things you liked about other groups' stations and why?

What different kinds of feeding interactions did the stations point out?
Animals eating plants, animals eating animals, and animals drinking water are examples of feeding interactions.

Ongoing Assessment

Student Reflections

Have students fill out a copy of the "Group Work Evaluation" (page 42). They could also fill out a "Scoring Sheet" for their own study stations. This is also a good time to have them complete a "Reflections" sheet (page 41).

Teacher Reflections

As you assess the stations, think of yourself as a visitor wanting to learn how to "read" clues in nature to learn about what animals live in the area and what they eat. Putting yourself in the position of someone genuinely wanting to learn something from the station cards will help you determine rankings of High Quality, Meets Objective, or Falls Short, based on how successfully the cards engage and teach you. The most heavily weighted criteria on the "Scoring Sheet" are the two content items, since at this point students should be able to communicate correct information about what animals eat.

Module 1: *Who Eats What?*

NAME(S)_____ DATE_____

OUTDOOR STUDY STATIONS

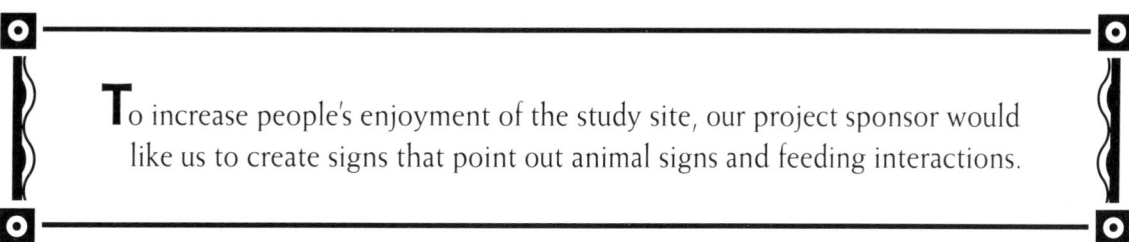

To increase people's enjoyment of the study site, our project sponsor would like us to create signs that point out animal signs and feeding interactions.

YOUR CHALLENGE:

Make 3 or 4 outdoor study stations that teach people about what animals eat. Choose interesting animals or animal signs to use as your stations. Make signs for people to read when they visit your stations. Each sign should have:

① A Title.

② A "To Do and Notice" section that helps people do and see something.

③ A "What's Going On" section that gives background information for people who want to learn more about what they are looking at.

RESOURCES:

You can use the *Who Eats What* guide and other resource books.

GOOD LUCK!

NAME(S)_____ DATE_____

Outdoor Study Stations

OBJECTIVES	POINTS				SCORE
	3 High Quality	**2** Meets Objectives	**1** Falls Short	**0** Not Done	
CONTENT					
1. Stations point out what animals eat.	_____	_____	_____	_____	___ x 2 =___
2. Information is correct.	_____	_____	_____	_____	___ x 2 =___
SCOPE					
3. Group has a variety of stations.	_____	_____	_____	_____	=___
4. Each sign includes facts and details.	_____	_____	_____	_____	=___
COMMUNICATION					
5. Writing is easy to understand and captures interest.	_____	_____	_____	_____	=___

COMMENTS:

FINAL SCORE: _____

Total Possible Score: 21
Overall Achievement:
    18-21   High
    14-17   Sound
    8-13   Limited
    0-7   Inadequate

    Module 1: *Who Eats What?*

1.6 Making Food Chains

Action Synopsis

Students make food chains for their study site organisms, and learn food chain terminology.

Session 1		**40–60 minutes**
1. Share thoughts about food chains.		*examining prior ideas*
2. Make a food chain as a class, using an example from the school lunch menu.		*introducing new information*
3. Work in groups to organize and make food chains for study site organisms.		*processing findings*
4. Present and discuss food chains.		*communicating*

Session 2		**40 minutes**
1. Review the process of photosynthesis.		*examining prior ideas*
2. Introduce food chain terminology.		*introducing new information*
3. Work in groups to label food chains.		*applying knowledge*
4. Analyze food chains to see that all parts can be traced back to plants and sunlight.		*reflecting*

Desired Outcomes

Throughout the lesson, check that students:

✓ Have a clear picture of the feeding relationships of animals on their study site.

✓ Recognize the strengths and weaknesses of different sources of information.

✓ Understand that plants make their own food.

✓ Are able to define food chain terms and give examples of organisms that fit in each category.

✓ Realize that plants are the ultimate source of food energy for all organisms in a food chain.

What You'll Need

Sessions 1 & 2

For the class:
- ❏ several copies of the *Who Eats What* guide (pages 355–382)
- ❏ other resource books (see "Resource List," pages 51–55)

Vocabulary

CARNIVORE - An animal that eats meat.

CONSUMER - An animal or microbe that gets food by eating things.

DECOMPOSER - An animal or microbe that uses dead plants and animals as food.

FOOD CHAIN - A diagram that shows the flow of food from producers to all types of consumers. The original food source for all organisms in a food chain can be traced to plants.

HERBIVORE - An animal that eats plants.

OMNIVORE - An animal that eats both plants and animals.

PHOTOSYNTHESIS - The process by which plants make sugars in their leaves.

PREDATOR - An animal that kills and eats other animals.

PREY - An animal that is eaten by other animals.

PRODUCER - A green plant that makes sugar for food using the process of photosynthesis.

Getting Ready

Session 1
♦ Plan to use the same student groups as for Lesson 1.3.

Action Narrative

Session 1

Today we're going to make Food Chains using our study site organisms. Who can tell me what a food chain is?

Students sometimes confuse food chains with nutrition and the four food groups, explaining food chains as *Like what's written on the label — sodium, nutrition, fat, cholesterol, all that stuff.* Or, *It's like placing the foods in sections, like the steaks and pork chops are in the meat family.* Children who have a more accurate idea about food chains typically say something like, *A big thing eats a smaller thing, and that thing eats something smaller, and it keeps on going like that.* Notice where your students' ideas about food chains fall on the continuum from purely intuitive notions, to a vague understanding of the structure of food chains, to a thorough understanding of how sun's energy is turned into food energy by plants, then passed along the food chain.

A food chain is a way to describe how matter and energy in food get passed along from plants to animals when one thing eats another thing. Why is it important to understand food chains?

Spend a few minutes helping students think about the larger significance of food chains. Some of the reasons they might mention are: for human health protection — understanding how chemicals like pesticides get into our food and then into us helps save lives; to prevent extinctions — knowing about ecological linkages helps people evaluate the consequences of their actions and modify them to prevent the extinction of plants and animals; to preserve biodiversity — understanding how plants and animals are linked in food chains helps people make sure that organisms in an area have what they need to stay alive.

Let's make a food chain together. What is on the lunch menu today?

Write a menu item (e.g., *FISH*) on the board, leaving space to construct a chain up and/or down depending on whether the item is a plant or animal.

If it is an animal, start the food chain by working downward, listing what organism students suggest it might have eaten, then what that organism could have eaten, and so on until you have a plant at the base of the list.

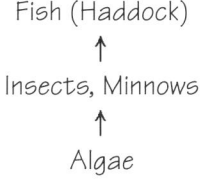

Fish (Haddock)
↑
Insects, Minnows
↑
Algae

You can record just one item at each level of the food chain or several possibilities.

What do you notice about the direction I've drawn the arrows?

Help students see that the arrows point from the item being eaten into the "mouth" of the animal that eats it.

To continue a food chain for an animal, or to begin a food chain for a plant, work upwards, listing what organism eats the item, what eats the organism that eats it, and so on until the students get to an organism that they say nothing eats. Stretch their thinking toward decomposers by asking what might eat the top level organism after it dies.

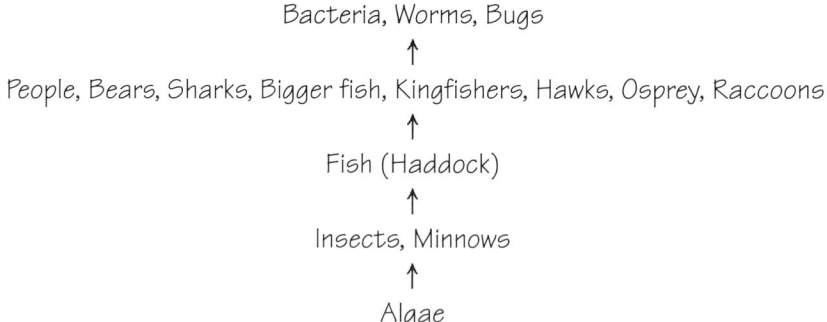

Bacteria, Worms, Bugs

↑

People, Bears, Sharks, Bigger fish, Kingfishers, Hawks, Osprey, Raccoons

↑

Fish (Haddock)

↑

Insects, Minnows

↑

Algae

There could be disagreement and uncertainty about what eats what. This creates a great opportunity for students to practice scientific thinking. Even though the point of this activity is to show the structure of a food chain rather than to teach the specific diets of certain animals, it's good to get students in the habit of supporting their claims with evidence or a knowledge source. Model the process by asking a few students where they got their information about what something eats. Then encourage students to ask one another to share how they know something, before you add new suggestions to the board. This will help them internalize the habit of looking for evidence behind claims, rather than seeing this as something only the teacher does. It's important that this be done in the spirit of intellectual curiosity, so students don't feel put on the spot and turn defensive when asked to elaborate on their ideas. List whatever ideas the class finds plausible, and tell them that it's okay to go with hunches so long as they acknowledge that the idea is uncertain and needs further research.

Work in groups to make food chains using the organisms you found on our study site. Start each food chain with an animal someone in your group saw (or saw evidence of) in your study plot. You can use the *Who Eats What* guide and other references to find out what each animal eats.

If you find out that an animal eats or is eaten by something nobody found in your plot, put a star by it when you include it in your food chain. That way we'll know which things we don't know for sure are on the site.

It will take students a while to decide how to organize their food chains: horizontally or vertically; in boxes or on lined paper; with a predetermined number of steps or going as far as they can. Groups will also need to determine how many food chains to make, and whether to work on each one together or have each person make one. If after an initial planning period some groups are frustrated or overwhelmed, suggest that they begin with three steps:

Step 2: Step 1: Step 3:

What it eats → **An animal you saw** → **What eats it**
or saw signs of

Encourage students to use specific names of organisms in their chains if they can: "robin" rather than "bird;" "ant lion" rather than "bug;" "palmetto leaves" rather than "leaves." For plants, be sure to have them name the plant part (e.g., leaves, stems, seeds, roots) that an animal eats — this is more important than including the species name of the plant.

Students will need to use a lot of organisms they didn't find to make complete food chains for those they did find. Before they include something they didn't see on the study site in a food chain, ask them to think through how possible it is that the organism lives there. (Have them use a list of common organisms in your region if you have one.) If it does not seem likely that it would live on the site, encourage students to find out if there is another kind of food that their organism eats. The goal is to make plausible food chains.

This activity could extend into two periods, especially if students take seriously the need to research information so that their food chains are accurate. When they complete their work, have pairs of groups show each other the food chains they made.

 Afterwards, engage the whole class in a discussion of questions such as the following:

How did you know what an animal eats?
Help students become aware of the variety of sources of information they used. They probably made many of the food chains based on some general knowledge they already had. This knowledge might be grounded in experience (a direct observation), or vague. Students might have used books, but what did they do if a book said something they didn't believe, or if it left out something they know is true? Perhaps they relied on an "expert," either someone they know or someone on television. Discuss which sources students consider to be the most reliable and why.

How did you resolve any differences of opinion within your group about what something eats?
Scientists always have to provide evidence for claims they make. Have students think about what made some people's claims more convincing than others. Making clear how one has come to know something, and stating how strong the evidence is for a conclusion, are two of the most central practices of science.

Did any two groups have a different food chain for the same animal?
Most animals eat and are eaten by more than one thing, so it is possible that several different food chains for one animal could be correct.

Were you surprised by anything you found out?
Students may read things that surprise them. For example, large carnivores such as foxes eat a lot of berries and insects, and daddy-longlegs are insects with six legs, not spiders — in fact they eat spiders.

Session 2

Let's look again at the example of a food chain we made from the lunch menu. (Draw it on the board if it has been erased). **Does anyone know what ecologists call plants like the one that is at the base of our food chain?**

Students are probably familiar with the word PRODUCER. Write it next to the plant at the base of the food chain.

Why do you think scientists call plants producers?

Plants use the process of PHOTOSYNTHESIS to produce sugars that they and animals use as food.

If your students have not yet developed a basic understanding of photosynthesis, you might want to take a few periods to focus on photosynthesis now or at the end of the module. One technique to help students examine their ideas is to ask them to jot down a response to a question such as: "How do plants meet their food needs?" Then have each student talk over their response with a partner, and together write a revised statement. Then have each pair get together with another pair, and repeat the process as a group of four. Finally have two groups of four share their statements and write a new version. Debrief as a class, targeting unresolved issues and differences of opinion that need to be addressed. (See "Children's Ideas about Food for Plants," page 119, and "Sugar Factory Skit," page 121.)

What are other terms ecologists use for organisms at each level in a food chain?

Move up the food chain written on the board, seeing if students can identify the ecological term to describe each category.

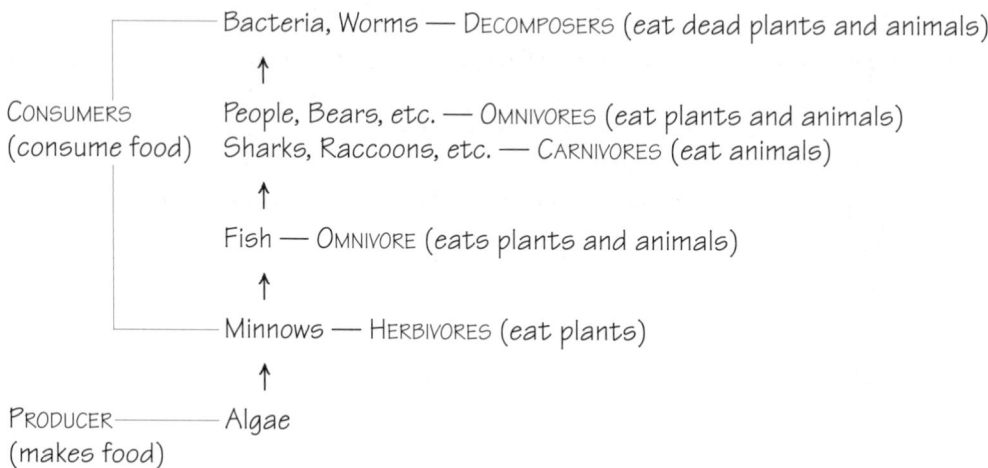

Also introduce the term Predator (an animal that eats another animal — a carnivore or an omnivore) and Prey (an animal that is eaten by another animal).

Now label each organism on your food chains using these new words: producer, herbivore, carnivore, omnivore, decomposer.

Sometimes students get stuck on what to call dead plants and plant parts such as berries, bark, or roots. These can be labeled producers.

Who can find something in your food chains that is not connected to sunlight?

Some students might suggest things that aren't linked to living plants, such as an earthworm that eats dead leaves, a beetle or fly that lives on animal droppings, or a carnivore such as a spider. In each case, ask them what the organism they mentioned eats, what that organism eats, and so on until they realize that food for all organisms starts with the sun's energy that plants use to make food.

No matter where an organism is on a food chain, you can always trace its food back to plants and sunlight. Could we survive in a world without plants?

Hopefully students' answer will be a resounding *No!* Expect however, that some students will not be fully convinced that all life depends on plants for food, although they might agree that we couldn't survive without plants because we need the oxygen that they release. Watch in future discussions to make sure they develop the understanding that even animals that don't eat plants depend on them for food.

Children's Ideas about Food for Plants

Plants' ability to make food from raw ingredients in nature is one of the most essential biochemical processes on earth. Photosynthesis provides all of the energy that makes food chains possible.

Children draw a natural and sensible parallel between food that people and other animals ingest, and the things plants take in from the environment. They wonder why adults say that plants make their own food, yet also admit that plants take in sunlight, air, water, soil nutrients, and "plant food." From a child's point of view, there is not a clear difference between the materials plants take in and the hot dogs and cookies they eat. Scientists, on the other hand, accept that soil nutrients, water, and air are not food because they do not contain food energy that can be measured in calories.

It is not unusual to hear students — from primary grades up through high school and even into college — state that plants use soil and water as food, yet in the next breath dutifully recite that *plants make their own food*. The following interchange between two sixth graders highlights how two incompatible sets of beliefs — their own and a scientific one — can coexist in children's minds.

Dominick: *Maybe the soil is its food. Maybe. It doesn't have a mouth, but maybe it goes inside of it.*

James: *It does!*

Dominick: *You're right. But the green plants don't really eat.*

James: *They do, they do. They drink, they eat. Like they get the food through the roots. Roots suck up water, it goes to the stem, the sun gives off light into the leaf which sends it in together and it makes food for the plant.*

Although James has some understanding of photosynthesis, he calls it eating, and indicates that both what the plant takes in through its roots and what it makes in its leaves are its food. Dominick on the other hand is reluctant to call soil food, but since it goes inside of the plant, he decides that food might be the best thing to call it. He also hesitates to call a plant's process of taking in soil and water eating. Both of these boys are struggling to reconcile their everyday understanding of "food," "eating," and "drinking" with a scientific explanation of photosynthesis.

Thinking and talking about their beliefs are exactly what students need to do in order to revise their naive notions into scientifically accurate conceptions. As students express their ideas about photosynthesis, tell them that scientists often use terms differently than we do in everyday conversation. This will help them begin to bridge the two worlds of understanding.

For more background on children's ideas about photosynthesis and suggestions for teaching the concept, see page 51 for information on *The Power Plant* by K. Roth and C. Anderson.

Ongoing Assessment

Student Reflections

Have students send a C-Mail message or record thoughts in their journals. Optional writing prompts include:

What would I have to do to be positive about what an animal eats?

I was surprised to learn...

Teacher Reflections

❏ How much effort did students put into making their food chains accurate?

❏ Were they able to articulate what sources of information they find most reliable?

❏ Do they understand that plants make their own food?

❏ Did students label their food chains correctly? Which items did they find difficult to categorize?

❏ Do they understand that the ultimate source of energy for every living thing on a food chain is sunlight?

Extensions

Sugar Factory Skit. Challenge students to develop and perform skits demonstrating the process of photosynthesis. They can portray leaves as "sugar factories" that have: 1) raw materials (carbon dioxide and water); 2) energy to make the factory run (sunlight); 3) a manufacturing process (combining carbon dioxide and water with the aid of chlorophyll in leaves); 4) a product (sugar); and 5) a byproduct (oxygen).

Sunlight for Supper? For a homework assignment, ask students to trace everything they eat for supper back to sunlight.

Ode to Plants. Have students write a song, poem, or rap thanking plants for providing all living things with the food energy they need to survive.

Personal Food Connections. Help the class draw a map of food relationships. Encourage students to make a list of what they eat during one day, then look in encyclopedias or go to the grocery store to find out where these foods are grown, or in the case of animals, what they eat. On a map of the world mark the locations of these food sources with pictures, then draw lines connecting them to your location. Have students measure the distances across which humans are able to obtain food and compare these to the food-getting habits of the organisms on their study site.

Food Chains Everywhere. Categorize everything encountered in stories, in lunch boxes, in magazine ads, etc. as a product of a producer, consumer, decomposer, or the non-living environment.

DDT Danger. Have students look up Rachel Carson in the library to learn how she made the public aware of the dangers of the pesticide DDT. Make food chains that show how DDT got into predators such as eagles, falcons, and hawks.

1.7 Food for Thought

Action Synopsis

Students sort items into food and non-food categories, then play a game to get enough food — nutrients and energy — to support six ecosystem organisms.

Session 1	40 minutes

1. Sort items into food and non-food categories.   *examining prior ideas*

2. Talk about definitions of food.   *examining prior ideas*

3. Burn a peanut and a vitamin pill to show that food has energy and nutrients do not.   *introducing new information*

Session 2	40 minutes

1. Play a game that requires six organisms to get the nutrients and energy they need to survive.   *applying knowledge*

2. Compare the flow of nutrients and energy in an ecosystem.   *reflecting*

Desired Outcomes

Throughout the lesson, check that students:

✓ Understand that all living things need nutrients and energy.

✓ Know that food is a substance that provides both nutrients and energy.

✓ Realize that nutrients alone don't contain useable energy.

✓ Realize that their bodies are made of the same substances that food is made of because food becomes part of the body — you are what you eat!

✓ Know that nutrients cycle in an ecosystem, whereas energy eventually is lost as heat.

✓ Know that plants get energy from sunlight and nutrients from soil, and animals get them both from their food.

What You'll Need

Session 1

For the class:
- ❑ various food and non-food items:
  - Food: peanuts, sugar, flour, beef jerky, potato chips, candy, vegetables, fruit, bread, oatmeal, apple juice, grass or leaves, an insect or other small critter
  - Non-food: salt, water, potting soil, sand, rock, metal, sugar-free vitamin pills, fertilizer
- ❑ pair of safety goggles
- ❑ pair of tweezers
- ❑ match or lighter
- ❑ small cup of water

Session 2

For each group of 6 students:
- ❑ set of 6 "Organism Sheets" (pages 141–146)
- ❑ set of "Game Cards" (pages 131–140) (see "Getting Ready")
- ❑ copy of "Game Rules" (page 130)

Vocabulary

CALORIE - A unit for measuring the amount of energy that food supplies to the body.

ENERGY - The ability to make things move or change.

FOOD - A substance that gives both nutrients and energy to a living thing.

NUTRIENT - A substance that does not provide energy, but supplies minerals that living things need to stay healthy.

Getting Ready

Session 1

♦ Collect food and non-food items and arrange them on a table so that they are intermingled.

♦ Cut a sheet of paper into thirds. Write "FOOD," "NON-FOOD," and "?" on them to use as category labels for the sorting activity.

♦ Practice the peanut burning demonstration described on page 126.

Session 2

♦ Plan groups of six students. If the number of students in your class doesn't divide evenly by six, plan to have two students in a group work together on one "Organism Sheet," or have one student be responsible for two sheets.

♦ Make one set of thirty "Game Cards" for each group of six students, using a photocopy machine that can make double-sided copies. It is best if you can copy them onto card stock, or laminate them.

Action Narrative

Session 1

We've been talking a lot about the food that animals eat to survive, but we haven't talked about what FOOD is. Before I tell you a scientific definition of food, work with your group to decide which of the things on this table are food, and which are not. When you're done, write down your group's definition of food.

Hold up and name each item, or have each group send a recorder to the table to make a list of what's there. Help them articulate the criteria they used to decide which are and are not food as they write their definitions.

When they're done, put all of the items on one end of the table and display the three category labels ("FOOD," "NON-FOOD," and "?") across the table.

Let's sort the food items from the non-food items.

Hold up each item and ask each group whether it decided it was food or not, and why. If the whole class agrees on its category, then place it next to the appropriate label. If they disagree, place it next to the "?" label.

Module 1: *Who Eats What?*

Some disagreement could arise over the grass or leaves and the insect or other small critter, because they are not food for people. Tell students that you want a broad definition of food for any living thing, and let groups that had decided these aren't food change their minds. Including food for any living thing in the definition could open the door to groups changing their minds about how they categorized soil, water, and fertilizer, if they still think of these as food for plants. Other possible miscategorizations include calling potato chips, and candy non-food because they are "junk food" and food is what's good for you; calling water, salt, and vitamins food because they are part of food or because people take them into their bodies; calling apple juice a non-food because it is a drink; or calling flour and sugar non-food because they are just ingredients of food.

Once all of the items are categorized, ask for each group's definition of food and perhaps write them on the board. Point out any definitions that contradict one another and ask the groups that wrote them to try to work out their differences. Challenge the class to agree on one definition, then go back to the items in the "?" category and decide if they are food or not based on the class definition.

Now I'll tell you the scientific definition of food: Food is a substance that gives both nutrients and energy to a living thing. A NUTRIENT is a mineral that organisms need to stay healthy, but nutrients don't provide energy that living things need to be active. So for something to be food it has to have ENERGY, expressed as CALORIES, in addition to nutrients.

Let's check what you put in the food and non-food categories to see if they belong there according to this new definition.

As students reconsider how they categorized the items, you might need to tell them which items have food energy as well as nutrients, and which do not, since it is not possible to tell this by visual clues alone. They might question why you categorize "junk food" such as chips and candy as food, since they don't have nutrients in them. Tell them that it is true that most junk food has very few nutrients, but it does have some. This is why junk food is called "empty calories," because it provides energy but few nutrients.

This is also a good time to check on students' understanding of photosynthesis. They may have put potting soil, plant fertilizer, and water into the food category, as foods for plants. Explain that these things are not food because they don't have any calories — they contain nutrients, but do not provide energy to plants. The sugar that plants make has calories as well as nutrients, so it fits the definition of food.

Children's Ideas About Food, Nutrients, and Energy

Every fifth and sixth grader knows what food is. Or do they?

They readily accept and recite that *Every living things needs nutrients to grow*, and *Nutritious food gives you energy*. They know that healthy food has vitamins and minerals that are good for you, and that junk food does not. What most fifth and sixth graders don't

understand is that food without many essential vitamins and minerals can contain more energy than food with these nutrients. They don't distinguish between nutrients and energy. Whereas "nutrient" is a technical term for the building blocks of organisms, "nutritious" is an everyday term that refers both to the nutrients and energy of food.

Children tend to blur nutrients and energy not only because everyday language is vague and confusing, but also because nutrients and energy are invisible and abstract. The following statements by fifth and sixth graders show how they confuse food, nutrients, and energy:

A nutrient is healthy food.

Nutrient is like a food or like a flavor.

On the wrappers it says nutrients. It powers you up, it's energy, it boosts you.

A nutrient is something that gives energy.

Nutrients come from the sun.

These students do not see food as chemical compounds that contain matter (atoms) and chemical energy (the molecular bonds between atoms). Energy and the particulate nature of matter are two of the most difficult, and yet most fundamental, concepts to understand in science. We can't expect students to master the principles of chemistry by sixth grade, but we can give them stepping stones towards these understandings.

By being aware of children's everyday understanding of food, nutrients, and energy, you can help them expand these definitions to incorporate more accurate, scientific views. The technical definition of food as a substance that contains both nutrients and energy is an important underpinning of the ecological concepts of nutrient cycling and energy flow. Take advantage of the inherent interest children have in food, and lay a foundation for ecological literacy.

One way to find out if something has food energy is to burn it. Do not try this at home! If we are correct that the peanut is food, then it should burn. Let's see what happens.

Hold the peanut with tweezers over a cup of water on a cleared table or desk, well away from students. Wearing a pair of safety goggles, light the peanut with a match or lighter. It should ignite immediately and burn for about two minutes. Drop the residue into the water after the peanut burns out.

Module 1: *Who Eats What?*

The food energy in the peanut was what burned. The black residue is the nutrients that were in the peanut. If you would have eaten the peanut, those nutrients would have become part of your body, and the energy would have been used up or stored as fat.

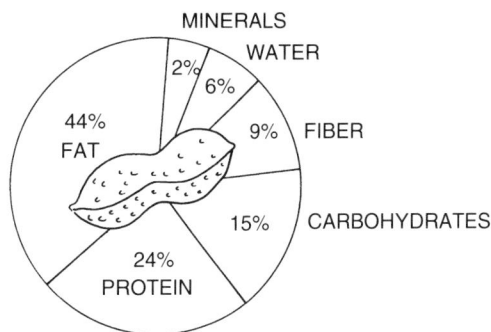

You might want to repeat the demonstration with a non-food item, such as a sugar-free vitamin pill or a pebble, to show that it does not contain energy.

 Conclude with questions such as:

How did your definitions of food differ from the scientific definition I gave you?

What is confusing or difficult about the scientific definition of food?

What does the phrase, "You are what you eat" mean?

Session 2

Now that we know that food is a substance that provides nutrients and energy, we are ready to play "It's All in the Flow." In this game, each player is an organism in an ecosystem that needs to get nutrients and energy to survive.

Put students into groups of six, then give one copy of the "Game Rules" to each group. Read the rules aloud, and help one group demonstrate how the game is played.

Once students understand the directions, give each group a set of "Organism Sheets" and "Game Cards," and let them begin. The game usually ends up being both cooperative and competitive as students within groups help one another decide what cards to choose, but compete with other groups to get all of their "Organism Sheets" filled in first.

While students are engaged in the game, write the name of each "Organism Sheet" on the board, and under each make two columns:

Mouse

Gets Nutrients From Gets Energy From

Circulate among the groups and listen to the reasons students mention for choosing certain cards for their organisms. Remind them to answer the bonus question on their "Organism Sheets."

When all groups are finished, fill in the columns on the board as students read off the sources of nutrients and energy for each organism.

 Conclude the activity with questions such as:

How did you know which cards to pick? What reasoning did you use?

What surprised you?

What is the difference between where plants and animals get their energy and nutrients?

Plants get nutrients from soil and energy from sunlight, whereas animals get both nutrients and energy from the food they eat.

How does energy escape from an ecosystem?

Living things use the energy in their food to live (e.g., to grow, reproduce, and move). This process is a little like burning, and releases heat that escapes into the atmosphere.

What is meant by the statement "Nutrients have a round-trip ticket in an ecosystem, but energy is on a one-way trip"?

The nutrients that are in organisms get recycled by decomposers, then taken up again by plants. Energy enters an ecosystem as sunlight, but escapes as heat. It has to be replenished by more sunlight.

Ongoing Assessment

Student Reflections

 Have students send a C-Mail message or record their thoughts about the lesson in their journals. Some prompts to guide their reflections are:

All the things I eat or drink that aren't food are:

The hardest Organism Sheet to fill in was _____ because:

The game we played is called "It's All in the Flow" because:

Teacher Reflections

❑ Did students consider one another's viewpoints about what constitutes food in order to agree on a definition?

❑ Were they able to adjust their intuitive definitions of food to accept a more scientific viewpoint?

❑ Did they share ideas and opinions productively with group members as they played the game?

❏ Do they realize that when one thing eats another thing in a food chain that nutrients and energy are passed along?

Extensions

Questions Jigsaw. Ask students to help you write several questions that will give them a chance to summarize their new knowledge about food, nutrients, energy, and ecosystems. List the questions on the board, then split the class into groups that contain as many students as there are questions. Have the groups write answers to each question. Then have each student take one of the questions and answers, and join a new group made up of one person from each original group who has chosen the same question (i.e., all the students with question #1 get together, all the students with question #2 get together, and so on). In their new groups, students should share their original group's answer to the question, discuss the variety of responses, then write a revised answer. Finally, have each of the new groups share its question and answer with the whole class.

Calorie Counting. Help students use a calorie chart to count the total number of calories in a school lunch. Look at an exercise chart to see how many of those calories will be burned throughout the afternoon.

IT'S ALL IN THE FLOW

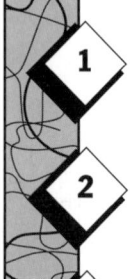

1 The object of the game is for each team to get all of the nutrients and energy its six organisms need.

2 Give one Organism Sheet (Dandelion, Grass, Cricket, Mouse, Owl, or Bacteria) to each of the players on your team.

3 Spread out the Game Cards so that the name on the back of each card shows.

4 When it's your turn, think about which of the things on the cards your organism would use to get nutrients and energy. Choose one card and read it aloud.

5 If the card gives nutrients or energy to your organism, then use a pencil to check off that number of nutrient and energy boxes, and write the name of the card on the "Source" lines. If you get more nutrients and energy than you need, keep track of extra ones in the margin to use if you lose some later. Then put the card back, facedown. No player can choose the same card twice.

6 If the card you chose was not right for your organism, put the card back, facedown.

7 When a card says that your organism has to lose energy, then erase that number of energy checkmarks. If you do not have that many energy checkmarks, erase as many as you have, then replace the card. If you don't have any checkmarks to erase, then just put the card back.

8 Players take turns. Since you are working as a team, you can help each other decide which would be the best card to choose for each organism.

9 When you have filled your own Organism Sheet, continue to help your group members. The game is not over until all six sheets are filled, including the Bonus Question!

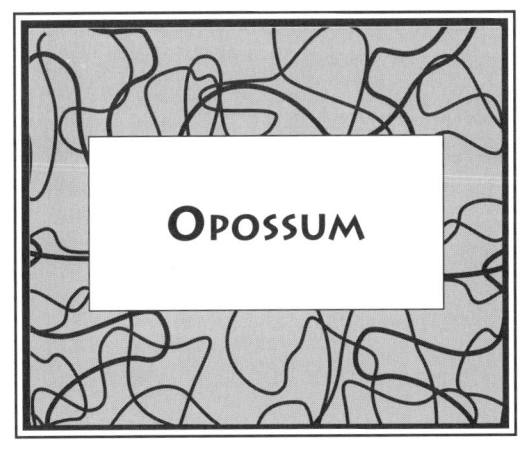

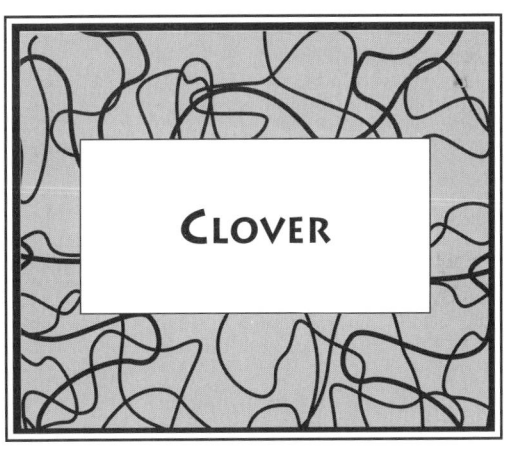

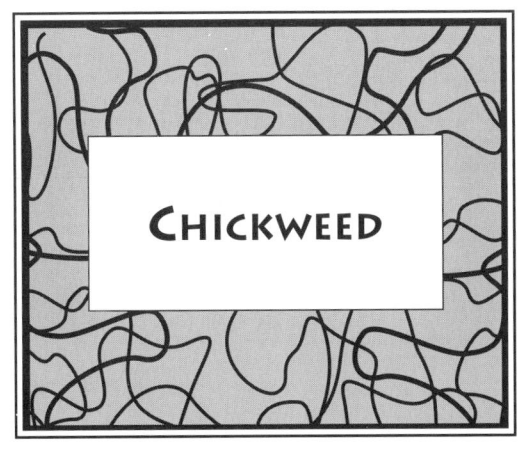

Bacteria eat a dead beetle.

Bacteria gain:

1 Nutrient
1 Energy

The Owl gets the
flying squirrel one night.

Owl gains:

2 Nutrients
2 Energy

Cricket eats clover.

Cricket gains:

1 Nutrient
1 Energy

This opossum is a big,
fat meal for Owl.

Owl gains:

3 Nutrients
3 Energy

Someone dropped an
apple core, and Bacteria
are having a feast.

Bacteria gain:

1 Nutrient
1 Energy

Chickweed plant dies
and decomposes.

Dandelion gains:

1 Nutrient

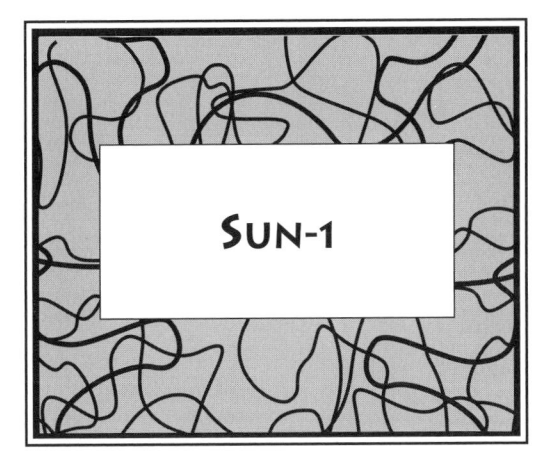

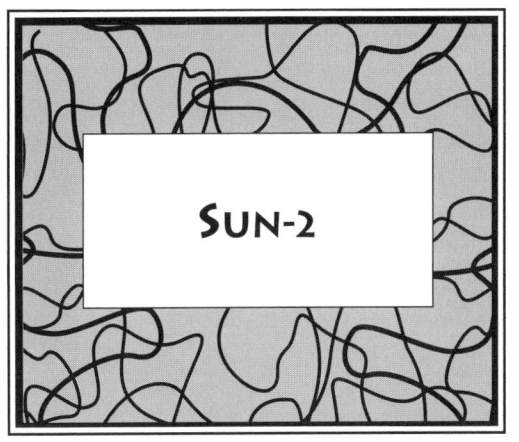

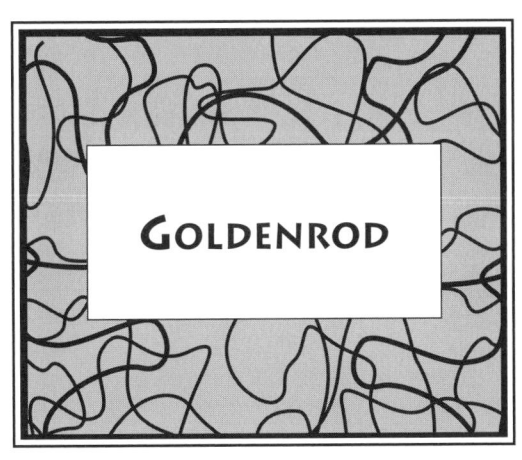

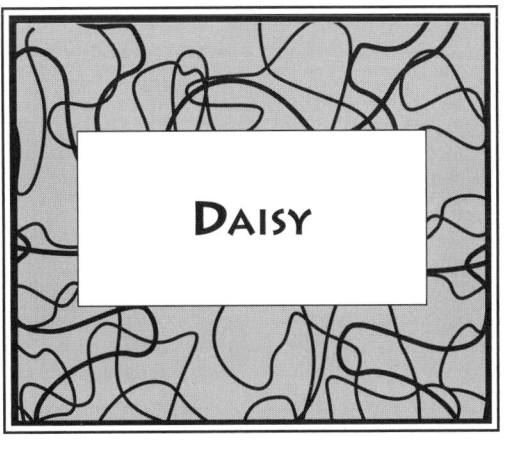

© Institute of Ecosystem Studies, 1994   **133**

It is a partly cloudy day. Plants use sunlight to make food.

Grass or Dandelion gain:

2 Energy

It is a sunny day. Plants use sunlight to make food.

Grass or Dandelion gain:

4 Energy

Mice love acorns!

Mouse gains:

2 Nutrients

2 Energy

Goldenrod leaves die and decompose.

Dandelion gains:

1 Nutrient

Cricket eats part of a daisy.

Cricket gains:

1 Nutrient

1 Energy

Maple tree branch falls to the ground and decomposes.

Grass gains:

1 Nutrient

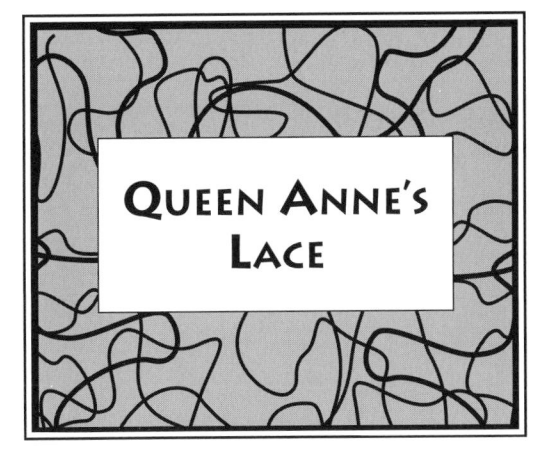

QUEEN ANNE'S LACE

BLUEBERRY SHRUB

BLACK BEAR

DEAD LEAF

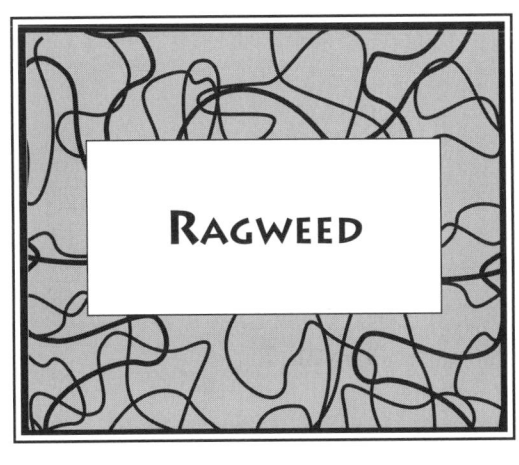

RAGWEED

RACCOON

Blueberries are plump
and juicy.

Mouse gains:

1 Nutrient
1 Energy

Love those little seeds!

Mouse gains:

1 Nutrient
1 Energy

Bacteria work over
the dead leaf.

Bacteria gain:

1 Nutrient
1 Energy

This bear died, and
Bacteria wasted no time
invading the body.

Bacteria gain:

2 Nutrients
2 Energy

Raccoon urinates next
to Dandelion.

Dandelion gains:

2 Nutrients

Cricket eats
ragweed seeds.

Cricket gains:

1 Nutrient
1 Energy

     Module 1: *Who Eats What?*

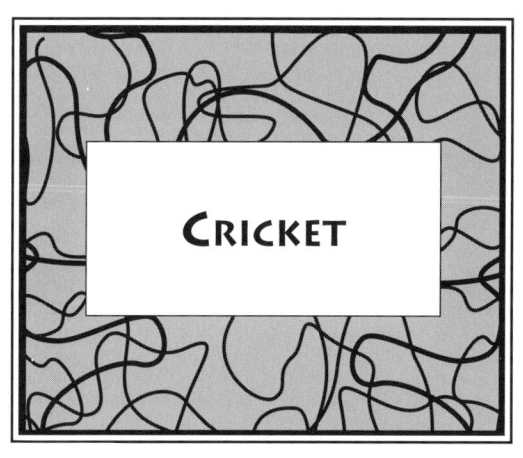

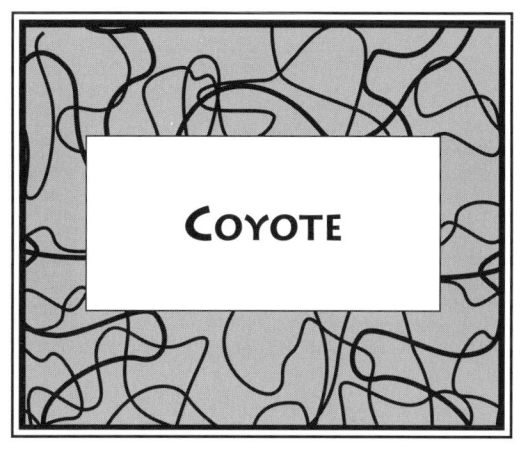

Yumm ... Owl's
favorite meal.

Owl gains:

1 Nutrient
1 Energy

Snakes can be fast, but
sometimes not fast enough!
Owl got this one.

Owl gains:

1 Nutrient
1 Energy

Strawberries fall to the
ground and rot.

Grass gains:

1 Nutrient

Cricket devours
another cricket.

Cricket gains:

1 Nutrient
1 Energy

Young apple trees have
tender bark—just right
for Mouse's meal.

Mouse gains:

1 Nutrient
1 Energy

Coyote releases feces
on Grass.

Grass gains:

2 Nutrients

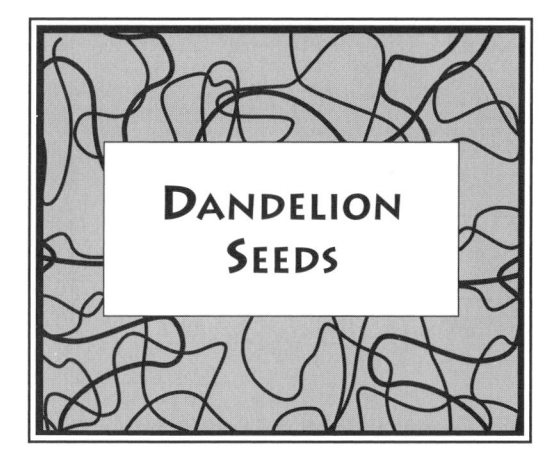

DANDELION SEEDS

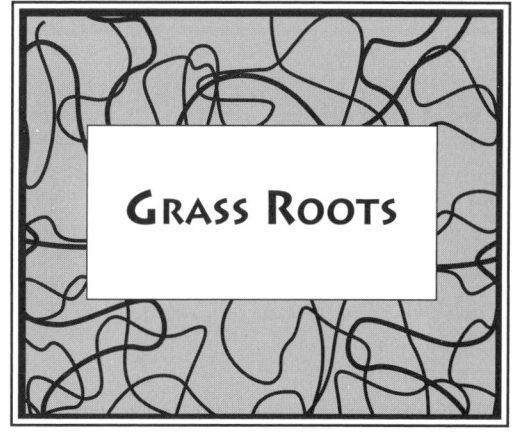

GRASS ROOTS

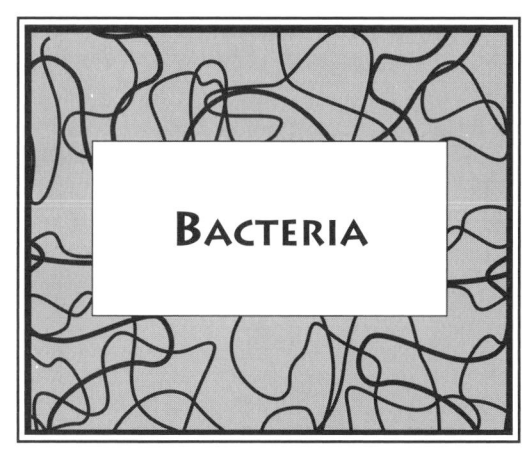

BACTERIA

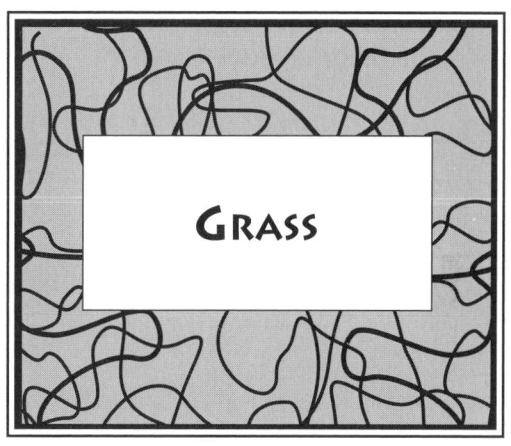

GRASS

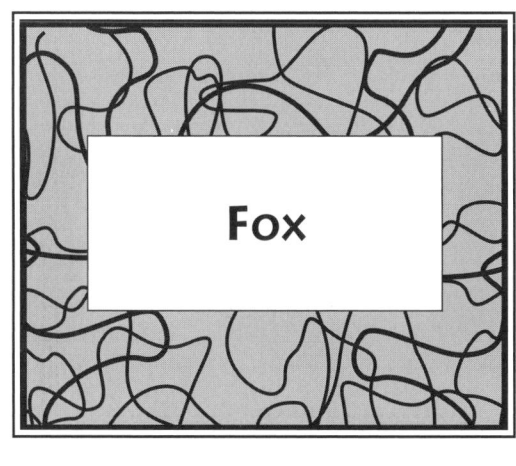

FOX

RABBIT

Grass uses energy
to make more roots.
Energy escapes as heat.

Grass loses:

1 Energy

Dandelion uses energy
to produce seeds.
Energy escapes as heat.

Dandelion loses:

1 Energy

Cricket uses energy
hopping through Grass.
Energy escapes as heat.

Cricket loses:

1 Energy

Bacteria used energy
reproducing more bacteria.
Energy escapes as heat.

Bacteria lose:

1 Energy

Owl uses energy
flying after a rabbit.
Energy escapes as heat.

Owl loses:

2 Energy

Mouse loses energy
running from a fox.
Energy escapes as heat.

Mouse loses:

2 Energy

OWL

NUTRIENTS

Check here when filled

Source:

_____

Check here when filled

Source:

_____

Check here when filled

Source:

_____

Check here when filled

Source:

_____

Check here when filled

Source:

_____

Check here when filled

Source:

_____

Check here when filled

Source:

ENERGY

Check here when filled

Source:

_____

Check here when filled

Source:

_____

Check here when filled

Source:

_____

Check here when filled

Source:

_____

Check here when filled

Source:

BONUS QUESTION   **H**ow does energy escape from an ecosystem?

_____

_____

GRASS

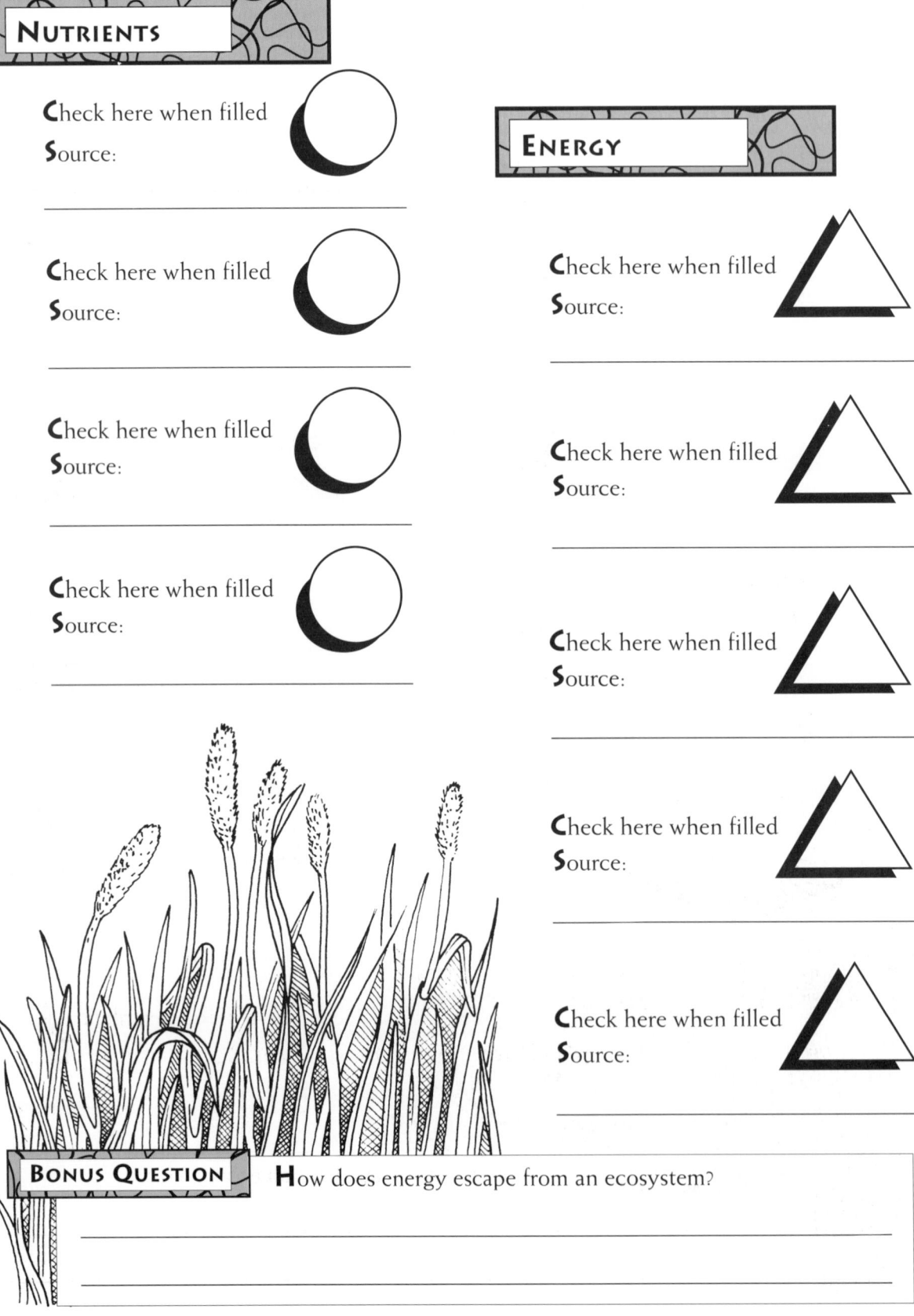

NUTRIENTS

Check here when filled
Source:

Check here when filled
Source:

Check here when filled
Source:

Check here when filled
Source:

ENERGY

Check here when filled
Source:

Check here when filled
Source:

Check here when filled
Source:

Check here when filled
Source:

Check here when filled
Source:

BONUS QUESTION **H**ow does energy escape from an ecosystem?

DANDELION

NUTRIENTS

Check here when filled
Source:

Check here when filled
Source:

Check here when filled
Source:

Check here when filled
Source:

ENERGY

Check here when filled
Source:

Check here when filled
Source:

Check here when filled
Source:

Check here when filled
Source:

Check here when filled
Source:

BONUS QUESTION   **H**ow does energy escape from an ecosystem?

CRICKET

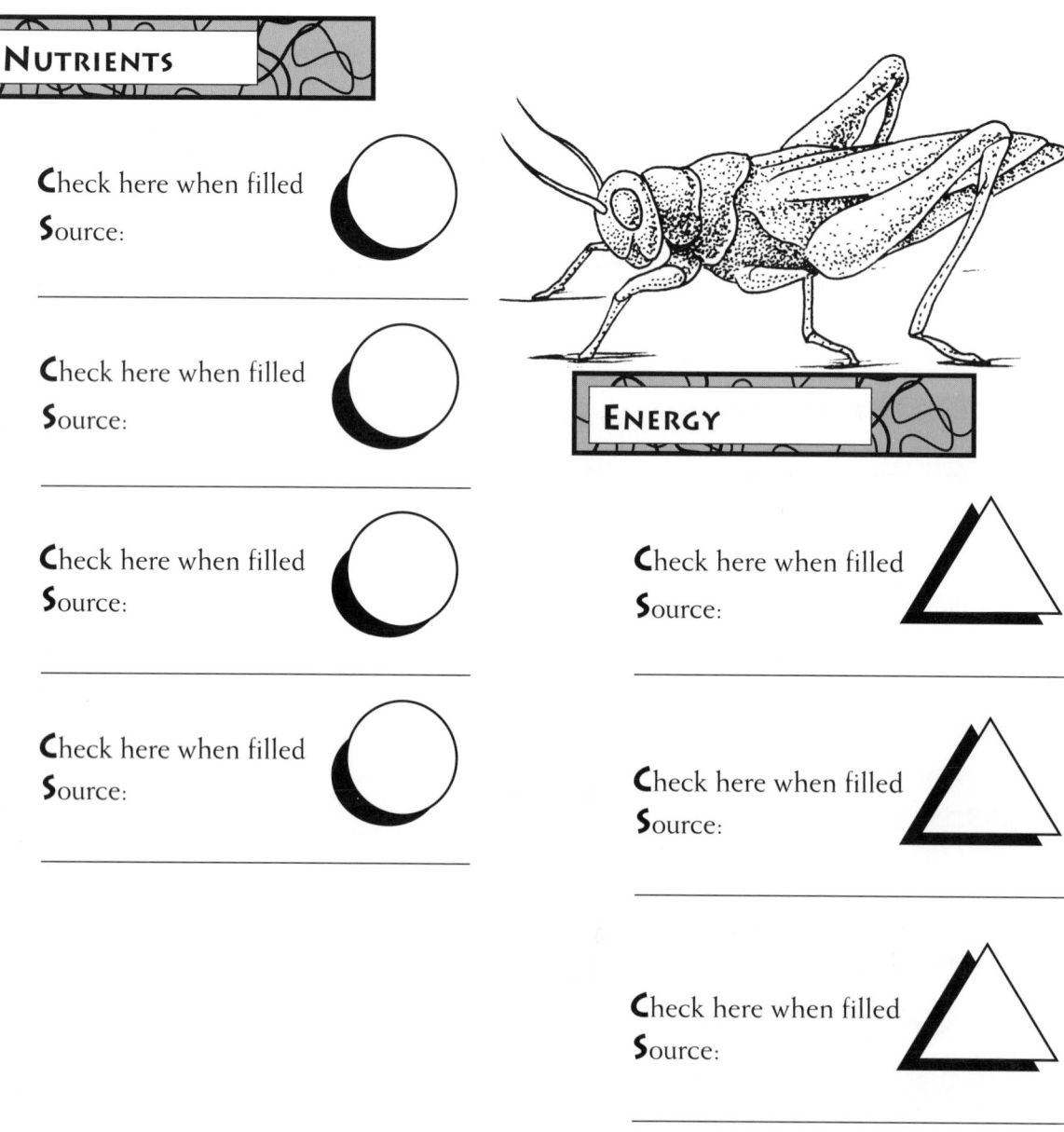

NUTRIENTS

Check here when filled
Source:

Check here when filled
Source:

Check here when filled
Source:

Check here when filled
Source:

ENERGY

Check here when filled
Source:

Check here when filled
Source:

Check here when filled
Source:

BONUS QUESTION   **H**ow does energy escape from an ecosystem?

BACTERIA

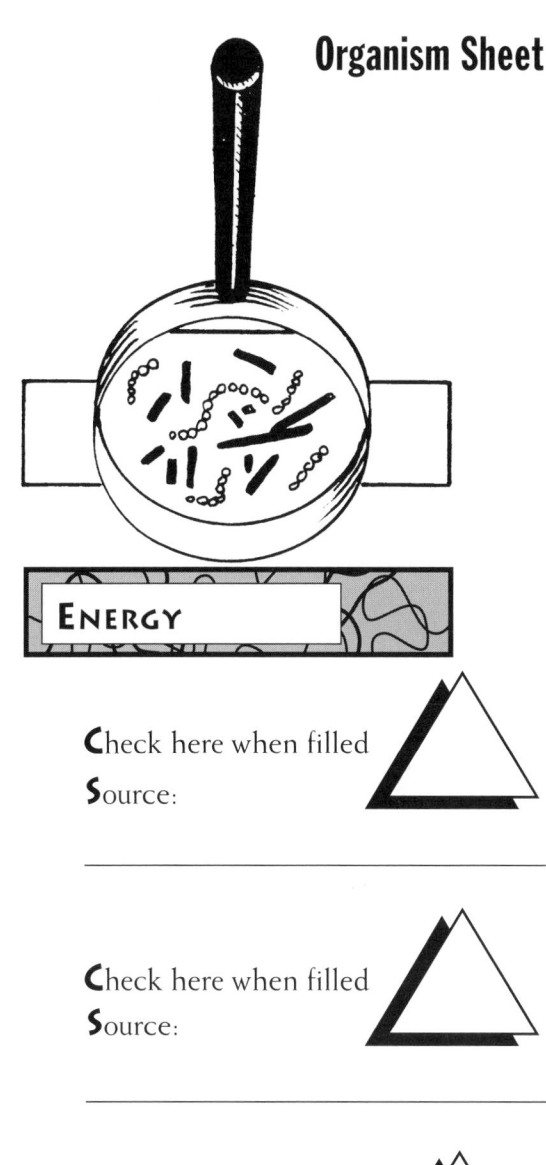

NUTRIENTS

Check here when filled
Source:

_____

Check here when filled
Source:

_____

Check here when filled
Source:

_____

Check here when filled
Source:

_____

Check here when filled
Source:

_____

ENERGY

Check here when filled
Source:

_____

Check here when filled
Source:

_____

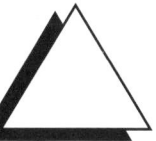
Check here when filled
Source:

_____

Check here when filled
Source:

_____

BONUS QUESTION   **H**ow does energy escape from an ecosystem?

_____

_____

MOUSE

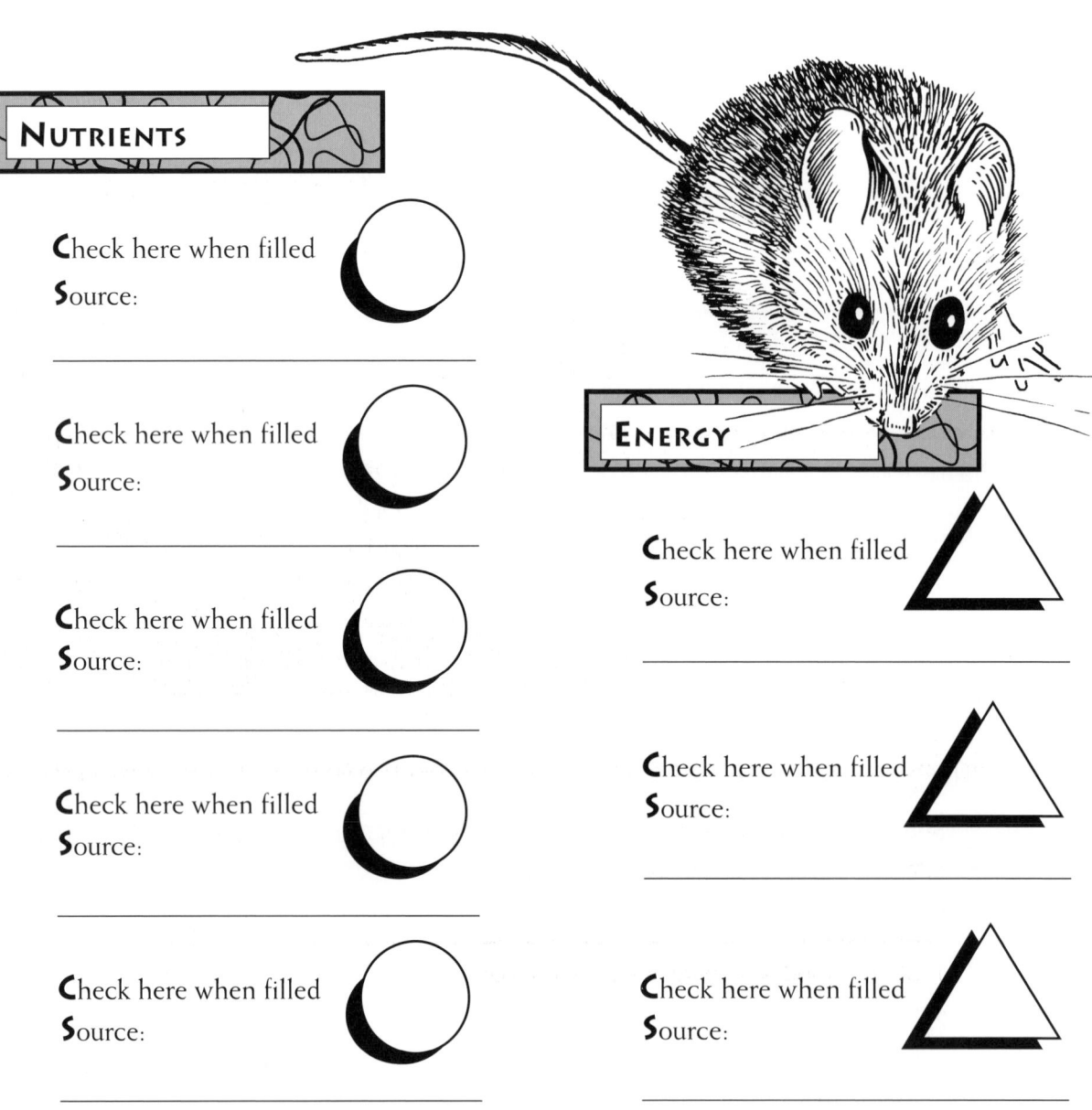

NUTRIENTS

Check here when filled
Source:

_____

Check here when filled
Source:

_____

Check here when filled
Source:

_____

Check here when filled
Source:

_____

Check here when filled
Source:

_____

ENERGY

Check here when filled
Source:

_____

Check here when filled
Source:

_____

Check here when filled
Source:

BONUS QUESTION   **H**ow does energy escape from an ecosystem?

_____

_____

1.8 Making Food Webs

Action Synopsis

Students make food webs of their study site, then trace how a change in one population could affect other populations within the web.

Session 1		**40 minutes**
1. Show a food web made by a team of ecologists.		*linking to real world*
2. Discuss populations and food webs.		*introducing new information*
3. Work in groups to make food webs using study site organisms.		*processing findings*

Session 2		**40 minutes**
1. Talk about how changes in one part of a food web can cause changes in other parts of the web.		*introducing new information*
2. Prepare and exchange "What if ... " food web scenarios.		*applying knowledge*
3. Summarize and discuss how people's actions can affect food webs.		*reflecting*

Desired Outcomes

Throughout the lesson, check that students:

✓ Know that most animals eat and are eaten by more than one thing.

✓ Understand that a food web shows all the likely feeding relationships at a location.

✓ Are able to explain the different ways a change in one population can ripple through a food web.

What You'll Need

Sessions 1 & 2

For the class:
- ❏ overhead transparency of "Food Web" (page 155)
- ❏ overhead marker
- ❏ 20–30 buttons or beans, two colors (optional)
- ❏ food chains from Lesson 1.6
- ❏ master list of study site organisms from Lesson 1.3
- ❏ several copies of the *Who Eats What* guide (pages 355–382)
- ❏ other resource books (see "Resource List," pages 51–55)

For each group of 3–4 students:
- ❏ materials for making food webs (see "Getting Ready")

Vocabulary

FOOD WEB - The connections among everything organisms in a location eat and are eaten by.

POPULATION - A group of the same kind of organism living in the same place.

Getting Ready

Session 1

◆ Gather materials for groups to use to make food webs, such as large sheets of butcher paper, slips of paper or self-stick removable notes in two colors, and markers.

◆ Plan to use the same student groups as for Lesson 1.3 and Lesson 1.6.

♦ Consider reading a food web story to your students to provide additional examples of how a change in one population can affect an entire food web. See *Wolf Island* and *The Day They Parachuted Cats on Borneo* in the "Resource List" (pages 54–55).

Action Narrative

Session 1

Today we're going to make FOOD WEBS. Here is a picture of one.

Show the "Food Web" overhead.

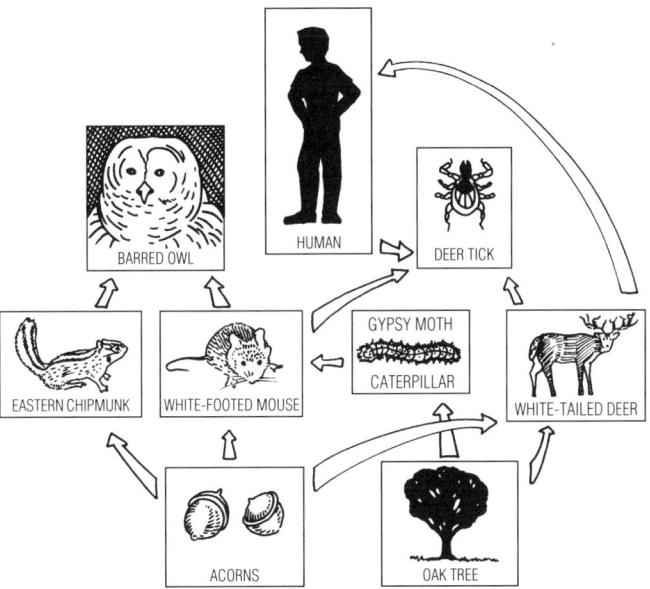

What do you notice about the difference between a food chain and a food web?

A food chain shows just one thing that each animal eats and is eaten by; a food web shows all the things an animal eats and is eaten by.

This food web was made by a group of scientists who work at the Institute of Ecosystem Studies, an ecology research center in New York state. They figured out this food web by studying plants and animals that live in oak forests. Some of the things living in the forest are: oak trees, white-footed mice, chipmunks, white-tailed deer, barred owls, Lyme ticks, and gypsy moths. Each scientist has a different specialty — plants, mammals, and insects. They work together to try to figure out how changes in one population of plants or animals affects the other populations in the food web. Do you know what I mean by a POPULATION?

A population is a group of the same kind of organism living in an area. You can illustrate this by spreading two colors of buttons on a table. All of the (red) buttons represent one population, such as deer mice, and all of the (blue) buttons represent another population, such as Lyme ticks. Have students count how many organisms there are in each population. Students might be familiar with the Federal Census Bureau which counts the population of people living in the United States.

A lot of people are interested in the size of the populations of the organisms in this food web. Can you think why?

Students might suggest some of the following reasons: 1) Lyme ticks carry Lyme disease which makes people very ill; 2) gypsy moths can destroy whole forests by eating all the leaves off of trees; 3) when there are a lot of deer they eat people's shrubs, gardens and crops, and cause accidents when they run in front of cars, but some people like having a lot of deer to watch or hunt for meat; and 4) oak trees make valuable lumber.

If ecologists can figure out what makes the populations of these organisms grow or shrink, they can help people manage forest resources. Let's see what the food web tells us about what each animal eats.

Go over the food web, asking students to interpret what each organism eats and is eaten by. The arrows in a food web point away from the thing being eaten, towards ("into the mouth of") the organism that is eating it. Food webs are often organized like food chains, with producers on the bottom, herbivores in the middle, and carnivores on the top.

Now you'll work in groups to make food webs using your research findings, just like the scientists who made this web. Start your webs with an organism you saw in your study plot. Work in your groups to decide what to include in your food web, and how to organize it. You can use the *Who Eats What* guide, resource books, and everyone's food chains for information about who eats what.

Show students the materials they can use to make their food webs. It will take them a while to decide how to organize their webs. It is usually easiest for them to choose one organism, then work outward to form a web above, below, and around it. After they have a core web, you can suggest that they look at their list of study plot organisms, and at the master list of study site organisms, to see if they can make any other connections to their web. They don't have to make a web of the entire study site.

You might suggest that groups figure out some way (e.g., two different color removable notes or paper slips) to indicate which plants and animals they know are on the site, and which they just assume are there because of evidence they saw. Students can also indicate how sure they are of each food link by using a dotted line to show connections of which they aren't sure, and a solid line for those of which they are sure. It's best if students use a pencil to draw connections initially, then use a pen or marker to darken the lines once they are satisfied that everything is correct.

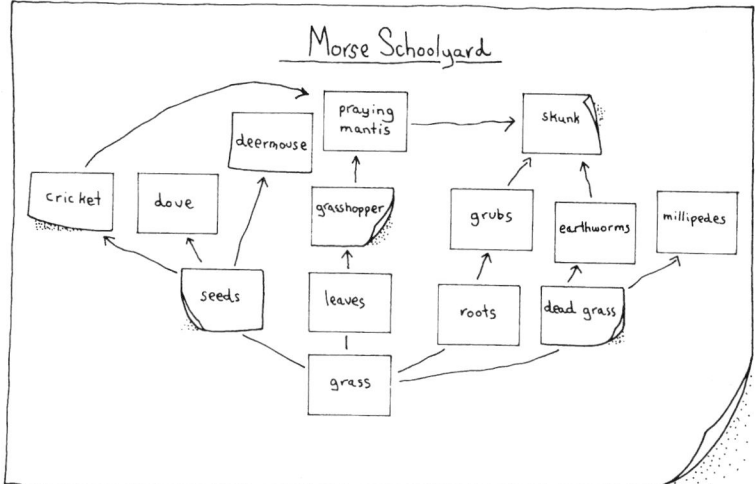

NOTE: Since different parts of a plant are food resources for different animals, students should specify the plant parts that each animal consumes.

Session 2

The next step in understanding food webs is to think of a "What if . . . " sequence of events.

Show the food web overhead transparency.

For example, what would happen if one year all the oak trees in the forest produced a huge crop of acorns?

Work through the food web putting a plus or a minus sign on the overhead next to organisms that students predict will increase or decrease in the first year after acorn production increases.

Next talk about what would happen the following year. If herbivores (e.g., mice, chipmunks) increase the first year because they have more acorns to eat, then their predators (e.g., owls) will gradually increase because they will also have more food. Once predators increase, the populations of the herbivores they eat will decline.

Encourage students to think about how a change could affect organisms on both ends of the arrows, to emphasize that effects ripple through a food web in all directions. For instance, an increase in mice might lead to a decrease in gypsy moth caterpillars, since mice eat them. But it might also lead to an increase in owls, since there are more mice for them to eat.

What would happen if a lot of mice died over a very hard winter?

Put a big X through the mouse picture and discuss the effects on the food web.

Thinking Like Food Web Scientists

A lot of questions and complications will arise in discussing how a change in one population could affect an entire food web, which are exactly the kinds of issues that make food web scientists' work challenging! For instance, if mice decrease, will there be more acorns for deer to eat so that they are able to have more offspring? And if deer increase as mice decline, will tick populations change? Will some of these population shifts "even out" so that top level predators are not affected?

Through raising questions and making predictions, students will realize that they need to know how much each organism depends on another one for food. For instance, do enough people depend on deer for food to really make a difference in the human population size if deer increase? Students also might begin to think about how the forest itself could change if herbivores eat all the acorns and oak saplings. If gypsy moths eat oak leaves, letting light onto the forest floor that used to be shady, will new types of plants grow where oak saplings once did? Help students to realize that scientists begin their research by making predictions, just as they are doing, but they can't be sure what really happens in nature until they actually study these communities in the forest.

The scientists doing the food web study in New York predict that in years when oak trees produce a lot of acorns, mice populations will increase. Then their populations will crash the next year when the oak trees have fewer acorns. When this happens, there will be fewer animals to eat gypsy moth larvae, so the gypsy moths will hatch and eat the leaves off of the oak trees. This means that the oak trees won't have enough energy to produce acorns. Also, with no leaves on the oak trees a lot more sunlight will hit the forest floor, making it possible for new kinds of plants to grow there. Since the oak trees aren't producing many seeds, and new kinds of trees are starting to grow, the whole forest could change. All this because of food web links among acorns, mice, and gypsy moths!

Read students a food web story to provide other examples of ripple effects in food webs. (See "Getting Ready," page 149.)

Now work with your group to write a "What If . . . " question about your food web. On a separate piece of paper, record what you think would happen to every organism on your food web. Then exchange your web and question, but not your answers, with another group. When both groups have written predictions about each other's food webs, get together to compare your answers.

Encourage students to express and justify the reasoning behind their predictions of how a change will ripple through their food web. After they exchange answers with another group, don't let them just "correct" and hand back one another's papers. Ask them to talk through differences of opinion by presenting the reasoning behind their predictions. Encourage them to achieve consensus by deciding which arguments make the most sense, or which have the most evidence to back them up. In some cases, two predictions may be equally valid, which is acceptable so long as students see that they are both based on sound reasoning.

 Conclude the activity with questions such as:

What are the different ways a change in one population can ripple through a food web?

1) If a predator increases, its prey decreases; 2) If a predator decreases, its prey increases; 3) If prey increases, its predators increase; 4) If prey decreases, its predators decrease; 5) Predators can indirectly benefit their prey's food (e.g., an owl eating mice helps gypsy moths) or their prey's competitors (e.g., an owl eating a chipmunk helps mice).

What would be the advantages and disadvantages of eating one or many things?

Animals that have adaptations for using one particular food source often can out compete animals that are less well equipped to use that food. However, relying on one food source makes an animal vulnerable when the food becomes scarce.

What investigations could you do to figure out if your predictions are correct?

Students might feed or remove organisms, then watch what happens to the size of populations of other organisms. Encourage them to think about how they could count organisms. Scientists usually do this by sampling a population rather than counting every individual. This is the difference between a U.S. population census that counts every head, and an opinion poll that takes a sample that represents the whole population.

In what different ways could people's actions affect your food webs?

People often cause wildlife populations to increase or decrease. For instance, when human populations increase, raccoon populations often increase because people's garbage is a food resource for raccoons. Deer populations increase where people change the landscape in ways that make more deer browse available. The population of timber wolves has been greatly decreased because of hunting pressure, and loss of habitat when people built towns and cities.

Are there any organisms on your webs that people might want to control?

People like to control plants and animals that they consider pests, as well as those that they can use to make their own lives better or more enjoyable.

Should people try to manage and control nature?

Some might argue that since people already have a large impact on plants and wildlife, we should try to balance protection and use of natural resources. One example of using knowledge of who eats what in nature is biological control, in which farmers and gardeners introduce insects or bacteria to eat or infect pests that eat their crops, instead of using pesticides.

Ongoing Assessment

Student Reflections

Have students send a C-Mail message or record thoughts in their journals. Optional writing prompts include:

What kind of changes to the outdoors have I seen that could have affected the food web in that place?

What does the food web that I am part of look like?

Teacher Reflections

❏ Do students understand the difference between a food chain and a food web?

❏ Did they make correct linkages in their food webs?

❏ Were they able to predict how organisms directly linked to a changed population could be affected, as well as how those several steps removed might change?

❏ Could they express their reasoning for the changes they predicted in their webs, and were they able to change their minds when someone else presented a stronger argument?

❏ Can they make general statements about the different ways changes can ripple through a food web?

Extensions

Concept Maps. Introduce concept mapping to students (see pages 25–27) if they are not already familiar with the process. Select all or some of the concept map cards on pages 43–44, then copy one set of cards for each group of 3–4 students. Have them construct concept maps that display their understanding of interrelationships within an ecosystem. Help students compare their new concept maps with those they made after Lesson 1.3 to see how their ideas have changed.

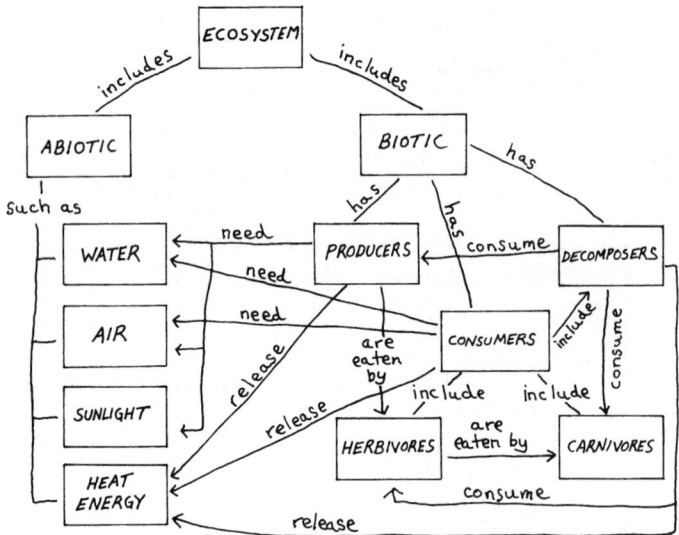

Pollutant Pathways. Have students pick a pollutant, such as lead or PCBs, and find out how it gets into food chains. Trace it through an entire food web.

Food Web Drama. Challenge students to write and perform a play that shows food web interactions before and after a disturbance to the web.

FOOD WEB

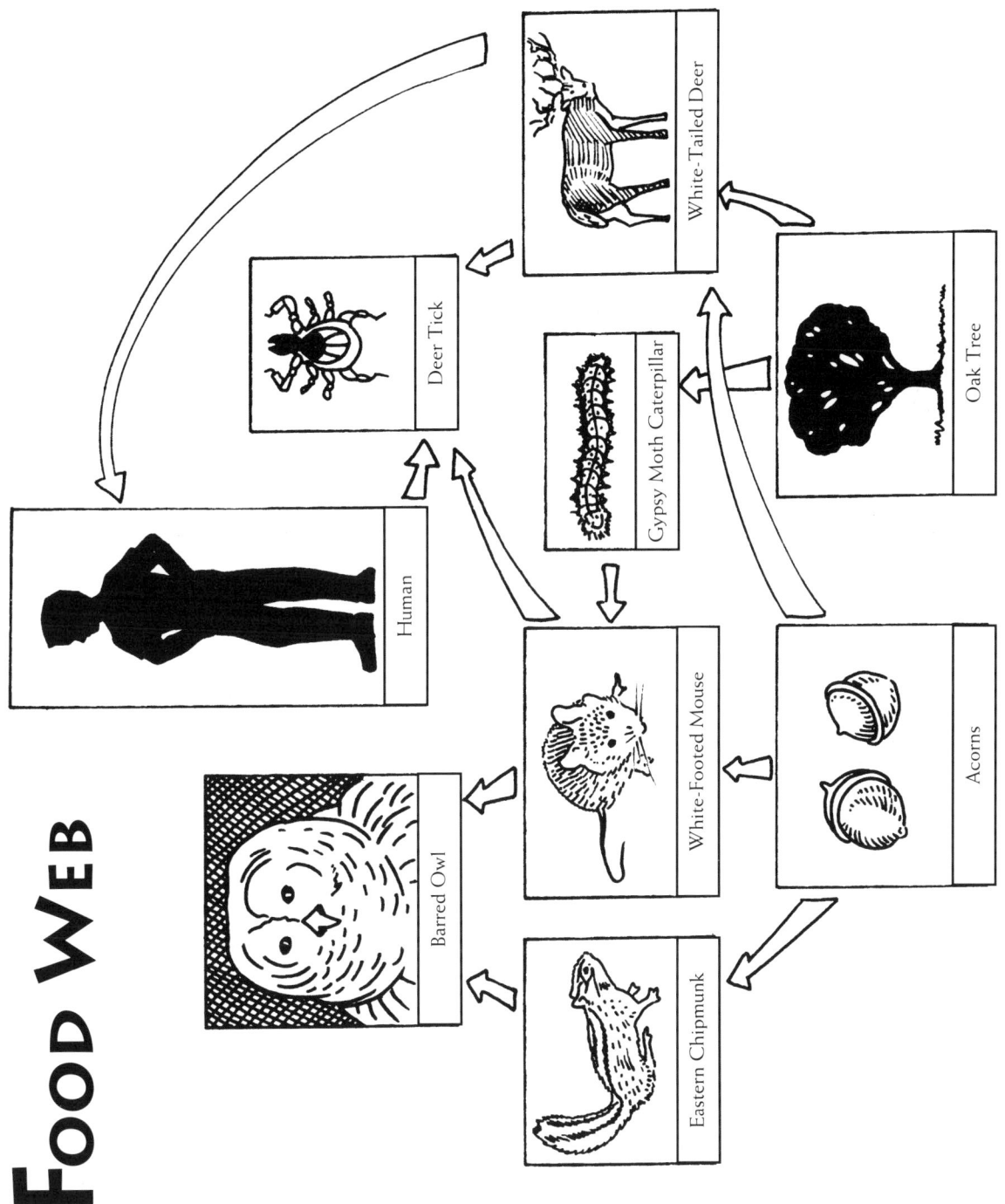

1.9 Environmental Impact Statements—Written Assessment

Action Synopsis

Students write predictions of how a proposed change to their study site would affect the organisms that live there.

One Session		40–60 minutes

1. Talk about what causes changes in the environment. *examining prior ideas*

2. Describe Environmental Impact Statements.  *introducing new information*

3. Present the challenge of assessing the impact of a study site alteration. *posing a challenge*

4. Discuss criteria for high quality work. *setting standards*

5. Share ideas in pairs, then write Environmental Impact Statements for the landowner. *applying knowledge*

6. Share and discuss the written statements. *reflecting*

7. Evaluate work and select samples for a portfolio. *assessing*

Desired Outcomes

By the end of this assessment activity, students should:

✓ Be able to predict how changes in a landscape could ripple through a food web.

✓ Understand why it's important for people to consider the food web of a piece of land before they alter it.

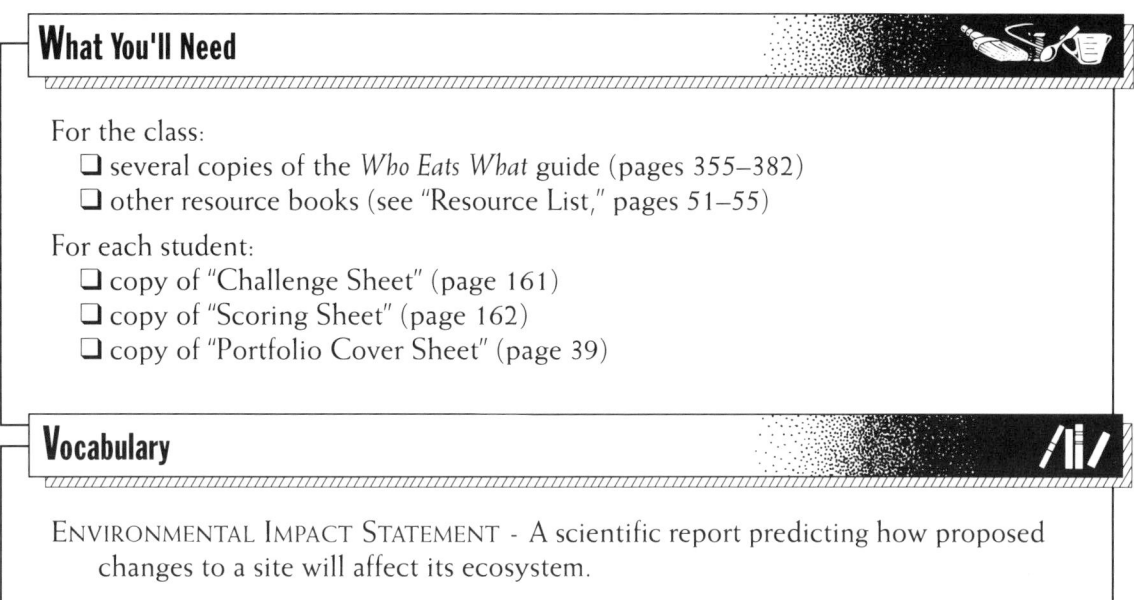

What You'll Need

For the class:
- ❑ several copies of the *Who Eats What* guide (pages 355–382)
- ❑ other resource books (see "Resource List," pages 51–55)

For each student:
- ❑ copy of "Challenge Sheet" (page 161)
- ❑ copy of "Scoring Sheet" (page 162)
- ❑ copy of "Portfolio Cover Sheet" (page 39)

Vocabulary

ENVIRONMENTAL IMPACT STATEMENT - A scientific report predicting how proposed changes to a site will affect its ecosystem.

Getting Ready

♦ Instead of using the "Challenge Sheet" and "Scoring Sheet" provided, consider writing your own challenge statement that is tailored to your study site, and devising your own scoring criteria in collaboration with your students. Some possible site alterations for students to evaluate are: paving a pathway or rerouting a road through the site; fencing around the site to keep out deer or people; mowing; cutting down trees; building a playground; spraying for mosquitoes; erecting a tall building; or introducing a new plant or animal species.

Action Narrative

One of the good things about knowing how different animals use plants, other animals, and the non-living environment to survive, is being able to predict how they

will be affected if the place where they live is changed. What are some of the things that cause an environment to change?

Students might mention natural disasters such as floods, earthquakes, wind, and fires, as well as changes caused by humans such as cutting down trees, building roads and structures, and paving parking lots.

Has anyone heard of ENVIRONMENTAL IMPACT STATEMENTS?

After students have offered their ideas, share with them that these are reports that scientists do when someone wants to change a large or special piece of land. Their job is to survey the living and non-living features of the site, and predict how the proposed changes will affect these things. Emphasize that the purpose of these reports is not to stop all development, but to help people shape their plans so that damage to the environment is minimized.

You might want to point out that people place different values on different things in nature. For instance, if a rare or endangered species is on a site, a development project might be halted. On the other hand, if habitats for common organisms such as sow bugs, earthworms, squirrels, and "weeds" will disappear, people won't mind as much because plenty of these things live in other locations.

Today you are going to write an Environmental Impact Statement about the food web of our study site. Here is the situation you'll write about.

Give a copy of the "Challenge Sheet" to each student and discuss it. Make sure students understand that they should try to trace how the proposed action could ripple through the food web of their site. Encourage them to refer to the food webs they've already made of the site for ideas.

How should we evaluate your work?

Have students generate standards for their work. Either formalize their suggestions into an assessment sheet, or give them a copy of the "Scoring Sheet," if it is an appropriate summary of what you and they feel is important.

You can start out in pairs to share ideas, then everyone will write his or her own Environmental Impact Statement in the form of a letter to the landowner.

Let students brainstorm ideas in pairs for about ten minutes and then write their own letters. This allows both for idea interchange to jog and expand thinking, and for individual accountability. As pairs talk, listen to make sure that they are using the assignment as an opportunity to demonstrate their understanding of the concepts they've learned over the past several weeks.

Students will need 20–30 minutes to write their letters. When they're finished, ask volunteers to read their letters aloud.

Dear Smith Street Vacant Lot Owner,

Our class has been studying your lot on Smith Street and we've discovered that it is not vacant! There are lots of amazing things living there, such as caterpillars, grubs, earthworms, sowbugs, 2 kinds of trees, and even a woodpecker.

This is why we have a problem with Clean Up Crew 2's plan for your lot. Lots of the animals depend on the dead leaves and branches, and even some of the trash that's there, too. Like if the Crew cuts the dead branches, the grubs won't be there anymore, and then the woodpecker that eats the grubs won't come around.

? Conclude with questions such as:

How certain do you feel that the changes in the food web you described would really occur after the Clean Up Crew Two did its work?
There is always an element of uncertainty in an Environmental Impact Statement. The environmental specialist writing the statement must provide as much support for the claims as possible, for instance by describing the outcome of a similar case.

How important is it if the organisms you mentioned die or leave the site?
Some students might make a case for why the benefits of the Clean Up Crew Two's work (e.g., a tidier landscape) outweigh the possible costs. Placing values on the decline or disappearance of organisms from a site is a key factor in deciding what action to take once an Environmental Impact Statement is written.

What is the best way to decide what to do when human preferences conflict with what's best for other parts of nature?
This question will help students think about the extent to which they feel that parts of nature that don't have an immediate benefit to people do or do not have rights.

Ongoing Assessment

Student Reflections

Have students evaluate their own work by completing a "Scoring Sheet" for the Environmental Impact Statement they wrote. This is also a good time to have them select work samples for a portfolio, and complete a "Portfolio Cover Sheet" (page 39). Review the purpose and structure of a portfolio, and set a due date.

Teacher Reflections

As you evaluate students' work, look for descriptions of food web impact that begin with the dead matter that decomposers eat, and then expand to include animals that eat decomposers. For example, if a dead branch is removed, the grubs feeding on it might die, and the woodpeckers who eat grubs might go somewhere else to find food. Students might also trace food web impacts that begin when animals that use dead plants for shelter, egg laying, or as hiding places for food, decline. The "Scoring Sheet" gives the highest points for true food webs (e.g., tracing how each organism eats and is eaten by more than one thing), rather than for a series of independent food chains.

Since students' food web studies have not emphasized nutrient cycling, don't expect them to include the effect that removing dead plants from the site could have on soil fertility and the health of living plants. It's a bonus if someone does mention this, since it will broaden the class's understanding of the impact of removing dead organic matter from a site, and set the stage for investigations in Modules 2 and 3.

NAME_____ DATE_____

ENVIRONMENTAL IMPACT STATEMENTS

A new business called the Clean Up Crew Two has made a special offer to the owner of your study site. After its parent company, the Clean Up Crew, picks up any trash on the site, Clean Up Crew Two will clear away all the dead leaves, branches, logs, and all other dead material on the ground. Clean Up Crew Two will also remove dead branches from living plants, and dead plants that are still standing.

They say that their work will make the site a neater, cleaner, and safer place for people to enjoy. Their first visit will be free, then the landowner will pay a discount price for a cleanup every six months.

YOUR CHALLENGE:

Write an Environmental Impact Statement in the form of a letter to the study site landowners. Say what you predict would happen to the things that live on the site if they accept the offer. Mention organisms that could lose their food, die outright, or increase. Give examples of how each thing affected could cause other changes in the food web.

Recommend whether the landowner should accept the offer, and explain why or why not.

RESOURCES:

You can use your food chains, food webs, and resource books to help you figure out how Clean Up Crew Two's work could affect your study site.

GOOD LUCK!

NAME(S)_____ DATE_____

ENVIRONMENTAL IMPACT STATEMENTS

OBJECTIVES	POINTS				SCORE
	3 High Quality	**2** Meets Objectives	**1** Falls Short	**O** Not Done	
CONTENT					
1. Mentions organisms that would die or lose their food source.	_____	_____	_____	_____	=___
2. Mentions organisms that could increase.	_____	_____	_____	_____	=___
3. Uses food chain vocabulary.	_____	_____	_____	_____	=___
SCOPE					
4. Describes how one change could affect more than one food chain in a food web.	_____	_____	_____	_____	___ x 2 =___
5. Correctly traces a food chain through at least two steps.	_____	_____	_____	_____	=___
COMMUNICATION					
6. Overall, presents a clear, detailed, and convincing argument for why to accept or not accept Clean Up Crew Two's offer.	_____	_____	_____	_____	=___

COMMENTS:

FINAL SCORE: _____

Total Possible Score: 21
Overall Achievement:

18-21	High
14-17	Sound
8-13	Limited
0-7	Inadequate

1.10 Who Eats What Exhibition—
Performance Assessment

Action Synopsis

Students plan, prepare, and present an exhibition of their work to an audience.

Session 1		**40 minutes**
1. Discuss what the person or group who requested the food web study wanted to know.	🐝	*linking to real world*
2. Talk in groups about ways to present findings.	🌐	*planning*
3. Discuss criteria for excellence in exhibitions.	🐝	*setting standards*
4. Begin preparations for the exhibition.	🌐	*applying knowledge*

Session 2		**1½ hours**
Complete preparations for the exhibition.	🌐	*applying knowledge*

Session 3		**40 minutes**
1. Present the exhibition to an invited audience.	🌐	*communicating*
2. Evaluate the presentations.	🌐	*assessing*

Desired Outcomes

By the end of this assessment activity, students should:

- ✓ Have a sense of how much they've accomplished and the significance of their work.
- ✓ Know how to target a presentation to the needs of a specific audience.
- ✓ Be familiar with the organization of scientific reports.
- ✓ Have experience with a variety of ways to communicate information.
- ✓ Have stronger project organization skills.
- ✓ Be more poised as public speakers.

What You'll Need

Sessions 1, 2, & 3

For each group of 3–4 students:
- ❏ copy of "Scoring Sheet" (page 168)
- ❏ materials for making visual aids (see "Getting Ready")

For each student:
- ❏ copy of "Group Work Evaluation" (page 42)

Getting Ready

- ♦ Set a date for the exhibition. Invite the project sponsor (see Lesson 1.1) and other guests, such as parents, environmental specialists, scientists, and school administrators, to attend.

- ♦ Gather materials for groups to use to make visual aids, such as mural paper, oak tag, construction paper, blank overhead transparencies, markers, yarn, and tape.

Action Narrative

Session 1

We'll use the next few days for you to prepare an exhibition of your work. First, let's think about why we did our studies, and what people will want to find out from our presentation.

Engage students in a discussion about the original purpose of their studies. Talk about why they made a food web of a local outdoor site, and ask why knowing who eats what in nature could be important. This discussion will raise issues about organisms' life support systems, and people's positive and negative impacts on the environment.

Discuss what the person or group who requested the study hoped to find out, and how they'll use the information. Emphasize that a very important part of science is communicating results so that they can be used by other people. You might want to make a list of the things students think are important to include in their final presentation.

If we work in groups, how can we present our findings?

Have students run this discussion by soliciting ideas from their peers, discussing each option, then deciding who would like to do what. Their choices range from presenting pieces of work they've already done (e.g., lists, maps, food chains, food webs) to preparing new products, such as one giant food web, a mural of the study site, or displays of animal signs. Options they might suggest include:

- Traditional scientific meeting format, with different groups presenting their own work, or a piece of a whole class report (e.g., introduction, methods, findings, conclusions, ideas for future research).

- Creative presentations, such as a play about themselves as scientists or the food interactions on the study site.

- Visual displays, such as an enhanced map or a mural, an illustrated food web of the whole study site, technical drawings of organisms, or samples of animal food clues.

- Interactive stations where visitors are invited to make observations or do activities.

Students might also want to create a written summary of their work to give to their guest. A copy could be placed in the school "archives" for future classes' use. Make sure that the work the groups agree to produce requires equivalent effort. For instance, a task such as presenting ideas for future research can be made more challenging by having the group responsible interview all the students in the class for ideas, then refine, organize, and elaborate on them.

Before you get started, let's think about what makes a presentation excellent.

Have students generate their own criteria for high quality work. Suggest categories for them to discuss if necessary, such as oral delivery, visual aids, and content.

You might want to formalize the students' suggestions into an assessment checklist, or show them the "Scoring Sheet" and explain how you will use it. Talk over if and how they will receive a grade for their exhibition, or for any additional written products you request (see page 167).

Tell students the date you've arranged for the exhibition, so that they know how much time they have to make preparations. Then let them get started.

Session 2

Spend this period working within your groups to prepare your part of our final presentation.

While groups are making preparations, it might be helpful to have a committee of students organize the overall presentation, deciding who should do what when.

Encourage students to rehearse their oral presentations, using you or their friends as an audience.

Session 3

I am pleased to introduce our guests who are here for the exhibition of your work.

Once you've made introductions, let students run their presentation while you fill out a "Scoring Sheet" for each group, or for the class as a whole (see "Teacher Reflections").

After the exhibition is over and guests have left, discuss with students how things went and what they'd do differently next time.

Ongoing Assessment

Student Reflections

Have students complete a "Scoring Sheet" for their work, and a "Group Work Evaluation" (page 42).

Teacher Reflections

How you use the "Scoring Sheet" will depend on how students organized their exhibition. If each group makes its own presentation, then it makes sense to fill out a separate sheet for each group. If the whole class worked cooperatively and each group had a different responsibility, then you might want to complete one assessment sheet for the entire class. In this case, you could ask each student to submit a piece of work that s/he worked on, so that you can give them an individual grade as well.

NAME(S)_____ DATE _____

WHO EATS WHAT EXHIBITION

OBJECTIVES	POINTS				SCORE
	3 High Quality	**2** Meets Objectives	**1** Falls Short	**0** Not Done	
COMMUNICATION					
Organization: logical order of ideas—easy to follow, smooth transitions	_____	_____	_____	_____	= ____
Delivery: speaks clearly, loudly, and at a good pace; good eye contact; stands tall—doesn't fidget; confident, direct, serious (no giggling!), and friendly	_____	_____	_____	_____	= ____
CONTENT					
Scope: covers all important aspects of work thoroughly	_____	_____	_____	_____	= ____
Thinking: accurate and broad thinking; good insights about findings; thoughtful responses to questions	_____	_____	_____	_____	= ____
Creativity: shows originality, clever ideas, and inventive approaches	_____	_____	_____	_____	= ____
Visuals: products made with care and attention to detail	_____	_____	_____	_____	= ____
Group Process: used work time effectively; everyone had a role; respect and attention shown to others	_____	_____	_____	_____	= ____

COMMENTS:

FINAL SCORE: _____

Total Possible Score: 21
Overall Achievement:

18-21	High
14-17	Sound
8-13	Limited
0-7	Inadequate

DECOMPOSER DYNAMICS

Module 2

DECOMPOSER DYNYAMICS

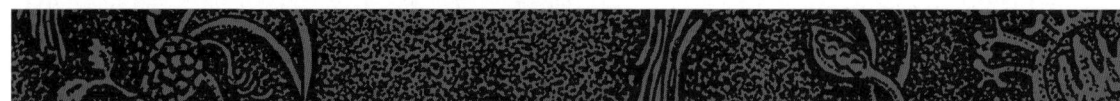

Contemplating Decay

If you're like most of us, you probably haven't given much thought to rot. Mold-covered leftovers, odorous garbage, a faded and drooping bouquet of flowers—we see and smell them daily, but don't usually pause to consider them indicators of the ongoing and crucial ecological process of decomposition.

Children think about decomposition perhaps even less than we do. Yet when asked to explain what happens to dead things in nature, they propose an array of possibilities. They realize that dead things disappear over time, but attribute this to causes they can see, such as rain, trampling, or large scavenger animals.

The main cause of decomposition eludes us because the primary perpetrators are invisible. From a brown apple core to a rotting fence post to a road-killed animal, it is microbes—organisms too tiny to see with the naked eye—that are doing the bulk of the deed of decomposition.

Whereas larger decomposer organisms with which children are often familiar (e.g., termites, earthworms, and millipedes) accomplish a lot of the physical breakdown of dead plants and animals, it is microbes like fungi and bacteria that are largely responsible for returning the once living materials to their basic elements. This module reveals the fascinating world of decomposer microbes to your students, and sets the stage for further exploration of nutrient cycling in Module 3.

Overview of Students' Learning Experiences

In this module students learn about microbes as decomposers, develop experimental design skills, and apply their knowledge to a variety of everyday situations.

Students set up a controlled experiment, or "fair test," culturing bacteria and fungi on non-living items to discover the invisible causes of decomposition. Then they use their investigation skills to design experiments to figure out what environmental factors favor the growth of microbes. This sequence of investigations moves from basic to applied research, as students use the results of their second investigation to set up compost in the classroom. They also apply their experiment design skills to critiquing hypothetical science fair projects.

Assessment activities provide other opportunities for students to apply their work in real-world contexts. They design exhibits to teach others about what causes dead leaves to "disappear;" become engineers to tackle an environmental problem by designing decomposition-friendly landfills; and help resolve a legal dispute involving a composting business. These experiences enrich students' understanding of decomposition while challenging them to put their knowledge, skills, and inquiry habits into action.

Module 2 Overview Chart

	DECOMPOSER DYNAMICS	
Mode	**Lesson Title**	**Activities**
Activating Ideas	**2.1** Introducing Microbes as Decomposers	**Day 1:** Students propose how dead plants disappear over time, then examine mold, and talk about microbes as decomposers.
Investigating and Processing for Understanding	**2.2** Stalking the Unseen	**Days 2–3:** Students hear a story of a scientist who studies microbe decomposers, then go outside to collect non-living items and observe evidence of decomposition.
	2.3 Culturing Bacteria and Fungi Decomposers	**Days 4–9:** Students design and carry out controlled experiments to culture microbes.
	2.4 Dead Leaf Storyboards— Performance Assessment	**Days 10–11:** Students work in groups to create displays that show what happens to a dead leaf over time.
	2.5 Testing Conditions That Promote Decomposition	**Days 12–17:** Students test factors that promote the growth of microbes, then use their findings to make compost
Applying and Assessing	**2.6** The Bag That Wouldn't Go Away— Performance Assessment	**Days 18–19:** Students design and set up model wasted disposal systems that will help biodegradable plastic bags decompose.
	2.7 A Jury's Dilemma— Written Assessment	**Day 20:** Students analyze a trial involving a dispute about a composting business, then outline how a Special Investigator could gather evidence to help settle the case.

Planning Ahead

GROW MOLD SPECIMENS About five days before you begin this module, seal small, moist chunks of squash or pumpkin in sandwich-size ziplock baggies. You'll need one baggie for every two students in your class. Keep the baggies in a warm place to encourage mold to grow.

CHOOSE AN OUTDOOR STUDY SITE If your students explored an outdoor site during Module 1, try to use the same study site for this module to deepen their understanding of that piece of land. Otherwise, look around the schoolyard for a place where students can collect non-living (organic and inorganic) items, and samples of leaves at different stages of decomposition. If you live in a semi-arid environment, try to find a relatively moist location, such as at the bottom of a slope or near a streambed. If no place in the schoolyard is suitable, make arrangements to take the class to a nearby park or other piece of land where students can collect things.

REVIEW VOCABULARY Many of the vocabulary words that were introduced and defined in Module 1 are used in Module 2 (e.g., *ecosystem, producer, consumer, decomposer, nutrient*). If your students haven't experienced Module 1, you might want to review these vocabulary words before beginning this module, and/or spend more time on the terms during lessons (see Appendix pages 390–392 for a list of vocabulary definitions).

GATHER MATERIALS A list of materials used in this module is provided in the Appendix (pages 386–387). Although locally available or homemade options are always provided, it is sometimes more convenient to order equipment made especially for science experiments, such as petri dishes for Lesson 2.2. Have each student bring in a 1-liter plastic soda bottle for Lesson 2.6.

COLLECT RESOURCE BOOKS Students find microbes fascinating, so a classroom collection of trade books on microbes will get well used. See the following resource list for suggested titles for both you and your students.

RESOURCE LIST

For Teachers ■ ■ ■ ■ ■ ■ ■ ■ ■ ■

REFERENCES AND BACKGROUND READING

Life in a Bucket of Soil
by R. Rhine (Lothrop, Lee & Shepard, 1972)
Each chapter is devoted to a common soil organism, and includes information on breeding, interactions, feeding, defense, and the organism's effect on soil. Helpful information on methods of collecting, keeping, and studying soil critters.

Microbes and Man
by J. Postgate (Cambridge University Press, 1992)
A good introduction to microbes for the general reader. Focuses on the omnipresent microbes and their varied activities, such as making the soil fertile, cleaning up the environment, changing our food, protecting humans from other microbes, and causing diseases. Also describes how to handle microbes, and includes a chapter on decomposition.

The Rodale Guide to Composting
by M. Hunt and J. Minnich (Rodale Press, 1979)
A readable book for those wanting to know everything about composting. Offers a comprehensive treatment of the history, benefits, techniques, materials, and technology of composting.

Worms Eat My Garbage
by M. Appelhof (Flower Press, 1982)
A practical guide to setting up a worm composting system. Although written for household use, its information is easily adapted to the classroom. Contains detailed information on the care of worms and other compost organisms, as well as how to recycle worm castings.

For Students ▪ ▪ ▪ ▪ ▪ ▪ ▪ ▪ ▪ ▪ ▪ ▪

SCIENCE BOOKS

Discovering Fungi
by J. Coldry (Bookwright Press, 1987)

Over forty large color photographs with text focus on the life history, ecological role, and economic importance of fungi. Includes a variety of beautiful and bizarre examples. From the twenty-three-volume "Discovering Nature" series.

Earthworms, Dirt and Rotten Leaves: An Exploration in Ecology
by M. McLaughlin (Atheneum, 1986)

The opening chapters draw in even the most squeamish students with information on earthworms' ecological importance and how to get started studying them. Subsequent chapters include inquiries about earthworms' adaptations, interrelationships, behavior, and body structure.

Lots of Rot
by B. Schatell (Lippincott, 1981)

This humorous and informative book tells where to find rot, what causes it, and how to grow your own. It includes easy experiments that help students discover facts about mold, bacteria, and mildew. The author emphasizes the importance of rot in natural cycles.

Microbes and Bacteria
by F. Sabin (Troll, 1985)

A simple, brief, illustrated overview of microbes and their reproduction, including protozoans, algae, fungi, slime molds, bacteria, and viruses.

Scavengers and Decomposers: The Cleanup Crew
by P. Hughey (Atheneum, 1984)

Looks at scavengers and decomposers in a few different environments, including oceans, freshwater, and the African plains.

The Smallest Life Around Us: Exploring the Invisible World of Microbes
by L. Anderson (Crown, 1978)

A basic introduction to microbes. It emphasizes the importance of microbes in the cycle of life, as well as in making foods such as cheese and bread. Also includes simple experiments.

Throwing Things Away: From Middens to Resource Recovery
by L. Pringle (Crowell, 1986)

This historical, precise, and straight-talking overview informs students about the development of human waste disposal practices in the United States. Includes staggering statistics on the amount of waste we generate.

STORIES

The Fall of Freddie the Leaf
by L. Buscaglia (C.B. Slack, 1982)

Brightly illustrated story about the life cycle of leaves. It emphasizes growth and change as necessary processes for living things.

The Paperbag Prince
by C. Thompson (Knopf, 1992)

The story of an old man who makes an abandoned dump his home. Colorful and detailed illustrations enhance a warm and wonderful story that encourages a new way of looking at our world, and highlights the rejuvenating power of nature.

2.1 Introducing Microbes as Decomposers

Action Synopsis

Students propose how dead plants disappear over time, then examine mold, and talk about microbes as decomposers.

One Session		1 hour	
1. Look at dead plant material and record ideas about what happens to it over time.			*examining prior ideas*
2. Discuss decomposition and animal decomposers.			*examining prior ideas*
3. Observe mold on plant material.			*observing & recording*
4. Talk about microbes as decomposers.			*introducing new information*

Desired Outcomes

Throughout the lesson, check that students:

✓ Are curious and have questions about what happens to plants after they die.

✓ Are able to accept that dead plants break down because decomposers use them for food.

✓ Begin to see how microbes growing on dead plants can make the plants disappear over time.

What You'll Need

For the class:
- ❑ paper grocery bag of dead plant material (see "Getting Ready")
- ❑ sheet of newsprint
- ❑ copy of *Who Eats What* guide (optional — pages 355–382)

For each pair of students:
- ❑ sandwich-size ziplock baggie of moldy squash or pumpkin (see "Planning Ahead," page 171)
- ❑ 2 hand lenses

Vocabulary

BACTERIA - Living things that have only one cell, and are so small that they can be seen only with a microscope.

DECOMPOSITION - The breaking down of dead things into their basic materials by decomposers that use them as food.

FUNGUS - An organism that uses other living or dead organisms as food by secreting chemicals that break it down, and then absorbing the substances into its cells.

HYPHAE - Threadlike, food-absorbing strands of a fungus.

MICROBE - A living thing (or "microorganism") whose individuals are too small to see with the naked eye. Fungi and bacteria are two kinds of microbes.

MOLD - A fungus that produces a fuzzy growth.

SPORES - Structures that can grow into new individuals, and can often survive harsh conditions.

Getting Ready

♦ Gather enough dead plant material outdoors (e.g., fallen leaves, grass clippings, twigs) to fill a paper grocery bag about one third to half full.

♦ Decide on pairs of students to work together, or plan to let them choose partners.

Action Narrative

I want you to predict the future of the items in this bag.

Dump the dead plant material out of the paper bag.

 **Imagine that we put these dead plants on the ground outdoors. Think about what would happen to them over the next few years. Work with a partner to make your predictions. Be specific — mention everything that could happen to them. Will the way they look change? What could cause them to change? Jot down your ideas in your journals. In a few minutes we'll share ideas.**

As pairs of students share their ideas, listen to make sure that they understand their task and are being specific. Help them articulate their prior ideas without suggesting possibilities to them. Students will probably need less than five minutes to generate predictions.

Let's hear your thoughts. I'll record a class list.

After a few students share their ideas, ask others to contribute ideas that aren't already on the list. Copy their wording as closely as possible. Treat this as brainstorming, accepting all new offerings and holding questions and comments until later.

<u>What Happens to Plants After They Die?</u>

they rot

they get stepped on and crushed

worms take them underground

they blow away

birds put them in nests

rain and wind rip them into pieces

they turn black

they dissolve and go into the ground

beetles make holes in them

someone rakes them up and burns them

dirt blows over them

they get slimy, smelly, and disgusting

Use students' own language in questions that ask them to elaborate on their suggestions, such as:

What makes a dead leaf "rot"?

Students' responses will tell you whether or not they associate rot with the fungi and bacteria that cause it.

What makes plants "dissolve"?

Students might attribute dead plant disappearance primarily to physical factors (weathering) or to biological processes (animals and microbes using the material as food).

Why do beetles "make holes" in dead leaves?

Students' responses will reveal whether they connect the disappearance of leaf tissue to the insect's need for food.

 *It is best not to tell students answers or correct their thinking at this stage. The point is for you and them to become aware of their prior ideas, and of how well these ideas explain decomposition. Expect that some students will have elaborate explanations that are contrary to how scientists describe and explain decomposition.*

Children's Ideas about Decomposition

When pressed to explain what makes a dead thing disappear, students usually list physical factors that cause it to break up, or say that it happens with nothing more than the passage of time. Consider these fifth and sixth graders' comments:

Dead branches fall off the trees and you step on 'em and they break up.

When it's been dead a long time and gets real old it breaks up and disappears.

The dirt breaks it down. It's something I can't explain in words, but I know about it.

When the rain and wind come the dead plant spreads out into the dirt.

It takes a lot of years for a dead tree to disappear. Just like with a rock, the wind hits it and breaks it down.

When we die they put us in a coffin and bury us, and while we're in the coffin we dissolve.

Some students will mention that bugs eat dead things, but do not necessarily see this as a cause of decomposition. They might also say that things "decay" or "rot away" without realizing that microorganisms cause these processes as they use dead things for food.

The investigations in Modules 1 and 2 give students direct contact with the organisms that cause decomposition. These experiences go a long way toward helping them view decomposition as primarily a biological, rather than a physical process. Expect however, that even once they tune into the world of decomposers, most students will still place too great an importance on the contribution of physical battering and "weathering" to decomposition.

Encouraging students to articulate their ideas and refine their language so that it expresses their thoughts accurately will help them think more clearly about the largely invisible process of decomposition. Teaching that decomposition is simply a matter of organisms eating food lays the groundwork for the central idea of Module 3: that the "stuff" that dead matter was made of never really goes away — it becomes part of the body of its consumer, or is released into the environment and is eventually used by other organisms.

We'll keep this list of ideas up so that we can see how your ideas grow and change after we've had a chance to do some investigations. We'll be studying DECOMPOSITION for a few weeks. Can anyone define decomposition?

Encourage students to build on one another's ideas to create a definition. Write their definition on the board, and then add and emphasize whatever they have omitted from the following definition: "Decomposition is the natural process of dead things breaking down into the basic materials they are made of, when living things use them as food."

Why is it important to study decomposition?

Students might mention the garbage crisis as a good reason to know more about how things break down. If they know something about nutrient cycling they might say that when dead organisms decompose, they fertilize the soil so new plants can grow. If students have no ideas, explain that decomposition is important to understand because it is nature's way of recycling the materials all living things need to grow and stay alive.

Our definition states that dead things decompose because living things eat away at them. An animal that eats dead things is called a decomposer. What eats dead things like these (leaves)?

If students have experienced Module 1, they'll be familiar with lots of soil organisms that consume dead plants. If not, you might need to mention a few for them, such as earthworms, beetles, and termites. If students mention an animal that you aren't sure is a decomposer, have someone look it up in the *Who Eats What* guide.

I have a kind of decomposer to show you that is quite different from the animals we've mentioned.

Give one baggie of moldy material and two hand lenses to each pair of students.

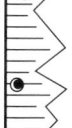

> **Caution!** Some students may be allergic to molds. During this activity, and throughout this module, have students keep moldy material sealed or covered.

Look closely at this decomposer. Work with your partner and jot down your observations in your journals. In a few minutes we'll share observations.

Encourage students to write adjectives, descriptive phrases, and questions in their journals as they make observations.

What are your observations and questions?

Students will probably recognize the mold, but will have lots of questions and ideas about what they are seeing.

The MOLD you've described is a kind of FUNGUS. The white fuzz you see is called HYPHAE. The hyphae are threadlike strands of a fungus that absorb food. If you see any colored or powdery surface on the fuzz, then you are seeing SPORES, the fungus's way of reproducing.

Can you see how the material the fungi are feeding on would eventually disappear into the body of the fungus?

In addition to the mold, there are also BACTERIA on the (pumpkin)**, but even a whole colony of them are usually too tiny for us to see without a microscope. Fungi and bacteria are called MICROBES because they are so small. They are important kinds of decomposers because they eat things that animals don't eat, and break down small pieces of other decomposers' leftovers even further.**

What have you heard about fungi, bacteria, or microbes before?

Most students know that the mushrooms they eat are a kind of fungus. They commonly associate bacteria and microbes with "germs" or disease, although do not necessarily think of them as living things. (Viruses, "germs" that are very different from bacteria and fungi, are in fact not living things — they need to invade living cells to function.)

Students might also confuse microbes with deterioration itself, rather than seeing them as the cause of deterioration.

Facts about Fungi and Bacteria

  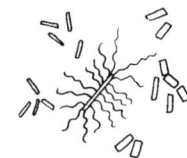

How many different kinds are there?

Fungi: There are approximately 66,000 different species of fungi classified into five major groups.

Bacteria: About 5,000 species of bacteria have been described, but scientists believe this is only a fraction of the actual number of different kinds of bacteria.

Do they make people sick?

Fungi: Some people are allergic to molds and other fungi. In rare occurrences, some kinds of microscopic fungi can be toxic to humans. Many mushrooms are also poisonous to humans. Some skin infections, such as athlete's foot, are caused by fungi. However, fungi also benefit humans by being a food source (e.g., mushrooms), and by making beverages ferment and bread rise.

Bacteria: Some bacteria cause human diseases such as strep throat, rheumatic fever, whooping cough, leprosy, and cholera. But bacteria also do a lot of good for people. They help digest food inside the stomach, and are used in making foods such as cheese and yogurt.

How do they get around?

Fungi: Fungi produce spores that travel great distances in wind, water, or on animals.

Bacteria: Many species of bacteria can move through water by whipping long strands called flagella. They can also move great distances carried by wind, water, or animals.

How do they reproduce?

Fungi: Fungi produce spores that grow into hyphae, which eventually make fruiting bodies (e.g., mushrooms) that produce new spores. Yeasts reproduce by budding.

Bacteria: Usually bacteria divide to make copies of themselves, although sexual reproduction is also used.

How do they eat?

Fungi: Fungi send out little threads called hyphae. Chemicals come out of the hyphae and break down their food, then the fungi absorb the food into their bodies, although some of it also leaks out into the surroundings.

Bacteria: Decomposer bacteria feed on dead organisms by secreting chemicals into their food source to break it down. In this way they absorb food directly from what they are growing on.

At the end of the period, collect the baggies of mold and throw them away without opening them. Return the dead plants that were in the paper bag to the outdoor area where you collected them.

Ongoing Assessment

Student Reflections

Have students send a C-Mail message or record thoughts in their journals. Optional writing prompts include:

What did I learn about microbes that I never knew before?

What would life as a decomposer be like?

I was surprised to learn that decomposition...

Teacher Reflections

❑ How detailed and realistic were students' descriptions of what happens to plants after they die?

❑ Did students name mostly physical or biological causes for changes in dead plants?

❑ Did students accept that decomposition happens because decomposers eat dead things?

❑ Did observing molds make students curious? What kinds of questions did they have?

❑ What ideas do students already have about microbes, and what do they want to know?

Extensions

Concept Maps. Introduce concept mapping to students (see pages 25–27) if they are not already familiar with the process. Select all or some of the concept map cards on pages 43–44, then copy one set of cards for each group of 3–4 students. Help them construct concept maps that display their ideas about decomposition. Have students save their concept maps so that they can compare them to maps they'll make as an extension to Lesson 2.5, to see how their knowledge grows.

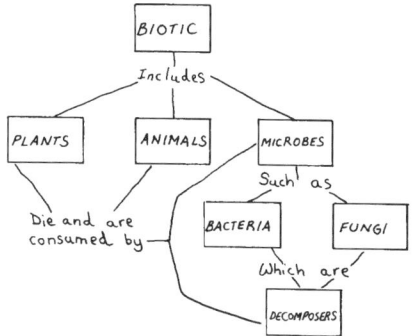

Mountains of Leaves. Ask students to measure the height of a stack of a given number of dead leaves from a deciduous tree. Then challenge them to count the leaves on one branch of the tree, and figure out a way to estimate how many branches there are on the tree. Help them multiply these numbers to estimate how many leaves there are per tree. Finally, students can use all of this information to figure out how many trees and how many years it would take to get a stack of leaves as high as different major mountains in the world, if deciduous leaves piled up each year instead of decomposing.

Bacteria and Fungi Festival. Set up stations for learning more about bacteria and fungi. These could include:

#1: Prevention! Display containers from foods that are pickled, dried, salted, frozen, vacuum-sealed, candied, smoked, and that say "refrigerate after opening". Challenge students to record how the foods' processing or packaging creates difficult growing conditions for bacteria and fungi.

#2: Treats from Other Kingdoms. Set out containers or wrappers from foods that use microbes in their processing, such as vinegar, cheese, mushrooms, bread, yogurt, tofu, wine, and soy sauce. Have students write a menu or recipe using as many of the bacteria and fungi products as possible.

#3: Spore Patterns. Select mushrooms from the store whose caps are just beginning to open. Have students cut off a cap and place it facedown on a white piece of paper. Check it in two days to see the dark spores that have fallen on the paper.

#4: Microscope Slides. Set up prepared slides (commercially available through science supply catalogs) of fungi and bacteria under a microscope for observation.

#5: A Cow's Stomach. Set out a large baggie and an assortment of fresh grass clippings, green leaves, lettuce, and spinach. Have groups of students add a handful of plants to the baggie to create a cow's stomach. Challenge them to figure out how to get all of the air out of the bag, then seal it. This simulates the part of a cow's gut where millions of bacteria can live without oxygen. The bacteria help to break down the stems and other things that cows eat. Watch what happens to the cow's stomach contents after one day, one week, and one month.

Fungus Farmers. Leaf cutter ants grow fungus to eat, just like farmers grow crops. Have students research and make a book showing leaf cutter ants farming fungus.

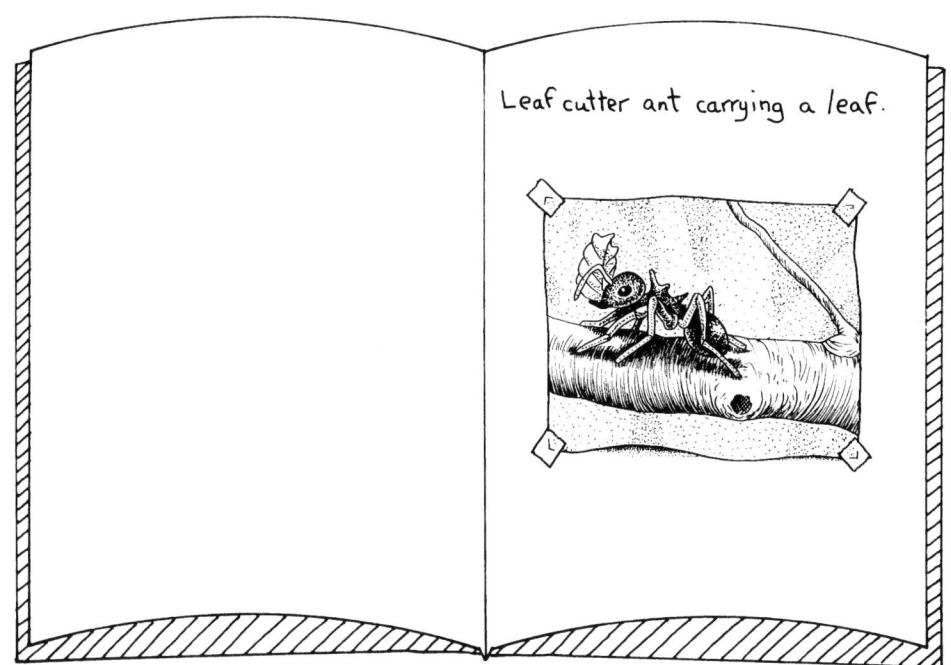

Leaf cutter ant carrying a leaf.

2.2 Stalking the Unseen

Action Synopsis

Students hear a story of a scientist who studies microbe decomposers, then plan and take a trip outside to collect items for culturing microbes.

Session 1		1 hour
1. Read and discuss the story of Dr. Elaine Ingham's microbe research.		*linking to real world*
2. Predict the best places to look for decomposition, and which non-living things will have many and few microbes.		*examining prior ideas*
3. Categorize list of non-living things as biotic and abiotic.		*generating ideas & questions*
4. Plan for trip outside, and learn field techniques.		*demonstrating methods*

Continued

Session 2   **1 hour**   **OUTDOORS**

1. Discuss how to behave like scientists while doing field work. *setting standards*

2. Get oriented to the outdoor site. *familiarizing*

3. Observe and record evidence of decomposition. *observing & recording*

4. Collect non-living items. *investigating*

5. Share and discuss observations. *processing findings*

6. Sequence leaves in various stages of decomposition. *applying knowledge*

Desired Outcomes

Throughout the lesson, check that students:

✓ Realize that scientists study decomposition to create knowledge that people can use to make wise decisions about how to manage land so it stays fertile.

✓ Can give examples of biotic and abiotic items.

✓ Are able to find evidence of decomposition outdoors.

What You'll Need

Session 1

For the class:
- ❑ petri dish or other clear container with flat bottom and cover
- ❑ newsprint sheets for class lists
- ❑ sandwich-size ziplock baggie
- ❑ small eraser or piece of chalk

Session 2

For the class:
- ❑ newsprint for leaf continuum (see "Getting Ready")

For each pair of students:
- ❑ 2 sandwich-size ziplock baggies
- ❑ masking tape or permanent marker
- ❑ 2 hand lenses (optional)
- ❑ ruler (optional)

Vocabulary

CULTURE - To grow living things in a prepared substance.

Getting Ready

Session 1

♦ Choose an outdoor location where students can collect non-living items (see "Planning Ahead," page 171).

Session 2

♦ Prepare a sheet of newsprint for a class leaf decomposition continuum. Position the sheet horizontally and draw a horizontal line across it. Label the left end of the line "Least Decomposed" and the right end "Most Decomposed".

♦ Decide on pairs of students to work together, or plan to let them choose partners.

Action Narrative

Session 1

We're going to spend several days doing an experiment to learn more about microbes that are decomposers. First I'm going to read a story about a scientist who studies microbes.

Read "Mad About Microbes: The Work of Ecologist Dr. Elaine Ingham" (pages 194–195), pausing where indicated for discussion.

Follow up with questions such as:

What does Dr. Ingham try to find out through her research?
She looks at what different microbes are in different habitats, and at which ones are eating what. She also studies how the way people use land affects these microbes.

What are some of the things she has discovered?
1) Even in a small outdoor area the decomposers you find can be completely different depending on where you look.

2) Bacteria typically eat food that is easy to digest, whereas fungi eat wood and tougher material, so more active fungi than bacteria are usually found in soil near dead trees.

3) Many bacteria on dead plants are in a resting state, waiting for food or conditions that are just right.

4) After forests are clear-cut, there are fewer fungi living in the soil and breaking down the dead plants.

5) When farmers spray crops, they can kill microbes in the soil that they didn't intend to harm.

Why do only a fraction of the microbes that are in a soil sample show up when Dr. Ingham stains them?
The stain only shows microbes that have eaten recently. A lot of microbes "rest" where they land until conditions are just right for them to begin eating.

What does Dr. Ingham's study of microbes have to do with living plants?
When microbes break down dead plants, the nutrients that were inside of the plants eventually get back into the soil where new plants can take them up. If it wasn't for microbes breaking down dead plants, living plants wouldn't get the nutrients they need.

During our next session, we're going outside to look for evidence of decomposition, and to collect items that might have decomposer microbes on them.

Tell students where they'll do their outdoor study. If they're familiar with the site, ask them to describe it. You might want to make a list of characteristics they mention.

If the site is not familiar, describe what you saw when you visited it.

Help students think about searching for decomposition with questions such as:

What could we see that would tell us if decomposition is occurring?
Students might mention that dead leaves, mushrooms, and small critters such as sow bugs and earthworms are indicators of decomposition. They might also see large items like leaves broken into smaller pieces. Remind them of the threadlike hyphae they saw when they looked at mold, and tell them that they might see thin white strands on dead leaves, on or just below the soil surface. Students might smell slightly pungent odors in a pile of moist leaves, which could also indicate decomposition.

Are some places more likely to have evidence of decomposer action than other places?
Students might have an intuitive sense that decomposers prefer moist environments, although they won't confirm this until later in this module when they test conditions that promote decomposition. Students might also suggest dark, shady spots, which are good for decomposers because they retain moisture.

Where do you think will be the best spots to look for decomposition?
Decomposition happens where there is food for decomposers to consume, so students might suggest looking among dead plant material. If students are familiar with the study site, they might have specific spots in mind for finding decomposition. They might also suggest places that you know are unlikely to have evidence of decomposition. The point is for them to have a plan and reasons in mind for where to look. Later they'll compare what they actually find with what they thought they'd find.

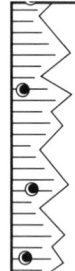

Caution! If students mention that dead animals are a good place to find evidence of decomposition, tell them that they are not allowed to go near, touch, or collect a dead animal. The kinds of microbes that grow on them can make humans sick. Also do not allow students to touch or collect animal feces, since some of the microbes that can grow on them are also pathogens (disease-causing agents).

When we're outside, you'll work in pairs. Your task will be to find one non-living thing that you think has a lot of decomposer microbes on it, and one that you think does not. Each has to be small enough to fit in these containers.

Show students a few empty petri dishes.

We're going to CULTURE the microbes that are on the things we collect. In other words, we're going to make the microbes grow.

Let's make a list of non-living things we might find on the study site.

Expect that students will raise the distinction between "natural" non-living things, and non-living things made by people.

Remember that scientists use the term *biotic* for things that are alive or used to be alive. They call things that were never alive *abiotic*. Let's divide our list of non-living things into two categories: biotic and abiotic.

Items made by people, such as a wooden ice cream stick and a plastic wrapper, do not all fall into the same category. For instance, if the item is made of wood it is biotic. If it is made of metal, it is abiotic. If it is made of plastic, it is technically biotic, because plastic is made from petroleum which comes from dead plants. However, the chemical structure of plastic is so different from that of the plants from which they are derived, that it makes more sense to categorize plastic items as abiotic.

Non-living Things

<u>Biotic</u>	<u>Abiotic</u>
dead leaves	rocks
sticks	potato chip bag
seed pod	penny

What non-living things should we collect that you predict will have many and few microbes on them?

As students offer suggestions, have them explain why they think some non-living items will have many microbes, and other items will have few. You might want to remind them that microbes only grow on things that they are using for food.

Some students might want to compare the amount of microbes on two biotic items, while others will want to compare a biotic and an abiotic item. Although microbes don't consume abiotic items such as bottle caps, candy wrappers, and pebbles, there are often residues (e.g., sugar, vegetable oil, or soil with dead plant particles) on non-living items that microbes do consume. If students decide to collect these items, this is something you'll have to explain later to help them interpret their culture test results.

Make a list of the comparisons they suggest.

> <u>Non-living Things to Compare for Microbes</u>
> two different kinds of dead leaves
> soil from the surface and soil from below ground
> two samples of the same kind of leaf, one newly fallen and one partly decomposed
> a pebble and a stick
> two samples of the same kind of leaf, one from a wet place and one from a dry place
> a plastic wrapper and a leaf
> soil beneath plants and soil from an area with no plants
> a pine needle and a leaf

When we're outside, each pair will have two plastic bags — one for the non-living item you think has a lot of decomposer microbes on it, and the other for the item you think has few microbes on it.

Keep the bags sealed until you are ready to pick up an item. Then invert the bag over your hand to pick the item up, so that you don't touch it with your bare hands.

Demonstrate the method by picking up a piece of chalk or a small eraser with a plastic bag over your hand.

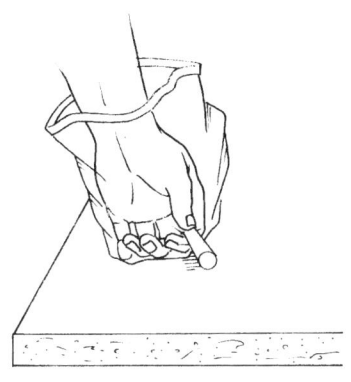

Why is it important not to touch the item or the inside of the bag?

Decomposer microbes feed on our dead skin flakes and body oils. Shielding hands with plastic will prevent microbes, skin, and oils from getting inside the bags.

What do you think will be important information to record in your journals when we're outside?

Have students offer suggestions for what they should record when they collect their items. Recording the date, the name of the item, where they found it, and what it looks like are some possibilities.

Session 2

Before we go outside, let's review how scientists behave while doing research.

Have students generate suggestions for how to behave as field ecologists. If your class has not done ecology field work before, see the suggested list of outdoor research behaviors in Lesson 1.2 (page 69).

Each pair needs to label two plastic bags, and each person should bring a journal and a pencil outdoors.

Hand out the baggies and masking tape or permanent markers. Keeping them sealed, have students label them as "Many" and "Few" along with their initials, by writing directly on the bags or on a masking tape label.

In addition to the baggies and journals, you might want students to bring rulers and hand lenses outside to enhance observations.

We also need to review the purpose of our study trip.

Have students tell you the goal of the outdoor excursion — collecting one non-living thing that they think has a lot of decomposer microbes on it, and one that they think does not.

When you arrive at the study site, gather students in a central meeting location. Point out key landmarks that serve as site boundaries.

When you hear this signal (demonstrate a whistle, hand clap, or some other attention-getting signal), **come back to this meeting place. Go ahead and look for evidence of decomposition. Then look for items that you think have a lot and a few decomposer microbes on them. Collect one of each item and take field notes.**

While pairs are working, listen to their discussions as they decide where to look for decomposition, and what items to collect. Encourage them to make careful observations and thorough journal entries about the items they collect. It is especially important that students record where they collected something. For instance, a rock found in a pile of leaves might have plant particles and microbes on it, whereas one found in the open playground on pavement might not.

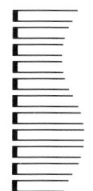

If your students haven't experienced Module 1, encourage them to look for non-microbe decomposer organisms (e.g., sow bugs, beetles, termites, worms) in leaf litter and upper soil layers. You could also collect some soil and leaf litter to extract hidden invertebrate decomposers using a Berlese funnel (see page 84).

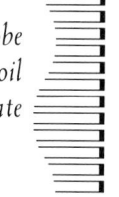

Everyone come to our meeting place to describe the evidence of decomposition you observed.

Students will probably be ready to share their findings with the whole class after about twenty minutes of collecting and notetaking.

FIELD NOTES   MARCH 12

Blue Jay Feather - I found it underneath some dead leaves over by the fence. It was kind of wet and looked old like it was sitting there for a long time.

Now let's try to find examples of leaves at different stages of decomposition — from hardly decomposed to almost completely decomposed. We'll arrange them along the line on this sheet, from least to most decomposed.

Lay the sheet of newsprint you've prepared for the decomposition continuum on the ground and anchor it with rocks. As each student brings back a sample, let him/her decide where to put the leaf in relation to the others collected. Challenge students to see if they can make an entire time line using the same species of leaf. When you have a complete continuum, have the class discuss it.

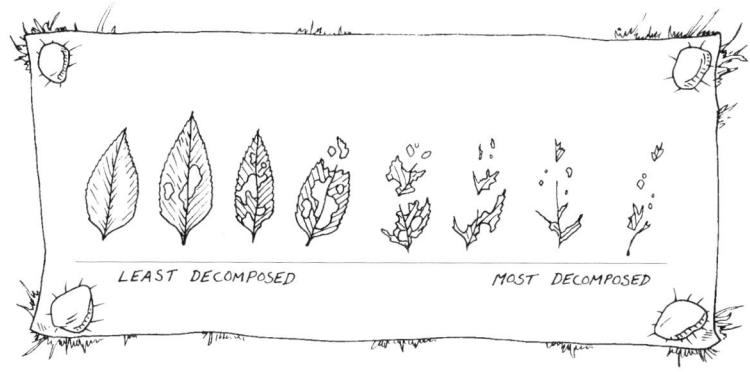

How do leaves change as they decompose?

Students might mention that leaves get more holes in them, the edges get eaten away, they break into small pieces, they get black spots on them, they get softer, thinner, and lighter.

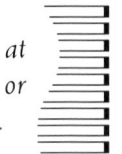

If you live in an arid or tropical environment, students may be unable to find leaves at various stages of decay. Have them discuss whether decomposition isn't happening, or whether things decompose so quickly that no examples of the various stages are available.

Although physical battering by rain and wind might cause some wear on leaves, the break down is caused primarily by decomposers — small animals and microbes — that are using the dead leaves as food.

At the end of the period, have students put the leaves back on the ground.

When back indoors, have students store their baggies of non-living items in an area of the classroom that is cool and dark (i.e., not on a windowsill or near a heater).

Ongoing Assessment

Student Reflections

Have students send a C-Mail message, or record thoughts in their journals. Optional writing prompts include:

Being a scientist who studies microbes for a living would be _____ because...

The best part about doing field work is...

I learn the most when I _____ because...

Teacher Reflections

❑ What did students' reasons for why different non-living items would have many or few decomposer microbes reveal about their understanding of decomposition?

❑ Did students' ideas about where they would find evidence of decomposition change after they went outside?

❑ Did students stay focused on their outdoor tasks and take good field notes?

Extensions

Soil Sample Cultures. Help students replicate Dr. Ingham's work. Collect the top 5 cm of soil — about the length of a thumb — from different spots, such as under and several meters away from a shrub, tree, or dead plant; under and between grass clumps; next to two different kinds of plants; from woods and a field. Sprinkle a small amount of each soil sample over dishes of Jello, then compare how many and what types of microbes grow on each.

Module 2: *Decomposer Dynamics*

Soil Layer Cake. Demonstrate how the dead plants that decomposers break down help build soil. (Note: This works best in non-arid environments where there is pronounced soil development, especially in woods or grasslands. In arid environments, try it under shrubs.) Cut a 20 cm square template out of cardboard. Lay the square on the ground, and cut around it with a sharp knife, penetrating as deeply as possible. Remove the cardboard and use a trowel to lift the square of soil intact onto a tray. Have students identify the layers, from whole leaves on the top, to partly decomposed leaves, to small organic particles mixed with soil, to paler layers of mineral soil where there is little organic matter. Look for white, threadlike strands of fungal hyphae between layers of moist leaves near the top of the layer cake. Look also for plant roots concentrated in the enriched upper layers of the soil. Students can help you replace the materials back in the hole.

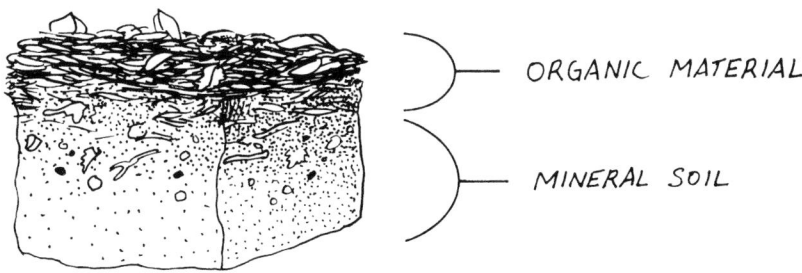

ORGANIC MATERIAL

MINERAL SOIL

MAD ABOUT MICROBES:
THE WORK OF ECOLOGIST DR. ELAINE INGHAM

When Elaine Ingham was in her last semester of college, she took a course called Microbiology and knew from that moment that she wanted to spend her career studying microbes — living things that are so tiny you need a microscope to see them. "The world of life under a microscope is fascinating, and the microbes are cute!" she says. "When you are able to recognize the different kinds of organisms, it's like saying hello to your old friends! Plus there are always new things to look at that you haven't seen before, so it's exciting."

Dr. Ingham is now a soil ecologist working at Oregon State University. The soil is a good thing to study if you're interested in microbes, because lots of microbes live there. In just a teaspoon of soil there can be more microbes than there are people living on the earth — over 500 million individual bacteria (about 40,000 different species), and up to 6,000 meters of hyphae from fungi.

Some microbes that live in soil, such as certain kinds of fungi and bacteria, are decomposers; they eat dead plants that fall to the ground. Other tiny soil organisms eat the fungi and bacteria that are eating the dead plants. Dr. Ingham tries to figure out what different kinds of microbes live in the soil in different places, such as in a forest, a grassland, and a mountain meadow. She calculates how many microbes there are and what they eat.

When Dr. Ingham gets to a site, the first thing she does is decide where to collect soil samples — near a tree, under a dead log, beside a blueberry bush, between patches of grass, and so on. These decisions are very important. Different areas, even when less than half a meter away from each other, can have completely different microbes. One reason is that bacteria are better than fungi at eating "fast food" — material that is high in energy and easy to digest. But when the food is tougher — like bark and logs — fungi win out. Do you think you'd find more fungi or bacteria in soil close to a dead tree?

Pause for discussion.

Once she decides where to sample, Dr. Ingham uses trowels and soil corers to collect the top 5 cm of soil where the microbes are most concentrated. She puts the soil samples in plastic bags. which are stored in coolers with ice to slow down the microbes until she gets back to the lab.

At the lab, Dr. Ingham puts a measured amount of sterilized water in a measured amount of soil, mixes it well, and looks at it under a microscope to identify the kinds of microbes that are there. She also wants to know how many of the microbes she sees have been eating dead plant material, instead of just resting. To find this out she helped invent a way to use dyes that turn color only on the microbes that are actively using food they've eaten recently. Imagine that someone poured a similar dye over you. While you were sleeping, it wouldn't turn color, but right after you ate, you would turn neon green!

When Dr. Ingham stains the samples she finds that only 2 to 20% of all the bacteria she sees are actually eating and breaking things down. This is because many bacteria are picky eaters, and particular about their living conditions. A lot of microbes are carried by wind, water, or animals to new places, but they stay in a sleeping stage unless everything is just right — they might need a certain kind or part of a plant, or food with a lot of iron in it, or a certain temperature. But if one kind of microbe doesn't like the food and conditions around it, there are usually others there that do!

Dr. Ingham also studies how the things people do to the land affect the microbes that live there. In one study, she compared un-cut forests to ones that people have clear-cut for lumber. She found out that after one year, the clear-cut forest had 10 times fewer fungi in its soil than the un-cut forest. After five years it had 100 times fewer fungi! This is because once the trees are gone, the forest floor is exposed to the sun. The soil dries out, making conditions that are too harsh for the fungi to live in. How do you think this could affect the land where the forest once grew?

Pause for discussion.

When there are less fungi to break down the leftover leaves, branches and trunks of trees in clear-cut forests, then nutrients (minerals that all living things need to stay healthy) don't get returned to the forest soil. So the land that was clear-cut might not be a good place for growing trees in the future.

Dr. Ingham also studies crops and other places where chemicals such as herbicides and pesticides are sprayed. She found that when a chemical is sprayed to control weeds or a disease that is attacking plants, it often kills microbes in the soil that it wasn't designed to kill. When one kind of microbe, such as bacteria, is wiped out, then the whole underground food web of microbes changes. Since microbes perform a very important step in returning nutrients to the soil that living plants need, it is important for scientists like Dr. Ingham to help farmers understand how crop spraying affects soil fertility.

Dr. Ingham has lots of adventures while she works, and some mishaps. "Sometimes when I'm walking around a plot in a clear-cut forest," she says, "I'm carrying my cooler and looking ahead for my plot markers. The next thing I know 'BOOM!' — I fall over a log and spend the rest of the day hobbling around on a sprained ankle. It's quite a comical sight!"

One of the forests where Dr. Ingham works has a lot of "widow makers" — trees that have big branches that fall whenever the wind blows, posing a danger to anyone below. Dr. Ingham has also been caught in mud slides while working in the mountains. "All of the sudden a heavy rain comes down, and the path gives way and you're zooming down the side of the bank along with the mud," she says.

But all of this outdoor adventure still isn't as exciting to Dr. Ingham as the world under her microscope. She knows that her work on microbes is important because it helps people like foresters and farmers understand how what they do to the land affects whether plants will get the nutrients they need to stay alive.

2.3 Culturing Bacteria and Fungi Decomposers

Action Synopsis

Students do a controlled experiment to culture microbes living on items they collected outside.

Session 1   **40 minutes**

1. Write predictions for growth of microbes in Jello culture when microbes from non-living items are added.   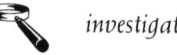 *generating ideas & questions*

2. Introduce fair test methods and rationale.   *introducing new information*

3. Set up culture dishes of Jello and non-living items.   *investigating*

Session 2   **40 minutes**

1. Discuss class predictions.   *reflecting*

2. Label list of non-living items as biotic or abiotic.   *applying knowledge*

3. Observe culture dishes and record results.   *observing & recording*

Continued

Sessions 3–5		**20–40 minutes**

1. Observe microbe growth and record results.

2. Evaluate weaknesses of experiments described in "Science Fair Stories."

observing & recording

applying knowledge

Session 6		**40 minutes**

1. Share and discuss results of investigations.

2. Compare findings to predictions of microbe growth.

processing findings

reflecting

Desired Outcomes

Throughout the lesson, check that students:

✓ Are able to explain what a fair test is and why scientists use controlled experiments.

✓ Are developing the habit of using their journal for recording observations and questions.

✓ Can relate experimental evidence back to their predictions and give possible reasons for the outcomes.

✓ Understand that microbes grow on their food source, causing decomposition as they consume it.

What You'll Need

Session 1

For the class:
- ❑ newsprint sheets for class lists
- ❑ 1–2 3-oz. boxes of flavored Jello (lemon, lime, or orange)
- ❑ bowl
- ❑ spoon
- ❑ boiling water
- ❑ paper towels
- ❑ measuring cup

For each pair of students:
- ❑ 3 petri dishes or other clear containers with flat bottoms and covers
- ❑ clear tape
- ❑ masking tape

Session 2

For each pair of students:
- ❑ 2 hand lenses

Continued

Sessions 3–5

For each pair of students:
- ❑ 2 hand lenses
- ❑ copy of "Science Fair Story #1" (page 206)
- ❑ copy of "Science Fair Story #2" (page 207)

Vocabulary

CONTROL - The unchanged item or group in an experiment.

FAIR TEST - An experiment in which everything is kept the same except for the one condition being tested.

MEDIUM - A substance in which an organism lives.

TREATMENT - The item or group that has been manipulated in an experiment.

VARIABLE - Something that is changed in a fair test.

Getting Ready

Session 1

♦ Prepare petri dishes with Jello as follows:

1. Sterilize the dishes, bowl, measuring cup, and spoon using boiling water. Place them upside down on paper towels until you're ready to use them.

2. Add 1 box of Jello to the bowl, then add 1 cup of boiling water and stir until Jello dissolves.

3. Add 1 cup of cold water.

4. Pour or spoon the liquid into the petri dishes to fill them half way (about 3–4 mm deep). Cover them immediately. [There should be enough for about 25 dishes (8 cm in diameter).]

5. Keep the filled dishes in a cool place (a refrigerator is best) until students are ready to set up their experiments.

6. If necessary, repeat the procedure to make enough for each pair of students to have three dishes.

Action Narrative

Session 1

Today we're going to culture the microbes on the non-living items we collected. We'll put the items into a culture **MEDIUM** that gives the microbes on them extra food. We're using Jello which has a lot of sugar in it — a product of plants that were once alive — as well as protein, minerals, and water that microbes need.

What do you think will happen when you put extra food in with a non-living item that has a lot of microbes, and with an item that has fewer microbes?

Students' expectation will probably be that the microbes that are on both items will grow and multiply, but those that started with more microbes will show more overall microbe growth than those that started with fewer. Help them consider that the amount of microbe growth could turn out to be the same, either because the items had the same amount of microbes on them to begin with, or because microbe growth expands to the same level once extra food is added. It could also turn out to take longer for microbe growth on some items to reach the density of that on other items. Another possible result is that students will see different kinds, rather than different amounts of microbes.

Before we start, write your predictions in your journal.

○	I predict that more microbes are on the leaf than on the rock.

You might want to have students record their predictions on a class chart as well.

Predictions

Pairs' Initials	Items with <u>Many</u> Microbes	Items with <u>Few</u> Microbes
L.M. & B.J.	lollipop stick	dry leaf
K.L. & A.M.	surface soil	deep soil
T.H. & K.T.	twig	pine needle
J.T. & J.L.	dead grass	bottle cap

Here is the procedure. Each pair will get three dishes of Jello. Put an item from your baggie labeled "Many" on top of the Jello in one dish without touching your fingers on the item, the inside of the dish, or the Jello. Make sure the item touches the Jello completely. Tape down the cover with clear tape. Then label the dish "Many" and write the name of the item on masking tape. Repeat the process with an item from your baggie labeled "Few". The third dish doesn't get anything added to it.

Why do you think you need a dish with just Jello in it?

Introduce the notion of an experimental CONTROL if students are not familiar with it. The control dish is needed since there might be microbes in the dish, the air, or the Jello itself. If microbes grow in this dish, students will know that they can't attribute all of the microbe growth in the other dishes to the non-living items they added.

Another name for an experiment is a FAIR TEST. To make an experiment fair, you have to do everything the same to the control as you do to the TREATMENT, except for the one VARIABLE you are testing. What is the variable in our test?

The non-living items are the variables.

Should we do anything to the control dish to make sure we treat it just like the other dishes except for adding the item we're testing?

Help students realize that they should expose the Jello in the control dishes to the air for the same amount of time the Jello in the treatment dishes are open to air while they add their items.

Have students get their dishes of Jello and baggies of items, then set up their experiments. Keep the dishes in a warm, but not hot and sunny, location to encourage microbe growth.

Once they've set up their tests, have students record their activities, new observations, and ideas as a dated journal entry. Also have them add what they think will happen in the dish of plain Jello to the predictions they wrote earlier.

◯	March 26th
	We added a leaf to the "Many" dish of Jello.
	Then we put a rock in the "Few" dish. We have
	one more dish that has nothing but Jello. Keisha
	timed how long we opened each lid for 5 seconds.
	I think something like mold will grow on the plain
	Jello, too.

 *An interesting sideline experiment is to boil several of the items collected outdoors to sterilize them. Then students can compare the growth of microbes on a sterile and non-sterile sample of each item in Jello culture dishes.*

Session 2

Before you observe your experiments today, let's talk about the predictions you recorded on the class chart yesterday.

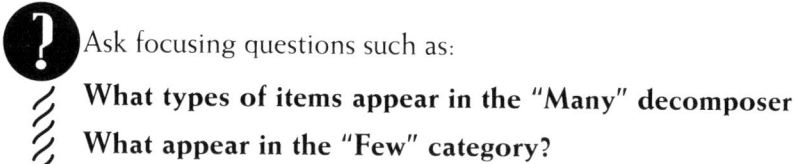Ask focusing questions such as:

What types of items appear in the "Many" decomposer microbes category?

What appear in the "Few" category?

Do some appear in both?

Ask students to share the reasoning behind their predictions. As they consider the validity of reasoning that differs from their own, cultivate and reinforce their habits of open-mindedness and critical reflection (e.g., *José said something that makes me think something new. Putting the bottle cap in the "Many" microbes category doesn't make sense to me because I don't think microbes eat metal.*).

Let's label each thing on our chart as biotic or abiotic.

Predictions

Pairs' Initials	Items with <u>Many</u> Microbes	Items with <u>Few</u> Microbes
L.M. & B.J.	lollipop stick - B	dry leaf - B
K.L. & A.M.	surface soil - A and B	deep soil - A and B
T.H. & K.T.	twig - B	pine needle - B
J.T. & J.L.	dead grass - B	bottle cap - A

Soil and water (except for tap water) can be considered both biotic and abiotic because they contain living and dead plants and animals, as well as minerals.

Once everything is labeled, have the class notice whether or not there is a trend for biotic items to be in one category and abiotic in another.

**Get your culture dishes and hand lenses to make observations. Make a chart in your journal for recording what you see.**

Each pair can come up with its own format for recording observations, or you can suggest a format. Also encourage students to make drawings, and to write ideas and comments as well as observations.

	Date	"Many" Dish: Leaf	"Few" Dish: Stick
○	March 27	It has spots on it.	The bark is peeling.

2.3 Culturing Bacteria and Fungi Decomposers

Sessions 3–5

Observe your culture dishes and keep a record of your observations in your journals. Hold the dishes up so you can see through the bottom, where the microbe growth might look different than it does from the top.

Give students 10–15 minutes for observations and notetaking each day for three to five days. If you have a weekend break during the experiment, make sure students observe their dishes on Friday and Monday since a lot of microbe growth can occur during the two days that they are away.

What to Expect

For the first few days, changes will be subtle. There might be clear, circular patterns around the items that are the beginning of microbe colonies. By the third day, students should see white fuzzy growth of fungi at the point of contact between the organic items and Jello. From the fourth to seventh days, the white fuzz will thicken, cover the entire item, and extend beyond it. Shades of green, black, gold, and grey will appear as the fungi begin to produce spores. Dark specks of bacterial colonies might be visible as well. If you let the experiment run for an eighth day, the Jello could begin to liquify, so will no longer be a firm substrate for the colonies.

There will also be microbe growth in the control dishes, but in small, neater-looking, round colonies. The amount of microbes from abiotic items will depend on how "dirty" they were (i.e., whether they had plant, soil, sugar, or residues on them).

Each day when you're done taking notes on your experiments, work with your partner on these "Science Fair Stories." They are about students your age who are doing science fair projects, and your job is to help them improve their experiments.

Give each pair of students "Science Fair Story #1" and "Science Fair Story #2" to work on together and/or complete on their own for homework. Here are some things to look for in their responses, and to go over in a class discussion:

Science Fair Story #1: Sam's Soil (Focus: Specifying a Plan)

1) Each funnel could have 1 cup of material total (e.g., a half cup of soil plus a half cup of other material), or 1 cup of soil to match the amount of soil in the first funnel, plus a measured amount of additional material. Either approach is acceptable, so long as students standardize the amount of each ingredient across treatments.

2) Other things Sam should do include making sure he tamps down each one the same amount, pouring the same amount of water in each funnel, and waiting the same amount of time after pouring the water in each before measuring how much water came through.

3) Sam should measure the amount of water that came through the funnel and subtract it from the amount of water he added to the funnel.

4) Students' suggestions for improvements will vary. Be sure to ask them why each of their ideas improves the experiment, such as by making it more accurate or by increasing the amount of information Sam will gain.

Module 2: *Decomposer Dynamics*

Science Fair Story #2: Alyssa's Algae (Focus: Controlling Variables)

1) The weaknesses of Alyssa's experiment are that the amount of pond water and algae was not the same in the different size jars, and they were not kept in the same conditions.

2) Alyssa should set up her test in equal size jars, and measure everything she puts into the jars so she can make them all the same. She should keep them all the same place — probably in sunlight since real ponds are exposed to sun.

Session 6

Take a few minutes to review your notes, then we'll share our findings with one another.

Display all of the dishes so everyone has a chance to see and compare them. Encourage pairs to share their results with the class. Students can put symbols such as plus and minus signs next to the items on the class predictions chart to show the relative amount of microbe growth on the items each pair tested. Also have students describe the different kinds of microbe growth they observed — this might be a more obvious result than the amount of microbe growth.

 Help them process their findings with questions such as:

Did anything grow on the plain Jello in the control dishes? If so, why?
Since students did not do their experiments in sterile conditions, the plain Jello dish most likely had microbes that came from the air, fingers, or the dishes themselves. Students can consider the type and amount of microbe growth in the control dishes as the "background" amount of microbe growth for all the dishes. In order to attribute microbe growth to the decomposers on the non-living items they collected, the growth in the dishes with these items should look different from the growth in dishes with plain Jello. Students should also notice whether the microbes started growing on Jello in parts of the dish far away from the item, rather than spreading there.

What kinds of items do you think had the most microbes on them when you put them in the dishes, and why?
Decomposer microbes should have been more abundant on items that are high in energy and nutrients, and are easy to digest. For instance, Jello to which tender plant tissues were added should show more microbe growth than Jello with tough, woody items. Jello to which plastic and metal items were added should show no microbe growth, unless the items had sugars, oils, or other residues on them. Help students understand that microbes are similar to all living things — they thrive best on high quality food.

How did your results compare to your predictions?
Fifth and sixth graders often have a hard time with results that don't turn out as they expected, in part because they don't like being "wrong". For instance, they are often surprised and disappointed that microbes grew on Jello to which abiotic items were added. But when they see that a lot of microbes also grew in their control dishes, they realize that they would need to improve their experiment

(e.g., by using sterile conditions) before they could draw conclusions. Asking students to explain why they think things turned out differently than they predicted is a good way to explore their understanding of the concepts that underlie the experiment. Help them understand that results that are contrary to a prediction are just as helpful to a scientist as positive results, and are often more thought provoking.

Does it look like different kinds of microbes grew on different items? If so, why?

Students will most likely see different shapes and colors of microbes on Jello to which different items were added, since the kinds of microbes differ in different locations and on different types of food sources. However, one dominant type of microbe might have thrived on the Jello regardless of the type of item added, masking the different kinds of microbes suited to digesting different materials.

What would happen to the items on which the microbes are growing after a long time?

Hopefully students will predict that the microbes will "eat them all up." This is true. After the microbes consume the Jello, the process of consuming the items themselves will slow down. Different kinds of microbes will take over at different stages of decomposition, as some are best suited to consuming fresh material, and others attack the more difficult to digest leftovers. Eventually, however, the materials that were once alive should get so small that they are no longer visible. The basic chemicals they were made of will be inside the microbes, or in the wastes the microbes have released.

The most important thing to make sure students come away with from this investigation is that dead things decompose because microbes use them as food. They should also understand that the matter the materials were made of may disappear from sight, but not from existence. It is just in different forms and in different places.

Either throw out the petri dishes without opening them, or if you want to save them, submerge them unopened in a bucket filled with hot water and about 2 cups of bleach. After they've soaked for a day or two, remove them and wash with hot water.

Ongoing Assessment

Student Reflections

Have students send a C-Mail message, or record thoughts in their journals. Optional writing prompts include:

A result of the experiment that surprised me was...

What would life as a microbe be like?

Module 2: *Decomposer Dynamics*

Teacher Reflections

❏ Do students understand why a control helps make an experiment a fair test?

❏ How detailed were their observations and journal records?

❏ Were they able to respect evidence that didn't match their predictions, and offer possible explanations for their results?

❏ Do they understand that microbes grow on dead things that they are eating, and that this causes the dead things to decompose?

Extensions

Leaf Chambers. Have students gather different kinds of leaves, or the same kinds of leaves from different environments (e.g., a place with more and less air pollution — this could involve exchanging samples with students at a different school). Wrap the leaves in wet paper towels, then put them in baggies and keep them in a warm place. Check on them at one-week intervals to see which have more fungal hyphae growing on them.

Micro Views. Put a small sample from a microbe culture dish in a drop of water on a microscope slide, cover it with a cover slip, and let students examine it under a microscope.

I Believe in Microbes! Students can have fun creating pins (with a pin-making machine if the school owns one, or with circles of white contact paper for stick-on buttons) that feature a drawing of a microbe and an appropriate slogan.

SAM'S SOIL

Sam was curious about soil. For his science fair project he decided to mix different things into garden soil, then compare how much water each mixture could hold. Here is the plan that Sam wrote:

"I'll get 4 funnels and put each one in a jar. Then I'll put some garden soil in the first funnel, some soil mixed with peat moss in the second funnel, some soil mixed with sand in the third funnel, and some soil mixed with leaves in the last funnel. I'll pour some water over each one, then see how much comes out the other end."

Sam's plan sounds pretty good, but it is not specific enough. Please help him be more specific.

1 If Sam put 1 cup of soil in the first funnel, how much soil, peat moss, sand, and leaves should he add to the other funnels?

_____

2 What else should Sam do exactly the same to make a fair test?

_____

_____

3 What should he measure to find out which material held the most water?

_____

_____

4 Can you suggest anything else Sam could do to improve his experiment? Explain.

_____

_____

SCIENCE FAIR STORY #2

ALYSSA'S ALGAE

Alyssa has a pond in the back of her house, so for her science fair project she decided to study algae. She heard people say that fertilizers from people's lawns got into the pond and made a lot of thick, green algae grow. Alyssa decided to test whether fertilizer helps algae grow.

She found six jars. Some were mayonnaise jars, some were peanut butter jars, and some were large pickle jars. Alyssa filled each jar with pond water and put in some strands of algae. Then she added 1 teaspoon of fertilizer to three of the jars. She put these three jars on her bedroom windowsill. Since there was no more room on her windowsill, she put the other three jars of pond water and algae on her bookshelf.

1 > What is wrong with Alyssa's experiment?

_____

_____

_____

2 > What should she do to make her experiment a fair test?

_____

_____

_____

2.3 Culturing Bacteria and Fungi Decomposers

2.4 Dead Leaf Storyboards —
Performance Assessment

Action Synopsis

Students work in groups to create displays that show what happens to a dead leaf over time.

Session 1		40 minutes
1. Present the challenge of making a dead leaf storyboard.		*posing a challenge*
2. Discuss criteria for high quality work.		*setting standards*
3. Plan storyboards in groups.		*planning*

Session 2		1 hour
1. Make storyboards in groups.		*applying knowledge*
2. Display and view storyboards.		*communicating*
3. Summarize and discuss the decomposition process.		*reflecting*

Desired Outcomes

By the end of this assessment activity, students should:

✓ Know how the appearance a dead leaf changes during decomposition.

✓ Understand that the primary cause of decomposition is decomposers that use dead material as food.

✓ Know that the matter a leaf is made of does not vanish during decomposition; it all can be accounted for even though it is in new forms and places.

✓ Be able to communicate their knowledge of decomposition in a way that engages and teaches others.

What You'll Need

Sessions 1 & 2

For each group of 3–4 students:
❏ materials for making storyboards (see "Getting Ready")
❏ copy of "Challenge Sheet" (page 213)
❏ copy of "Scoring Sheet" (page 214)

For each student:
❏ copy of "Group Work Evaluation" (page 42)
❏ copy of "Reflections" (page 41)
❏ copy of "Scoring Sheet" (page 214)

Getting Ready

Session 1

♦ Gather materials for groups to use to make storyboards, such as poster board, markers, paints, construction paper, leaf samples, glue, and tape.

♦ If you'd like students to share their storyboards with an audience beyond their classmates, make arrangements to display the projects in a public space within or outside of school, or invite guests to your classroom to view them.

♦ If possible, make arrangements with the art teacher for students to spend additional time working on their storyboards in art class.

♦ Plan groups of 3–4 students.

Action Narrative

Session 1

We're going to spend the next couple of days on an activity to see how much you've learned about what makes a dead leaf disappear. You're going to make Dead Leaf Storyboards. A storyboard is a display that uses pictures and words to tell a story, sort of like a comic strip. Here is your challenge.

Give a copy of the "Challenge Sheet" to each group and discuss the activity. Tell students where they'll display their work and/or who their audience will be. Emphasize that they should use the storyboards as an opportunity to show you and others everything they've learned so far about the causes of decomposition.

What are some different ways you've seen pictures and words used to explain something or tell a story?

Students might mention museum displays, science fair project backboards, comic strips, and textbook illustrations. Discuss the style and purpose of these examples.

What do you think would make a storyboard effective?

Help students establish standards and a vision for their final products. They might suggest that the storyboards should be eye-catching, make information easy to understand, and teach people something.

Your storyboards will be evaluated using several criteria.

Give a copy of the "Scoring Sheet" to each group and go over the scoring so students know what is expected of their finished storyboards. Point out that Objective 2 ("Correctly explains what causes a leaf to change") is worth three times as many points as the other criteria.

You can use the rest of this period to plan your storyboards in groups. Later you'll have more time to make them.

Show students the materials you have on hand, and let them know where, when, how, and if they can get other materials (e.g., by going outside to collect leaf samples, getting supplies from the art teacher, or bringing things from home).

Students' initial planning will probably focus on the physical characteristics of their storyboards. You might want to help groups brainstorm formats (e.g., a poster or a three-dimensional display), size, and materials. Remind them that their knowledge and ideas about decomposition are important "raw materials" for constructing their boards, too. Suggest that they appoint a notetaker to record everyone's ideas.

Help students come up with questions that they can ask each other to generate the content for their boards, such as:

Who knows how the looks of a decomposing leaf change?

What makes leaves decompose?

Where does the stuff the leaf was made of end up?

Module 2: Decomposer Dynamics

Creating a storyboard is as much a learning experience as an assessment, so encourage students to look up or ask for information they don't have.

By the end of the session, each group should have a sketch of each frame of their storyboard. Make sure they agree on the final format and the things they'll need to finish the project during the next session.

Session 2

Review your plans for your storyboards, then gather your materials and get started.

You might need to remind students not to leave any information off their boards in the excitement of creating an attractive display.

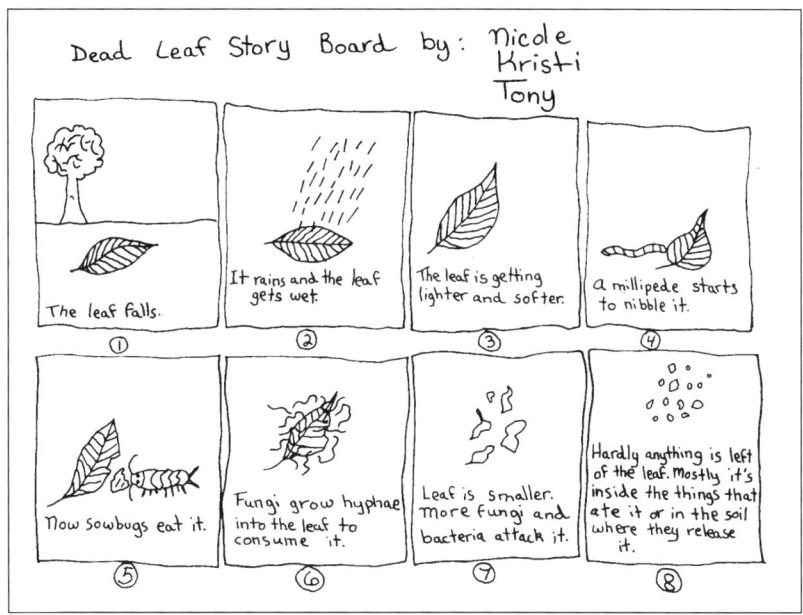

After the storyboards are finished, display them, and give students and any invited guests time to view everyone's work. Have each group leave a "Scoring Sheet" with their names on it by their storyboard for you to fill out later.

 Conclude the activity by posing questions such as:

What changes in decomposing leaves do the storyboards show?
Leaves might dry up and wither, get holes in them, get nibbled around the edges, get skeletonized so that only the veins and stem are left, break into smaller pieces, get brown, get black spots on them, get slimy, get white fuzz on them, smell rotten or pungent, etc.

? **What causes of decomposition did different groups illustrate?**

The major cause of decomposition is the organisms that use dead leaves as food. Invertebrates such as earthworms, termites, beetles, sow bugs, and millipedes consume leaves, and also leave behind pieces of the leaves they've chewed. Bacteria and fungi attack the leaf particles in the soil organisms' droppings and leftovers, breaking them down further. The direct effects of physical factors such as wind, rain, and trampling are minuscule compared to the biological factors that cause decomposition. However, physical conditions such as warmth and moisture do make it easier for microbes to eat dead material and multiply.

Do the materials that a decomposed leaf was made of still exist?

Students' responses will reveal whether or not they understand the conservation of matter. Students who have not yet grasped that matter can neither be created nor destroyed are likely to say that only the "bits of the leaf that have gone into the soil" still exist, and that in one way or another the rest of the leaf vanishes during decomposition.

Do dead leaves really "disappear"?

Decomposing leaves might disappear from sight, but the material they were made of does not disappear from existence. Decomposition is a good example of the conservation of matter. The leaf matter becomes part of the organisms that ate it, or is released from the organisms as waste into the soil, water, or air. Help students realize that all of the matter can be accounted for; nothing has vanished.

Ongoing Assessment

Student Reflections

Have students fill out a "Group Work Evaluation" (page 42) to reflect on their group process. They could also complete a "Scoring Sheet" for their own or another group's work. This is also a good time for them to complete a "Reflections" sheet (page 41).

Teacher Reflections

As you evaluate students' work, look for storyboards that show that leaves decompose because animals and microbes use them for food. These should receive higher scores than those that emphasize physical wear and tear. All of the storyboards should illustrate the role of microbes, but whether they include invertebrate decomposers depends on if your students observed them during earlier field trips.

NAME(S)_____ DATE_____

DEAD LEAF STORYBOARDS

Many people think that dead leaves just magically disappear after they die!

YOUR CHALLENGE:

Make a storyboard that shows people what causes a dead leaf to break down.
Your storyboard should have:

(1) Drawings, paper cut-outs, and/or samples to show how a dead leaf looks from the time it falls, until it is too tiny to see.

(2) Words that explain what is making the leaf change.

GOOD LUCK!

© Institute of Ecosystem Studies, 1994   **213**

NAME(S)_____ DATE_____

DEAD LEAF STORYBOARDS

OBJECTIVES	POINTS				SCORE
	3 High Quality	**2** Meets Objectives	**1** Falls Short	**0** Not Done	
CONTENT					
1. Shows how a dead leaf looks at a variety of points in time.	_____	_____	_____	_____	___ x 2 =___
2. Correctly explains what causes the leaf to change.	_____	_____	_____	_____	___ x 2 =___
CLARITY					
3. Made with care and attention to detail.	_____	_____	_____	_____	=___
4. Presents a clear, easy-to-follow sequence.	_____	_____	_____	_____	=___
5. Captures interest with creative use of materials and layout.	_____	_____	_____	_____	=___

COMMENTS:

FINAL SCORE: _____

Total Possible Score: 21
Overall Achievement:
   18–21 High
   14–17 Sound
   8–13 Limited
   0–7   Inadequate

2.5 Testing Conditions That Promote Decomposition

Action Synopsis

Students test factors that promote the growth of microbes, then use their findings to make compost.

Session 1		**40 minutes**

1. Present the challenge of testing conditions to make dead plants decompose.

 posing a challenge

2. Brainstorm factors that might promote microbe growth and decomposition.

 generating ideas & questions

3. Work in pairs to choose a variable to test and outline experiment plans on a "Research Proposal."

 designing experiments

Session 2		**40 minutes**

1. Set up experiments.

 *investigating*

2. Record experimental setup in journals.

 *documenting*

Continued

Sessions 3–5		**40 minutes**

1. Monitor experiments and keep records. *observing & recording*

2. Evaluate weaknesses of experiments described in "Science Fair Stories." *applying knowledge*

Session 6		**1 hour**

1. Discuss results of experiments. *processing findings*

2. Draw conclusions about best conditions for microbe growth. *reflecting*

3. Design and set up a decomposition (compost) chamber. *applying knowledge*

4. Make plans for monitoring compost over time. *planning*

Desired Outcomes

Throughout the lesson, check that students:

✓ Understand that invisible spores of microbes are in the air, water, and on all non-sterile surfaces.

✓ Discover that certain physical conditions, such as moisture and warmth, help microbes grow.

✓ Can explain the connection between the growth of microbes on dead plants and decomposition.

✓ Are refining their experimenting skills, such as defining a research question, controlling variables, using replicates, making measurements, documenting results, and drawing conclusions.

What You'll Need

Sessions 1–6

For the class:
- ❏ 2.5 gallon (30 x 15 x 17 cm) plastic animal cage with cover (or a similar clear plastic container to use as a decomposition chamber)
- ❏ clear plastic bag large enough to line the decomposition chamber
- ❏ 6 cups of alfalfa hay
- ❏ 6 cups of hardwood shavings
- ❏ materials to vary conditions for growing microbes (see "Getting Ready")

Continued

Session 1

For each pair of students:
❑ copy of "Research Proposal" (pages 230–231)

Session 2

For the class:
❑ miscellaneous containers (see "Getting Ready")

For each pair of students:
❑ 4 sandwich-size ziplock baggies
❑ masking tape or permanent marker

Sessions 3–5

For the class:
❑ measurement and observation tools (see "Getting Ready")

For each pair of students:
❑ 2 hand lenses
❑ copy of "Science Fair Story #3" (page 232)
❑ copy of "Science Fair Story #4" (page 233)
❑ copy of "Science Fair Story #5" (page 234)

Vocabulary

COMPOST - Decayed plants, usually used for improving garden soil.

REPLICATES - Identical copies of an experiment.

Getting Ready

Session 1

♦ Gather a variety of materials that students can use to vary the conditions of their hay samples, such as soil, decomposing leaves, water, mushrooms, freezer packs, non-electric heating pads, black construction paper, and "compost starter" (a commercial product that contains microbe spores).

♦ Decide on pairs of students to work as research teams, or plan to let them choose partners.

Session 2

♦ Collect some containers for students to use while conducting their experiments, such as plastic cups for carrying water and trays on which to examine compost.

♦ Display the hay, baggies, and materials for varying experimental conditions on a centralized table so that students can quickly identify and get what they need.

♦ Assemble measurement and observation tools for students to use to monitor their experiments, such as rulers, a balance, measuring cups, dropping pipettes, thermometers, and a microscope.

Action Narrative

Session 1

How could we imitate the decomposition that happens outdoors right here in the classroom? Your challenge over the next week is to test conditions that will make these dead plants decompose.

Show students the bags of hay and wood shavings, and the empty container that they'll make into a decomposition chamber. Discuss why hay and wood shavings are dead plants (i.e., hay comes from plants that are mowed, harvested, dried, and then baled; and wood shavings come from trees).

What do you think you'd have to do to make the hay and wood shavings decompose in this container? Think about what causes decomposition, and what the conditions were like in places outdoors where you saw the most evidence of decomposition.

Make a class list of students' suggestions. Probe for the reasoning behind their ideas, asking questions such as *Why do you think adding water would help?* Their responses might reveal lingering misconceptions. If so, remind them that dead plants break down because microbes consume them, so they'll want to create conditions that will help decomposer organisms live and multiply.

<u>What conditions will make the dead plants decompose?</u>

Make the plants wet

Keep the plants in a dark place

Put the plants under pressure, like when they're under stuff outside

Add soil

Add a mushroom

Add manure

Put the plants between layers of soil

Add microbes

Give them sunlight

Keep the plants warm

Rip the plants into tiny pieces

Give them lots of air

These are ideas for variables you could test. The next step is to plan experiments so that we know the best way to make this container into a "decomposition chamber" for our dead plants.

You and a partner will use small samples of hay to test the conditions you think are the most important or interesting. Then when we figure out what conditions make microbes grow the best, we will use our findings to set up the decomposition chamber with all of the plant material, and whatever else you decide to add.

Make sure students follow the reasoning of using microbe growth as an indicator of optimal conditions for decomposition. Since it would take too long to wait for the sample material to decompose completely, students will need to assume that conditions that make the most microbes grow are the best for creating a decomposition chamber.

With your partner, choose a variable you'd like to test and write your names beside it on our list, or add a new idea you'd like to investigate. More than one pair can test the same variable. In fact, it is better that way. Does anyone know why?

See how much intuitive sense students have about why experiment REPLICATES are important, then introduce the term to them. Scientists set up more than one trial of an experiment so they can be more sure of their conclusions. If something happened once, it might have been by chance. If it happened 100 times out of 100 trials, then a scientist can be quite sure it happened because of the test conditions.

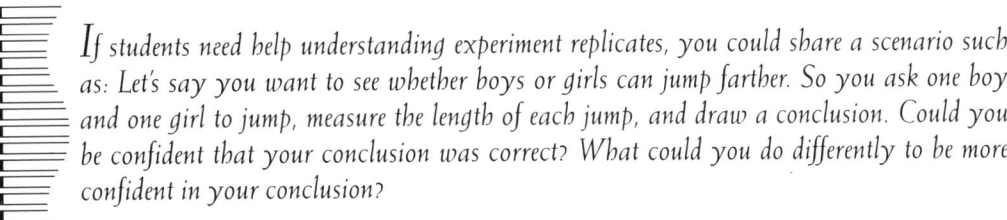

If students need help understanding experiment replicates, you could share a scenario such as: Let's say you want to see whether boys or girls can jump farther. So you ask one boy and one girl to jump, measure the length of each jump, and draw a conclusion. Could you be confident that your conclusion was correct? What could you do differently to be more confident in your conclusion?

Give pairs a few minutes to choose a variable and record their selections. Once students see what everyone has chosen, they might want to make adjustments to test a greater variety of variables, or to have at least two pairs replicate each test.

Each pair will get four baggies and a small amount of hay to put in each.

Show students the baggies, hay, and the materials they can use to vary conditions for growing microbes.

Notice that the hay includes seed heads, stems and leaves. What will you want to make sure of when you choose hay to add to your baggies?

To make their tests fair, students will want to use the same part(s) of the plant in each baggie. Microbes often grow better on the stems and leaves of alfalfa hay than on seed heads, so students might want to include a small piece of each part of the hay in each baggie to make sure that they'll see microbe growth.

You'll have the rest of the period to plan your experiment with your partner. Scientists usually have to write up a plan and have it approved by other scientists before they can proceed with their research. Write your plans on this "Research Proposal" and then go over it with me before you begin your experiment.

Planning Experiments

Some issues about experimental design that you might want to address with small groups or the class as a whole include:

Defining a Question. A good research question contains specific information about the kinds of comparisons that will be made in an experiment. For instance, the question *Will more microbes grow on wet hay than on a dry hay?* is more helpful than *Does water help microbes grow?* The question *Will adding soil to a baggie with hay make microbes grow on the hay more quickly than on plain hay?* is better than *What will happen when we add soil to hay in a baggie?*

Adding Microbes. Students might wonder where the microbes that are supposed to grow on the hay will come from. Remind them that microbes are everywhere. Reproductive spores of fungi and the resting spores of bacteria are already on the hay, waiting for the right conditions to grow. They can introduce more microbes by adding things to the hay, such as soil, moldy material, mushrooms, or compost starter .

Testing a Combination of Variables. Students might want to test several variables together, such as soil and water, or darkness and warmth. This is alright, but makes things slightly more complicated. If they combine soil and water for instance, they won't know if both conditions were really necessary for the microbe growth, or if they would have seen the same results by changing just one of the variables. Students can deal with this by having all four combinations (e.g., dry hay, wet hay, hay with dry soil, and hay with wet soil). They might not need to set up these extra tests themselves if other research teams are already doing them.

Creating Replicates. Students should set up at least two replicates in their experiments, especially if they have chosen a variable that nobody else in the class is testing.

Observing Evidence of Decomposition. From their experiments with Jello cultures, students should have a good idea of what something looks like when microbes are growing on it. Although bacterial colonies might form on the hay, students are more likely to see fungi. A slimy appearance and odors are also indicators of decomposition.

Predicting Results. The "Predictions" section of the "Research Proposal" asks students to list several possible results. Some students might just name three different types of changes for the treatment group (e.g., *the wet one will get fuzzy; it will get mushy; it will start to break apart*). Encourage them to consider the possibility that there could be no changes in the treatment as compared to the control, or that the treatment and control groups could both show changes.

Tomorrow bring in any materials you need that we don't already have.

Have students who finished their "Research Proposal" hand it in for you to review and initial.

Session 2

Today you'll set up your experiments. First, finish your "Research Proposal" if you haven't already. Once I've initialed it, go ahead and get started.

Expect that students won't realize difficulties with their plans or a better way to do things until they begin working with materials. Encourage them to refine their methods as necessary as they go along.

Sometimes students are less accurate in setting up their tests than their plans specify. Ask them if they are doing everything they can to create equal conditions in the treatment and control baggies, except for the variable they are testing. This could involve measuring or weighing the hay, measuring water so they know how much to add to each of their replicates, or keeping the baggies in the same conditions. If students forget to label their baggies, you might ask them how they'll be sure which is the treatment and which is the control.

After students use the materials they need to set up their experiments, clear away the leftovers and arrange the table with observation and measurement tools. It might help to tape labels to the table to show where each tool should be returned at the end of each period.

Help students find places to keep their experiments. Those who are testing conditions such as warmth, sunlight, or darkness might need special locations for their baggies.

 **When you're finished setting up your experiments, make an entry in your journals. Describe what you did, draw a picture of your setup, and record what the hay looks like now so you'll have something to look back on when you think it is showing signs of decomposing.**

Communicate the importance of keeping good records by giving students enough time during class to make a detailed journal entry, or by assigning journal writing for homework.

Sessions 3–5

Check your experiments and make careful notes of your observations. Use hand lenses to get a closer look at what's happening in the baggies.

In addition to writing descriptions, have students think about if and how they could quantify their results. One idea is to make a rating system for the amount of fungal growth.

> 0 - no fungi visible,
>
> 1 - a few strands of fungal hyphae are present
>
> 2 - fungi all over the sample
>
> 3 - fungi so dense that the hay is no longer visible

Students might want to base their ratings on the consensus of several people's opinions, to slightly reduce the subjectivity. You might want to help students develop a chart for recording results.

Date	Baggie #1 wet	Baggie #2 Dry	Baggie #3 wet	Baggie #4 Dry
5/3	0	0	0	0

Take time to look over students' journals and encourage them to show them to each other. This helps them value journal keeping as a way to develop and display creativity, documentation skills, and reflection. Their writing, charts, and drawings can also spark discussions about their work.

Let the experiments run over a weekend if possible, since the longer they sit, the more dramatic the results will be.

What to Expect

Fungi will grow most quickly on hay that is kept warm and moist. Students won't see any microbes after one day, although they might see discoloration of the leaves and a yellowish tint to the water they added, due to dissolved material leaching from the leaves. By the end of the second or third day they'll begin to see fuzzy molds and fungal hyphae, especially thin white networks of strands and black dots of spores along the hay stems, which will increase daily. If students added so much water to their baggies that the hay is saturated and no oxygen is available, bacteria that are "anaerobic" will grow, and a noticeable odor resulting from gases and other products they release could result.

Each day when you're done taking notes on your experiments, work with your partner on some more "Science Fair Stories."

Give each pair of students three more science fair stories to work on together and/or complete on their own for homework. Here are some things to look for in their responses, and to go over in a class discussion:

Science Fair Story #3: Paul's Pollution (Focus: Keeping Accurate Records)

1) Advice to Paul should concern improving his record-keeping habits.

2) Charts for Paul's data should have a place for the date and for the number of duckweed, snails, algae, and water fleas in the mini-ponds with and without laundry soap.

Science Fair Story #4: Juan's Wonderful Worms (Focus: Interpreting Results)

1) Juan lost points because he didn't take all of his data into account when drawing a conclusion.

2) The best conclusion is that the worms had no clear preference for either soil as measured in this study. However, students might also reason that: a) the worms liked the woods soil better because there were more in it two times out of three that he checked; b) the worms liked the woods soil better because there were more in it the last day; or c) the worms liked the field soil better because an average of 10.3 worms were found there per day, and only an average of 9.7 per day were found in the woods soil.

Science Fair Story #5: Maritza's Marigolds (Focus: Planning a Whole Investigation)

1) Maritza's research question could be something like: *Do marigolds watered with water that egg-shells have soaked in grow taller (or look greener, or flower sooner…) than marigolds watered with plain water?* The question should include more specific terminology than "grow better".

2) Students will probably predict that the marigolds receiving eggshell water will grow taller (or look greener, or flower sooner…), since that's what Maritza's grandmother claims.

3) Students should define how many plants to use as a treatment and how many as a control, pot sizes, amount of soil, size of marigolds to start with, and amount of water each will receive. They should define a watering schedule for the duration of the experiment. Students should plan to observe and measure indicators of plant health, such as height, number of leaves, greenness of leaves, and size of flowers.

4) Charts should include a space for dates and sections for recording measurements of 32 treatment and control plants.

Session 6

Prepare to share your results with the class by discussing these questions with your partner.

Write several questions on the board to focus students' discussions.

1) What variable did you test?

2) Did your treatment change in comparison to your control? In what ways?

3) Were the results of your replicates the same?

As each pair reports its results, summarize the findings on a class chart. You might want to list those that tested the same variable together for easy comparison.

| | | Microbe Growth | |
Research Team	Variable	Treatment	Control
B.K. & L.T.	soil	2	0
T.J. & M.L.	soil	3	0
S.T. & J.H.	water	3	0
T.H. & A.R.	mushroom	2	0

(0 none; 1 little; 2 medium; 3 lots)

 Facilitate a discussion of the results with questions such as:

Was there variation in the replicates?

Students may have seen variation in how samples of hay responded to the same variable. Their challenge is to decide whether the variation among replicates was so great that they can't draw a conclusion about the kind of change their variable causes, or whether the variation was small enough that a clear trend was still evident.

Which variables created the best conditions for microbes to grow?

Any variable that added moisture to the hay should have promoted microbe growth. If students added moist items (e.g., soil, a mushroom, moldy leaves) ask them how they could figure out if it was the moisture or something else about the items (e.g., microbe spores on them) that promoted microbe growth in their experiment. They might suggest testing dry and moist samples of the items as variables. Moisture plus warmth promotes even more microbe growth, but warmth alone does not. Like all living things, microbes need moisture to carry out life functions.

What are some examples of how people try to keep plant material dry to prevent decay?

Students might mention farmers who try to cut, bale, and store hay in dry weather.

What would happen if you treated a dead plant with a chemical that prevented decomposers from attacking it, and then exposed it to rain and wind?

Students' responses will reveal whether or not they still harbor the misconception that physical factors alone can cause decay. Normal rain and wind might cause some physical breakdown, but it will be minuscule in comparison to the breakdown caused by decomposers. For example, fence posts, telephone poles, and wood decking that are treated with preservatives to deter microbial decay last longer than untreated wood, despite being exposed to the same weather.

Did some variables cause changes to happen more quickly than others?

Since students monitored their experiments on a regular basis, they can compare notes to see which variables caused changes to appear sooner than others.

Now it's time to use our findings to design a decomposition chamber. What conditions should we create in the chamber to cause the dead plant material to decompose?

This is a good opportunity for students to think through and use what they've learned about decomposition. Encourage them to challenge and elaborate on one another's suggestions until everyone agrees on what to do.

Water is the only essential ingredient to add to the contents of the decomposition chamber, but students might make strong arguments to add other ingredients as well.

The next step is to set up our decomposition chamber. We'll need to line it with a plastic bag. Every few days we'll remove the bag, close it up, and shake it to expose the bottom and center of the rotting plant material to air.

If the moist material doesn't get air, bacteria that can live without oxygen start growing. They give off smelly gases (like ammonia and hydrogen sulfide), and other chemical products that will stink up the classroom.

How much water should we add?

Too much water will fill up all the air pockets, so again only the bacteria that don't need oxygen and produce a rotten odor will take over. It is best to add 1 cup of water at a time until the hay feels like a squeezed out sponge.

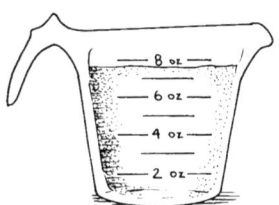

Does anyone know what gardeners call the material they get by letting dead plants rot?

Introduce the word COMPOST if students are not familiar with it.

We'll keep some observation tools by the decomposition chamber, so you can monitor what happens as dead plants turn into compost.

Show students the materials you've gathered, such as a thermometer, spoons and petri dishes, hand lenses, and a microscope. Have students take the temperature of the center of the compost just after they set it up, and each time they shake it. Keep a notebook or chart by the decomposition chamber where students can record their observations.

Compost Happenings

Temperature. Much heat is released by microbes as they consume dead plants. Students should be able to detect temperatures in the compost that are higher than air temperature. When microbes have optimum food and moisture, compost temperatures can reach as high as 65° C (150° F). Brush turkeys in Australia and some kinds of crocodiles bury their eggs in piles of decomposing plants to use the heat produced as an incubator.

The Compost Community. If students have added soil to the compost, they've probably introduced some invertebrates as well as microbes. By examining samples of compost with hand lenses and a microscope, students might find some of the organisms pictured below.

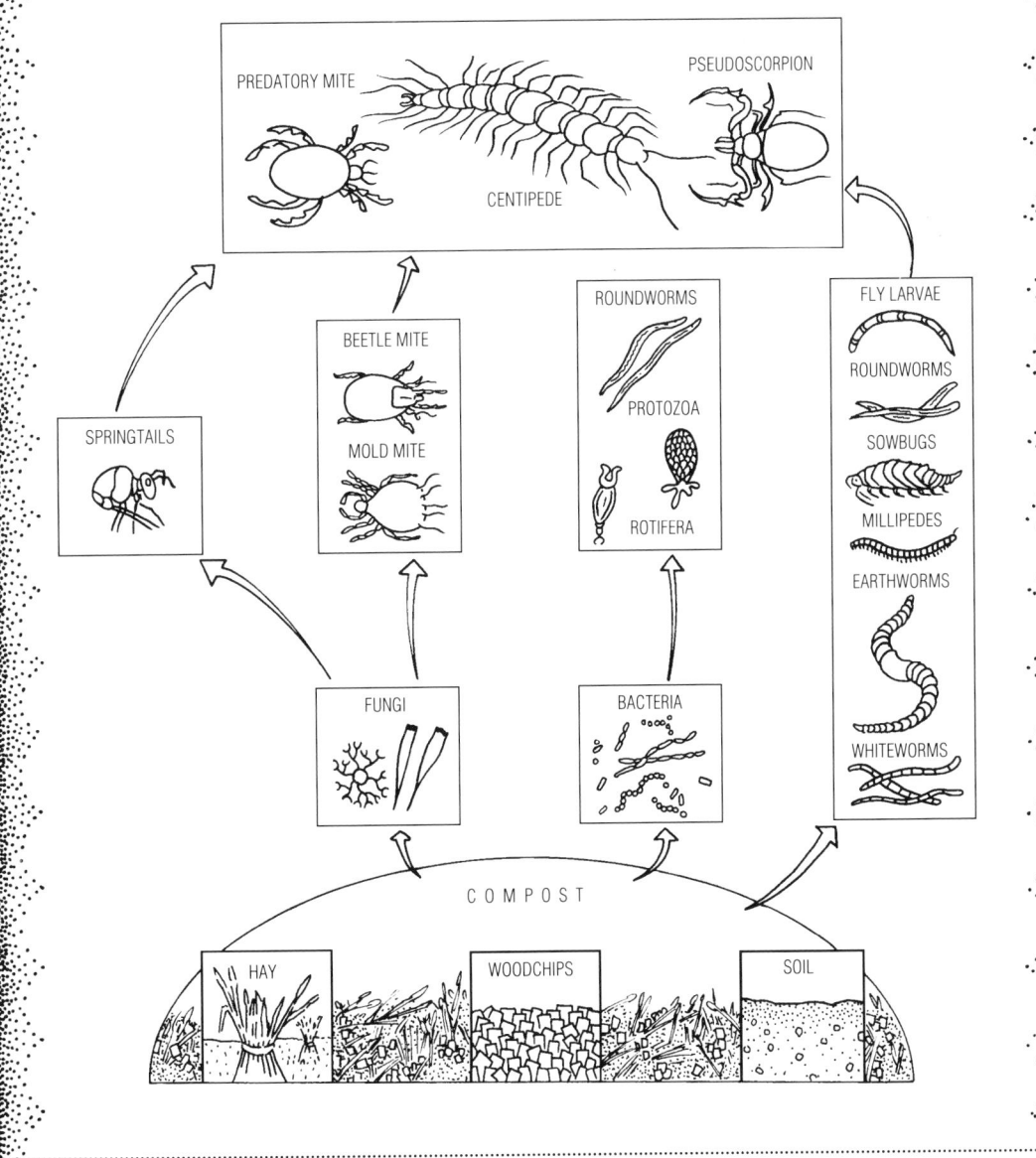

After students have observed the compost for a few weeks, bring out the class chart made during Lesson 2.1, listing ideas about what happens to plants after they die. Have students revise and enhance the list to reflect their new knowledge about decomposition.

The compost will be used during Module 3. If you don't plan to do Module 3, keep the decomposition chamber going as long as students are interested, then talk with them about what they could do with the compost (e.g., add it to the soil around plants near the school building).

Ongoing Assessment

Student Reflections

Have students send a C-Mail message, or record thoughts in their journals. Optional writing prompts include:

How did you feel while doing the experiment (e.g., excited, frustrated, impatient, curious, disgusted, overwhelmed, creative)? Why?

If there were no decomposers on earth, then...

Teacher Reflections

❑ Are students comfortable with and able to use the logic and methods of controlled experimentation?

❑ Do they understand that physical conditions such as moisture and warmth can make it easier for microbes to consume their food and reproduce, but that these conditions alone do not cause decomposition?

❑ Did they show thoughtful use of results when deciding how to set up the decomposition chamber?

Extensions

Burial Studies. Help students bury equal size samples of the same item, such as spinach leaves, in the top 5 cm of soil in different locations. Mark the locations with a stick or ribbon. Check back every few days to see how the materials have changed. Try a variation by burying the samples in a coarse mesh such as cheesecloth or plastic screening, to exclude larger soil organisms, and in a tight mesh such as panty hose, to exclude all but microbes. Students could also bury different biotic and abiotic items in the same location and compare their rates of decomposition.

Concept Maps. Introduce concept mapping to students (see pages 25–27) if they are not already familiar with the process. Select all or some of the concept map cards on pages 43–44, then copy one set of cards for each group of 3–4 students. Have them construct concept maps that display their ideas about decomposition. Help students compare their new concept maps with those they made after Lesson 2.1, to see how their ideas have changed.

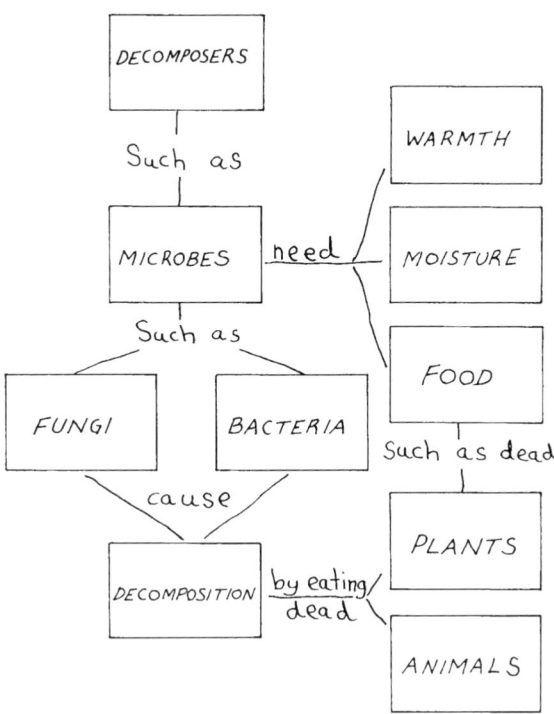

Do Not Rot. Challenge students to figure out what conditions *prevent* microbes from growing on organic matter. Keep one piece of a fruit or vegetable, unenclosed and unaltered, at room temperature as a control. Have students take other pieces of the same item and treat them in a variety of ways that might prevent them from decaying.

Desert Decomposition. If you live in an arid region, have students find a shrub with dead leaves beneath it. Use a watering can to wet the leaves and the ground beneath them. Check back daily. Termites should respond to the moisture and consume the dead leaves quickly.

Test Writing. Have groups of students write several questions and answers on microbes and decomposition, then submit them to you for possible use on a class quiz.

RESEARCH PROPOSAL

QUESTION
▼▼▼▼▼▼▼▼▼▼▼▼▼▼▼▼▼▼▼▼▼▼▼▼▼▼▼▼▼

⟨1⟩ Write the question that you want to answer.

_____

_____

FAIR TEST
▼▼▼▼▼▼▼▼▼▼▼▼▼▼▼▼▼▼▼▼▼▼▼▼▼▼▼▼▼

⟨2⟩ Describe a fair test you'll do to answer your question.

_____

_____

_____

_____

⟨3⟩ What variable are you testing?

_____

⟨4⟩ Draw and label your experimental setup. Circle the variable that you are testing.

Remember, everything should be exactly the same in the treatment and the control except for the variable you're testing!

TREATMENT

CONTROL

How many of these will you set up?_____   How many of these will you set up?_____

    Module 2: *Decomposer Dynamics*

MATERIALS
▼▼▼▼▼▼▼▼▼▼▼▼▼▼▼▼▼▼▼▼▼▼▼▼

⟨5⟩ List everything you'll need. Specify exact amounts.

_____ _____ _____

_____ _____ _____

_____ _____ _____

OBSERVATION AND CARE PLAN
▼▼▼▼▼▼▼▼▼▼▼▼▼▼▼▼▼▼▼▼▼▼▼▼

⟨6⟩ WHAT	HOW	WHEN	WHO
What will you do, watch, and measure to answer your research question?	How exactly will you make observations and measurements?	How often?	Who will do each job?
_____	_____	_____	_____
_____	_____	_____	_____
_____	_____	_____	_____
_____	_____	_____	_____

PREDICTIONS
▼▼▼▼▼▼▼▼▼▼▼▼▼▼▼▼▼▼▼▼▼▼▼▼

⟨7⟩ What do you think the result of your experiment will be? Why?

_____

_____

What other result could there be?

_____

_____

Can you think of another possible result?

_____

_____

☐ Check here when this plan has been reviewed.

Reviewer's Initials: _____

PAUL'S POLLUTION

Paul wanted to study water pollution for his science fair project. He got two 1-gallon jars and made them into mini-ponds. He added the same amount of pond water, duckweed, snails, algae, and water fleas to each jar.

Paul then added a small amount of dissolved laundry soap to one pond, and left the other pond alone. He kept the jars near the window in his bedroom for two months to observe what things grew or died.

The first time he collected data, Paul counted the amount of duckweed in each jar. His notebook and pencil were downstairs, so he kept the numbers in his head. Then he counted how many snails were still alive in each jar. As he was adding up numbers, Paul decided that he better get his notebook. On his way through the living room he saw that his brother was watching his favorite television show, so he sat down to watch. After the show he got his notebook and wrote down the numbers he could remember.

A week later, Paul used his microscope to see how many water fleas were in samples of water he took from each of his ponds. He jotted down the numbers on the back of a bubble-gum wrapper. A few days later, Paul realized that he had thrown out the gum wrapper by mistake.

1 > How can Paul improve his experimenting skills?

_____

_____

2 > Make a chart or charts that Paul could use for keeping track of his data. Use the back of the sheet.

SCIENCE FAIR STORY #4

JUAN'S WONDERFUL WORMS

Juan loved to fish, and was good at digging up earthworms. When it came time to do a science experiment, he decided to investigate what kind of soil earthworms prefer.

Juan dug up some soil from the woods, and some soil from a field. Then he put the piles of soil next to each other in his backyard. He put 20 worms in between the two piles.

Here are Juan's findings:

Date	Woods Soil	Field Soil
April 25	12 worms	8 worms
April 30	6 worms	14 worms
May 5	11 worms	9 worms

Juan decided that the clearest differences were on April 30th, so he concluded that worms prefer field soil.

1 ▷ Why do you think Juan lost points from the Science Fair Judge for his conclusion?

_____

_____

2 ▷ What should Juan have concluded from his experiment? Explain your answer.

_____

_____

_____

MARITZA'S MARIGOLDS

Maritza's grandmother always lets eggshells soak in the bottom of her watering can. She says that the eggshells add something to the water that helps her plants grow better.

Maritza wants to test her grandmother's eggshell method for a science fair project. She has 32 marigold plants to use for her test.

Plan an experiment that will help Maritza find out what she wants to know:

 1 Write a research question that Maritza can test.

_____

_____

 2 Make a prediction.

_____

 3 Describe a fair test Maritza could do. Remember to include:

- What materials she should use
- How she should set up the experiment
- What she should do to keep the experiment running
- What observations and measurements she should make

_____

_____

_____

_____

_____

4 Make a chart that Maritza could use to record her data.
Use the back of the sheet.

 Module 2: *Decomposer Dynamics*

2.6 The Bag That Wouldn't Go Away—Performance Assessment

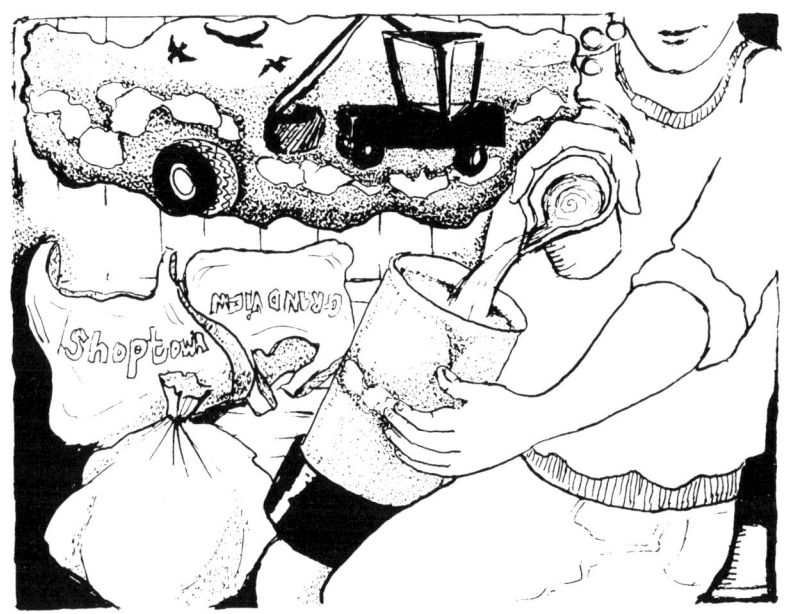

Action Synopsis

Students design and set up model waste disposal systems that will help biodegradable plastic bags decompose.

Session 1		40 minutes

1. Discuss whether trash decomposes.   *examining prior ideas*

2. Discuss biodegradable bags and trash disposal systems.   *generating ideas & questions*

3. Set up a model landfill.   *demonstrating methods*

4. Present the challenge of becoming engineers to design waste disposal systems.   *posing a challenge*

5. Discuss criteria for high quality work.   *setting standards*

6. Work in groups to plan waste disposal systems.   *planning*

Continued

1. Set up model waste disposal systems in soda bottles.   *applying knowledge*

2. Complete design specifications and present   *communicating*
   designs to the class.

3. Summarize and discuss waste disposal and   *reflecting*
   the garbage crisis.

Desired Outcomes

By the end of this assessment activity, students should:

✓ Be able to explain why biodegradable items don't always decompose after they're thrown out, and suggest ways to promote their decomposition.

✓ Be able to communicate and support their ideas using a model and written design specifications.

✓ Be aware of the complexity of the garbage crisis, and the potential roles of technology and citizens in solving it.

What You'll Need

Sessions 1 & 2

For each student:
- ❑ copy of "Challenge Sheet" (page 243)
- ❑ copy of "Design Specs Sheet" (page 245)
- ❑ copy of "Scoring Sheet" (optional—page 244)

Session 1

For the class:
- ❑ several non-biodegradable plastic bags
- ❑ several biodegradable plastic bags (see "Getting Ready")
- ❑ 1-liter plastic soda bottle
- ❑ 2 cups of soil
- ❑ watering device (see "Getting Ready")
- ❑ piece of a biodegradable plastic bag, approximately 13 x 20 cm

For the teacher:
- ❑ pushpin
- ❑ pair of sharp, pointed scissors
- ❑ pair of plastic gloves (optional)

Session 2

For the class:
❏ large bag of soil (see "Getting Ready")

For each group of 2–4 students:
❏ 2-liter soda bottle
❏ pair of scissors
❏ piece of a biodegradable plastic bag, approximately 13 x 20 cm
❏ cup for scooping soil

For each student:
❏ copy of "Portfolio Cover Sheet" (page 39)
❏ copy of "Group Work Evaluation" (page 42)

Vocabulary

BIODEGRADABLE - The ability to be broken down by being consumed by living things.

ENGINEER - A person who uses scientific knowledge to make products and solve problems for people.

SPECS - Short for "specifications" that provide design details.

Getting Ready

Session 1

◆ Look for biodegradable plastic trash or sandwich bags in the grocery store. Make sure that the bags you choose are biodegradable (contain an additive such as cornstarch), and not photodegradable (made with chemicals that break down when exposed to the sun's ultraviolet rays).

If you can't find biodegradable plastic bags, use paper grocery bags instead. Although paper decomposes more readily than plastic, landfill conditions inhibit its decomposition, so this lesson's challenge to improve landfills will still be appropriate.

◆ To prepare to make a model landfill for a class demonstration, cut off the top of a plastic soda bottle by piercing it with a pushpin, and then inserting sharp scissors into the hole for cutting. Set aside a few cups of soil to use for your model landfill as well.

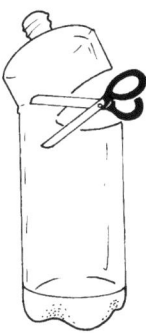

♦ For a landfill watering device, locate a watering can with a sprinkler head or a spray bottle. You can also make a sprinkler by punching holes in the metal top of a soda bottle with a pushpin.

♦ Plan student groups. Decide whether you'll have them hand in one "Design Specs Sheet" for a group grade, or individual sheets describing their group's model.

Session 2

♦ Each group will need a minimum of 3 cups of soil for its landfill. Bring in a small trash bag of outdoor soil, or have on hand a few large bags of potting soil, plus a small amount of soil from outdoors. Since potting soil may be sterile, you'll need to add outdoor soil to it to inoculate it with microbes.

Action Narrative

Session 1

We've explored how things decompose in nature. Now let's think about the trash we throw away. Does it decompose?

Students usually predict that organic trash items like food scraps will be more likely to decompose than inorganic or manufactured items like toys. Have them think about things they've thrown out in the past 24 hours, or look through the classroom wastebasket (wearing plastic gloves), to see what percentage of items they throw away are likely to decompose.

People manufacture a lot of things that aren't good food for decomposers. Plastic is one of those things. When people started getting concerned about the "garbage crisis" — too much trash and no place to put it — manufacturers decided to make BIODEGRADABLE plastic bags. What do you think biodegradable means?

The definition for biodegradable — the ability to be broken down (degraded) by being consumed by living things (bio) — should make sense to students who now understand that decomposition is a biological process.

Since not many microbes can eat plain plastic, some manufacturers started adding cornstarch to their plastic bags to make them biodegradable. Cornstarch is a powdery substance made from the sugars that corn plants produce during photosynthesis. The idea is that when cornstarch is added to plastic bags, microbes will eat the cornstarch after the bag is thrown out. Scientists are still trying to figure out if microbes eat the plastic, too. If not, maybe the bags break into tiny pieces that stay in the soil or water where they were buried.

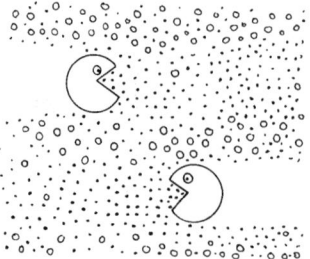

Module 2: *Decomposer Dynamics*

Pass around the biodegradable and regular plastic bags so students can see and feel how they differ.

Will It Rot or Not?

Claims that plastics biodegrade are hotly debated among scientists. In one study done at Cornell University, scientists put plastic household products labeled biodegradable (e.g., diapers, garbage bags, and magazine mailers) into "bioreactors" full of bacteria so potent that they could reduce a paper bag to carbon dioxide and water within a day. The scientists concluded that the plastic in the products did not break down into natural elements, although it may have broken into smaller pieces. The amount of mass lost was equal to the amount of cornstarch or sugar that had been added to the products. Meanwhile, some plastic companies report that their tests have shown that the actual plastics do break down into their basic elements.

So maybe manufacturers are onto something by making plastic bags out of material that microbes can use as food. But as we found out, microbes work best when their surrounding conditions, as well as their food, are just right for them to grow. Does anyone know in what conditions our trash ends up after it is thrown away?

Some students might know how trash is disposed of in your community. If not, ask them to find out and report back to the class during the next session. Typically, trash is either buried between layers of soil in a landfill, burned (and the ash buried), or dumped into the ocean or a big lake.

I'm going to make a model of a landfill to show you the conditions that many plastic bags end up in after they're thrown away. Does anyone know how a landfill is constructed?

After students have shared what they know about landfills, make a model landfill in the soda bottle you've prepared. Put about a cup of soil in the bottom, then a piece of a plastic bag, then another cup of soil on top. As you make the model, explain that landfills often start as big pits in the ground. They are sometimes lined so that nothing leaks out. Workers use dump trucks, tractors, bulldozers, and other machinery to cover new trash with soil every day. Eventually, the pit fills up with layers of trash and soil, until in some cases the landfill becomes the tallest mountain around.

What else should I do to imitate landfill conditions?

When students suggest that landfills are exposed to weather, sprinkle some water on top to simulate rain.

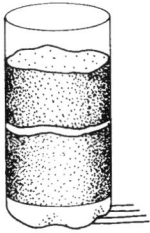

Your challenge is to become ENGINEERS to create a waste disposal system that is better at helping biodegradable plastic bags decompose than this typical landfill. You can also think of ways to alter the bag itself so it is more likely to decompose.

Make sure that students understand that engineers are people who use scientific knowledge to make products or solve problems. Discuss examples of what engineers do.

Here is a description of your challenge.

Give each student a copy of the "Challenge Sheet" and talk about the activity.

Every group will get one soda bottle and a piece of a biodegradable plastic bag. There will also be soil and water available. You may ask my permission to use other materials in the classroom or school, and you can bring things from home.

Hand out and discuss the "Design Specs Sheet," explaining that SPECS is short for "specifications". Emphasize that students might come up with ideas for conditions that are impossible to include in their classroom model. They should sketch and explain these ideas on their "Design Specs Sheet." Tell students whether you want each person to complete a sheet or if they will submit one per group.

Your disposal system design will be evaluated using several criteria.

Discuss how students' work will be scored, either by giving them a copy of the "Scoring Sheet," or by having them decide on scoring criteria.

Start talking over ideas in your groups, then tomorrow you can make your models and fill out your "Design Specs Sheet."

 If some groups don't know where to begin, suggest that they discuss why the landfill model you made might not be the best place for microbes to grow. Remind them to stay focused on what they know causes decomposition. Each time someone suggests a landfill improvement, the group should discuss how it will help make the bag decompose. Recommend that at least one person in each group take notes.

Session 2

Today you'll have time to make your biodegradable bag disposal system models and complete your "Design Specs Sheet." Near the end of the period we'll share our designs with one another.

Help students cut their bottles by using a pushpin to make a hole, then insert sharp scissors into the hole to start the cut for them. Students can finish cutting the bottle using blunt scissors.

Circulate as students make their models to get a sense of the rationale behind their designs.

Now let's share our designs with one another.

Module 2: *Decomposer Dynamics*

After each group explains its model, have students attach the "Scoring Sheet" (unless you're using other criteria) to their "Design Specs Sheet" to hand in for your review and feedback.

Conclude with a discussion of questions such as:

Would your solutions be practical for dealing with tons of trash?
Help students analyze whether their disposal systems would be effective when plastic bags are mixed in with other types of garbage. They should also consider the cost of materials and labor required to handle garbage in the ways they suggested.

Would any of the designs create new problems?
Students might suggest ideas such as leaving bags unburied could increase odors and rats.

If microbes are everywhere, why don't the biodegradable plastic bags degrade right on the grocery shelf?
Have students think about the conditions within a box of plastic bags, and compare these to the conditions they know favor growth of microbes (e.g., moisture). Even after biodegradable bags get moist and are filled with food scraps that have microbes attacking them, it takes a very long time for the microbes to consume the cornstarch in the bags to the point where the bag falls apart.

Even if the bags decompose, do they really "go away"?
The bags might disappear from sight, but the material they were made of does not disappear from existence. The tiny particles of matter that the bags were made of become part of decomposers' bodies, or enter the soil, water, or air. Matter is recycled through decomposition, not destroyed.

Some scientists are trying to create new kinds of microbes that can eat all kinds of plastic, using a technique called genetic engineering. What are the pros and cons of this work?
Students might suggest that one benefit is that the microbes could help reduce the build-up of garbage. A negative aspect is that it's hard to predict what will happen once the microbes are let loose in the environment. Also, some of the particles the microbes release from the plastic bags could harm the environment.

Is technology the only answer to the garbage crisis? What else can be done?
Have students consider the strengths and limitations of technological solutions. If students suggest that another approach would be reducing the amount of garbage entering landfills, ask them for ideas of what they personally could do to make this happen.

Students can keep their landfills in the classroom or at home to periodically check on how well the bags are decomposing.

Ongoing Assessment

Student Reflections

Have students fill out a "Group Work Evaluation" (page 42) to reflect on their group process. They could also fill out a "Scoring Sheet" for their group's disposal system model. This is also a good time to have them select work samples for a portfolio, and complete a "Portfolio Cover Sheet" (page 39). Review the purpose and structure of a portfolio, and set a due date.

Teacher Reflections

The main thing to look for in each "Design Specs Sheet" is evidence that students understand that: 1) microbes cause decomposition; 2) microbes grow best on materials that are easy to digest and provide lots of nutrients and energy; and 3) conditions such as warmth and moisture promote growth of microbes.

Examples of conditions students might have included in their models to favor decomposition are:

   adding additional microbes;

   adding sugar, protein, or nutrients to or around the bag;

   adding moisture (but not too much water);

   exposing decomposing bags to oxygen that most microbes need;

   supplying warmth;

   cutting the bag into smaller pieces so there is more surface area for microbes to attack; or

   adding invertebrate decomposers.

When explaining how they could know if their system works better than a typical landfill, students might suggest:

   comparing their results with research data about how long it takes things to decompose in a real landfill;

   assessing the bag's strength, weight, or transparency before and after being in the landfill;

   seeing if the bag is intact or in pieces;

   looking at the bag under a microscope to see if microbes are growing on it; or

   using the bag in the demonstration model landfill as a comparison.

Module 2: *Decomposer Dynamics*

NAME(S)_____ DATE_____

THE BAG THAT WOULDN'T GO AWAY

Do biodegradable plastic bags decompose? Some people don't think they do, especially in the landfills or large bodies of water where they usually end up.

YOUR CHALLENGE:

Design a disposal system that you think will give biodegradable plastic bags the best possible chance of decomposing. You can change the conditions of the place where the bag ends up, and/or change the bag itself. Make a model of your system, and complete the "Design Specs Sheet."

SCORING:

You will be scored on how well you put your knowledge of decomposition to use in your design, not on how well the bag decomposes — that would take too long!

GOOD LUCK!

NAME(S)_____ DATE_____

THE BAG THAT WOULDN'T GO AWAY

OBJECTIVES	POINTS				SCORE
	3 High Quality	**2** Meets Objectives	**1** Falls Short	**0** Not Done	
APPLICATION OF KNOWLEDGE					
1. Shows understanding of what causes decomposition.	_____	_____	_____	_____	___ x 2 =___
2. Shows understanding of physical conditions that favor microbe growth.	_____	_____	_____	_____	___ x 2 =___
3. Has ideas of how to judge the success of the design.	_____	_____	_____	_____	=___
CREATIVE THINKING					
4. Designed a clever, inventive solution.	_____	_____	_____	_____	=___
DOCUMENTATION/ COMMUNICATION					
5. Labeled drawing accurately to reflect entire design.	_____	_____	_____	_____	=___
6. Wrote a complete list of what was done.	_____	_____	_____	_____	=___
7. Thoroughly explains reasons for each action.	_____	_____	_____	_____	=___

COMMENTS:

FINAL SCORE: _____

Total Possible Score: 27
Overall Achievement:
23–27 High
18–22 Sound
9–17 Limited
0–8 Inadequate

    Module 2: *Decomposer Dynamics*

DESIGN SPECS SHEET

1 Draw your biodegradable bag disposal system in the box below. Label everything you used or would like to use.

2 List everything you did to make a better disposal system, and explain why. Be sure that what you write shows how much you understand about decomposition.

What You Did:_____   Why: _____

_____   _____

_____   _____

_____   _____

_____   _____

3 Explain how you could know if your system works better than a typical landfill:

_____

_____

2.7 A Jury's Dilemma—
Written Assessment

Action Synopsis

Students analyze a trial involving a dispute about a composting business, then outline how a Special Investigator could gather evidence to help settle the case.

One Session		1 hour
1. Present the challenge of a court case about composting.		*posing a challenge*
2. Discuss criteria for high quality work.		*setting standards*
3. Generate ideas about the case in groups, then work independently to write detailed opinions about the case.		*applying knowledge*
4. Share and discuss completed work.		*communicating*
5. Summarize and discuss ways to solve the case.		*reflecting*

Module 2: *Decomposer Dynamics*

Desired Outcomes

By the end of this assessment activity, students should:

✓ Show that they can think broadly and accurately about factors that influence the biological process of decomposition.

✓ Be better able to explain and justify their ideas.

✓ Realize how scientific knowledge can be used in everyday life.

What You'll Need

For each student:
- ❑ copy of "Challenge Sheet" (page 251)
- ❑ copy of "Scoring Sheet" (page 252)

Getting Ready

♦ Plan groups of 3–4 students.

Action Narrative

Today we're going to read a court case that requires knowledge about decomposition before it can be settled.

Give each student a copy of the "Challenge Sheet." Make sure that students know what a plaintiff and a defendant are, then read the dilemma aloud. Have students summarize the two sides of the argument to make sure that they've picked up on all of the details.

Since you are specialists in decomposition, the jury needs your help. What is your challenge?

After students have summarized their challenge, explain that they'll work in groups at first, because talking with others is a good way to generate ideas. Then they'll have a chance to demonstrate individually that they can solve a problem by applying knowledge about decomposition and research methods. Emphasize that when students outline tasks for the Special Investigator, they should suggest possible experiments to do, as well as observations to make.

What do you think I should look for when I score your responses?

Have students think through what knowledge and skills this assessment is asking them to demonstrate. Hand out the "Scoring Sheet," and revise or enhance it as needed to reflect what you and the class feel are important elements of the challenge.

Go ahead and begin working in your groups. After you've jotted down all of the ideas everyone can think of, work alone to complete the assignment.

Listen in as students generate ideas. Once they start working on their own, make sure they're pushing themselves to write down everything they can think of that a Special Investigator could do. Many students tend to stop writing after they've described what came to mind first.

Let's hear your ideas.

After students have completed their work, have volunteers describe the one reason for the slow decomposition that made the most sense to them, and the tasks they outlined for the Special Investigator. Encourage other students to react to and build on their ideas.

 *An alternative way to share their work which students enjoy is to set up a mock trial, with students playing roles of plaintiff, defendant, witnesses, special investigator, judge, and jury. This takes one or two additional periods.*

 Conclude the activity with questions such as:

If you were on the jury, what evidence would make you vote in favor of Bud?
    Students might cite evidence such as: the Special Investigator discovered that Leaf Busters' leaves in the city don't really turn into compost faster; or Leaf Busters isn't treating its compost pile at Bud's the same way it treats its compost in the city; or the leaves in the two locations are different kinds.

What would make you vote in favor of Leaf Busters?
    Some reasons students might give are: the Special Investigator found out that Leaf Busters was treating the compost at Bud's the same as it treated the compost

Module 2: *Decomposer Dynamics*

in the city; or the compost pile on Bud's land was being sabotaged (e.g., with chemicals that killed microbes or by drying it).

How could they settle the problem?

Students might suggest ways to speed up the decomposition process (e.g., turning the pile to aerate it; keeping it moist, but not soaked; adding more microbes; adding food that is higher in nutrients and energy) so that the compost can be sold and profits shared more quickly.

Have students hand in their group brainstorm list with everyone's names on it, as well as their individual work with a "Scoring Sheet" attached for your feedback.

Ongoing Assessment

Student Reflections

Have students fill out a "Scoring Sheet" to assess their own work.

Teacher Reflections

Groups might list some of the following reasons why leaves turned into compost more slowly at Bud's than at Leaf Busters' city location:

it's usually a few degrees warmer in the city, which would favor microbe growth;

there might be more kinds of leaves in the city pile that are tender and easier for microbes to consume;

perhaps there is more air, soil, and water pollution in the city that somehow weakens the leaves, making them easier for microbes to break down;

maybe pollution adds something to the leaves that makes them more nutritious for microbes;

maybe the leaves in the city get trampled on more before Leaf Busters collects them, so they are in smaller pieces that give microbes more surface area;

maybe there are more microbes or invertebrate decomposers in the city;

maybe Leaf Busters does things to the city compost pile to speed up decomposition, like keeping it moist, turning it, adding microbes, or adding food that is higher in nutrients and energy; or

maybe Bud is sabotaging the compost pile on his land, by adding chemicals to kill the microbes, soaking it, or drying it out.

In selecting a reason, students should make a strong case for why that factor is the most likely cause of slower decomposition. There is no one best reason to explain why decomposition is slower at Bud's than in the city, so the strength of students' responses depends on the understanding of decomposition they exhibit.

Some observations which students might suggest the Special Investigator could do include:

determining how long the leaves have been in each pile, and how decomposed each pile is;

measuring or looking up the average air temperature and rainfall at each site;

using a moisture meter to see how moist each compost pile is;

seeing what kinds of leaves are in the piles in the two sites;

seeing what shape the leaves are in when they first go into the two piles;

looking for invertebrate decomposers, fungal hyphae, bacterial colonies (under a microscope), and odors that indicate decomposition;

looking for chemical residues, or evidence of other tampering in either pile; or

interviewing employees of Bud's Wonderland and Leaf Busters, Inc. to see if they've observed anything unusual happening with either of the two piles.

Some experiments which students might suggest the Special Investigator could do include:

taking newly fallen leaves from the city and putting them in a pile on Bud's land, and taking newly fallen leaves from Bud's region and putting them in the city, to see if the leaves themselves decompose differently;

doing things to the leaf pile at Bud's to make the conditions exactly the same as those for the pile in the city (e.g., making it warmer), then comparing the two piles; or

making two piles of leaves at Bud's, keeping one the same as the current leaf pile and doing things (e.g., turning the leaves, adding water) to the other pile to see if Leaf Busters could do anything to speed up the decomposition rate.

NAME(S)_____ DATE_____

A JURY'S DILEMMA

THE PLAINTIFF'S STORY: BUD'S WONDERLAND

Bud, the owner of Bud's Wonderland, entered into a deal with Leaf Busters, Inc. Bud told Leaf Busters it could use land next to his amusement park out in the country for five years to keep the leaves that people pay the company to collect from their yards. Instead of paying rent on the land, Leaf Busters agreed to give Bud half of the profits it made from selling leaf compost to gardeners.

Bud brought Leaf Busters to court because a year has gone by and no profits have come in. Bud says Leaf Busters is guilty of fraud by claiming that leaves naturally turn into compost that can be sold. He also claims the company is guilty of negligence by not doing all it can to help the leaves decompose. Bud wants to throw Leaf Busters off his land, and make the company pay to have its tons of leaves hauled away.

THE DEFENDANT'S STORY: LEAF BUSTERS, INC.

Leaf Busters argues that it isn't guilty of fraud. The company says it expected the leaves to turn into compost faster than they have, because at its other business site located in the city the leaves decompose quickly.

In fact, Leaf Busters thinks it should sue Bud! The company claims that he is sabotaging the compost pile by making the conditions unsuitable for decomposition. Leaf Busters believes the real reason Bud wants to break the agreement is so that he can put a miniature golf course on the land and make more money.

YOUR GROUP'S CHALLENGE:

Make a list of the possible reasons why Leaf Busters' leaves are turning into compost more slowly on Bud's land than at the company's other location in the city.

YOUR CHALLENGE:

Choose one reason, and explain why it makes the most sense to you.

Describe what a Special Investigator could do to figure out if the reason you chose is correct. Remember, to help the jury solve its dilemma, the Special Investigator's research needs to be detailed and fair.

GOOD LUCK!

NAME(S)_____ DATE_____

A JURY'S DILEMMA

OBJECTIVES	POINTS				SCORE
	3 High Quality	**2** Meets Objectives	**1** Falls Short	**0** Not Done	
LIST OF POSSIBLE REASONS 1. Includes a wide variety of reasons, both environmental and human-caused.	_____	_____	_____	_____	___ x 2 =___
2. Shows understanding of what causes decomposition.	_____	_____	_____	_____	___ x 2 =___
EXPLANATION OF ONE REASON 3. Selects a reason that makes sense.	_____	_____	_____	_____	=___
4. Shows understanding of decomposition processes.	_____	_____	_____	_____	=___
SPECIAL INVESTIGATOR TASKS 5. Includes things to do at both compost sites.	_____	_____	_____	_____	=___
6. Suggests relevant observations.	_____	_____	_____	_____	=___
7. Includes a fair test or experiment Special Investigator could do.	_____	_____	_____	_____	=___

COMMENTS:

FINAL SCORE: _____

Total Possible Score: 27
Overall Achievement:
   23–27 High
   18–22 Sound
   9–17 Limited
   0–8 Inadequate

      Module 2: *Decomposer Dynamics*

Cycles—From Rot to Radishes

Module 3

CYCLES—FROM ROT TO RADISHES

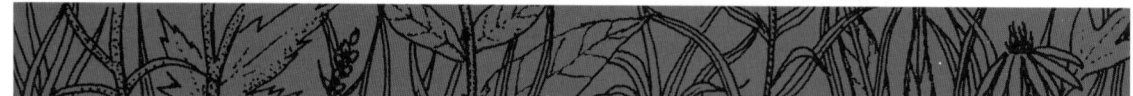

Envisioning the Invisible

Imagine that you have the ability to see particles so tiny that they elude even the most powerful microscopes. Suddenly, the room is full of movement. You watch oxygen and carbon dioxide molecules flowing in and out of people, pets, and plants. You glance out the window and see streams of atoms and molecules going from dead plants to microbes, from microbes to soil and air, from soil and air to living plants, and from plants to animals and air.

The particles you're watching are nutrients, particular kinds of atoms and molecules that enable living things to grow and function. Their pathways back and forth between living things and the physical environment are called nutrient cycles. These cycles are driven largely by biological processes, such as eating, respiring, and decomposing.

Even though (imaginations not withstanding) none of us can see nutrient cycles on a molecular level, it is possible to observe evidence of cycling. During this module students look for such evidence by comparing the growth of plants with and without the addition of compost tea. Through their investigations and discussions, students learn that all living things are made of the same basic building blocks—nutrients; that decomposers release these nutrients from dead organisms into the environment; and that living plants take up the nutrients and build them into their tissues.

Overview of Students' Learning Experiences

This module builds on the knowledge about decomposition that students developed during Module 2, or through other prior experiences (see "Make compost," page 256). Its central investigation helps students answer the question *Where does the stuff living things are made of go after those organisms die?* Throughout the module, students grapple with the notion that matter is neither created nor destroyed, but that it takes different forms as it cycles—as part of a living thing at one point in time, then as part of the non-living environment at another.

Along with helping students develop a fundamental understanding of nutrient cycling, this module provides the opportunity for the class to function as a scientific community. Groups of students co-plan an experiment, then give feedback on other groups' plans using a peer review process. Discussions throughout their experiment help students realize that they create their own knowldege through action and reflection. If their results end up not showing clear evidence of nutrient cycling, which can often happen when students are given the freedom to design and run their own experiments, then the whole experience becomes even more thought-provoking. Students are challenged, just as scientists are, to figure out what factors could have been responsible for their outcomes.

Finally, this module provides real-world contexts for students' learning. Their experiment is motivated by a request for knowledge about using dead plants as fertilizer from a company called Green Resources of the World, Unlimited.

Students also extend and apply their nutrient cycling concepts by exploring soil, leaf litter, and living plants in a familiar outdoor setting. Through assessment tasks, students recommend where a community club should plant shrubs, develop advertising campaigns to teach the public about research and nutrient cycling, and review the qualities of three scientists to decide whom they would hire.

Module 3 Overview Chart

CYCLES: FROM ROT TO RADISHES		
Mode	**Lesson Title**	**Activities**
Activating Ideas	**3.1** A Challenge from GROW	**Day 1:** Students receive a letter from Green Resources of the World, Unlimited (GROW) asking them to test a claim that dead plants can be used as a fertilizer for garden plants.
Investigating	**3.2** Plans and Peer Reviews	**Days 2–3:** Groups write research proposals, and exchange them for peer review. The whole class finalizes its research strategy for GROW.
	3.3 Up and Running	**Days 4–5:** Research groups set up experiments.
		Days 6–26: Students water, treat, measure, and observe their plants, and keep records of developments.
	3.4 Exploring Plant and Soil Connections	Three sessions during **Days 6–26:** Students hear about the work of scientists who study how soil and decomposing plants affect living plants in an ecosystem, then go outside to compare soil and plants in different areas.
	3.5 Planting Preferences— Written Assessment	One session during **Days 6–26:** Groups review the descriptions of four sites and rank them according to their suitability for planting shrubs.
Processing for Understanding	**3.6** Radish Results	**Days 27–28:** Groups summarize and share compost tea experiment data, then the class discusses trends and conclusions.
Applying and Assessing	**3.7** GROW Gets an Answer— Performance Assessment	**Days 29–31:** Students develop creative ways to share what they've learned with GROW, and produce fact-based promotional materials that highlight GROW's research and products.
	3.8 Hiring a Scientist— Written Assessment	**Day 32:** Students evaluate the job applications of three scientists, then decide whom they would hire and why.

Planning Ahead

SCHEDULE THE MODULE Try to schedule the module so that the three-week period during which students grow plants (Lesson 3.3) does not include a school vacation. Also, if you don't plan to use supplementary grow lights, it's best to do this module in early fall or late spring when the plants will get more hours of sunlight.

MAKE COMPOST If your class hasn't done Module 2, you'll need to make compost before beginning this module. You can accomplish this either by spending about a week doing Lesson 2.5, or by setting up a decomposition chamber as a class demonstration using alfalfa hay, hardwood shavings, and water (see pages 225–227). The plant material needs about three weeks to turn into usable compost. Since students don't begin using compost tea until after the cotyledons of their seedlings have unfurled (about 12 days into the module), you can begin Lesson 3.1 about a week after setting up the decomposition chamber.

CREATE A COMPANY IN THE CLASSROOM If you haven't already established a classroom research company, consider doing so for this module (see "The Company Option," pages 15–16). The company creates an ideal real-world context for doing research, and for completing the module's three assessment activities.

REVIEW VOCABULARY Many of the vocabulary words that were introduced and defined in Modules 1 and 2 are used in Module 3 (e.g., *ecosystem, producer, consumer, decomposer, microbe, nutrient*). If your students haven't experienced the preceding modules, you might want to review these vocabulary words before beginning this module, and/or spend more time on the terms during lessons (see Appendix pages 390–392 for a list of vocabulary definitions).

CHOOSE AN OUTDOOR STUDY SITE Most of this module is done indoors, but Lesson 3.4 provides an opportunity for students to connect the cycling they're studying in the classroom to a local ecosystem. As in previous modules, taking students to a familiar, everyday setting, such as the schoolyard or a neighborhood park, helps them realize that ecological processes are at work all around them. You don't need a large area for the outdoor study, but the site should include some diversity, such as soil with and without plants growing. This will allow students to compare soils in places with different features. You'll need to get permission from landowners for students to dig soil samples, which could result in uprooting plants.

GATHER MATERIALS A list of materials used in this module is provided in the Appendix (pages 388–389). Both recommended and alternative materials are included when possible, to make it easy for you to obtain what's needed.

COLLECT RESOURCE BOOKS Both stories about growing plants and factual references on nutrient cycling will enhance students' learning during this module. See the following resource list of suggested titles for both you and your students.

Resource List

For Teachers ∎∎∎∎∎∎∎∎∎

REFERENCES AND BACKGROUND READING

Earth: The Stuff of Life
by F. Bear, H. Pritchard, and W. Akin (University of Oklahoma Press, 1986)

A lengthy but readable book on how soil influences plant growth. It covers what soil is made of; different soil types of the U.S.; how air and rain affect the soil and plant growth; and the connection between nutrients in soil, and plant and animal nutrient requirements.

Plant Ecology: Plants, the Soil and Man
by M. Staefelt (William Clowes, 1972)

Focuses on the relationship between plants and their environment. Includes several in-depth chapters on decomposition and nutrient cycling.

For Students ∎∎∎∎∎∎∎∎∎∎

SCIENCE BOOKS

Death is Natural
by L. Pringle (Morrow Junior Books, 1977)

This book portrays death as a natural part of life. The first chapter follows the journeys of atoms released from a dead rabbit, revealing that matter is not destroyed when something dies or is eaten—it cycles back and forth between living and non-living things. Other chapters address population fluctuations and species extinctions.

Flowers, Trees and Other Plants
by A. Royston (Franklin Watts, 1991)

This question-and-answer book provides a basic introduction to plants. Each page is packed with facts and beautiful color illustrations that make complex processes such as photosynthesis, respiration, and reproduction understandable. Activity suggestions and a glossary are also included.

Linnea's Windowsill Garden
by C. Bjork (R&S Books/Farrar, Straus & Giroux, 1988)

Linnea describes everything from seeds to cuttings to potted plants in her indoor garden. Through friendly narration this book gives information on caring for plants throughout their life cycles, and invites readers to try the activities and games.

STORIES

Promise of the Faraway Flower
by T. Parks (Kendall/Hunt, 1993)

Erin, a sixth grade budding botanist, plants a mysterious seed that came from the rain forest via her uncle's muddy clothes. She nurtures the seed for her science fair project, using compost and testing a range of growing conditions. Although her project doesn't win a science fair prize, her plant eventually creates a stir among scientists, who find that she's discovered a new genus and species from the rapidly diminishing rain forest.

Top Secret
by J. Gardiner (Little, Brown, 1984)

A determined fourth grader investigates human photosynthesis for his science fair project. Despite discouragement and skepticism from adults, Alan begins to turn himself into a plant, and in the process includes his overbearing science teacher in his experiment.

3.1 A Challenge from GROW

Action Synopsis

Students observe soil samples, talk about where soil nutrients come from, receive a letter from a company that wants to know if dead plants can be used as fertilizer, then develop research questions.

One Session		**1 hour**	
1. Discuss what plants need to grow.			*examining prior ideas*
2. Examine soil samples to decide which would be best for plant growth, and jot down observations and ideas.			*observing & recording*
3. Talk about plants' needs for nutrients, and nutrient cycling.			*introducing new information*
4. Read a letter from a company requesting research on the potential for using dead plants as fertilizer.			*linking to real world*
5. Write and discuss research questions.			*developing research questions*

Desired Outcomes

Throughout the lesson, check that students:

✓ Understand that nutrients are the invisible building blocks that make up all living things.

✓ Know that all living things need nutrients to grow and stay healthy.

✓ Have ideas about where nutrients in soil come from.

✓ Can form a research question.

What You'll Need

For the class:
❑ houseplant

For each group of 3–4 students:
❑ small clear bag or container of poor soil, such as sand or clay (see "Getting Ready")
❑ small clear bag or container of good potting or garden soil (see "Getting Ready")

For each student:
❑ copy of the letter from GROW (page 267)

Vocabulary

NUTRIENT CYCLE - The transfer of nutrients back and forth between living things and the non-living environment (soil, water, and air).

Getting Ready

◆ Students need to be familiar with compost before this lesson, and will need compost for this module's central experiment. If you haven't done Module 2, see "Planning Ahead" on page 256 for information on setting up compost in the classroom.

◆ Decide on groups of 3–4 students.

◆ Before photocopying the letter from GROW for each student, make one copy of the original. Personalize the letter by typing the class research company name (optional, see pages 15–16), and the school's address in the space provided above the salutation.

◆ Put a few tablespoons of the two types of soil in separate bags or containers for each group. You can get rich soil from a garden, woods, or a landscaped area, or purchase potting soil. If you use potting soil, mix in some compost or decomposed plants you find outdoors to give students clues about where soil nutrients come from. You can find poor soil that has little organic matter in places such as driveways or parking lots, or you can purchase sand. Label each of the bags of poor soil "A," and each of the bags of rich soil "B."

Action Narrative

During the next few weeks, we'll be experimenting with plants to learn how they get what they need in an ecosystem. What do you already know about what plants like this one need to grow?

Show students a houseplant, then make a class list of their ideas.

<u>What Plants Need to Grow</u>

Sunlight

Air

Water

Soil

I have some soil samples for you to look at. Talk with your group about which soil would be better for growing plants and why.

Assign students to groups, and give each a sample of both kinds of soil. Suggest that they appoint a recorder to jot down their observations, choice, and reasons. They'll need about 5 minutes.

 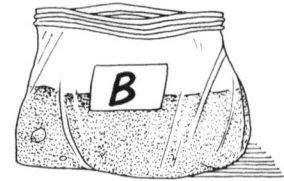

If you are in an arid region where plants such as cacti grow in sandy soil, you might want to have students think about garden plants rather than native plants for this exercise. But if you prefer to have them consider native plants, you can have an interesting discussion about the two resources plants take in through their roots: water and nutrients. Explain that some plants are more suited to growing in sand because they need well-drained soil. The trade-off is that they get fewer nutrients from sand than they would from soil that contains more organic matter and also holds more water.

Let's hear what you think.

Ask which groups chose soil A and which chose soil B, then ask for their reasons. Most students will choose the soil that looks richer. Their reasons could include: it's darker, it's more like a garden, it's easier to grow roots in, it's fluffier, it will give them better "food," it has more good stuff in it, it will hold more water, etc.

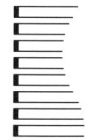 *If your students' comments reveal naive ideas about soil being food for plants, you might want to take time during this module to review photosynthesis. See pages 119–121 for more information.*

You've mentioned a lot of different reasons why some soil is better for plants. We're going to focus on one of those reasons— that plants need to get nutrients from soil. Plants need nutrients—invisible mineral particles —for the same reasons that people do: the bodies of every living thing are made of tiny nutrient particles. Also, we need nutrients to grow and stay healthy. Do you have any ideas about where the nutrients that plants get from soil come from?

Have students look at the soil sample they decided was better for plants. Ask them to look for clues about where the many invisible nutrients in it might have come from. They will most likely say that the nutrients came from weathered rocks, and from plants and animals that have decomposed, which is true. (In addition, air is a source of some soil nutrients, such as nitrogen, but the complexities of nutrient cycles that occur partially in the air won't be addressed in this module.)

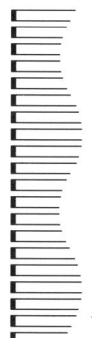 *Discussing where plants get nutrients will help you begin to assess students' prior ideas about nutrient cycling. Their ideas will continue to surface during later activities, which will provide opportunities for you to help them confront and revise their naive notions. A key realization that students should develop is that unlike animals, plants (with a few exceptions, such as Venus flytraps) can't digest living or dead plants or animals. Plants need to take up particles that have already been broken down ("pre-digested") by decomposers. See the passage below for information on some of the ideas and confusion your students might reveal about nutrient cycling as the module progresses.*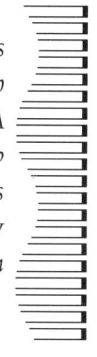

Children's Ideas About Nutrient Cycling

Many children have an intuitive idea that dead plants make soil better for living plants, but their understanding of how this happens can be quite vague. Consider this interchange between two sixth-grade boys:

David: *Like when a plant falls down, it's dead, the dirt covers it. So then it connects to the root of a tree and helps the tree get bigger.*

Luis: *It makes the tree healthier, grow. The dead plant still helps.*

David: *It's like it's not dead, it still lives.*

These boys don't mention that decomposers break down dead plants, nor do they seem to have any idea that decomposition releases nutrients from dead plants, that in turn become part of living plants. They imagine a dead plant connecting to the root of a living plant, but do not yet have concepts and images necessary to explain what happens on an invisible level.

Understanding nutrient cycling requires being able to imagine and accept that all matter is made of particles that are so tiny that they're impossible to see, even with the most powerful microscopes. These particles—atoms and molecules—are the building blocks of all living and non-living things. Some of these building blocks, such as nitrogen, phosphorus, carbon, and potassium, are called nutrients because they're essential to all life. Nutrients cycle back and forth between non-living substances and organisms' bodies.

Children have a difficult enough time accepting the basic principle of the particulate nature of matter, but can find it especially unbelievable that both living and non-living things are made of the same basic "stuff." Here is an example of one fifth- grade girl grappling with this notion at two different points in time:

> How can something alive be made of atoms and molecules? "Made of" makes it sound like someone made it, and plants, they just grow, nobody makes them out of anything.

> I thought before atoms and molecules were only in non-living things. But I saw a book with pictures of circles and stuff, atoms and molecules, and next to them there were children jumping. But children are living. So then I said, atoms and molecules can't be in non-living things if they're in living things like children.

Because this girl imagines that living and non-living things must be made of fundamentally different substances, she would have a hard time accepting that the same particles that make up the non-living environment actually become part of living things, and vice versa. Even though it would be helpful for her to know that all matter is made of the same basic building blocks before she studies nutrient cycling, it is also possible that first-hand investigations and discussions about cycling could help her develop the concept of the particulate nature of matter.

Another confusing nutrient cycling issue for children can be the distinction between microbes and nutrients. Since both microbes and nutrients are invisible parts of compost, children sometimes think that microbes fertilize plants, rather than the nutrients that microbes release. Hopefully if students have cultured microbe colonies during Module 2, they will understand that microbes are living things. The exact nature of nutrients may be less clear, however, as it is for this sixth-grade boy:

> Hold it, are nutrients living or non-living? I'd like to know, I'm not sure. How can they help plants if they're dead?

His use of the word "help" when explaining what nutrients do for plants is revealing. Children tend to think of nutrients as assisting in a process of keeping an organism alive and making it healthy, but are unaware that nutrients also make up the tissues of living things. Students' understanding needs to be expanded to include a structural, as well as a functional, role for nutrients.

Many challenging subconcepts, such as the particulate nature of matter, conservation of matter, the cause of decay, the nature of growth, and even photosynthesis and respiration, make nutrient cycling a particularly complex concept for children to grasp fully. It's essential to give students the opportunity to explain and work through their ideas as they do nutrient cycling investigations. This will help them develop a basic mental model of nutrient cycling. When they take biology and chemistry courses in high school they'll be able to add more abstract details to this basic framework. The following explanation of nutrient cycling by a sixth-grade Eco-Inquiry student illustrates a solid, basic level of understanding:

> *Let's say you bury a dead pig. Decomposers like microbes, mushrooms, worms, and ants eat it up, break it down, and put nutrients back into the soil. Then plants take the nutrients up and we eat the plants. Or the plants die and decompose. The others around them are happy and living while they're getting rotten. Then the living plants have offspring, then those have babies, then maybe in like, a million years, the nutrients will all still be going.*

When we observed our decomposition chamber, we talked about what could be happening to the matter that the dead plants were made of. Do you remember any of our ideas?

Have students review their thoughts about the fate of dead plant matter that emerged during the discussion suggested on page 218, and compare these with the ideas they've just offered about where soil nutrients come from.

Every living thing is made of invisible nutrients. When nutrients go from the non-living environment—the soil, air, or water—to being part of living things, and then back to the non-living environment, this is called a NUTRIENT CYCLE. Nutrients go back and forth between non-living substances and living things over and over and over.

Students don't need to absorb or completely understand this definition of nutrient cycling yet since they'll have a chance to work through the concept as they do their upcoming experiment. If, however, you feel they would benefit from more elaboration on the concept at this point, you could draw an explanatory diagram such as:

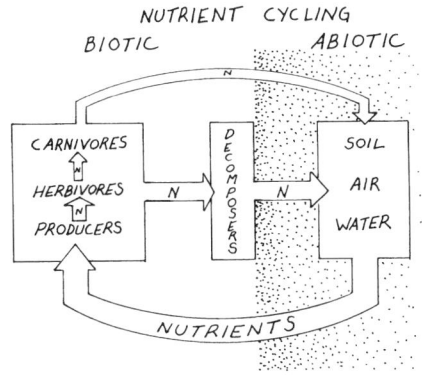

NOTE: Some nutrients leak, leach, or are released as wastes from plants and animals, and enter into the abiotic environment without passing through decomposers.

This diagram simplifies nutrient pathways (e.g., some animals eat decomposers but there is not an arrow from decomposers to carnivores). It also does not include oxygen, carbon dioxide, or water cycles.

We've received a letter from a company that wants you to help them figure out if dead plants can be used as fertilizer for living plants. This will give us a chance to try to complete a whole nutrient cycle right here in the classroom.

Hand out and go over the letter from GROW. The ideas for advertisements mentioned in the letter will be the basis for students' final performance assessment, so you don't need to explain this aspect of the challenge yet. Tell students they'll come back to it after they've fulfilled GROW's first request—doing research on the effects of decomposed plants on the growth of living plants.

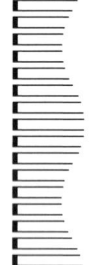 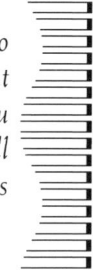

Students will ask whether the GROW company really exists. Play up the simulation to whatever extent you feel is appropriate. Students usually know that GROW isn't real, but depending on the personality and maturity of the group, they sometimes enjoy having you play along as though GROW is an actual company. Another approach would be to tell students that this is a simulation of the kind of work scientists are asked to do as consultants or when they are employed in industry.

Scientists always begin their investigations with a question. Take a minute to put GROW's request into the form of a research question. Use your journal to help you think. Write and revise a question until you have it in a form that tells others what kind of comparison you want to make.

If students didn't get practice forming research questions by doing Module 2, give them examples of an explicit and a vague research question and have them tell you how they differ. For instance, *Will a bean plant grow taller after one month in potting soil than in sand?* is a more helpful question for guiding research than *Is potting soil or sand better for plants?* Using these examples, students can generate a few criteria for a good research question.

Have students work on their own to write a question. If they aren't accustomed to using writing as a tool for clarifying thoughts, encourage them to get a phrase down on paper and then add to, delete, or change the words to make their research question more specific.

Let's hear the questions you wrote.

Write the first few questions on the board. As a class, refine the wording until you have a question that students feel reflects GROW's request the best.

Do plants watered with compost tea grow taller than plants watered with plain water?

Are there any other related questions you're interested in studying?

Some students might want to study the effects of compost tea (nutrients dissolve in water before plant is watered), while others might be interested in testing the effects of compost as a soil additive (nutrients dissolve in water as plant is watered). They might also have ideas for testing different types of compost or dead leaves collected from outdoors, using composts at different stages of decay, using different strengths of compost tea, comparing plant growth with compost tea versus commercial fertilizer, or testing compost's effects on different types of plants.

Decide with the class whether all groups should study the same question or if they prefer to do a variety of studies for GROW. If everyone does the same study, students will have a lot of replicates of the experiment, giving them more confidence in their results. Also, the whole class can have discussions focused on the same issues. One possibility is to have each research team set up the same basic experiment, and then have those who are interested do a sideline experiment as well.

For homework, write down ideas of ways to set up an experiment to test our question. Tomorrow you'll share your ideas with your group and then work together on a "Research Proposal."

Ongoing Assessment

Student Reflections

Have students send a C-Mail message or record thoughts in their journals. Optional writing prompts include:

If I was a plant root that could think and talk, what would I say about living in the two types of soil we looked at?

Where does my body get nutrients and what does it use them for?

Working for GROW is going to be _____ because...

Teacher Reflections

❑ Are students aware of what plants need to grow?

❑ How much intuitive sense did they already have that nutrients in soil come partly from dead plants that decomposers have broken down?

❑ How successful were they at using the process of writing to develop a research question?

❑ Which of the possible research topics seems to intrigue them the most?

Extensions

Concept Maps. Introduce concept mapping to students if they are not already familiar with the process (see pages 25–27). Select all or some of the concept map cards on pages 43–44, then photocopy one set of cards for each group of 3–4 students. Have them construct concept maps that display their ideas about nutrient cycling. Ask them to save their concept maps so that they can compare them to maps they'll make as an extension to Lesson 3.6.

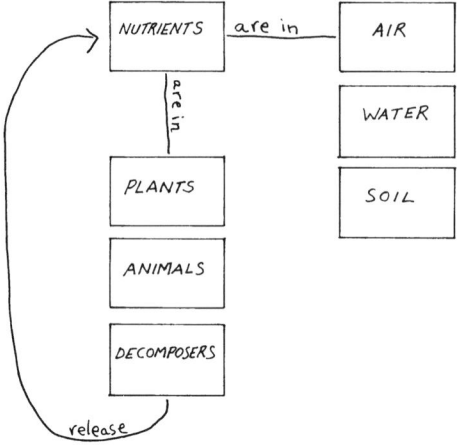

Soil Organic Matter Test. Have students put the two soil samples they examined in two small jars of water and shake them. Then let the jars sit undisturbed. After 20–30 minutes the sample will have separated into layers according to the density of different soil particles. Soil that contains organic matter will show a dark layer of these particles floating on or just below the water surface. Below these will be clay particles suspended in the water, making it cloudy. On the bottom of the jar there will be a profile of particles: silt on top, then fine sand, coarse sand, gravel, and finally pebbles on the very bottom. Students can add a pinch of alum (an inexpensive powder available at pharmacies) before they shake the jars to promote a more marked separation of organic matter and heavier minerals.

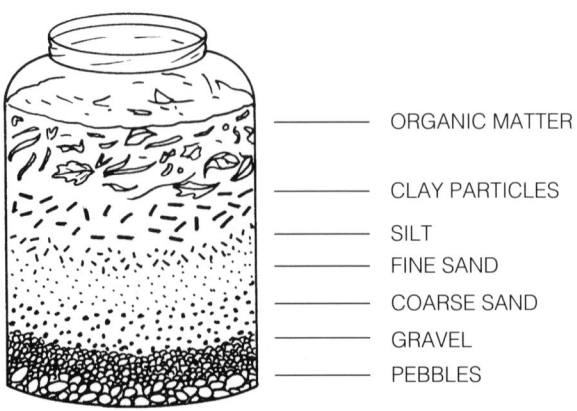

Green Recources of the World, Unlimited

Dear Researchers,

GROW is a company that makes and sells products to help people grow healthy plants. Our latest idea is to sell fertilizer made from dead plants. Our problem is that we aren't completely sure if dead plants make good fertilizer.

Since we don't have any scientists on our staff, we'd like you to do some research for us. Could you figure out if decomposed plants help living plants grow? People like to use liquid fertilizer. So, we'd like to see if "compost tea," made from decomposed plants soaked in water, can be used as a fertilizer.

After you finish your experiments, we'd also like your ideas for advertisements we could do to tell the public about your research and the products we develop from it. We'd also like the ads to teach people about nature's way of recycling nutrients.

I hope you'll help us out. All of us at GROW are eager to hear your results.

Thank you!

Sincerely,

Mary Gold
President

3.2 Plans and Peer Reviews

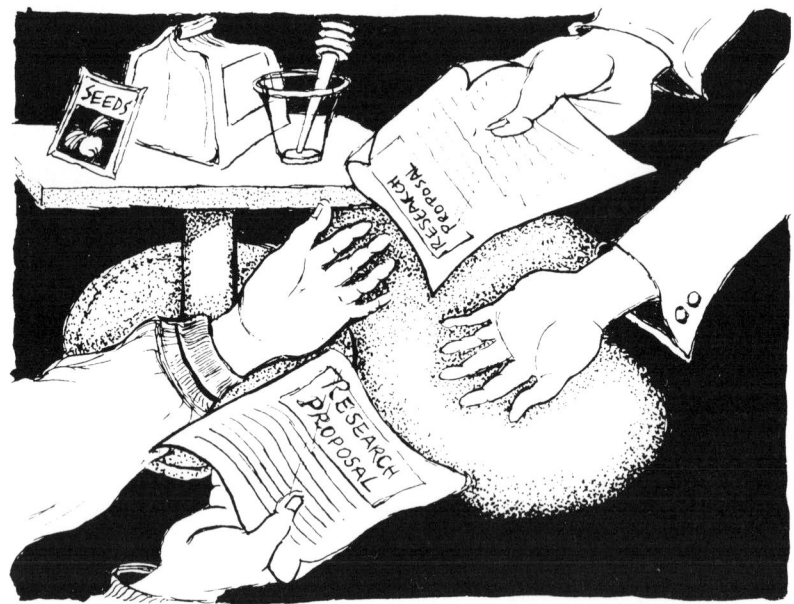

Action Synopsis

Students work in groups to design a fair test that will yield information for GROW, then review one another's plans and decide on a final design.

Session 1		40 minutes
1. Go over the research proposal and peer review process.		*familiarizing*
2. Work in groups on research proposals.		*designing experiments*
3. Exchange proposals to begin peer reviews.	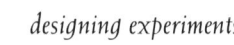	*applying knowledge*

Session 2		40 minutes
1. Complete and discuss peer reviews in groups.		*communicating*
2. Decide as a class on experiment procedures.		*designing experiments*
3. Discuss predictions.		*examining prior ideas*

Desired Outcomes

Throughout the lesson, check that students:

✓ Can design a fair test to answer a research question.

✓ Can give constructive feedback on experimental design to their peers.

✓ Have ideas about what indicators of plant health could be useful to measure and observe.

What You'll Need

Sessions 1 & 2

For the class:
- ❏ samples of experiment materials:
  - packet of radish seeds
  - 4 6-oz. clear plastic cups
  - bag of vermiculite
  - 2 plant pot markers
  - measuring cup
  - 2 dropping pipettes
- ❏ large sheet of newsprint

For each student:
- ❏ copy of "Research Proposal" (pages 230–231)
- ❏ copy of "Peer Review" (page 275)

Vocabulary

PEER REVIEW - Scientists' process of reviewing each other's work to make sure their methods and conclusions are as valid as possible.

Getting Ready

Session 1

♦ Decide on groups of 3–4 students. Try to make an even number of groups so it's easier to organize the peer review process.

♦ If your students haven't previously learned how to design controlled experiments, review the information on pages 200 and 220 to share with them before you begin this lesson.

Action Narrative

Session 1

Before we set up experiments to get information for GROW, we have to make plans. We'll do that in two steps. First, you'll work in groups to write research proposals. Second, each group will exchange its proposal with another group for feedback. Scientists call having their work reviewed by other scientists PEER REVIEW. Why do you think peer review is important?

Students might mention that other scientists who have done the same kind of work would have ideas to share, or someone else might see weaknesses in a plan that the person who developed it couldn't see.

You could draw a parallel to the word *peer* being used to refer to their friends and classmates to help them think of peer review as a friendly and supportive process, rather than negative and judgmental.

Here are the "Research Proposal" forms.

Assign students to groups, and hand out and go over the "Research Proposal." Make sure students remember how to design a fair test (see "Getting Ready"). If the class decided that all groups will test the same question, have students restate the question so that everyone can write it on his or her proposal.

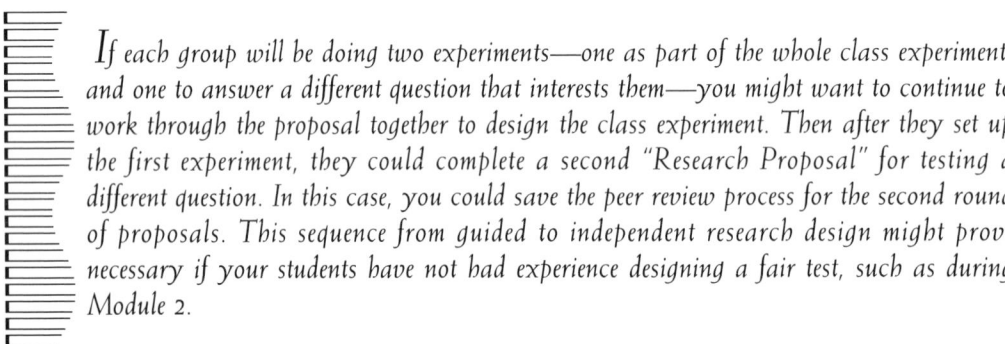

If each group will be doing two experiments—one as part of the whole class experiment, and one to answer a different question that interests them—you might want to continue to work through the proposal together to design the class experiment. Then after they set up the first experiment, they could complete a second "Research Proposal" for testing a different question. In this case, you could save the peer review process for the second round of proposals. This sequence from guided to independent research design might prove necessary if your students have not had experience designing a fair test, such as during Module 2.

What should you look for when you review another group's proposal?

List students' suggestions for review criteria so that they'll have them to refer to as they respond to the general items listed on the "Peer Review" form.

> <u>Things to Judge in a Peer Review:</u>
> their research question is clear, interesting, and important
> their test has a treatment and a control
> they changed only one variable
> their plan and drawing show exactly what to do
> they listed all the materials
> they gave exact amounts so anyone could set up the same experiment
> they thought of everything that needs to be done while plants are growing
> they know what is important to watch and measure
> they've predicted more than one possible result

When your group finishes its proposal, exchange it with another group. Use this "Peer Review" form to give them feedback.

Hand out and go over the "Peer Review" form. Encourage students to write specific suggestions right on the "Research Proposal" forms they're reviewing, in addition to filling out the "Peer Review" summary.

Scientists need to be good at giving and taking constructive criticism. What does that mean?

Have students discuss the importance of giving and receiving feedback in the spirit of sharing ideas and making improvements.

Here are the materials available for your experiments. Before you list anything other than these items on your materials list, make sure that I can get it for you, or that you can bring it in.

Show students the materials. Tell them what kind of seeds you have so that they'll know what kind of plants they'll be growing.

Get out the experiment ideas you wrote for homework. Share them with other members of your group, then work together on a "Research Proposal."

Announce who is in each group. This is a good time to establish permanent work areas for each group, as well.

Although each student can fill out a "Research Proposal," the group only needs one copy to exchange for peer review.

Listen as students make experiment plans. Since they'll be reviewing each other's work, you might want to hold back from playing the role of reviewer.

When groups finish their proposals, they can exchange their plans with another group to begin the peer review process.

Session 2

Finish reviewing each other's proposals. Then we'll talk about the ideas everyone has outlined.

Give students time to finish their peer reviews. Then have each pair of groups get together to go over the comments they made on each other's proposals.

If all the groups will be doing the same experiment, continue with the discussion below. If they'll be doing separate experiments, give each group a few minutes to describe its procedures to the rest of the class.

If we want each group's experiment to be a replicate for one big experiment, each setup needs to be the same. Let's go through the design step-by-step to decide on the best possible procedures.

Make sure that students understand that a replicate is a copy of an experimental setup, and that scientists do replicates so that they can be more sure of their conclusions (see page 219).

Who wants to describe the fair test your group planned?

Write, or draw and label, one group's fair test plan on a sheet of newsprint to save it for the next lesson. Encourage other students to make suggestions for improving the plan. Ask them to give reasons for design changes they propose, and let students talk together until they reach a consensus on one design. You could have a few students work with a set of experiment materials to specify the amount of vermiculite to add to each cup.

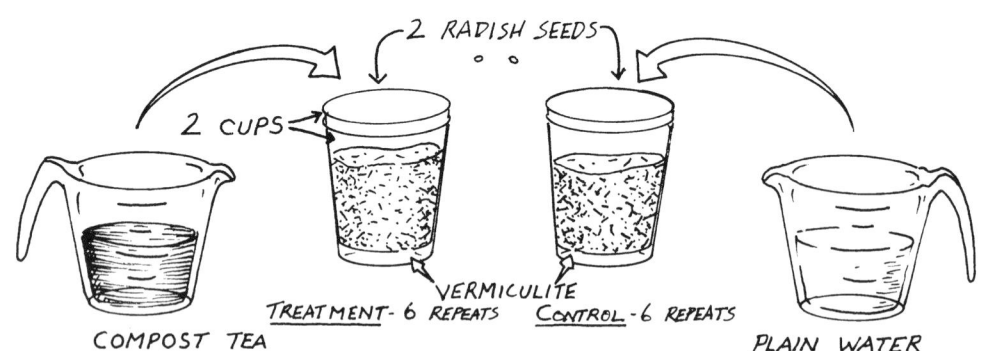

If your students are testing solid rather than liquid compost, tell them that sometimes seeds rot before they can grow, if they come into contact with fungus. Keeping the compost away from the seed should prevent this problem.

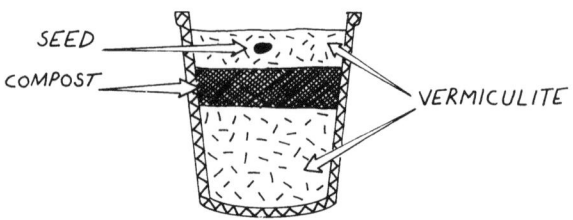

Now let's decide on an Observation and Care Plan. Remember, you'll use observations to answer your research question. So let's think about what kinds of evidence will be most helpful to measure and observe.

Students might have a variety of suggestions for what they should watch and measure, based on the physical characteristics they associate with healthy plants: plant height; the number, size, and color of leaves; or how "strong" or "droopy" each plant is. It is impossible for students to predict any one best indicator of plant health until they see the plants growing. Tell them they can decide to observe additional things as their experiments unfold. For instance, with radish seedlings the length of the true leaves (not the cotyledons) has proven to be one of the most useful ways of comparing plants with and without nutrient inputs, but students seldom think of this as a possible indicator until they notice it.

Record the procedures that the class agrees on.

<u>Observation and Care Plan</u>

What ...	How ...	When ...
1. give water to control plants	use a dropper to measure a certain amount	check every other day, water only if they're dry
2. give compost tea to treatment plants	use a dropper to measure	check every other day, water only if they're dry
3. see how tall they get	put a ruler on top of the soil and measure up to the top of the stem	every other day
4. see the leaf color	make a color chart with markers to compare with the leaves	once a week
5. see how healthy the plant looks overall	look at them and take notes	once a week

What are some of your predictions?

Students are likely to predict that plants given compost will grow better because they'll be getting more nutrients. They might wonder why they should consider other possible results. Help them realize that scientists need to keep an open mind in order to learn as much as possible from their experiments. See if students can think of reasons why compost tea might not help the plants in the expected ways (e.g., it doesn't contain enough nutrients, it contains too many nutrients so damages the plants, it contains fungus and bacteria that might harm the plants, the type of seedlings don't respond to nutrients).

Ongoing Assessment

Student Reflections

Have students send a C-Mail message or record thoughts in their journals. Optional writing prompts include:

How did it feel to review another group's work?

How did it feel to have my group's work reviewed?

If a group of scientists applied to me for money to support their research, I would/would not ask other scientists to review their proposal because...

Teacher Reflections

❑ Do students understand why only one variable is changed in fair tests?

❑ Are they able to accept suggestions from their peers, and change their ideas when warranted?

❑ Do they predict that nutrients from decomposing plants will benefit living plants?

❑ Do they have some mental images of how their treatment and control plants might differ as they grow?

Extensions

Review-o-Rama. Give students the opportunity to apply the peer review process to other subject areas, such as reviewing one another's creative writing. Branch out with the art of reviewing by having them write reviews of movies, television show episodes, or books.

Team Building. Give research groups a chance to build a positive working relationship by giving them a fun, non-academic, physical challenge. Have each group brainstorm and decide on something within the following categories to become:

a machine with moving parts (e.g., bicycle, old-fashioned sewing machine, windmill);

an animal (e.g., clam, grasshopper, insect at different stages of metamorphosis);

a plant going through its life cycle.

Groups will need to decide how each person can be a part of the whole machine or organism, then practice making it work. They can then perform for the class and let you and the other students guess what they are.

NAME(S)____ DATE__________

PEER REVIEW

We are reviewing the plans of:________________________________

The strengths of this proposal are:

____

____

____

____

Things that need to be improved are:

____

____

____

____

Suggestions we have are:

____

____

____

____

Questions we have are:

____

____

____

____

3.3 Up and Running

Action Synopsis

Students set up experiments to test the effects of compost tea on plant growth, learn about plant development, then monitor their experiments for 3–5 weeks.

Session 1		**40 minutes**
1. Demonstrate experiment techniques.		*demonstrating methods*
2. Work in groups to set up experiments.		*investigating*
3. Record experiment activities in journals.		*documenting*

Session 2		**40 minutes**
1. Check to see if seeds have germinated.		*observing*
2. Discuss ideas about what happens to seeds after they're planted.		*examining prior ideas*
3. Observe, draw, and discuss dry and soaked bean seeds.		*observing & recording*
4. Look at a drawing of the inside of a bean seed and name the parts of the seed, then discuss a drawing of plant development.		*introducing new information*
5. Answer questions about where a developing plant gets nutrients and energy.		*applying knowledge*

Continued

Ongoing Monitoring

1. Thin plants to one seedling per cup.  *investigating*

2. Make compost tea. *investigating*

3. Water, treat, and measure plants, and record observations. *observing & recording*

4. Share ideas and findings in periodic class meetings. *processing findings*

5. Share note-keeping strategies, and develop data charts. *documenting*

6. Relate the experiment to the concept of nutrient cycling. *reflecting*

Desired Outcomes

Throughout the lesson, check that students:

✓ Can set up an experiment according to plans.

✓ Know the parts of a seed and how seeds develop into a mature plant.

✓ Understand where plants get nutrients and energy as they grow.

✓ Can accurately make and keep records of observations and measurements.

✓ Are willing to exchange and reflect on information with peers.

What You'll Need

Session 1

For the class:
  ❑ newsprint poster of experiment design plan (see page 273)
  ❑ large bucket or dishpan
  ❑ several measuring cups or 8-oz. plastic cups
  ❑ cleanup supplies:
  • broom
  • whisk broom
  • dustpan
  • paper towels
  • sponges
  • bucket of water

For each group of 3–4 students:
  ❑ set of experiment materials (see "Getting Ready"):
  • 24 6-oz. clear plastic cups

Continued

- pushpin
- approximately 9 cups of vermiculite
- plastic bag, 1-gallon size (see "Getting Ready")
- 24 radish seeds
- mini paper cup
- 12 pot labels (see "Getting Ready")
- permanent marker

Session 2

For the class:
- ❑ overhead transparency of "Inside of a Seed" (page 293)
- ❑ overhead transparency of "Growing from Seed to Young Plant" (page 294)

For each student:
- ❑ 2 large beans—one dry, one soaked (see "Getting Ready")
- ❑ hand lens
- ❑ copy of "Growing from Seed to Young Plant" (page 294)

Ongoing Monitoring

For the class:
- ❑ compost tea materials:
  - compost (see "Getting Ready," page 259)
  - dishpan or bucket
  - measuring cup
  - a sheet of cheesecloth
  - rubber band
  - water dispenser (optional—see page 288)
- ❑ containers and potting soil for planting thinned seedlings (optional—see "Getting Ready")

For each group of 3–4 students:
- ❑ watering equipment:
  - distilled water (optional—see "Getting Ready")
  - 2 plastic dropping pipettes
  - 2 medium-size plastic cups (8–9 oz.)
- ❑ several rulers, preferably small 15 cm size

For each student:
- ❑ copy of "Compost Tea Experiment Data Chart" (optional—page 296)

Vocabulary

COTYLEDONS - Seed leaves; the leaves of the embryo in a seed.

EMBRYO - The early stage of development of an organism.

GERMINATE - To sprout; to begin to grow.

SEED COAT - Tough outer layer of a seed that protects the embryo.

SEEDLING - A plant in its first stages of growth.

Getting Ready

Session 1

♦ The quantity of materials listed in "What You'll Need" is enough for each group to set up 12 nested planting units—6 treatment and 6 control plants. This number could vary depending on your students' experiment design.

♦ Students need the plastic bag to carry from the distribution area to their desks. They could use a basin or cut-off gallon milk jug instead.

♦ Students can label their planting units by writing with a permanent marker on plastic pot labels, wooden craft sticks, or masking tape.

♦ Pre-moisten the vermiculite. Empty two 8-quart bags into a bucket or dishpan (or do it in two batches), shielding your nose and mouth from floating vermiculite dust particles. Hold the container under a faucet and add water (or use distilled water), mixing with a large spoon or your hands until all of the vermiculite is saturated, but not too wet.

♦ If you want seeds to germinate quickly after students plant them, cover them with water to soak overnight. The next day, drain the water and count 24 seeds into one mini paper cup for each group. Radish seeds are large enough so that students can handle them easily. If you are using smaller seeds, consider providing toothpicks that students can wet to pick the seeds from the cup in order to plant them.

♦ Set out experiment and cleanup materials on a table so that distribution can work like a buffet.

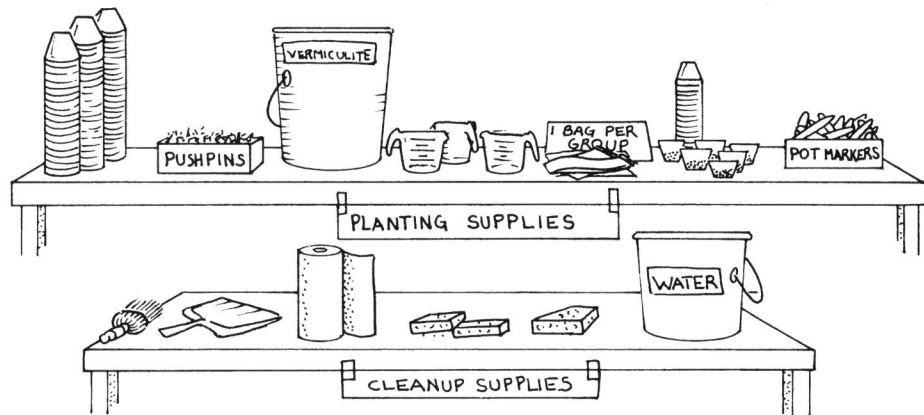

Session 2

♦ Soak one bean seed for each student overnight in water.

Ongoing Monitoring

♦ If students opt to save the seedlings they thin from their experiment planting units, they'll need containers such as paper cups, milk cartons, or margarine tubs to plant them in.

♦ If your water is high in nitrogen (greater than 5–10 parts per million), consider using distilled water for the experiments. Students' experiments will work best if the water they give control plants is low in nutrients. Some regions have a lot of nitrogen in their water supply, particularly agricultural and urban areas. You can check with your local soil and water agency to see if your water is likely to be high in nitrogen. You could also test your water using nitrogen test strips or a water test kit, available from science supply catalogs (or perhaps from a local high school teacher). You can purchase distilled water at pharmacies, or buy an inexpensive water deionizer from a science supply catalog.

Action Narrative

Session 1

I've posted the experiment design we made together so you can refer to it as you set up your experiments.

This teaching narrative assumes that each group will set up a replicate of a whole class experiment. The step-by-step planting instructions that follow will help assure that seeds will germinate and grow, and that all replicates will be set up identically. If your students have had prior experience growing plants, you can let them work out proper planting techniques on their own, rather than guiding them through the following methods.

Before you get started, I want to show you a few techniques to use. First, you need to make drainage holes in the cup that you'll plant seeds in. Then set that cup into another cup for water to drain into.

Turn one cup upside down and punch several holes in the bottom with a pushpin.

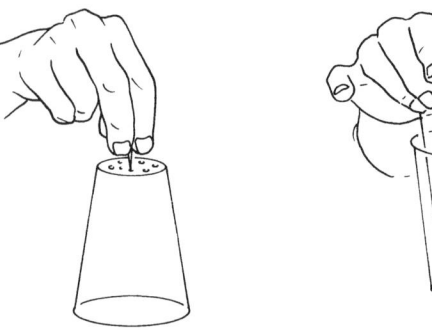

Next, fill the cups with vermiculite, then plant two seeds in each. If both seeds grow, you can remove one later.

Use a ruler to measure and mark a fill-line a few centimeters below the top of the cup. Or use a measuring cup to measure the vermiculite. If students are using solid compost as their experimental variable, then set up the cup as shown on page 272. It is important to tamp down the vermiculite in each cup the same amount—a gentle tap on the surface will do.

Next demonstrate seed planting. Most kinds of seeds should be planted only as deep as they are large, but check your seed packet for specific directions. Plant the two seeds near the center of the cup so that whichever one survives will have maximum room to grow.

Label each cup. What should go on the labels?

Show students the pot markers or masking tape they'll use as labels. One way to label the cups is to call the six Treatment cups T1–T6, and the six Control cups C1–C6. If students are using wooden craft sticks, they might want to color the tops of the sticks in treatment and control cups two different colors. Each group's name or initials should go on the labels, too.

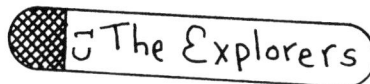

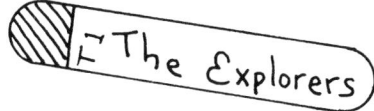

Send one person from your group to get materials, then work together to set up your experiment.

Have the delivery person from each group scoop about 9 cups of vermiculite into the gallon-size plastic bags or other containers to bring back to their desks. This way group members can work together to fill their 12 planting cups.

As students set up their planting cups, check to see if they have figured out a way to get the same amount of vermiculite in each cup. Two ways to accomplish this are to measure the vermiculite with a measuring cup, or to use a ruler and marker to measure and mark a fill-line on each cup.

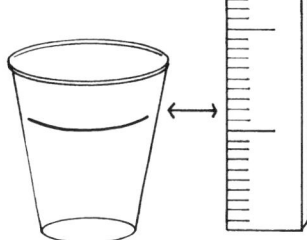

Make sure students don't plant seeds too deeply or else the seedlings will take a long time to emerge, or the seeds might not sprout at all.

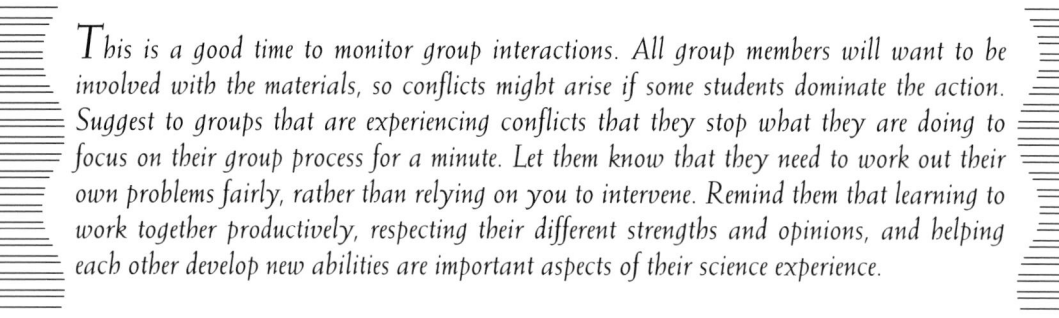

This is a good time to monitor group interactions. All group members will want to be involved with the materials, so conflicts might arise if some students dominate the action. Suggest to groups that are experiencing conflicts that they stop what they are doing to focus on their group process for a minute. Let them know that they need to work out their own problems fairly, rather than relying on you to intervene. Remind them that learning to work together productively, respecting their different strengths and opinions, and helping each other develop new abilities are important aspects of their science experience.

Check to see how moist your vermiculite is. Since I pre-moistened it, you probably won't have to add water to the cups today.

The cups most likely won't need water until the seeds germinate in about 2–3 days. The compost tea treatment shouldn't start until the cotyledons unfurl, since fungus from the compost can kill the tender seedlings while they're germinating.

If you have extra seeds, students might find it interesting to put a few in moist paper towels surrounded by plastic wrap, or in a plastic sandwich bag with a drop of water, so that they can observe them sprout.

Dry Seed   Soaked seed,   Soaked seed,
              24 hrs.   48 hrs.

Bring your cups to the windowsill, and clean your work area.

Cleanup is an important part of all science experiments. Help students get in the habit of taking responsibility for cleaning up efficiently. Have them shake out the plastic bags and/or wipe the containers they used for vermiculite into the trash can, then turn the bags inside out to dry so that you can reuse them.

Record what you did today in your journals.

 Once cleanup activities have settled down, create a quiet atmosphere so that students can concentrate on writing in their journals.

March 18
Today Tyrone, Rene, and I planted radish seeds. We made 12 cups and I punched the holes. We put the seeds not too deep. Each cup got a label. It was wet so we don't water them yet. I hope tomorrow they'll be up.

the Seed is under here

Creating Optimal Growing Conditions

Classroom conditions aren't always friendly for growing plants. To maximize plant survival, go over the following tips with students, so they can take responsibility for looking after their plants' health.

Protect from excessive heat and drying. If you are keeping plants near an active radiator, insulate the surface the plants sit on with material such as styrofoam, or a foam pad. Also put a pan of water on the radiator to add moisture to the air. If your windowsill area heats up because of intense sunlight, keep a window open to allow air to circulate. Draw the shades if plants show signs of wilting or leaf burn. Over weekends, and especially for longer school breaks, put plastic bags or sheets of plastic wrap loosely over the plants to conserve moisture. Students could also put a small amount of water in the outer cup of their planting units before weekends or vacations.

Provide plenty of light. The more light the plants get, the faster they'll grow and respond to nutrients. A south-facing window that provides 4–5 hours of sunlight a day is best, with east- or west-facing windows being second best. If you only have access to north-facing windows, consider using supplemental plant lights 6–8 hours a day. Plant lights are the best option overall, if at all feasible.

Don't overwater. Students have a tendency to love their plants to death by overwatering them. Before the seeds germinate, they can be easily washed out with a glut of water. Using dropping pipettes helps prevent overwatering. Vermiculite should be kept moist, but not soggy. Students can see through the cup to tell when the vermiculite is saturated. They can also watch for drainage into the outer cup, and stop adding water as soon as they see it dripping out the bottom of the inner cup. They should pour out excess water from the outer cup, except just before weekends.

Cover roots. When roots start to grow to the edge of the cup, cover the cup with black paper to keep the roots in darkness.

Handle gently. Plants often get mauled as students measure them. The experiment provides an opportunity to encourage students to develop their fine motor coordination. Let them know that scientists often have to learn to handle fragile or tiny things as they do experiments. Explain that they shouldn't ever squeeze the stem which might damage the tissues that transport water and sugars to all parts of the plant. Handling plants can affect their growth, so the plants should be handled minimally, and the same amount.

Session 2

Check on the cups of seeds you planted to see if anything looks different.

It takes a few days for seeds to germinate and emerge above the vermiculite, so students may or may not see any changes.

Let's think about what might be happening to the seeds in the cups, even if we can't see anything growing yet. Any ideas?

As students share their ideas, note how much prior knowledge they have about how plants grow from seeds. If you put some seeds to sprout in paper towels or plastic bags, have students check on them and speculate about whether or not these seeds reflect what is happening to the seeds beneath the vermiculite.

To learn more about what happens as seeds grow, everyone will get two bean seeds— a dry one and one that soaked up water overnight. Observe them both with a hand lens, then take the outside layer—the SEED COAT— off the soaked bean. Then you can gently pull the two halves of the bean seed apart and see what is inside. Draw what you see.

Hand out the bean seeds and lenses. Give students time to make and draw their observations. You could use one of their drawings later in lieu of the prepared overhead transparency of the inside of a seed, if you have a plain paper projector or if the student is willing to trace the drawing onto a transparency.

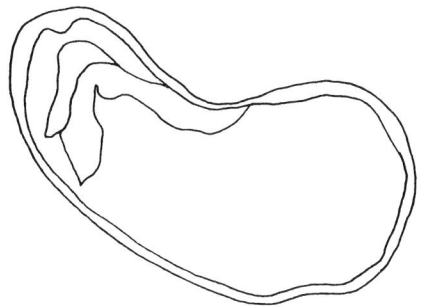

? After they have finished, ask questions such as:

What was the difference between the dry seed and the soaked seed?
Encourage students to use detailed and descriptive language to explain how the seeds look, feel, and smell.

Did the seeds you planted look more like the dry or the soaked seed? How do you think they look now that they've been planted for a day?
Students' responses will depend on whether or not you pre-soaked the seeds for their experiment. Since they were planted, the seeds have probably absorbed more water from the wet vermiculite, and have begun to expand.

Does anyone know what it is called when a seed begins to grow?
Students might use the term "sprout," which is another term for GERMINATE.

Here is a drawing of the inside of a bean seed. See if it looks like what you drew.

Show the "Inside of a Seed" overhead transparency, covering the vocabulary words with a sheet of paper.

Does anyone know what the parts of the seed the arrows point to are called?

Once students share their ideas, remove the paper that covers the terms and discuss them. The EMBRYO is the baby plant. One end will be the growing tip or shoot from which the leaves grow, and the other will be the root. COTYLEDONS are the seed leaves. They contain nutrients and energy that the embryo needs to start growing.

Now let's look at how this seed will change as it grows.

Show the "Growing from Seed to Young Plant" transparency, covering the bottom questions section with a sheet of paper. Explain the growth stages as follows:

A: The seed begins to absorb water. The cotyledons start to draw nutrients and food energy from the embryo.

B: The embryo sprouts roots and a shoot that begins to push above the soil.

C: The cotyledons burst out of the seed coat. The plant begins to use up the stored nutrients and energy to grow. Meanwhile, the plant is beginning to take in nutrients from the soil, and is beginning to make its own food energy through photosynthesis. This tiny plant is called a SEEDLING.

D: The first true leaves start to grow. The plant now takes in even more nutrients from the soil, and makes all of its own food energy. The cotyledons will turn yellow and die as the other leaves take over their job.

Here is a copy of the overhead, with questions for you to answer on the bottom.

Hand out a copy of "Growing from Seed to Young Plant" to each student. If there is time, they can work on it in class independently or in pairs. Or they can complete it for homework. See the "Growing from Seed to Young Plant—Teacher's Page" for examples of well-reasoned student responses. Discuss the completed sheets as a class. The basic idea students should understand is that plants need to take in nutrients through their roots once they use up the nutrients stored in their cotyledons.

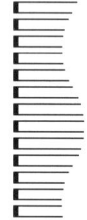 *You might want to review photosynthesis, and the terms* nutrients *and* energy *with the class. Students should understand that plants make their own food to use for energy, and that they also need nutrients from soil and water to stay healthy and grow. See Lessons 1.6 "Making Food Chains" and 1.7 "Food for Thought" for ideas on introducing these concepts.*

Ongoing Monitoring

Students will need ten to fifteen minutes two or three times a week for at least three weeks to water, treat, and measure their plants, and to record observations. You can also continue with Lessons 3.4 and 3.5 during this time period.

Thinning Seedlings

After plants have been growing about a week it is time to thin them to one seedling per cup.

Now that your seedlings have started to grow above the vermiculite, it's time to remove one of them from each cup so that the one left will have more room to grow.

Students should decide which seedling to keep in each cup for their experiment. They should keep the seedlings that are the healthiest and of similar size, so that all of their replicates are as similar as possible.

An easy way to thin seedlings is to cut them off with scissors at soil level. But students will probably not like the idea of killing the extras. An alternative is to remove an intact seedling from each cup. This risks damaging the roots of the remaining plant, so discuss the options with your class. If the plants are edible, such as radish, the students could eat the seedlings, which means they could cut them off at the soil surface.

If students decide to transplant, have them prepare cups of potting soil or a whole class planting tray for the seedling transplants. They can use pencils to make planting holes in the new containers.

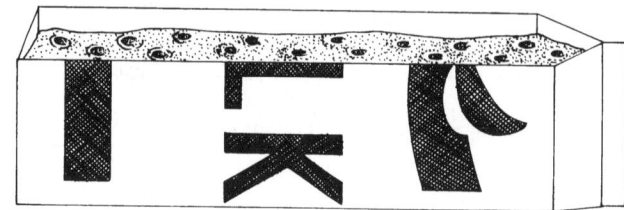

Module 3: Cycles—From Rot to Radishes

Have students carefully remove their unwanted seedlings by holding onto a leaf and pulling gently as they loosen the roots from the soil with a pencil, being careful not to disturb the other seedling in the cup. Students should also be sure not to squeeze the stem, which would damage the plant's ability to transport water and sugars.

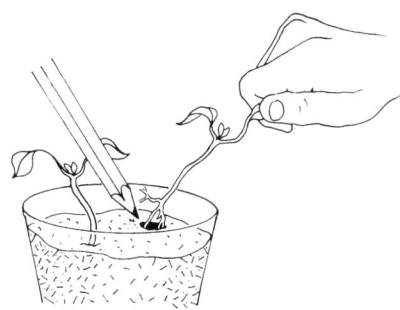

Finally, have students transplant their seedlings into the holes they prepared, making sure the holes are deep enough for roots to point straight down, and gently press the soil around the roots.

Watering and Beginning the Compost Tea Treatment

Gather the compost tea materials (compost, a measuring cup, cheesecloth, a rubber band, a bucket, and deionized or tap water) after the cotyledons have unfurled.

We've been waiting for the cotyledons to unfurl before giving the plants compost tea, because there might be molds in the compost that can make tiny plants rot. Now that the plants are taller and stronger, it is less likely that would happen. So we're ready to make a batch of compost tea for you to use on your treatment plants.

Have students help you make the compost tea as follows:

1. Measure a gallon of water into a bucket or dishpan.

2. Open a square of cheesecloth. Put 4 cups of compost into the center of the square.

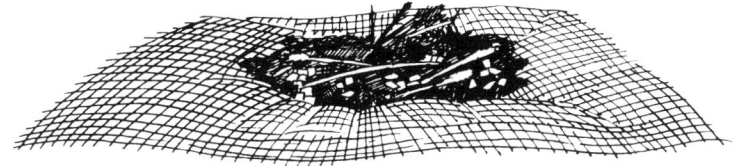

3. Gather the cloth into a bundle and fasten it with a rubber band.

4. Put the bundle of compost into the water, swirling it a few times to saturate it.

5. Let the compost soak in the water overnight. Remove and discard it the next day. The tea should be a light caramel color. If it is as dark as a strong tea beverage, dilute it with water. You can keep the compost tea in the bucket where students can scoop it out with cups as needed, or use a funnel to pour it into a water dispenser.

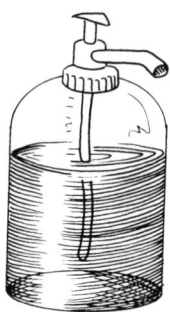

6. Repeat the procedure to make smaller batches of compost tea as needed, using a ratio of 1 cup of compost to 4 cups of water.

 **Caution!** Be sure students always wash their hands after handling compost and compost tea to remove bacteria and fungal spores.

 Students should record information about their treatment and control plants before beginning the compost tea treatment, so that they know how the plants are similar or different from the outset.

Students can decide whether to give their treatment plants only compost tea, or alternate tea treatments with plain water. If the tea is not too concentrated, there is no reason why they can't give it to the plants during every regular watering.

An easy way to manage watering the plants with a measured amount of liquid is for each group to have two cups to use as water reservoirs—one for plain water and one for compost tea—and two graduated dropping pipettes—one for plain water and one for compost tea.

What's In Compost Tea?

In addition to nutrients released from dead plants by decomposers, compost tea contains microscopic bacteria and fungi. There also will be plant-derived molecules such as tanins (used for tanning leather), which are much like the substances that flavor and color tea beverages.

To see if there are different atoms and molecules in plain water (tap and deionized) versus compost tea, students can dip blue litmus paper into each. The paper will turn red in the presence of nutrient molecules that make a solution acidic.

Class Meetings

Hold class meetings periodically for students to share observations and ideas. They can also demonstrate measuring techniques to one another to double-check that they are all measuring in the same ways.

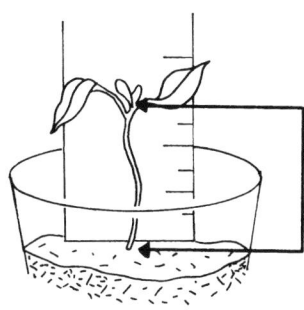

Class meetings can also be forums for sharing "news bulletins," such as when a group discovers a new indicator of plant health (e.g., the size of leaves) to observe and measure.

Focus some of the meetings on discussions of nutrient cycling. One way to do this is to have groups of students map out and then display the pathway they think nutrients are taking in their experiment. They can arrange a set of cards on paper, similar to concept mapping.

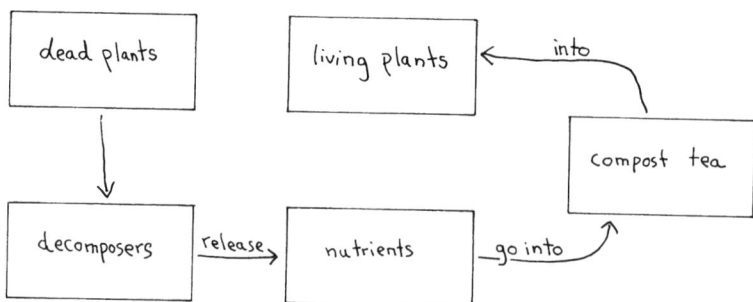

Challenge students to support the theory they've illustrated with evidence that is emerging from their experiments. If experimental results are not supporting the theory, ask them to speculate about, and perhaps illustrate, what else could be happening.

Keeping Records

Early on you might want to focus a class meeting on note-keeping strategies.

Let's share the different ways people are keeping records.

The compost tea experiment provides a rich opportunity for students to keep a variety of notes and drawings. Giving students a chance to share their notes helps them take pride in, and see the value of their records. It also shows them that there are many ways to record observations.

Date:	What I did:	What I noticed:	What I wonder about:
April 11	Started giving compost tea to treatment plants	The treatment and control plants look the same to start with	When will they start to look different?

In addition to encouraging creative notetaking, introduce data tables as a convenient format that scientists use to organize their data. Some students might have devised their own data charts that you can use as examples, or give each student a copy of the "Compost Tea Experiment Data Chart."

What to Expect

Students should begin to see subtle differences between treatment and control plants within two weeks, with differences continuing to get more obvious as time passes. The more light the plants get, the more quickly they'll grow, and the sooner untreated plants will show signs of nutrient deficiency. The most notable difference between treatment and control plants will likely be the width and length of leaves, with the control plants having smaller leaves. The control plants might also be paler, or even yellowish. All cotyledons turn yellow as they grow older, so it is better to compare color of true leaves. Also, you can compare when cotyledons fade and wither. If you are using radishes, students might notice a difference in the size of the radish developing at the base of the stems.

Trouble shooting. Too much of a good thing can be toxic! Especially under very low light conditions, plants might not be using the nutrients in the compost tea very rapidly. Thus, the nutrients could accumulate and act as toxins rather than as fertilizer. This could also happen if the compost tea is too strong. The toxic effect will show up as mottling on the surface of leaves. Other reasons that treatment plants might not grow well are mentioned on pages 283–284.

If the treatment plants begin to look worse than the control plants, students could speculate about why, but decide not to change their experiment. Or they could try a variation on the basic experiment using half of their treatment and control plants, diluting the compost tea to half-strength, or giving the plants more light.

Ongoing Assessment

Student Reflections

Have students send a C-Mail message or record thoughts in their journals. Optional writing prompts include:

What is good and what is bad about working in a team to do an experiment?

Ways our team could work better together are...

Things I've noticed about myself as a scientist are...

Teacher Reflections

❏ Are students working together productively and settling their own disputes?

❏ How clear are their ideas about where plants get nutrients and energy?

❏ Are they developing notetaking skills and a commitment to accuracy?

❏ Are they trying to make sense of their observations?

Extensions

Hydroponics. Have students find out how plants are grown without soil. If possible, visit a commercial grower that uses hydroponics. Try to grow plants, from houseplant cuttings to lettuce and beans, without soil.

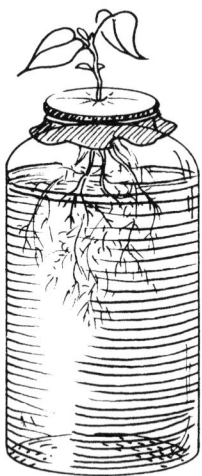

Sprouts to Eat. Students can sprout alfalfa and radish seeds, then add them to their lunches! Make sure to use seeds that have not been treated with a fungicide (often a brightly colored powder coating the seeds). They should soak the seeds in water overnight, then drain them. They'll need to rinse them every day, and keep the sprouts' jar in a dark place.

Home-based Experiments. Send home a list of plant experiment suggestions that students can do with their families, and then report their results back to the class. Some ideas are: a) test other homemade solutions (e.g., eggshells or manure soaked in water) to see if they help plants grow better than plain water; b) compare the growth of plants given different amounts of fertilizer; c) collect soils from different locations outdoors and compare how well plants grow in each.

Big Books. Suggest that students write, illustrate, and bind "big books" on plant growth for kindergarten or primary-grade students.

Farm Comparisons. Have students check the library or contact agricultural offices to find out the differences between farms that use compost and manure as fertilizers, and those that use only chemical fertilizers. Ask students to list the pros and cons of each approach (i.e., costs, environmental impact, quality and quantity of food produced). If possible, visit a local farm or an agricultural experiment station.

INSIDE OF A SEED

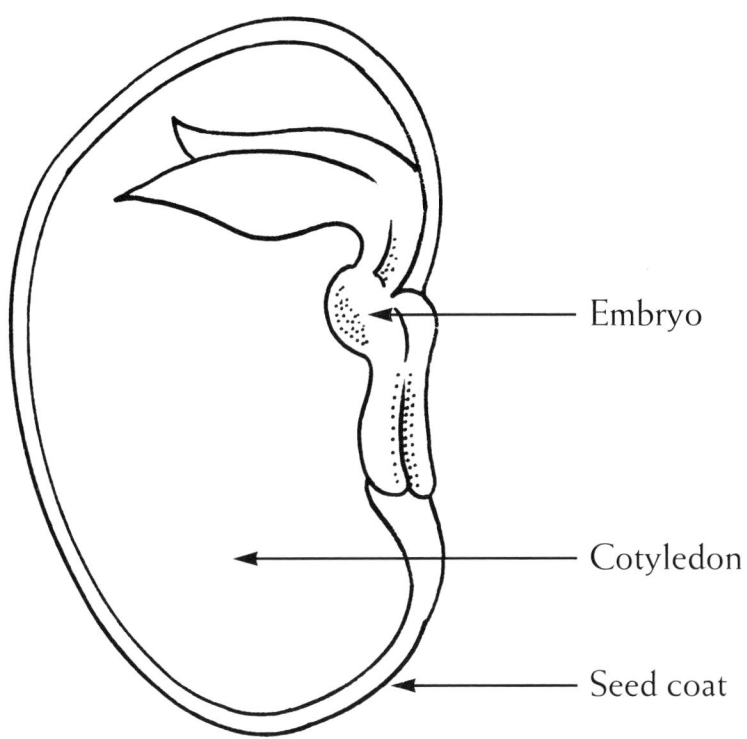

Embryo

Cotyledon

Seed coat

GROWING FROM SEED TO YOUNG PLANT

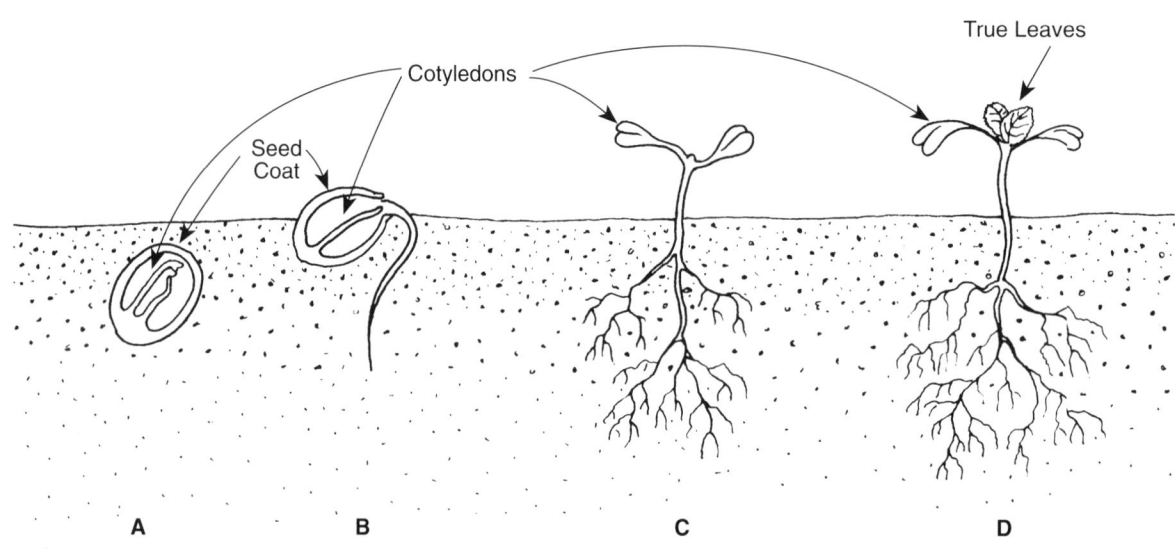

True Leaves

Cotyledons

Seed
Coat

A   B   C   D

1 In picture B, where is the tiny plant getting most of its nutrients and food energy?

_____

2 Where is the plant in picture D getting its nutrients?

_____

Where is it getting its food energy?

_____

3 If you sprouted a seed on a paper towel, what do you predict would happen to the seed after 3 weeks? Why?

_____

_____

4 If you wanted the seed you sprouted in the paper towel to grow into a healthy plant, what would you have to do with it? Why?

_____

_____

294   Module 3: *Cycles—From Rot to Radishes*

GROWING FROM SEED TO YOUNG PLANT — TEACHER'S PAGE

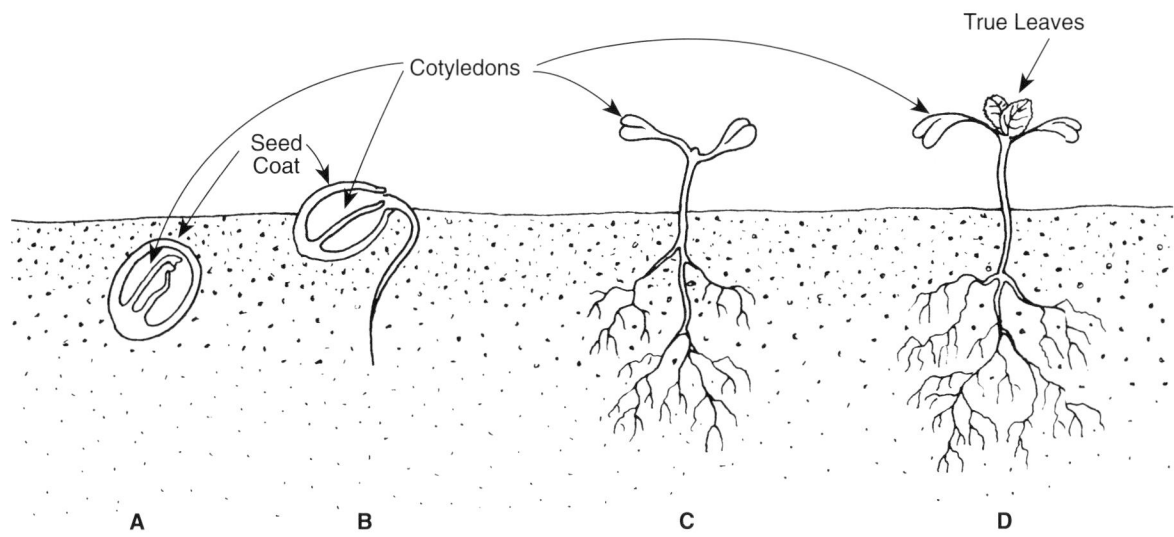

Cotyledons

True Leaves

Seed Coat

A   B   C   D

(1) In picture B, where is the tiny plant getting most of its nutrients and food energy?

Since the plant does not yet have well-developed roots or leaves, it still gets its nutrients and energy from the cotyledons.

(2) Where is the plant in picture D getting its nutrients?

The plant now has roots, so it is getting nutrients from the soil.

Where is it getting its food energy?

The plant is using its true leaves to make food through photosynthesis.

(3) If you sprouted a seed on a paper towel, what do you predict would happen to the seed after 3 weeks? Why?

It would probably die because it would have used up the food stored in its cotyledons without getting sunlight and nutrients.

(4) If you wanted the seed you sprouted in the paper towel to grow into a healthy plant, what would you have to do with it? Why?

You would have to plant the seedling in soil (or in a fertilizer solution, such as in hydroponic gardening) so it could get nutrients, and then put it in light so that it could make its own food.

Compost Tea Experiment Data Chart

Plant Height (in centimeters)

Date	Treatment						Average Height	Control						Average Height
	T1	T2	T3	T4	T5	T6		C1	C2	C3	C4	C5	C6	

3.4 Exploring Plant and Soil Connections

Action Synopsis

Students prepare for and do an outdoor investigation of soil in areas where plants and other landscape features differ, then use their findings to think about plant and soil connections.

Session 1		**1 hour**

1. Imagine being a plant outdoors.   *examining prior ideas*

2. Discuss how plants get nutrients, and what   *generating ideas & questions*
   conditions could affect where plants grow.

3. Hear and discuss a story about Dr. Charlie Canham,   *linking to real world*
   a scientist who studies plant communities.

4. Go over questions and procedures for outdoor   *familiarizing*
   soil investigation.

Session 2		**1 hour**	**OUTDOORS**

1. Review outdoor study rules and get   *familiarizing*
   oriented to the study site.

2. Work in groups to find two sites, write a   *investigating*
   research question, collect soil samples, and
   record observations.

Continued

1. Compile outdoor study findings in groups.   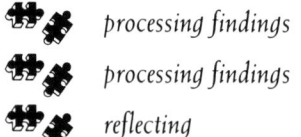   *processing findings*

2. Share research questions and findings as a class.   *processing findings*

3. Have a final discussion about plant and
   soil connections.   *reflecting*

Desired Outcomes

Throughout the lesson, check that students:

✓ Can envision roots growing in soil and taking in nutrients.

✓ Are aware of some ways that ecologists study plant communities and help people
   manage land.

✓ Can use visible differences in sites to predict differences in soil.

✓ Know how to look for patterns in their data in order to make generalizations.

✓ Can explain how soil could affect plant communities, and how living and dead plants
   could affect soil.

✓ Are familiar with a variety of factors that together determine what plants grow where.

What You'll Need

Session 1

For the class:
   ❑ overhead transparency of "Shrub Invaders" (page 311)
   ❑ overhead transparency of "Root Races" (page 312)

For each student:
   ❑ copy of "Plant & Soil Connections Data Sheet" (page 313)

Session 2

For each group of 3–4 students:
   ❑ tray (e.g., cookie sheet, foil pan, dishpan) lined with white paper
   ❑ trowel or large metal spoon
   ❑ piece of rigid plastic 2" pipe, about 50 cm long (optional)
   ❑ several hand lenses
   ❑ rulers

Vocabulary

COMPETITION - The interaction of two or more organisms seeking a limited resource that they both need.

FIBROUS ROOTS - Fine roots that branch in all directions with no central main root.

PLANT COMMUNITY - The group of different kinds of plants growing in the same area.

SHRUB - A low-growing woody plant that usually has many stems.

TAPROOT - A central root that grows downward and has smaller roots extending outward from it.

Getting Ready

Session 1

♦ Decide on groups of 3–4 students.

Session 2

♦ Scope out a study site by looking for an area that has several distinctive areas within it (e.g., with and without plants; grassy and forested areas; low/moist and high/ dry places). If you cannot find a suitable location for an outdoor excursion, you can modify the lesson by asking students to take a soil sample at home, and record observations on their data sheet. They can bring their soil samples to class, and share their observations within groups.

♦ Read the Extensions (pages 306–307) before going outdoors in case you would like to do any of them, or collect soil samples for them, during the field trip.

Action Narrative

Session 1

In your experiment, you're comparing how well plants grow with and without nutrients from decomposed plants. While the experiment is running, we're going to take some time to explore how decomposing plants affect soil and living plants outdoors—in an ecosystem.

To start thinking about plants growing outdoors, close your eyes.

It often helps to dim the lights while guiding students to use their imaginations.

Imagine that you're a plant growing outside. Picture what type of plant you are. Now imagine that your feet are your roots, your legs are your trunk or stem, and the rest of your body is the branches and leaves, or pads if you're a cactus.

Focus on the underground world around your roots. What is the soil like? Is it rocky, sandy, or smooth? Moist or dry? What are your roots like? Are they FIBROUS ROOTS, with a lot of thin hair-like strands? Or do you have woody tree roots, or a long TAPROOT like a carrot? What's coming in through your roots? How does that feel? Are any soil critters moving around your roots? Are any nibbling on them? Maybe there are strands of fungal hyphae growing near your roots. Are there any decomposing plants on top of, or in the soil around your roots?

Now look around in your mind's eye at where you're growing. Is it sunny or shady? Are there other plants near you, crowding or shading you? Or do you have a lot of space around you? What kinds of plants live nearby? Are they the same as you or different?

When you're ready, open your eyes and we'll share some of the images you had.

Call students' attention to the variety of plant and soil types, environmental conditions, and surrounding vegetation they imagined. Have them consider which of the images are most like plants and conditions common in your local region, and which are not.

 Continue the discussion with questions such as:

What did you imagine coming in through your roots?
See whether or not students have a picture of nutrients dissolved in water entering a plant through its roots. Whereas animals can break food down into simple nutrient particles in their guts, plants must take in nutrients from materials that have been pre-digested by decomposers. Make sure that students understand that even when plants aren't given liquid fertilizer or compost tea, they still take up soil nutrients dissolved in water. The nutrients that decomposers release from dead plants, and that come from weathered rocks, go into solution when they come into contact with water that enters the soil as rain or snowmelt.

A group of different kinds of plants that live in the same area is called a PLANT COMMUNITY. Did you imagine different kinds of plants around you? What did your plant community look like?
If you have a plant community outside your classroom window, have students describe it after they've discussed their imaginary communities. Otherwise, talk about other familiar areas where there is a natural area of plants, such as a nearby park.

Why do you think certain plants grow in some places, but not in others?
Encourage and expect a wide variety of preliminary ideas from students, which will grow and change when they do their outdoor exploration. Climatic conditions determine many of the patterns of plant distribution around the globe. Within a local environment, sunlight, temperature, wind, moisture, landscape features, and soil type and fertility are some of the physical factors that influence plant distribution. Biological factors, such as seed sources, presence of animals that transport seeds or eat seeds and seedlings, and interactions among plants themselves (e.g., shading each other, competing for water) also determine what plants live in a given spot.

Module 3: Cycles—From Rot to Radishes

**Would you expect more or different kinds of plants to grow where there are a lot of dead plants decomposing on the ground than where there is no leaf litter? Why or why not?**

Students will continue to explore this question when they go outdoors during the next session. Encourage them to articulate their prior ideas, but they don't need to settle on any definitive answers yet. In general, soil that is rich in decomposing plant material has more nutrients and retains more moisture, and thus is more favorable for plant growth. Plant communities in nutrient-poor, dry soils will contain plants that are adapted to these conditions, many of which will be different species than those that grow in rich soils. Amount of plant growth is influenced by factors in addition to soil, especially sunlight.

Before we make plans for doing an outdoor investigation of what the soil is like in different areas, I want to read you a story about the work of a scientist named Dr. Charlie Canham and his research team. They are interested in where different plants grow for an unusual reason—they want to help prevent tall trees from growing in certain areas.

Read aloud the story on pages 308–310.

Make sure students have understood the story by asking questions such as:

What are Dr. Canham and his colleagues studying and why?

They are studying how shrubs' use of critical resources such as sunlight, water, and nutrients might prevent tree seedlings from growing. They are studying this question to try to help electric utility companies figure out ways to prevent trees from growing beneath their power lines.

What did they find out from doing the experiment in which they planted tree seedlings in the middle of shrubs?

Dr. Canham and his team discovered that in poor soil, the tree seedlings benefited most from not having to compete with shrubs for water and nutrients. In rich soil, the trees benefited most from not having to compete with shrubs for sunlight.

What did Dr. Canham discover from doing the "Root Races" experiment?

He found out that plants that normally grow in soil that is poor in nutrients can grow towards patches of soil that are high in nutrients more quickly than the roots of plants that usually grow in soil that is high in nutrients.

Now let's make plans for our own outdoor study. For his outdoor experiment, Dr. Canham looked for areas where the soil had different amounts of nutrients and moisture. He found that this had a big effect on the plants growing in each area. We're going to do something similar to explore whether or not the soil is different in areas that look different above ground.

How do living and dead plants, and other conditions above ground, affect soil?

When we go outside, each group's challenge is to find two places where you think the soil might be different. What are some clues to look for above ground?

Some ideas students might mention include comparing locations: with and without plants; where different kinds of plants grow; where there is a leaf litter layer and where the ground is bare; under and between hummocks of grass; under shrubs or cactus and in the open; where the ground is rocky and where there are no rocks; or where the ground is trampled and undisturbed.

Help students understand that the purpose of their study is to see if they can detect any connection between the amount or types of living or dead plant material above ground, and the consistency, moisture, or nutrient richness of the soil below ground.

Here is a data sheet for recording your observations. Look it over in your groups, then be ready to summarize your tasks in your own words.

Assign students to groups and give each person a "Plant & Soil Connections Data Sheet." After they read and discuss the data sheet in their groups, have them summarize their challenge aloud. They might need help understanding what they should write as a question for item #2. If so, explain that once they are outside they can form a question about differences between two sites such as *Is the soil in a place covered with pine trees different from the soil in a place covered with grass?*

Session 2

What are some behaviors to keep in mind while doing field work?

Review field trip rules and safety reminders (see page 69).

Remember that we should try not to destroy the roots of plants when digging soil samples.

Have each group get its trowel, plastic pipe, tray, hand lenses, and data sheets to take outside.

When you arrive at the study site, gather students in a central meeting location. Point out prominent landmarks that mark the study site boundaries.

Look around with your group for two sites within the boundaries where you think the soil could differ. Decide on a specific question you want to answer, and write it on your data sheet. Then go to the first site, and complete Part 1 of your data sheet.

Each group's sites don't need to be far apart. For instance, the upper layer of soil directly beneath and one meter beyond a shrub could be different. Help students make and record detailed observations of above-ground characteristics, such as the depth of leaf litter and the types of prominent plants.

Next, dig a soil sample and put it on your tray to examine it. Record your observations of the soil in Part 2 of the data sheet. Follow the same procedures at your other site.

You might want to demonstrate a few methods of collecting soil samples. If the soil is moist or held together by a network of fine roots, students can cut out a square of soil to observe.

If the soil is dry, students can remove soil one scoop at a time, and display the scoops side-by-side on their tray to observe any differences in the samples from upper to lower layers of the soil.

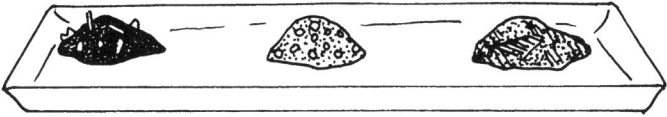

Another method for collecting soil samples is to push a piece of 2″ plastic pipe into the ground as far as it will go, then remove it. Students will have a soil core inside the pipe which they can push out carefully with a stick.

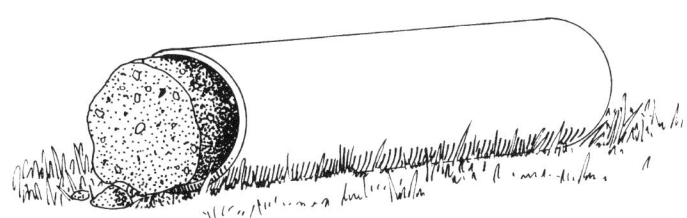

Soil Profiles

Soils have different layers, called horizons, between the uppermost decomposing organic matter at the surface of the soil, and mineral or bedrock at its base. These layers differ in texture and color because of the size and type of particles in them. Soil horizons form in part through the action of water that leaches and deposits different minerals and organic particles in different layers. Plowing, rototilling, or bulldozing and grading can eliminate or alter soil horizons.

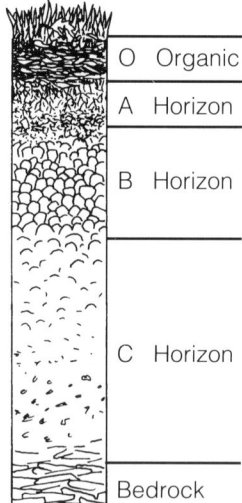

All soils have some sort of profile, although how thick and distinct the horizons are varies greatly from place to place. Students won't see an entire soil profile just by digging 10 centimeters or so into the soil, but they might notice that the color and/or texture of the soil changes the deeper they dig. Differences in the appearance or thickness of soil horizons might be one of their major findings when comparing soils in their two sites.

Help to focus students' observations on characteristics of their soil samples, such as texture, color, layers, organisms, fungal hyphae, and burrows. They could also measure the width of each distinct layer, and rate the moisture level of the soil.

Make sure students return their soil samples to the holes they dug, unless you want soil for the "Growth of Plants in Different Soils Test" (see page 307).

Session 3

Spend some time in your groups pulling together the information you collected outdoors. Be ready to share your research question and findings with the whole class.

Have students work in their groups to share and complete the notes they recorded on their data sheets, and decide which data sheet(s) to hand in at the end of class to represent their group's findings.

Let's share your questions and the answers you discovered.

You might want to record each group's question on a class list.

Is the soil under a rock different from the soil under a shrub?

Is the soil under the swing set different from the soil under the lawn?

Is the soil in a place with a lot of dead leaves different from the soil where the ground is bare?

Once each group has shared its findings, the class can try to find patterns in their observations, to see if they can make any generalizations. Help students realize that this is how scientists build knowledge. Encourage them to support their ideas with evidence.

Depending on the sites students investigated, they may or may not have noticed correlations between the character of the soil and the living or dead plants on it. This is truly an opportunity for your class to draw its own conclusions about the soil conditions different plants seem to grow in locally, and in turn how living and dead plants and other conditions above ground might be influencing the soil. However, students should realize that since they didn't do a controlled experiment, more than the one factor each group focused on (e.g., sites with and without leaf litter) varied between the two sites. This makes it difficult to attribute any differences in soil they observed to a single factor.

 Conclude with questions such as:

How do you think dead plants affect soil and the living plants that grow in it?
In general, dead plants enrich soil with nutrients. The organic matter also helps the soil retain moisture. In these ways, leaf litter enhances a soil's ability to provide two important resources for plants.

How would the ability to live in soil that is low in nutrients and moisture be beneficial to a plant?
There are many places where these conditions occur, so plants that can tolerate them can flourish there.

In addition to soil, what else could affect where plants grow?
It is important for students to realize that where plants grow is not just due to soil, but also to climate and other physical and biological factors. (See page 300 for variables that influence where plants grow.)

What new questions or ideas for investigations do you have as a result of your observations?
As students share their ideas, help them realize that scientists usually have many more questions after doing an investigation than they had to begin with.

Ongoing Assessment

Student Reflections

 Have students send a C-Mail message or record thoughts in their journals. Optional writing prompts include:

If I was a plant, I'd want to live _____ *because...*

To make perfect conditions for growing garden plants, I would...

Teacher Reflections

❑ In what ways did students' prior ideas about soil and plant connections change and grow?

❑ Do their data sheets reveal insight into why the soil in different sites might differ?

❑ Did they make and record thorough observations?

❑ Were they able to use the information they recorded to make generalizations and ask new questions?

❑ Do they understand that decomposing plants that become part of the soil benefit living plants by providing nutrients and retaining moisture?

Extensions

Root Races. Have students find out whether roots prefer growing in plain vermiculite, or in a mixture of vermiculite and compost. They can set up this investigation by taping a vertical plastic divider (e.g., plastic wrap) three-quarters of the way up the middle of a clear plastic cup that has bottom drainage holes. They should put vermiculite on one side of the divider, compost with vermiculite (1 part compost to 5 parts vermiculite) on the other side, and vermiculite across the top of both sides. Then students can plant a seed in the center of the cup within the upper layer of vermiculite. As the plant grows, they can compare the volume and length of roots showing through each side of the cup to see which planting medium encourages more root growth. Students will need to cover the sides of the cup with dark paper to keep the roots shaded.

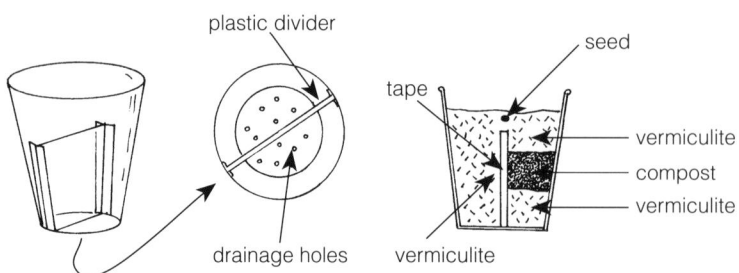

Plant Ups and Downs. Either dig up several plants with their root systems intact, or purchase root vegetables that still have their greens attached. Cut a hole in the bottom of a paper bag for each plant. Place the plants in the bags so that the roots come out through the holes, but the stems and leaves are hidden inside the bags. Have students guess what kind of plant is attached to each type of root. Another way to do this is to cut up pictures of plants, and have students try to match the upper and lower portions of the plants.

Soil Chemistry Tests. Purchase soil chemical test kits, such as for nitrogen, phosphorus, potassium, and pH, through a science supply catalog or gardening center. Students can work in groups to learn to use one type of test kit, then teach the procedures to the other groups. They can test soil samples in different outdoor locations, and/or test compost, vermiculite, and potting soil.

Growth of Plants in Different Soils Test. Have students collect soil from different outdoor locations, then set up a controlled experiment testing the growth of one kind of plant in the different soils.

Perc Tests. In order to have land approved for installing a septic system, soil must pass a "perc" (percolation) test to show that it has good drainage. Students can scope out two or more hypothetical housing sites and do perc tests on soil samples they collect from each. They can put a measured amount of soil in a funnel resting in a jar, then pour a measured amount of water at a constant rate on top of the soil. Students should time how long it takes for water to start dripping out of the soil into the jar, and how much water drips through over time. The soil sample that water flows through most quickly is the best for a septic system. Students can also experiment with how percolation differs when they modify the soil samples by adding materials such as sand, clay, or organic matter.

Mystery Soils. Collect three soil samples that have different textures and colors from an outdoor area. Take students to the area, show them the three samples, and challenge them to predict, and then find, where each one came from.

Biography of a Scientist. Have students do research on a scientist, either by interviewing a local scientist, or by consulting books and articles. They could present the story of that scientist's life and research in creative ways, such as through a scrapbook or diary. Students could also take on the persona of that scientist and be interviewed by their classmates.

Plant Happenings, Above and Below: The Work of Ecologist Dr. Charlie Canham

Dr. Charlie Canham, an ecologist at the Institute of Ecosystem Studies in New York State, has been helping to solve a big problem for electric companies—how to prevent trees from growing under their power lines.

Electric power companies run overhead power lines across miles and miles of land to bring electricity to their customers. In the northeastern United States, in places like New York, trees grow under the power lines. When the trees get so tall that their branches touch the lines and cause the power to short out, the utility company has to stop transmitting electricity.

Utility companies can spray the land under power lines with herbicides to kill tree seedlings. But since many herbicides are bad for the environment, they want to figure out better ways to manage their "right-of-ways"—the strips of land under the power lines. Another option is to cut down the trees, but a lot of hardwood trees sprout back up from stumps, so cutting them doesn't solve the problem.

Dr. Canham and his colleagues have been doing experiments for nearly ten years to figure out what kinds of natural conditions make it difficult for tree seedlings to survive underneath power lines. One of their studies began when Dr. Canham noticed that trees are less likely to grow where the land is covered with SHRUBS—woody plants that don't get as tall as trees. Dr. Canham decided to investigate what prevents trees from growing where there are shrubs, so that perhaps electric utility companies could make this work in their favor.

What do you think might prevent tree seedlings from growing where shrubs are already growing?

Pause for discussion.

Dr. Canham had several ideas. Maybe young trees don't grow well where there are shrubs, because the shrubs shade them so they don't get enough light. Or maybe the roots of shrubs take up so much water and nutrients that new trees can't get enough to survive. Another possibility was that maybe light and root COMPETITION together prevent tree seedlings from getting established in shrub communities.

To test these ideas, Dr. Canham and his colleagues chose two places that were covered with shrubs: 1) a dry site where the soil did not have many nutrients, and 2) a site where the soil had a humus layer, so was moist and had more nutrients.

Dr. Canham set up several plots in each site. In each he planted tree seedlings in the middle of a group of shrubs. In some of the plots at each site, he wired back the branches of the shrubs so the tree seedlings could get full sunlight. In other plots he dug a trench around the tree seedlings, and put down a special fabric to prevent the roots of the shrubs from getting the nutrients and moisture from the soil where the young trees were planted. In other plots he did both treatments: he gave the tree seedlings full sun, and he prevented shrub roots from competing with the young tree roots. Finally, he had a control group of tree seedlings planted in a clump of shrubs where nothing was altered.

Pause to show "Shrub Invaders" overhead, covering Part B with paper.

Where do you predict the tree seedlings would grow the most? The least? Why?

Pause for discussion.

Dr. Canham and his research team measured how much the tree seedlings grew in their study plots during a spring and summer. They found out that on the sites with poor soil, cutting out the roots of shrubs helped the tree seedlings grow better than giving them extra light. In sites with good soil, letting extra light in by wiring back the shrubs helped the young trees grow more than cutting back the roots of the shrubs.

Pause to show Part B of the "Shrub Invaders" overhead.

This information is useful to power companies because now they know that they should take the soil conditions into consideration when planning ways to keep tall trees from growing beneath their power lines.

Dr. Canham and his colleagues have also done greenhouse experiments to figure out what goes on underground in different soil conditions. They called these experiments "Root Races." They wanted to find out if roots of different shrubs and trees can find patches of nutrients in poor soil. Even in poor soil that is low in nutrients, there can be patches of nutrients where an animal died and decomposed, or where a dead log is rotting. Do you think plant roots would be able to find these patches?

Pause for discussion.

The scientists made big boxes in which to plant seedlings. One end of the boxes was wood and the other end had a root observation window made of Plexiglas. When the scientists weren't making observations they kept the window covered, since roots grow better in the dark.

Pause to show "Root Races" overhead, covering Part B with paper.

To set up the experiment, Dr. Canham and his team put sand in each box, and planted a tree or shrub seedling in the middle. In one half of the box they put different amounts of fertilizer, with the most fertilizer in the layer of sand closest to the observation window. This area imitated patches of soil outdoors that are high in nutrients. They didn't add any fertilizer to the sand between the seedling and the wooden end of the box. They kept the boxes in a greenhouse where the conditions were good for growing plants.

As soon as they saw that roots had reached the observation window in a box, Dr. Canham and his colleagues measured how much the plant had grown, and how many roots had grown in each section of sand. They found that the kinds of trees and shrubs that usually grow in soils without many nutrients grew more roots, more quickly, in the parts of the boxes that had the most fertilizer. That means that plants that grow in poor soil are good at finding patches where nutrients are concentrated, and can beat other plants to those patches.

Pause to show Part B of the "Root Races" overhead.

The scientists discovered that the roots of plants that grow in better soil didn't race to patches of good soil as quickly, perhaps because they usually get enough nutrients without having to use extra energy to grow more roots in a certain direction. This information helps utility companies identify which trees are most likely to grow tall and create problems where power lines are in places with poor soil.

The discoveries made by Dr. Canham's research team have helped utility companies and other scientists realize that what happens below ground, where plants get water and nutrients, can be as important in determining where plants can grow as what happens above ground, where plants compete for sunlight. Hopefully this information will help utility companies use the natural processes of plant competition to prevent tall trees from growing under their power lines.

SHRUB INVADERS

PART A — EXPERIMENT SETUP

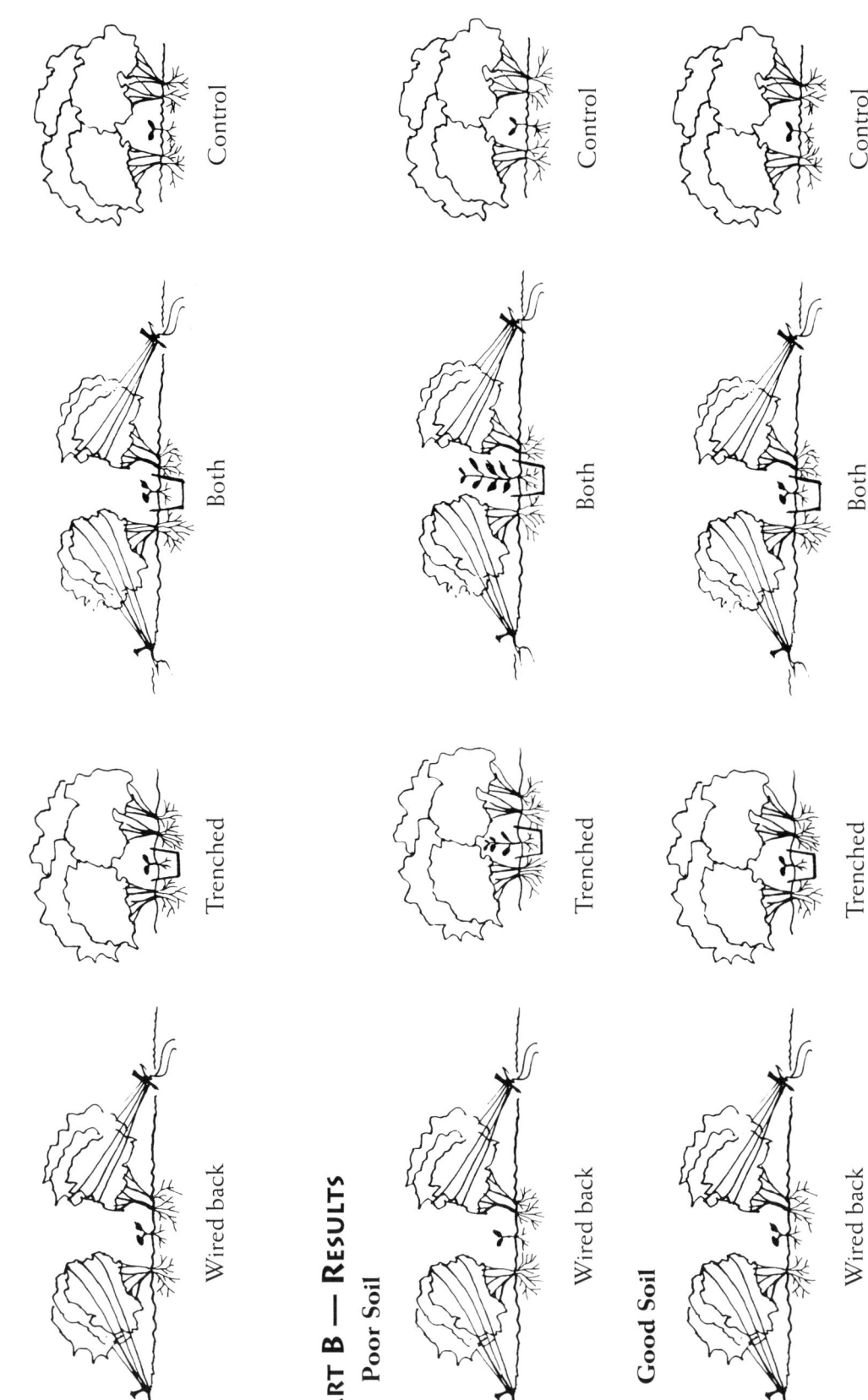

Wired back   Trenched   Both   Control

PART B — RESULTS
Poor Soil

Wired back   Trenched   Both   Control

Good Soil

Wired back   Trenched   Both   Control

3.4 Exploring Plant and Soil Connections

ROOT RACES

PART A — EXPERIMENT SETUP

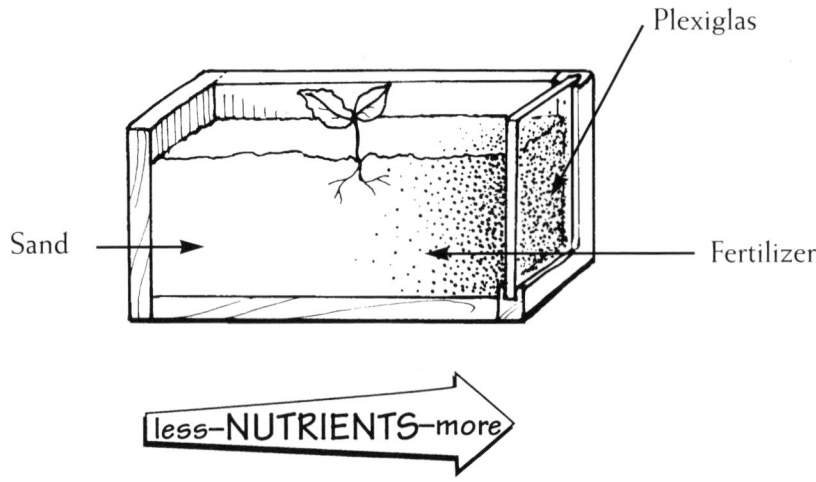

Plexiglas

Sand

Fertilizer

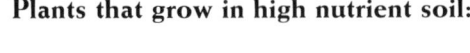
less—NUTRIENTS—more

PART B — RESULTS

Plants that grow in low nutrient soil:

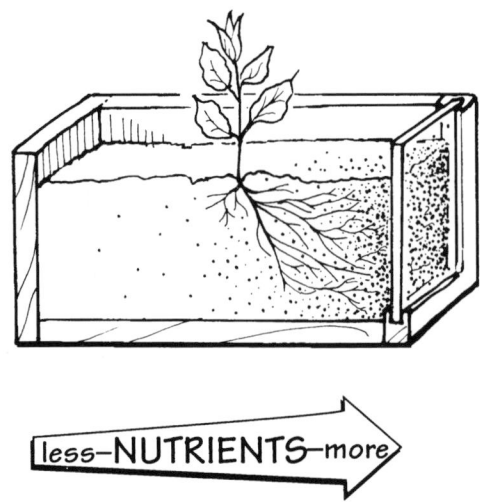

less—NUTRIENTS—more

Plants that grow in high nutrient soil:

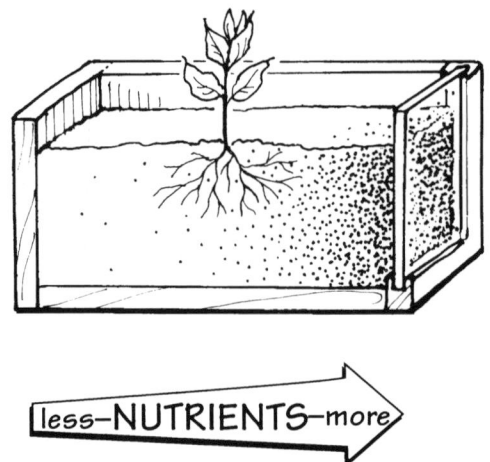

less—NUTRIENTS—more

           Module 3: *Cycles—From Rot to Radishes*

PLANT & SOIL CONNECTIONS DATA SHEET

Directions

1. Look for two sites where you think the soil will differ. Give each place a name. Write the names at the top of the two columns.

2. Write a question that you'd like to answer by comparing soils at your two sites:

   _____

3. At each site, first fill out Part 1 of the data table.

4. Dig a sample of soil from each site and put them on your tray. Observe the samples.

5. Fill out Part 2 with your observations of the soil.

	SITE #1 NAME:	SITE #2 NAME:
Part 1: SITE		
1. Describe features of the site that might affect the soil. *(Is it shady or bright? Flat or sloped? Are plants growing there? What types? Many or few? Is there leaf litter on the ground? How deep is it?)*		
2. What do you predict the soil will be like? Why?		
Part 2: SOIL		
3. Describe the soil. *(How does it look, smell, and feel? Is it moist or dry? Does it stick together or crumble? Are there roots in it? Are there living things in it? Are there layers?)*		

3.4 *Exploring Plant and Soil Connections*

3.5 Planting Preferences—
Written Assessment

Action Synopsis

Students work in groups to rank four sites according to their suitability for planting shrubs, then independently complete a diagram showing a nutrient cycle for the preferred site.

One Session		**40–60 minutes**
1. Read a challenge that requires choosing a planting site where shrubs will get adequate nutrients.		*posing a challenge*
2. Discuss scoring criteria.		*setting standards*
3. Work in groups to list the pros and cons of each site, and then rank them.		*applying knowledge*
4. Talk about rankings and share reasons for the choices.		*communicating*
5. Discuss the second part of the challenge—tracking the flow of nutrients—and complete it for homework.		*applying knowledge*

Desired Outcomes

By the end of this assessment activity, students should:

✓ Understand that the nutrients available on a site depend on the history and current conditions of the site.

✓ Be able to weigh pros and cons to make and support judgments.

✓ Be able to diagram steps in a nutrient cycle.

✓ Be able to judge their own work and reflect on their understanding of nutrient cycling.

What You'll Need

For each group of 3–4 students:
- ❏ copy of four "Planting Preferences Cards" (pages 322-323—see "Getting Ready")
- ❏ copy of "Scoring Sheet" (page 321—see "Getting Ready")

For each student:
- ❏ copy of "Challenge Sheet, Part 1" (page 319)
- ❏ copy of "Challenge Sheet, Part 2" (page 320)
- ❏ copy of "Scoring Sheet" (page 321)
- ❏ copy of "Reflections" (page 41)

Getting Ready

♦ If possible, laminate each set of "Planting Preferences Cards" you make.

♦ You'll need a copy of the "Scoring Sheet" for each group as well as one for each student, because students receive a group score for Part 1 of the challenge, and an individual score for Part 2.

♦ When you copy the two "Challenge Sheet" pages, don't collate them because you'll hand them out separately.

♦ You can plan to have students work in their research groups, or form new groups for this activity.

Action Narrative

We're going to do an activity that challenges you to use your knowledge about nutrient cycling. Here is the first part of your challenge.

Hand out and have students read the "Challenge Sheet, Part 1." Go over it to make sure they understand their task.

After you finish this part of the challenge in groups, I'll give you the second part for each person to do alone. What do you think I'll look for when I score your work?

Encourage students to articulate their ideas about what knowledge they can demonstrate by fulfilling the challenge. Make sure that they understand that there is not necessarily one right answer to the challenge. What is most important is how well they support their choices. Hand out a "Scoring Sheet" to each student, and review the objectives listed for Part 1.

Begin the challenge as soon as you get the cards that describe each location the Community Club is considering.

Assign students to groups, and give each a set of the four "Planting Preferences Cards." You might want to suggest that each group member read a different card aloud to the rest of the group, to involve everyone. They might also want to choose one student per group to record the pros and cons they generate.

As you circulate and listen to the groups' discussions, make sure they are encouraging each person to contribute ideas. If students get into heated arguments over differences of opinion, help them focus on using argumentation skills to explore and refine ideas. This requires good listening skills, open-mindedness, and critical reflection, as well as the ability to give the person advancing an idea positive acknowledgement, even while disagreeing with the idea itself.

Groups will need about 20 minutes to complete the challenge. Make a chart on the board to record how they rank the sites.

	1st	2nd	3rd	4th
Green Acre Gardens				
Brady Forest				
Office District				
Town Lot				

How many groups ranked Green Acre Gardens as your first choice? Your second? Your third? Your fourth?

Tally the class results for Green Acre Gardens, then repeat the process for each of the other sites.

	1st	2nd	3rd	4th
Green Acre Gardens	1	1	4	1

Once the chart is complete, have students share the reasons for their choices. See below for pros and cons students might mention. Hold a discussion to help them examine their ideas and assumptions.

Each group needs to hand in one completed "Challenge Sheet, Part 1" with everyone's names on it.

Attach a group "Scoring Sheet" to each, to use for scoring Part 1 of the challenge.

Now here is the second part of the challenge for you to do on your own as homework.

Give each student a copy of the "Challenge Sheet, Part 2." Go over it to make sure they understand that their diagram should show several steps in a nutrient cycle that is specific to the site where they've chosen to plant the shrubs.

Review the objectives listed under Part 2 of the "Scoring Sheet" so that students understand how their individual work will be evaluated. Have them attach their own "Scoring Sheet" to their "Challenge Sheet, Part 2."

After you score their completed homework assignment, you can transfer group scores for Part 1 to each individual's "Scoring Sheet" so that each student receives a combined score for group and individual work.

Ongoing Assessment

Student Reflections

Have students complete a "Scoring Sheet" to score their own group and individual work. This is also a good time for them to complete a "Reflections" sheet (page 41).

Teacher Reflections

Challenge Sheet, Part 1
The chart below lists some of the pros and cons of each site, to look for in students' work.

Site	Pros	Cons
A: Green Acre Gardens	• there might still be fertilizer or compost in the ground • some of the garden plants might have rotted and returned nutrients to the soil • land has been worked so will be easy to plant in	• harvesting garden plants might have used up all the nutrients in the soil • some weeds grow best in poor soil, so weeds might mean that the soil is low in nutrients • could be hard to get rid of the weeds • pesticides in the soil might have killed some of the decomposers that recycle nutrients

Site	Pros	Cons
B: Brady Forest	• lots of dead plants are there to provide nutrients • mushrooms and other decomposers are breaking down the dead plants and releasing nutrients	• logs and branches don't break down very quickly • it could be hard to clear the site to make room for the shrubs
C: Office District	• the ground is bare so it would be easy to plant shrubs	• probably all of the topsoil where there are the most nutrients was scraped away • since nothing has grown there in the year since the building came down, the soil must be low in nutrients or toxic
D: Town Lot	• leaves at the bottom of the layer are probably decomposing and returning nutrients to the soil • leaves could stay around the shrubs once they are planted to keep weeds from growing up, and to keep providing nutrients to the shrubs	• not sure what is under leaves—if it is pavement, it would not be good for the shrubs • it could be a lot of work to clear away the leaves to make room for the shrubs

Challenge Sheet, Part 2

The student's diagram below illustrates the steps in a nutrient cycle for the Brady Forest site. The diagrams for all sites should be similar, showing:

shrubs ← soil ← dead plants ← living plants.

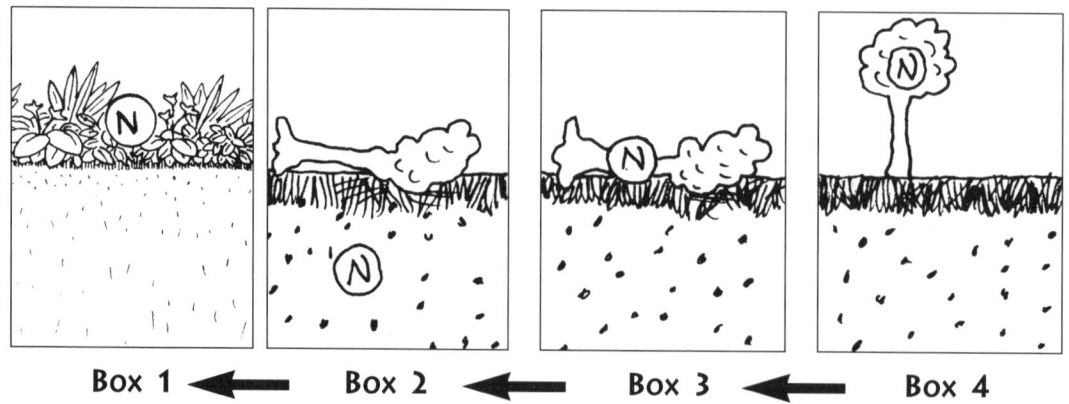

Students' explanation of how nutrients get out of dead plants and into soil (question #2) should mention that decomposers consume the dead plants and release the nutrients that were in the plants into the soil. They might name specific decomposers, such as mushrooms, which are mentioned in the Brady Forest site description.

NAME(S)_____ DATE_____

PLANTING PREFERENCES

The Community Club of Pleasantville received a donation of flowering shrubs. They had a meeting to talk about where to plant them. They thought of four possible locations. All four places:

- get sunlight all day;
- get the same amount of rain; and
- are where lots of people will see and enjoy the shrubs.

The club doesn't have any money for fertilizer, so they want to plant the shrubs where they'll get plenty of nutrients naturally.

YOUR GROUP'S CHALLENGE:

1. Read the descriptions of the four places on the Planting Preferences Cards.

2. Discuss and record the pros and cons of each place for growing shrubs.

3. Decide which place would be best for planting all of the shrubs. Give that place "1st" in the Rank column. Then rank the others as your 2nd, 3rd, and 4th choices.

		PROS	CONS	RANK
A	Green Acre Gardens			
B	Brady Forest			
C	Office District			
D	Town Lot			

4. Explain why your 1st choice is the best location. Use the back of the sheet.

NAME_____ DATE_____

PLANTING PREFERENCES

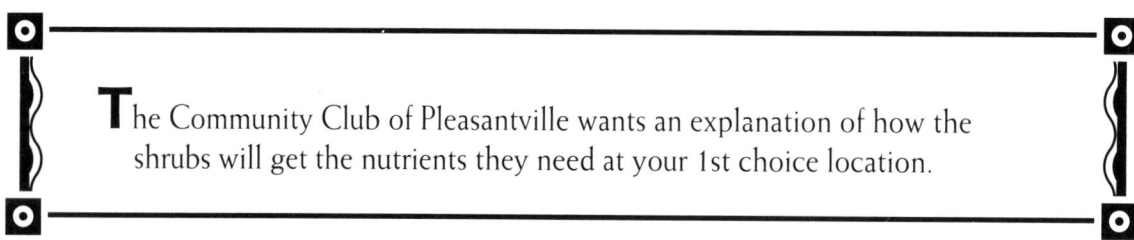

The Community Club of Pleasantville wants an explanation of how the shrubs will get the nutrients they need at your 1st choice location.

YOUR CHALLENGE:

1. In Box #2, draw a picture that shows where the nutrients (N) might have been before they became part of the shrubs. In Box #3, draw where the nutrients might have been before that. In Box #4, draw where the nutrients might have been before that.

Use this symbol (N) in your drawings to show where the nutrients are located.

Below each box, write what the nutrients were in.

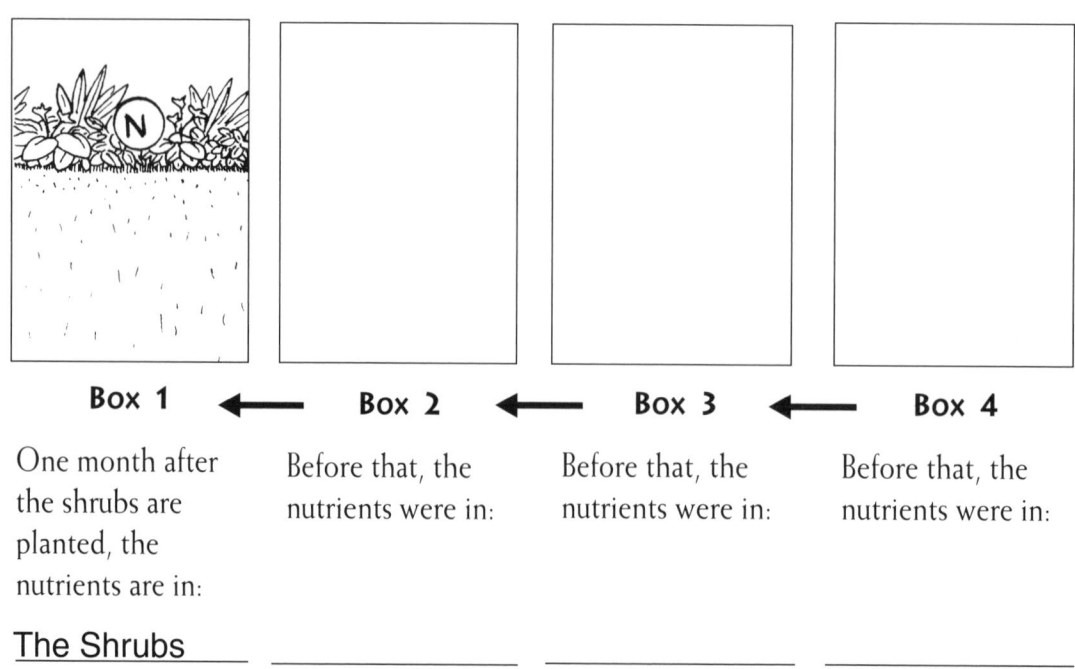

Box 1 ←	Box 2 ←	Box 3 ←	Box 4
One month after the shrubs are planted, the nutrients are in:	Before that, the nutrients were in:	Before that, the nutrients were in:	Before that, the nutrients were in:
The Shrubs	_____	_____	_____

2. Explain how nutrients get out of dead plants and into soil. Use the back of the sheet.

NAME(S)_____ DATE_____

PLANTING PREFERENCES

OBJECTIVES	POINTS				SCORE
	3 High Quality	**2** Meets Objectives	**1** Falls Short	**0** Not Done	
PART 1: **GROUP CHALLENGE** 1. Pros explain why some sites would have more nutrients.	_____	_____	_____	_____	___ x 2 =___
2. Cons explain why some sites would have fewer nutrients.	_____	_____	_____	_____	=___
3. Ranking of choices shows that all pros and cons were were weighed.	_____	_____	_____	_____	=___
4. Pros and cons include other reasons why sites are good or bad for planting shrubs.	_____	_____	_____	_____	=___
PART 2: **INDIVIDUAL CHALLENGE** 5. Drawings and labels correctly show steps in a nutrient cycle.	_____	_____	_____	_____	___ x 2 =___
6. Steps shown make sense for the chosen site.	_____	_____	_____	_____	=___
7. Explanation of how nutrients are released is clear and correct.	_____	_____	_____	_____	=___

COMMENTS:

FINAL SCORE: _____

Total Possible Score: 27
Overall Achievement:
   23–27 High
   18–22 Sound
   9–17 Limited
   0–8 Inadequate

SITE A
GREEN ACRE GARDENS

This site used to be a community garden. Four families shared it and grew vegetables here for ten years. They stopped using it three years ago. Now a lot of tall weeds grow here.

SITE B
BRADY FOREST

This site was a small forest. The town recently cut it down, leaving logs, leaves, and branches on the ground. A lot of mushrooms grow here.

322   Module 3: *Cycles — From Rot to Radishes*

SITE C

OFFICE DISTRICT

This site used to have an office building on it. The building was torn down about a year ago. All parts of the building were taken away. Now the ground is bare.

SITE D

TOWN LOT

This site is where the town crew dumps the leaves it collects from lawns. The crew spreads the leaves over the lot. The ground now has a layer of leaves about 15 cm deep.

323

3.6 Radish Results

Action Synopsis

Students make and process final observations of their plants, graph and discuss their data in groups, compile the whole class' data, discuss conclusions, then write letters to GROW.

Session 1		40 minutes
1. Discuss observations.		*processing findings*
2. Compare the color and lengths of treatment and control plants' leaves.		*observing & recording*
3. Demonstrate how to make bar and line graphs.		*introducing new information*
4. Graph plant height data.		*processing findings*

Session 2		1 hour
1. Finish and discuss graphs.		*processing findings*
2. Calculate average growth for treatment and control plants in groups, then put numbers on a whole class data chart.		*processing findings*

Continued

Module 3: *Cycles—From Rot to Radishes*

3. Average all of the class data to get final average growth for treatment and control plants. 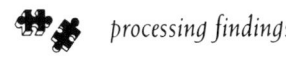 *processing findings*

4. Discuss variation among replicates. 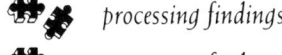 *processing findings*

5. Decide which indicators of plant growth were most useful. 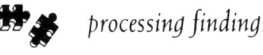 *processing findings*

6. Discuss and write conclusions. 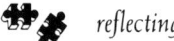 *reflecting*

7. Write letters to GROW for homework.  *communicating*

Desired Outcomes

Throughout the lesson, check that students:

✓ Can make insightful observations and accurate measurements.

✓ Can graph their data.

✓ Can use and interpret their graphs.

✓ Are willing to acknowledge and try to explain unexpected results.

✓ Are able to draw conclusions that are supported by their data.

What You'll Need

Session 1

For each group of 3–4 students:
- ❏ sample card of paint chips in shades of green (optional)
- ❏ rulers

For each student:
- ❏ 1–2 sheets of graph paper

Session 2

For the class:
- ❏ sheet of newsprint (see "Getting Ready")

For each student:
- ❏ 3–4 8-oz. paper cups (optional)
- ❏ copy of "Experiment Conclusions" (page 336)
- ❏ copy of "Group Work Evaluation" (page 42)

Getting Ready

Session 1

♦ Either make sample graphs on overhead transparencies (see pages 328–329), or plan to draw them on the board as you introduce them.

Session 2

♦ Make a whole class data chart on a sheet of newsprint:

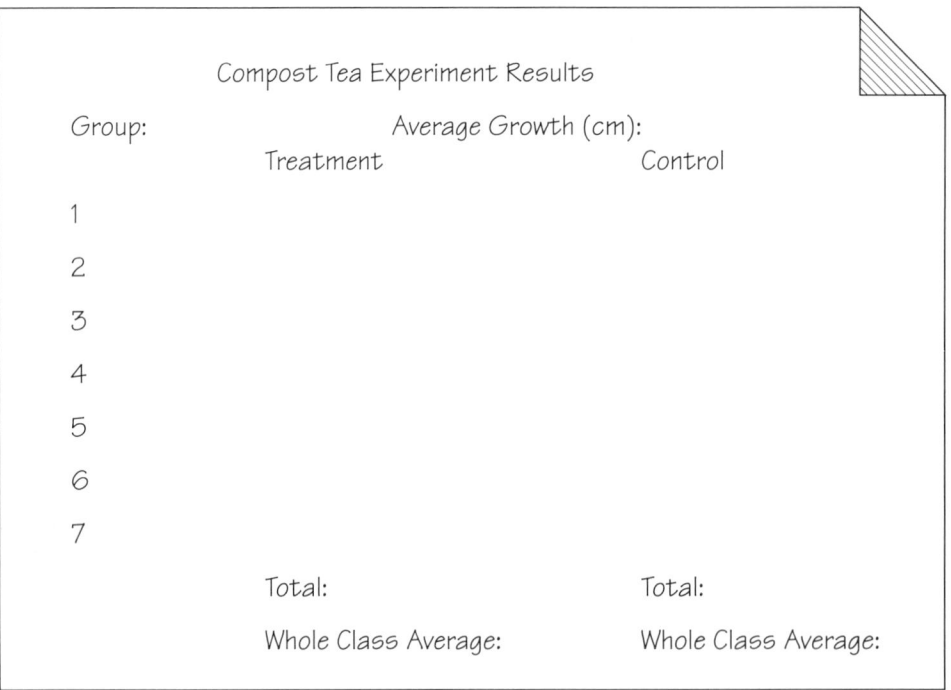

Compost Tea Experiment Results

Group:	Average Growth (cm):	
	Treatment	Control
1		
2		
3		
4		
5		
6		
7		
	Total:	Total:
	Whole Class Average:	Whole Class Average:

Action Narrative

Session 1

We're going to spend the next two periods looking at your data and drawing conclusions. Before we try to make sense of the numbers on your data charts, let's talk about your general observations.

What have you been noticing and keeping track of?
Have students talk about how their observations expanded beyond plant height as they watched the plants develop. For instance, they might have noted when the first true leaves appeared on the treatment and control plants, or how droopy or straight the plants were. Also encourage students to describe what they've found most interesting or surprising.

Are there any obvious differences in how the treatment and control plants look?

Encourage students to refer to the notes they've taken during the past few weeks, as well as to the plants themselves, in order to consider which characteristics of the plants may be the best indicators of treatment effects.

If students haven't been keeping track of the color or length of leaves, have them make these observations now. Encourage them to think of ways to make these measurements objective.

Comparing Leaf Colors

Students can use paint chips or make a color chart with markers to compare the shades of treatment and control plant leaves.

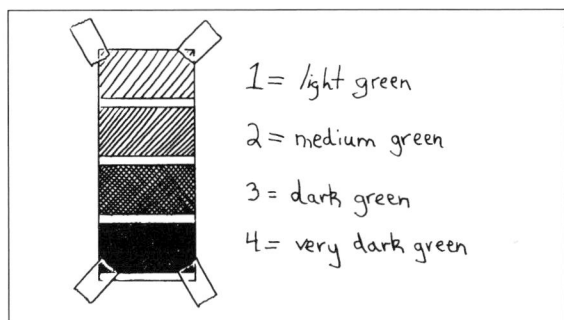

Students can average the scores for leaf colors on control plants, and on treatment plants, to see if there is an overall difference in color between treatment and control plants.

LEAF COLOR (1 = light green; 4 = very dark green)
Date: April 15th

Treatment:		Control:	
T1	3	C1	2
T2	4	C2	2
T3	3	C3	3
T4	3	C4	2
T5	4	C5	1
T6	2	C6	3
Total: 19		Total: 13	
Average: 3.2		Average: 2.2	

Comparing Leaf Lengths

In the compost tea experiment, leaf lengths are often a better indicator of plant health than plant height. One problem with plant height is that plants that do not get enough sunlight become "leggy," so can be tall even though they are not healthy.

To compare leaf lengths, students should choose the largest true leaf on each plant, and measure and record its length from the tip to its base where it attaches to the stem.

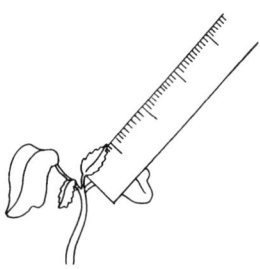

Students can then average the lengths of the largest true leaf on each control plant, and compare this number to the average length of the largest leaves on treatment plants.

LEAF LENGTH (cm)
Date: April 15th

Treatment:		Control:	
T1	4.0	C1	1.2
T2	3.2	C2	1.1
T3	3.4	C3	1.1
T4	3.5	C4	1.0
T5	3.8	C5	1.5
T6	3.3	C6	1.3
Total: 21.2		Total: 7.2	
Average: 3.5		Average: 1.2	

Have students discuss whether or not compost tea affected plant health based on leaf color and/or leaf length of treatment and control plants.

Now let's graph your plant height data. Scientists make graphs to get a clear picture of what happened during their experiment.

Show students how to make bar and/or line graphs to show the height of treatment and control plants over time.

Give each student a sheet of graph paper on which to graph plant height data. Making graphs will likely extend into the next period.

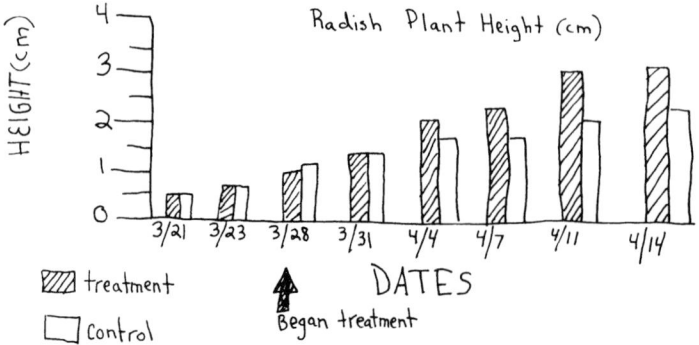

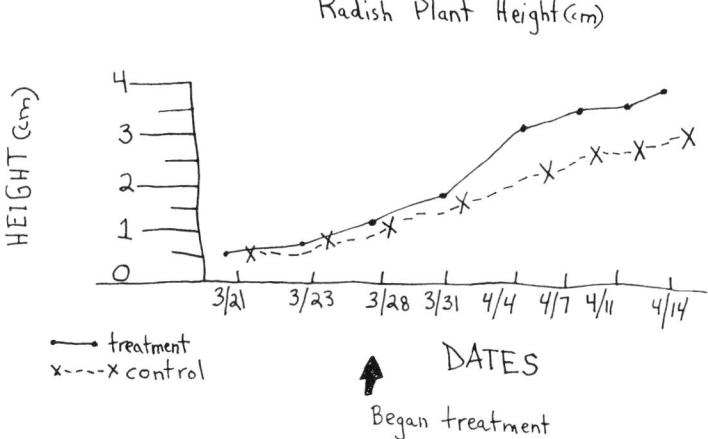

Radish Plant Height (cm)

HEIGHT (cm)

DATES

● — ● treatment
x - - - x control

Began treatment

Session 2

Finish making the graphs you started yesterday.

Students who have completed one graph can try the other type of graphing until everyone has made at least one graph. They can also compare their graphs to those made by the rest of their group. The graphs for each group should look similar if they used the same data.

Let's see what the graphs tell us.

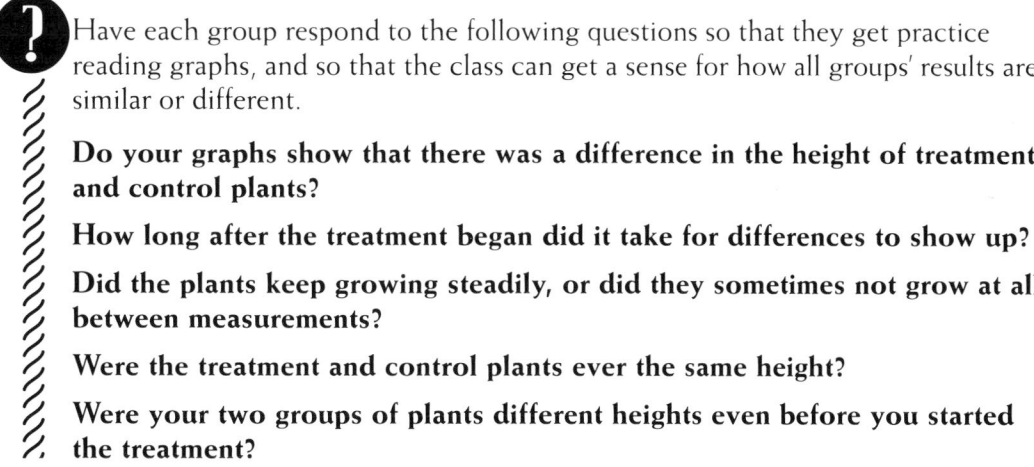

Have each group respond to the following questions so that they get practice reading graphs, and so that the class can get a sense for how all groups' results are similar or different.

Do your graphs show that there was a difference in the height of treatment and control plants?

How long after the treatment began did it take for differences to show up?

Did the plants keep growing steadily, or did they sometimes not grow at all between measurements?

Were the treatment and control plants ever the same height?

Were your two groups of plants different heights even before you started the treatment?

Each group now has a good idea of what happened to its own treatment and control plants during the experiment. But we still don't have the whole picture. What else do we need to do?

Since each group did a replicate of one big experiment, the class needs to compile its data. Results of one group's work might not reflect the overall pattern of class results.

I've made a chart on which each group can record its results so that we can get one final result for our whole experiment.

Show students the data chart you've prepared and point out its sections. Help the class realize that it can be more certain of results by taking into account all of the replicates.

Compost Tea Experiment Results		
Group:	Average Growth (cm):	
	Treatment	Control
1		
2		
3		
4		
5		
6		
7		
	Total:	Total:
	Whole Class Average:	Whole Class Average:

Each group needs to summarize all of its data to get just two numbers to add to the chart. How will you get the overall average growth for your treatment and control plants?

At first students might suggest that they should just record the final average heights for their treatment and control plants in the two columns. However, this will not reveal how much the plants grew. To calculate growth, as opposed to final height, students will need to subtract the average height of the treatment and control plants on the day they started the treatment, from the height the plants were on the last day they took measurements.

The reason that students should use total growth rather than final height to draw conclusions about their experiment is because the treatment and control plants might have started at different heights, so final height figures could be misleading.

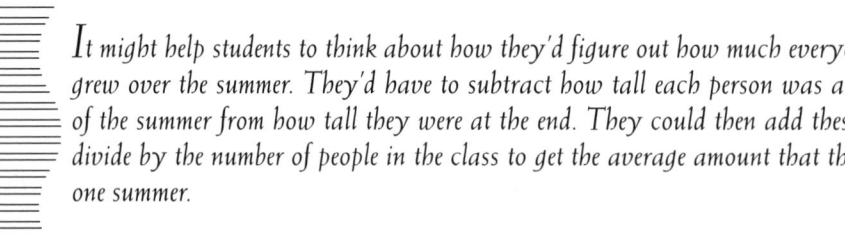

It might help students to think about how they'd figure out how much everyone in the class grew over the summer. They'd have to subtract how tall each person was at the beginning of the summer from how tall they were at the end. They could then add these numbers and divide by the number of people in the class to get the average amount that the class grew in one summer.

Work in your groups to make calculations, then choose someone to add your two final numbers to the class chart.

Once all of the groups' numbers are on the chart, have the class add them to get totals for each column, then divide the totals by the number of groups to get final averages.

Compost Tea Experiment Results

Group:	Average Growth (cm):	
	Treatment	Control
1	2.0	1.2
2	2.3	2.0
3	3.0	1.6
4	2.7	1.5
5	2.2	1.5
6	2.3	1.7
7	2.6	1.6
	Total: 17.1	Total: 11.1
	Whole Class Average: 2.4	Whole Class Average: 1.6

Students can make a bar graph on the board to display all of the groups' results.

Radish Growth (cm)

Help students analyze their results and draw conclusions with questions such as:

Were groups' results similar to or quite different from each other?
Have students look at the bar graph or class chart to see how much variation there is among different groups' results. It could be that just one or two groups' numbers are radically different from the rest.

If all of the groups' results are quite variable, have students think first about whether the differences could be due to different experimental methods—perhaps some groups kept their plants in a different part of the classroom, used stronger compost tea, or watered more frequently.

If students decide that their methods were as identical as possible, then they can attribute the differences to natural variation in the plants themselves.

Are the differences in the final averages you got for treatment and control plants large enough to say that the compost tea helped the plants grow?

Scientists use statistics to tell them how confident to be that differences in numbers they're comparing are significant, and not just due to chance. Since students won't be applying statistics to their numbers, help them to judge how big of a difference is large enough to allow them to say that the compost tea really affected plant growth. The key to making this judgment is to look at the variability of the data. The more spread out the results of the replicates are, the bigger the difference between the final averages for treatment and control groups should be in order to say with assurance that compost tea affected plant growth.

How do the height results compare with other indicators of plant health you observed?

Students might find that although treatment and control plants do not differ in height, the leaves of the treatment plants are bigger and/or greener than those of the control plants.

Considering all of the results, what conclusions can you draw?

Students have a tendency to focus on their own group's results, rather than on the combined results of the whole class to draw conclusions, especially if their treatment plants grew better than other students'. Remind them that scientists do a lot of replicates to be more sure of their conclusions, and that they don't ignore data that didn't turn out as they expected.

Often students' results are not clear-cut, due in part to the difficulties of growing plants in classrooms. If they decide that their experiment did not show that compost tea improved plant growth as they expected, and in some cases might have damaged the plants, challenge them to think about why. Some reasons they might mention include: the plants needed to grow longer before showing positive treatment effects; the plants' growth might have been affected by the vermiculite drying out or getting too soggy; the plants were handled too roughly; the cups were too small for the roots; the plants didn't get enough light, or got too much heat; there were too many or the wrong kinds of nutrients in the compost tea for the type of plant they grew; or the dead plants in the compost hadn't decomposed enough for nutrients to be released. Having students explain unexpected results provokes creative and in-depth thinking.

Since they are used to judging their success by getting the "right" answer, students might feel disappointed that all of their hard work and patience yielded negative or unclear results. Help them understand that scientists can learn as much from negative as from positive results. Also, scientists will often do an experiment over again to improve their methods.

Why is nutrient cycling important?

Even if students' experiment did not clearly demonstrate that nutrients flow from dead plants to living plants, it is important for them to understand that this does indeed happen in nature. Without nutrient cycling, all of the nutrients in the world would eventually be tied up in dead things, and then nothing could live or grow.

Here is an "Experiment Conclusions" sheet for each person to complete.

Students can write their conclusions in class or for homework. Information on evaluating the sheets is provided on page 334.

Your homework assignment is to write a letter to GROW. What information should your letters include?

Students might suggest that they tell GROW what they did and found out, and perhaps include drawings, photos, or graphs. They could also recommend what GROW should do next (e.g., do more experiments, begin marketing compost tea, or start a new line of research). See page 334 for tips on evaluating students' letters.

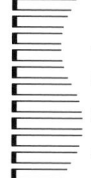 *Instead of having each student write a letter to GROW, you could have each person outline a letter, then meet as a group to decide on a final outline. Then each group member can write a different section of the letter. Before signing the letter, each person should read all of the sections to make sure the whole thing is satisfactory.*

Students can transplant their seedlings into soil in paper cups to take home, or continue growing them in class until radishes are ready to harvest and eat. Wash out the nested plastic cups for future use.

Ongoing Assessment

Student Reflections

 Have students send a C-Mail message or record thoughts in their journals. Optional writing prompts include:

I would convince someone that I kept the experiment fair by telling them that…

What strengths did I develop or find out I had while experimenting?

Something I know now that I didn't know when I began the experiment is…

Students could also complete a "Group Work Evaluation" (page 42) to reflect on their group's cooperation during the experiment.

Teacher Reflections

❏ Did students successfully make and read graphs?

❏ Were they able to consider more than one indicator of plant health in order to draw conclusions?

❏ Were they able to draw conclusions based on results from the whole class?

❏ Did they have reasonable explanations for why their experiment turned out as it did?

❏ Do their suggested experiment revisions show that they understand the importance of controlling variables and keeping accurate records?

Evaluating Students' "Experiment Conclusions" Sheets

Look especially to see if students are able to admit that the experiment turned out differently than they predicted, if in fact it did. Their explanations of why the experiment turned out as it did will reveal their critical thinking skills, as well as their knowledge about plant development and nutrient cycling. Their suggestions for how to make their experiments better will reveal if they understand the importance of controlling variables and keeping accurate records. Finally, their ideas for new research will show their curiosity and depth of thinking about plant growth and cycling issues.

Evaluating Students' Letters to GROW

Exemplary letters to GROW will include a description of research methods, results, conclusions, and recommendations. The methods should be detailed, and accurately reflect what the students did. The results section might mention their own group's results, but ultimately should focus on whole class results if each group did a replicate of a larger experiment. Conclusions should also reflect the whole class experiment. Some students might decide that the experiment was inconclusive, which is valid so long as they cite a reason for this interpretation other than that the experiment didn't turn out as it should have. Finally, the recommendations section will vary according to individual opinions and experiment outcomes. Some students might feel that GROW should sponsor more research; others might suggest they give up on developing a compost tea product; while others could encourage GROW to bottle and market compost tea immediately.

Extensions

Concept Maps. Introduce concept mapping to students if they are not already familiar with the process (see pages 25–27). Select all or some of the concept map cards on pages 43–44, then copy one set of cards for each group of 3–4 students. Have them construct concept maps that display their ideas about nutrient cycling. They might compare their new concept maps with those they made after Lesson 3.1, to see how their ideas have changed.

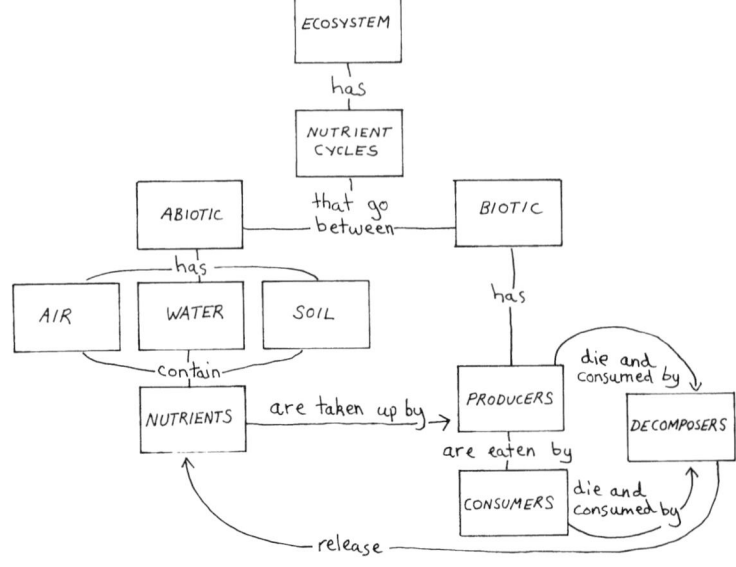

Surveying Gardeners. Have students interview experienced gardeners from a span of generations about their plant growing practices. This is an especially interesting project if your students have diverse cultural heritages with family members who came from other countries. Have students tape record their interviews for an oral history archive. They can also create a document that compares different gardening traditions, and how these have stayed the same or changed over the years.

Roving Responses. Post five to ten sheets of newsprint around the classroom, each with a different question written across the top. Have students circulate in groups to write a group response to each question. Their challenge is to elaborate on or refine what other groups have written, rather than parroting the same answers. Have each group use a different color marker. Possible questions include: *Where do plants get nutrients? Why do plants need nutrients? What happens to plants after they die? Would you recommend that gardeners use compost tea—why or why not? What are the most important things to remember when doing an experiment? What does it take to be a scientist?*

Journey of a Nutrient. Have students write creative, fact-based stories or poems tracing the pathway of a nutrient over a hundred years, beginning and ending inside of a dead plant. For instance, the nutrient can travel through the decomposition cycle, into living plants, and through food webs, as well as spend time in the non-living environment of soil, water, or air.

Experiment Conclusions

1 **W**hat was your research question?

_____

2 **W**hat did you *think* would happen?

_____

3 **W**hat actually *did* happen?

_____

4 **W**hy do you think it happened?

_____

_____

5 **W**hat would you do differently to make your experiment better?

_____

_____

6 **W**hat other experiments would you like to do to learn more about your topic?

_____

_____

   Module 3: *Cycles—From Rot to Radishes*

3.7 GROW Gets an Answer—
Performance Assessment

Action Synopsis

Students complete their work for GROW by working in groups to create advertisements that teach the public about nutrient cycling, and GROW's research and products.

Session 1		40 minutes
1. Share and discuss letters written to GROW.	🌐	*communicating*
2. Discuss possible themes and methods to use in creating advertisements for GROW.	🐝	*linking to real world*
3. Establish criteria for judging the success of the ads.	🐝	*setting standards*
4. Begin planning advertisements in groups.	🌐	*planning*

Session 2		40 minutes
Work in groups to create advertisements.	🌐	*applying knowledge*

Continued

Session 3   **40 minutes**

1. Present advertisements to the class.   *communicating*

2. Have a final discussion about the effects of the ads   *reflecting*
   and the impression the public gets of science
   through advertising.

Desired Outcomes

By the end of this assessment activity, students should:

✓ Be more skilled at cooperatively planning and completing a project.

✓ Be able to communicate their knowledge about nutrient cycling in an engaging way.

✓ Be able to judge their own work and reflect on their understanding of nutrient cycling.

✓ Have new perspectives on the representation of science in popular media.

What You'll Need

Sessions 1 & 2

For the class:
- ❑ overhead transparency of the letter from GROW (page 267)
- ❑ materials for making advertisements (see "Getting Ready")

For each group of 3–4 students:
- ❑ copy of "Scoring Sheet" (page 343)

Session 3

For each student:
- ❑ copy of "Scoring Sheet" (page 343)
- ❑ copy of "Group Work Evaluation" (page 42)
- ❑ copy of "Portfolio Cover Sheet" (page 39)

Getting Ready

Session 1

♦ Assemble materials students can use to create their advertisements, such as poster paper, cardboard, markers, paints, stencils, old magazines, a tape recorder and blank cassettes, and a box of clothing for costumes.

♦ Decide if you'd like to invite other adults to view and score students' finished ads.

Action Narrative

Session 1

Who would like to read the letter you wrote to GROW?

Have a few students read aloud the letters they wrote for Lesson 3.6 homework. This could result in some lively discussion if their recommendations to GROW differ. Encourage students to explain their reasoning, as well as to consider other viewpoints with an open mind. At the end of the discussion, have students hand in their letters and the "Experiment Conclusions" sheet they did for homework. (See page 334 for suggestions on evaluating these.)

Eco-Corp
Meeting Your Research Needs

Dear Ms. Gold,
   I'm glad to tell you that my personal opinion on the radish plants is that they grow better with compost tea. Not only do I think that but the majority of the company agrees to it also. This means that it won't cost you much to make your fertilizer because you can just soak the compost in water. Here is what we did.

   We split our company, Eco-Corp, up into 7 teams. Each team did the same thing so that we had 7 repeats of the experiment. We planted radish seeds in vermiculite. After they had cotyledons, each team gave six of their plants compost tea. These were the treatment plants. Everyone had 6 controls, too.

Now we're ready to complete our work for GROW. Let's look at their letter to remember what else they asked us to do.

Show the overhead of the letter from GROW. Have students summarize what they need to do to fulfill GROW's request: develop advertisements that teach the public about GROW's work to develop natural fertilizer products.

Given the results of your experiment, what do you think the ads should focus on?

If students' experiments showed that compost tea improved plant growth, then they might suggest creating ads to convince people to buy compost tea. If their experiments did not show that compost tea helps plants grow, then they might prefer to do a more general ad campaign focusing on how and why GROW is trying to develop natural fertilizer products. In either case, the ads should communicate some basic information about nature's way of recycling nutrients.

Now let's brainstorm different types of advertisements you could do.

Make sure students understand that a basic rule of brainstorming is that every idea is accepted without immediate comment or judgment. This encourages creativity and risk-taking. Have students think about the multitude of advertising approaches they encounter daily. It might help for them to think specifically about advertisements that show how a company uses scientific research to develop products, or that make claims about products based on scientific results. Record their suggestions on a class list.

> <u>Kinds of Advertisements</u>
>
> posters
>
> billboards
>
> magazine and newspaper ads
>
> flyers to send in the mail
>
> TV commercials (maybe with actors, puppets, cartoons)
>
> radio commercials
>
> eye-catching displays to put in stores

What should your GROW ads do to be successful?

In responding to this question, students will generate their own criteria for measuring the success of their work.

> A Successful Ad for GROW will...
>
> get people's attention
>
> show how nutrient cycling works
>
> stick in people's minds
>
> make them like GROW
>
> make them want to buy GROW's stuff

Either formalize students' list into a scoring chart, or hand out and discuss the "Scoring Sheet" so that students will know what is expected of them. Emphasize that their ads should not make unwarranted claims (e.g., that vegetables grown using compost tea taste better), and should include accurate information about nutrient cycling.

Each group can develop its own advertisement for GROW. Let's make a list of steps each group should take to create an advertisement.

Help students generate a checklist of steps for planning their projects. This could include deciding on: the target audience for the ad; what information to get across; the tone of the ad (e.g., serious, inspiring, entertaining, funny); what medium to use; an outline or script for the ad; what materials are needed; and who will do what.

Get started making plans in your groups.

Let students know when their projects are due so they can gauge how ambitious to make their plans. Also let them know what materials you have on hand, and help them figure out where they can get what else they need.

Circulate as they begin planning to observe their group process.

Session 2

Continue working on your advertisements.

Check in with each group to remind them to make sure their ads meet the scoring objectives. If any groups are doing live performances such as a television ad, make sure they're writing a script that they can hand in for scoring.

If some groups finish early, encourage them to create a second ad, or to elaborate on their existing one.

Next time, come prepared to present your ads to the rest of the class.

Students might need additional work time to complete or rehearse their ads.

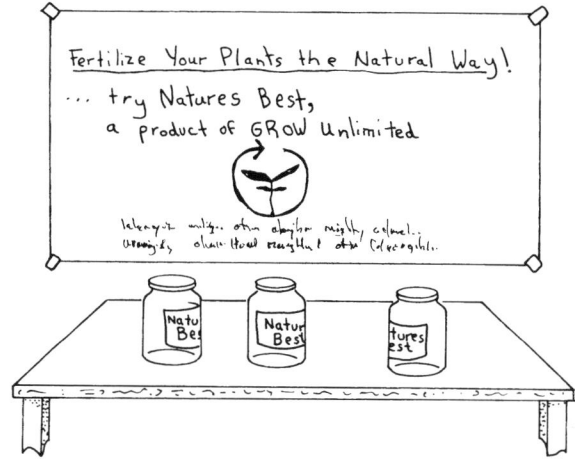

Session 3

Remember to give each group your full attention when they present their advertisement. Which group wants to go first?

Give each group time to display or perform its ad. You might want to begin filling out a "Scoring Sheet" for each group as they make their presentations.

 Conclude with questions such as:

What kind of impression of GROW did the advertisements convey?

What do the ads teach people?

Do you think people respond favorably when they know a company uses scientific research to help develop its products? Should they?

What was challenging about translating your science experience into a public awareness campaign?

What impressions do people usually get from popular media about scientific research and findings?

What do you think is important for the public to understand about science? About ecology?

Ongoing Assessment

Student Reflections

Have students complete a "Scoring Sheet" to assess their own work, and fill out a "Group Work Evaluation" (page 42). This is also a good time to have them select work samples for a portfolio, and complete a "Portfolio Cover Sheet" (page 39). Review the purpose and structure of a portfolio, and set a due date.

Teacher Reflections

With the exception of the content objectives, scoring most of the objectives for students' ads will be more a matter of opinion than a judgment of whether students' work is "right" or "wrong." Since the success of advertisements is usually judged by their effect on a large audience, you might want to invite several adults to view and score the students' ads as well, or have each student group score the other groups' work. You can then average the scores to determine final group scores.

If you want to give students an individual grade as well as a group score, consider having each person hand in documentation of the factual content of their ads, such as a diagram of a nutrient cycle.

Living Plant → Dead Plant → Decomposers → Nutrients (released) → Living Plant

NAME(S)_____ DATE_____

GROW GETS AN ANSWER

OBJECTIVES	POINTS				SCORE
	3 High Quality	**2** Meets Objectives	**1** Falls Short	**0** Not Done	
CONTENT					
1. Includes correct information about nutrient cycling.	_____	_____	_____	_____	___ x 2 =___
2. Has an important main point that comes across clearly.	_____	_____	_____	_____	=___
METHOD					
1. Uses a medium and tone suited to the message.	_____	_____	_____	_____	=___
2. Ambitious—did something challenging.	_____	_____	_____	_____	=___
3. Done with care and attentionto detail.	_____	_____	_____	_____	=___
OVERALL EFFECT					
1. Attracts attention and pulls audience in.	_____	_____	_____	_____	=___
2. Creates a positive impression of GROW.	_____	_____	_____	_____	=___
3. Ad is memorable.					

COMMENTS:

FINAL SCORE: _____

Total Possible Score: 27
Overall Achievement:
  23-27 High
  18-22 Sound
  9-17   Limited
  0-8   Inadequate

3.8 Hiring a Scientist—
Written Assessment

Action Synopsis

Students recommend who GROW should hire as a scientist after reviewing three job applications.

One Session		1 hour
1. Write a description of an ideal scientist, and share ideas with group members.		*examining prior ideas*
2. Read a challenge that requires ranking three candidates applying for a research position with GROW.		*posing a challenge*
3. Work in groups to review job applications, determine pros and cons of each candidate, and rank them.		*applying knowledge*
4. Have a final discussion about the choices, and reflect on scientists as people.		*reflecting*

Desired Outcomes

By the end of this assessment activity, students should:

✓ Understand that being a good scientist requires a range of skills and qualities.

✓ Be able to identify the weaknesses in an experimental design.

✓ Know that collaboration is an important aspect of science.

✓ Be able to modify opinions based on convincing arguments.

What You'll Need

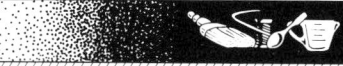

For each group of 3–4 students:
- ❏ copy of three "Job Applications" (pages 352–354)
- ❏ copy of "Scoring Sheet" (page 351)

For each student:
- ❏ copy of "Challenge Sheet" (page 350)
- ❏ copy of "Scoring Sheet" (page 351)

Getting Ready

♦ Decide on groups of 3–4 students.

Action Narrative

By doing research for GROW you've learned what it takes to be a good scientist. Now you'll have a chance to help GROW choose a scientist to hire. First, take a few minutes to write a description of an ideal scientist—someone you would like to have working for you or with whom you would like to work.

Have students develop their own descriptions independently. They can write descriptive narratives or lists of attributes. If they are having trouble getting started, have them think about the scientific standards they upheld while doing activities such as designing experiments, giving and receiving peer reviews, setting up and maintaining fair tests, keeping records, interpreting results, and collaborating.

Get together with your group and share your descriptions.

Assign students to groups. Encourage them to discuss how their lists differ, and to explain to one another why they think certain characteristics are or are not important for being a good scientist.

Now that you've thought about what you'd look for in a scientist, here is your challenge.

Hand out and go over the "Challenge Sheet."

What should I look for when I score your work?

After students share their ideas for scoring criteria, hand out and go over the "Scoring Sheet" to use or adapt according to their suggestions.

Here are applications from three job candidates. When you've completed the "Challenge Sheet" we'll make a final decision as a class about who GROW should hire.

You might need to explain the initials PhD, MS, and BS to students. They can look up unfamiliar words, such as *anthropology*, *zoology*, and *botany*.

Some groups might choose to have each person fill out pros and cons for a different candidate, then present his or her ideas to the group for additional input. Others might prefer to have someone read each "Job Application" to the group and generate pros and cons together. In either case, students should assign a recorder to make a copy of their work to hand in. Suggest that each person sign his or her name on the completed "Challenge Sheet" to indicate that they've read and approved it.

While the students work, make a class chart for recording their decisions.

Let's see how each group rated the candidates.

Record the number of 1st, 2nd, and 3rd ratings each candidate received.

	1st	2nd	3rd
Roberto Zack	1	0	6
Cicely Monroe	2	5	0
Leah Kleinman	4	2	1

What were some of the pros and cons that influenced your decisions?

Have students discuss the strengths and weaknesses of the three candidates' experimenting skills, as well as other factors they considered to be important, such as personality, ability to collaborate, academic background, and relevant experience. See pages 348–349 for pros and cons students might mention.

Now that you've heard each group's reasons for their choices, can we agree on one candidate to recommend to GROW?

Challenge students to come to a consensus rather than saying that the candidate with the most 1st choice votes "wins." If some groups won't change their minds, then the class might decide it would be best just to report its different opinions to GROW.

? Conclude with questions such as:

Did your images of an ideal scientist take into account that scientists have human strengths and weaknesses just like anyone else?

Help students see the importance of having high standards for science, while at the same time realizing it is not just a field for an elite group of people.

Can you imagine a lot of kinds of people being scientists?

Students should realize that anyone with an interest in science, and a willingness to work hard, can be a scientist. Also, different scientists have different styles and approaches to their work, all of which can be successful. Meeting scientists in their own community, as well as reading about scientists, would help to enrich students' images of scientists.

What sort of training would you give a scientist you hired?

Students' responses will reveal whether they think that scientists' collaborative skills and habits of mind are as important as technical skills and knowledge.

What advice would you give to the two people you didn't choose, to help them get jobs in the future?

Students should realize that people can develop and strengthen their scientific abilities.

Hand in your individual descriptions of an ideal scientist, as well as your group's "Challenge Sheet."

Before students hand in their scientist descriptions they could add new perspectives they gained as a result of the class discussion. See below for information on evaluating their work.

Ongoing Assessment

Student Reflections

Have students fill out a "Scoring Sheet" for their group's work.

Teacher Reflections

When reading students' descriptions of an ideal scientist, look for indicators that their own experiences doing science have enriched their perspectives beyond stereotypes. Typically students' descriptions include a combination of the following attributes:

Has a good education, knowledge, experience

Can help society by creating cures or inventions

Is interested in and enjoys science

Willing to work hard

Not afraid to do new things, reaches for the unknown and unexpected, is curious, asks a lot of questions

Can stick with something, can handle frustration and disappointment, is patient

Is accurate

Has a sense of humor, pride, imagination, creativity

Cares about the world, the environment, and other people

Is reliable, independent, organized, responsible, has common sense

Has skills with computers, microscopes, chemicals

Has experimenting skills like observing, making a fair test, keeping records, drawing graphs

Is logical, has good study habits, can solve problems

Is cooperative, works well with others, shares ideas, can give and take constructive criticism

There is no one right answer to the challenge of ranking job candidates. The chart below shows some of the pros and cons to look for in students' lists.

	Pros	Cons
Roberto Zack	• he models nutrient cycling on computer so must understand and be interested in it • he did a study testing dead plants as fertilizer • he's creative and can come up with new ideas • he's good at math, so will be good at analyzing data • he can use high-tech equipment like an electronic nutrient analyzer	• his experiment didn't have any replicates, yet he drew a conclusion anyway • he didn't measure the nutrients in the soil before he started growing grass to make sure they all started the same • he might draw the company down if he needs a lot of support when he gets discouraged • he might be too impatient to stick with experiments long enough, or he'll try to rush things to get results
Cicely Monroe	• she has degrees in ecology • she has studied how dead plants fertilize soil • she tested 25 of each kind of plot, so had a lot of replicates • she took a lot of samples • her experiment lasted for 3 years, so she's willing to take a long time to do things right	• she doesn't like to work with other people • she's not willing to share ideas, so she might not tell GROW what she discovers, and her work might not be as good if she doesn't ask for feedback from other people • she might spend more time and take more samples than is necessary to get reliable results

	Pros	Cons
Cicely Monroe (continued)	• she based her conclusions on solid evidence • she is precise and willing to stick with things even if they're boring • she knows a lot about plants	
Leah Kleinman	• she has worked for an industry that probably made things like fertilizer • she's curious about plants and has a degree in botany • she asks interesting questions • she has experience testing the effects of fertilizers on plants • she would be a good employee because she pitches in and works hard	• her experiment wasn't a fair test because she planted the corn in two very different kinds of places • she drew conclusions without considering that it might have been the soil near the riverbank, not the fertilizer, that made the plants produce more ears of corn • other scientists don't think her work is good, so GROW's scientific work would have less credibility

How students weigh the pros and cons to rank the candidates will depend on their opinions about the most important qualities of a scientist. For instance, many students choose Leah Kleinman as someone with whom they would prefer to work. Even though they realize that her experimenting skills are weak, they reason that skills can be taught, whereas the personality characteristics of the other candidates could make them difficult to work with and would be harder to change. This is a testament to students' own experience doing research in collaborative teams, and in fact reflects the importance of collaboration in professional science. Their supporting arguments for their 1st choice candidate should reveal that they've taken that candidate's shortcomings and strengths into consideration.

NAME(S)_____ DATE_____

HIRING A SCIENTIST

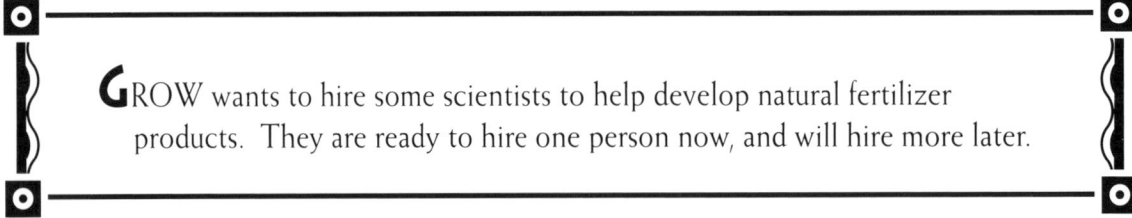

GROW wants to hire some scientists to help develop natural fertilizer products. They are ready to hire one person now, and will hire more later.

YOUR CHALLENGE:

1. Read the Job Applications and write down the pros and cons of each applicant.

2. Rank the candidates as your 1st, 2nd, or 3rd choice to help GROW decide who to hire.

	PROS	CONS	RANK
Roberto Zack			
Cicely Monroe			
Leah Kleinman			

3. Make a case for your 1st choice by explaining why GROW should hire that person. Use the back of the sheet.

NAME(S)_____ DATE_____

HIRING A SCIENTIST

OBJECTIVES	POINTS				SCORE
	3 High Quality	**2** Meets Objectives	**1** Falls Short	**0** Not Done	
CONTENT					
1. Pros explain the strengths of candidates.	_____	_____	_____	_____	___ x 2 =___
2. Cons explain the weaknesses of candidates.	_____	_____	_____	_____	=___
3. Ranking of choices shows that pros and cons were weighed.	_____	_____	_____	_____	=___
COMMUNICATION					
4. Case for 1st choice has good supporting reasons.	_____	_____	_____	_____	=___

COMMENTS:

FINAL SCORE: _____

Total Possible Score: 15
Overall Achievement:
13–15 High
10–12 Sound
5–9 Limited
0–4 Inadequate

JOB APPLICATION

NAME: Dr. Roberto Zack

EDUCATION:

PhD and MS in Zoology, East Central University
BS in Computer Science, Wexon College

MOST RECENT JOB:

Research Scientist at East Central University making computer models of
nutrient cycling

SUMMARY OF MOST RECENT EXPERIMENT:

I wanted to figure out if leaving cut grass to decompose on lawns would add extra
nutrients to the soil. I made three huge boxes in a greenhouse. I added soil and grass
seed to each one. After the grass grew in each box, I mowed it. In the first box, I
removed the cut grass. In the second box, I left the cut grass on top of the soil. In the
third box, I left the dead grass, and also added extra decomposers, like earthworms,
fungi, and bacteria, to the soil. After one month I tested the soil in each box using an
electronic nutrient analyzer. I found that the soil in the box with extra decomposers in
it had the most nutrients. The soil in the box that had no dead grass in it had the
fewest nutrients. I concluded that if people want healthy lawns they should not
remove the cut grass after mowing, and they should also add extra decomposers to
their soil.

HOBBIES:

Gourmet cooking, skiing

• •

COMMENTS BY PEOPLE WHO GAVE REFERENCES FOR THE CANDIDATE:

"Roberto is very creative when designing experiments. He has a talent for
thinking of amazing techniques that have never been used before."

"When things aren't going well, Roberto can get really sour. He likes things to
happen quickly, so doesn't have much patience with long experiments. He gets so
frustrated sometimes that he needs a lot of supportive people around to encourage
him to keep trying."

"Roberto is is a whiz with math and computers. He is very familiar with using
high-tech equipment."

JOB APPLICATION

NAME: Dr. Cicely Monroe

EDUCATION:

PhD and MS in Ecology, Radmore State College

CURRENT JOB:

Land Manager in Bixton State Park

SUMMARY OF MOST RECENT EXPERIMENT:

I tested the soils in areas of Bixton State Park where trees were being cut for lumber. In some of the areas the work crew chipped all of the leftover branches, then transported the wood chips away. In places where the workers couldn't bring in a wood chipper, they left the wood to rot on the ground.

I wanted to see how many nutrients were in the soil in the two kinds of places. I tested 50 different areas, 25 where wood chips were taken away, and 25 where wood was left to rot. I took thousands of soil samples for three years. After I did chemical tests on the samples, I found that in areas where all the wood was taken away, the soil didn't have many nutrients. Where dead wood was left on the ground, the soil had more nutrients. I concluded that when dead branches rot they return nutrients to the soil, helping new trees to grow. I recommended that branches should be left on the ground in all logged areas of the park.

HOBBIES:

Whitewater canoeing, organic gardening

• •

COMMENTS BY PEOPLE WHO GAVE REFERENCES FOR THE CANDIDATE:

"Although many people would find taking thousands of soil samples boring, Cicely never lets it get to her. She is always very precise when taking and analyzing her samples."

"Cicely would rather spend her time alone in the woods or in the laboratory. She is not what I'd call a sociable person. She is hesitant to share her ideas with others."

"She must know more about the plants and animals in this state than anyone else alive! She even knows the names of the different kinds of mosses—they all look alike to most people."

JOB APPLICATION

NAME: Dr. Leah Kleinman

EDUCATION:

PhD and MS in Botany, University of Windsor

CURRENT JOB:

Research Associate at TecPro Industries studying the effect of fertilizers on crop plants

SUMMARY OF MOST RECENT EXPERIMENT:

I designed an experiment to find out whether a certain fertilizer would increase the number of ears of corn a crop would produce. I planted corn in a 2-acre field near a riverbank, and gave this field the fertilizer. Then I planted the same kind of corn in another 2-acre field on the outskirts of town, and did not fertilize this field. At the end of the growing season I harvested the corn from both fields. I found that the fertilized field produced more ears of corn. I concluded that the fertilizer I tested makes corn plants produce more ears of corn.

HOBBIES:

Cave exploration, playing the flute, square dancing

♦ ♦

COMMENTS BY PEOPLE WHO GAVE REFERENCES FOR THE CANDIDATE:

"Leah is a real team player. She'll pitch in on a project, do more than her share, and encourage everyone else to do his or her best."

"Many of Leah's papers are turned down for publication by the scientists that review them."

"Leah has always been very curious about plants. She thinks of interesting questions, and is willing to do research to try to find answers."

WHO EATS WHAT

A GUIDE TO FOOD WEB CLUES IN SCHOOLYARD HABITATS

WHO EATS WHAT

A GUIDE TO FOOD WEB CLUES IN SCHOOLYARD HABITATS

COMPILED BY:
LISA MORGANSTERN
KATHLEEN HOGAN
ALAN BERKOWITZ

ILLUSTRATION:
CAROL MORLEY
LISA MORGANSTERN

ECO-INQUIRY APPENDIX A
© INSTITUTE OF ECOSYSTEM STUDIES, 1994

TABLE OF CONTENTS

    Appendix A

INTRODUCTION

A LAWN FOOD WEB

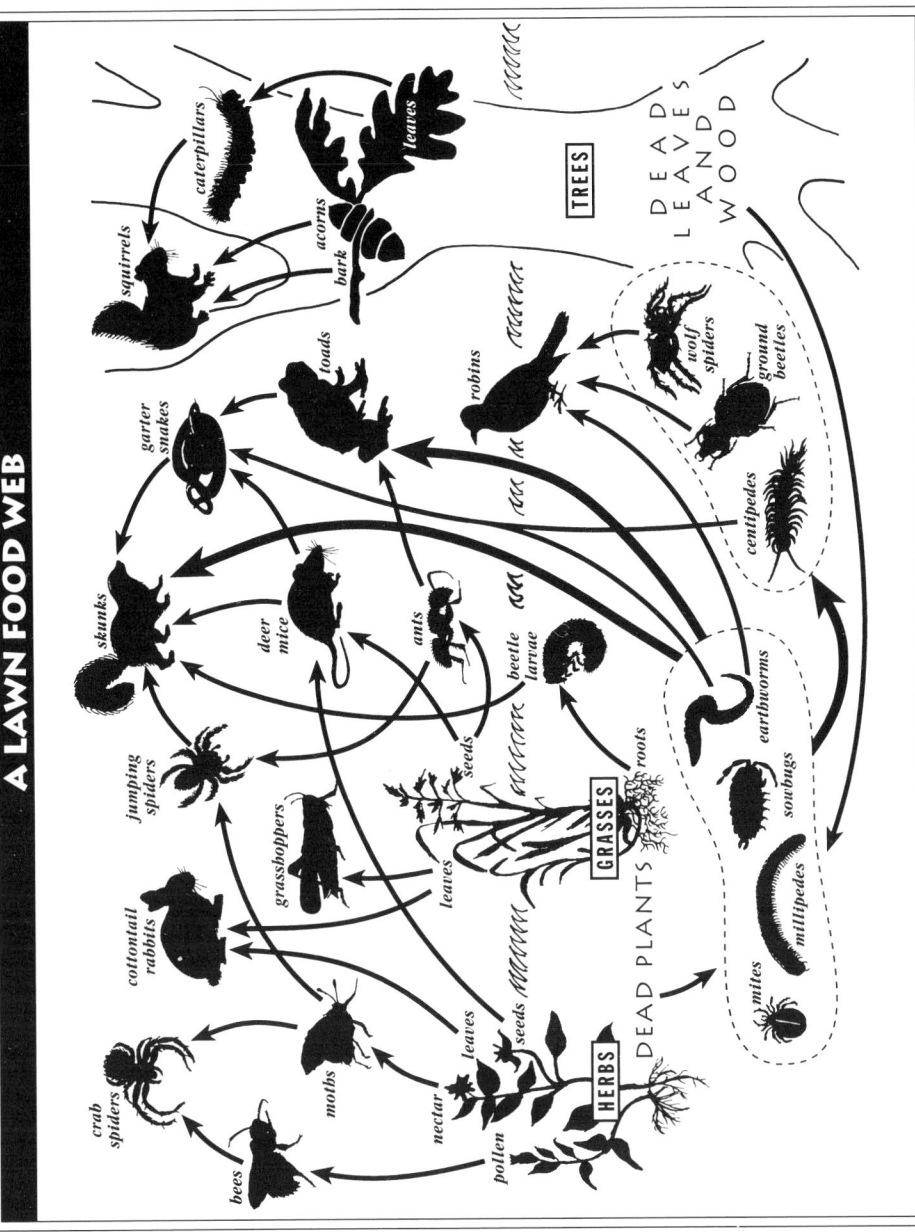

Even in seemingly barren schoolyards, lots of animals are busily getting the foods they need to survive. Although some animals are visibly active during the day, many others are either nocturnal or hard to see. Fortunately, there are often telltale signs of these animals and their activities. Once your students learn where and how to look for animals and their signs, they'll become aware of the wide variety of creatures within their everyday environment.

The *Who Eats What* guide will help you and your students find animals and their signs, and figure out what these animals eat. It will not necessarily help you identify all of the animals you find. For this you'll need field guides that provide keys, drawings, descriptions, and range maps for individual species. The Eco-Inquiry Module 1 "Resource List" suggests field guides for adults and young people that you can use to supplement the information provided here.

By using the information in this *Who Eats What* guide, your students will be able to make a food web that shows interactions in a local ecosystem, even if they never see a single animal in the act of eating!

⚠ This symbol means CAUTION and appears next to animals or animal signs that are potentially hazardous. They might be poisonous, transmit diseases, or cause harmful bites or stings. Students should avoid all contact with animals or signs marked with the caution symbol. It's a good idea for students to avoid touching with bare hands <u>all</u> living and dead animals, and animal droppings.

1. ANIMAL SIGNS

KNOWING WHERE TO LOOK

When searching for animals and their signs, students tend to look only on the ground. The "Where to Look" page helps them expand their focus. It provides tips on what animals and signs they might find in many locations.

KNOWING WHAT TO LOOK FOR

The "Signs of Animals Eating Plants" and other animal signs pages help students develop search images for evidence of animal activity. Although the signs illustrated on these pages are only a sampling of those likely to be found at your study site, they provide a starting point to help your students notice things they often overlook. This new perspective will help them piece together clues about interactions among animals and their food sources.

FINDING THE "WHAT" AND FIGURING OUT THE "WHO"

Once students have found an animal sign, they'll need to figure out who made it. The signs illustrated in the animal signs pages are labeled with the names of the animals that make them. If students find a sign that's not included here, they can compare it to the illustrations to try to narrow down the type of animal (e.g., an insect, a bird) that could have made the sign.

Some animal signs, such as a nibbled leaf or a seed-filled scat, are direct evidence of what an animal is eating. Other animals signs, such as a nest or a track, simply reveal an animal's presence. Once students trace either of these kinds of signs to the animal who made them, they're ready to consult the "Animals and Their Foods" chapter to complete their detective work!

WHERE TO LOOK

IN THE AIR
- ☐ up high for flying or soaring birds
- ☐ around plants for flying insects

IN SHRUBS, CACTI, AND TREES
- ☐ on branches, arms, and twigs for galls, eggs, nests, browse marks, insects, spiders, mammals, tree frogs, snakes, and bird droppings
- ☐ on trunks for woodpecker holes, scratch marks, cocoons, webs, and ant trails
- ☐ in holes, pleats, and crevices in bark for nests, scorpions, pseudoscorpions, beetles, daddy-longlegs, and other small organisms
- ☐ on flowers and fruits for insects and signs of eating
- ☐ on leaves, stems, and vines for tree frogs, insects, insect eggs, snails, galls, and signs of eating

AMONG LOW PLANTS
- ☐ in moss clumps for tiny animals
- ☐ in grass for trails, clipped leaves, and matted bedding
- ☐ in thickets for signs of rabbits, such as droppings, and clipped twigs or grass leaves
- ☐ on stems and leaves for insects, spiders, galls, insect eggs, bird droppings, and signs of eating
- ☐ on flowers for bees, flies, butterflies, moths, and spiders

ELSEWHERE
- ☐ on and around tree stumps, fence posts, and rocks (perches) for scat, nutshells, and other leftovers
- ☐ on fence posts and walls for birds, spiders, lizards, small mammals, snails, and insects
- ☐ in sunny areas for animals basking
- ☐ on building ledges and windowsills for birds, nests, and bat roosts
- ☐ in drainpipe ends, and holes in bricks and cinder blocks for spiders and insects
- ☐ on pavement and in sidewalk cracks for insects and other animals
- ☐ in wet areas for animals drinking

ON THE GROUND
- ☐ between plants for scat, worm castings, bird droppings and pellets
- ☐ under rocks, boards, logs, bricks, and trash for salamanders, toads, skinks, sow bugs, centipedes, millipedes, ants, snakes, scorpions, and beetles
- ☐ in leaf litter and surface soil for seed caches, earthworms, sow bugs, millipedes, beetles, and other small animals
- ☐ in sandy or muddy areas for tracks
- ☐ under plants for bird nests, mammal tunnels, mouse holes, rabbit dens, tracks, snakes, lizards, salamanders, and other animals
- ☐ in rotting logs, stumps, and under bark for termites, beetles, insect larvae, ants, skinks, and lizard eggs

SIGNS OF ANIMALS EATING PLANTS

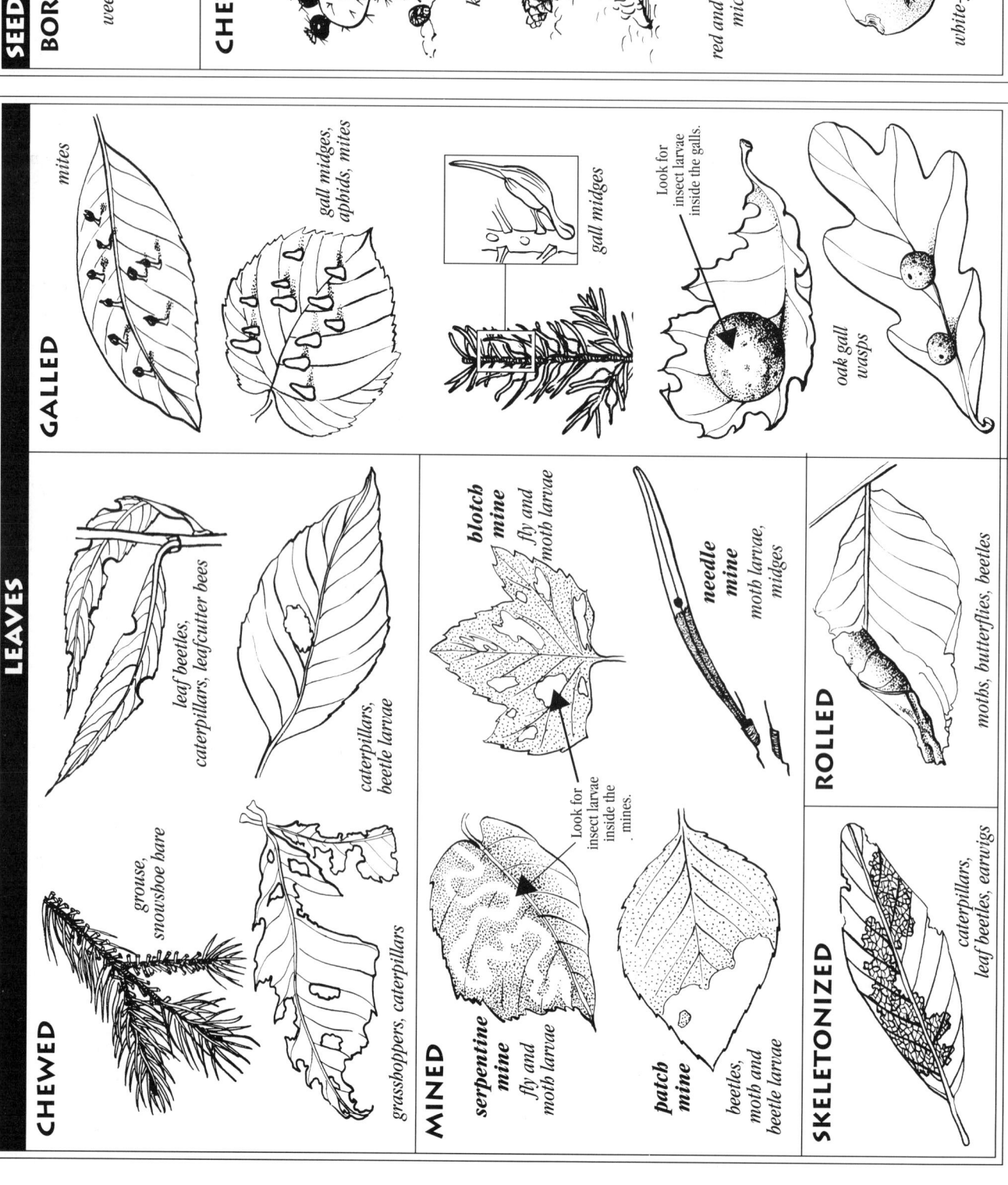

SEEDS, NUTS, AND FRUITS

BORED
weevils

Look for weevil larvae inside the acorns.

CHEWED
kangaroo rats, orioles, coyotes

red and gray squirrels, chipmunks, jumping mice, white-footed mice, deer mice

white-footed mice, deer mice, fox, deer, opossum, woodchucks

LEAVES

CHEWED
grouse, snowshoe hare

leaf beetles, caterpillars, leafcutter bees

caterpillars, beetle larvae

grasshoppers, caterpillars

MINED

serpentine mine
fly and moth larvae

blotch mine
fly and moth larvae

Look for insect larvae inside the mines.

needle mine
moth larvae, midges

patch mine
beetles, moth and beetle larvae

GALLED
mites

gall midges, aphids, mites

gall midges

Look for insect larvae inside the galls.

oak gall wasps

ROLLED
moths, butterflies, beetles

SKELETONIZED
caterpillars, leaf beetles, earwigs

---

360   © Institute of Ecosystem Studies, 1994

Appendix A

TRUNKS, LIMBS, AND LOGS

BARK STRIPPED

porcupines

deer

bark beetles

cottontails, jackrabbits, ground squirrels, tortoises, woodrats, pocket mice

woodchucks, squirrels

rabbits, hares

BORED

sapsuckers

CHEWED

cottontail rabbits

SIGNS OF ANIMALS EATING PLANTS *continued*

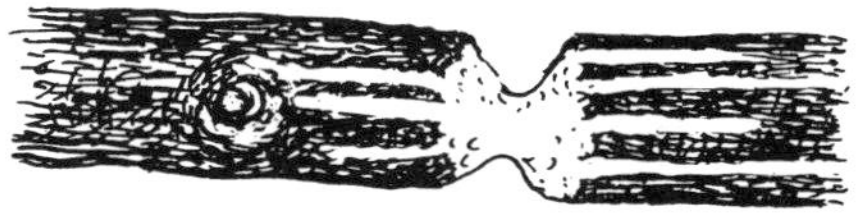

STEMS AND TWIGS

CLIPPED

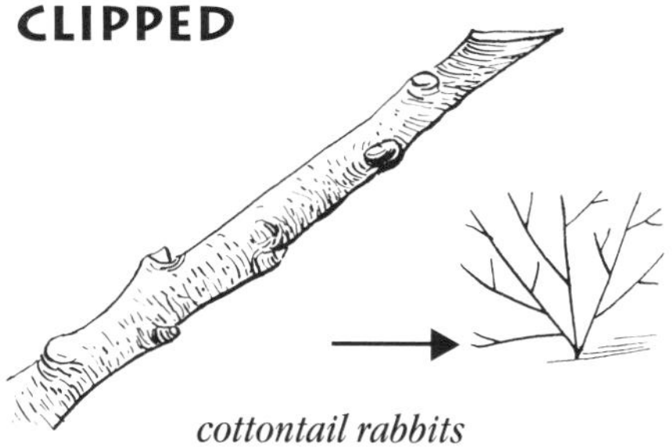

cottontail rabbits

CHEWED

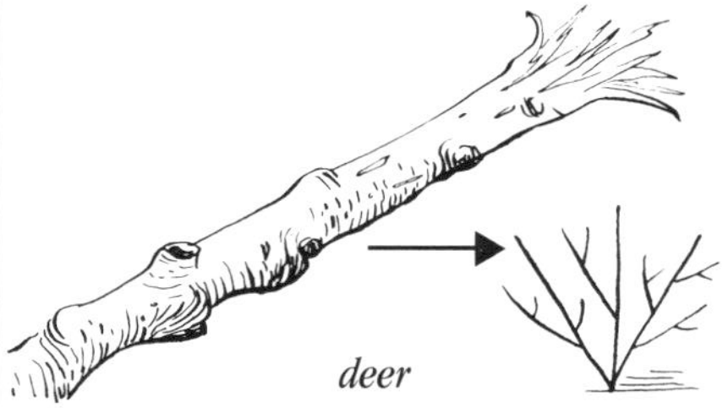

deer

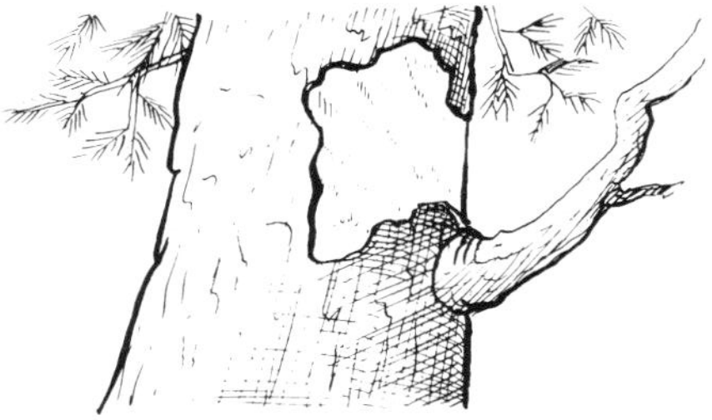

PRUNED

porcupines; red squirrels, beetles

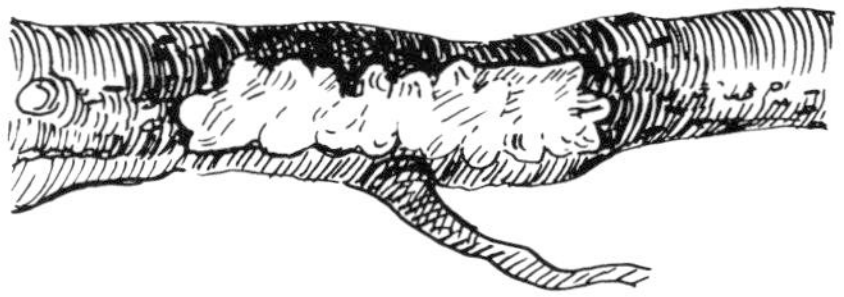

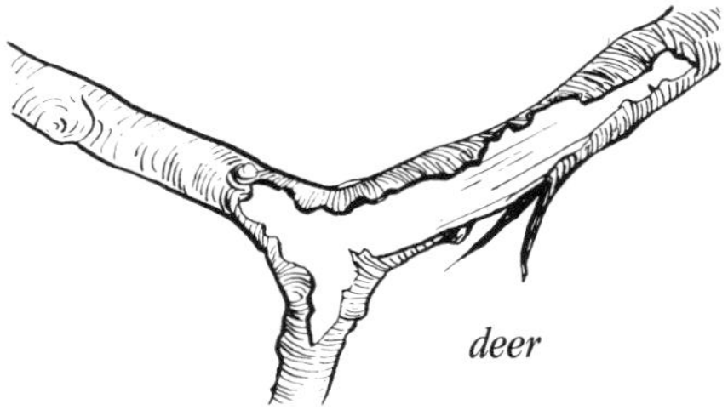

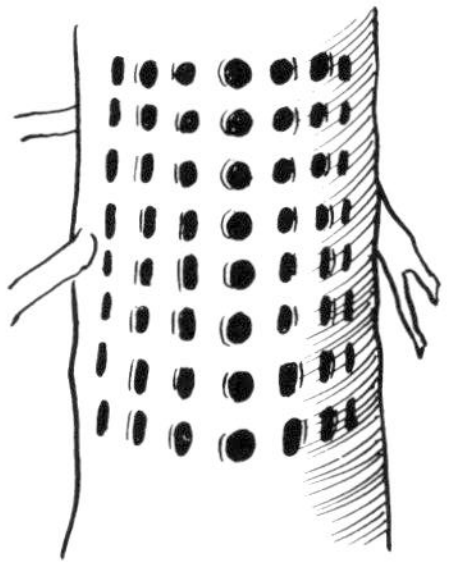

GNAWED

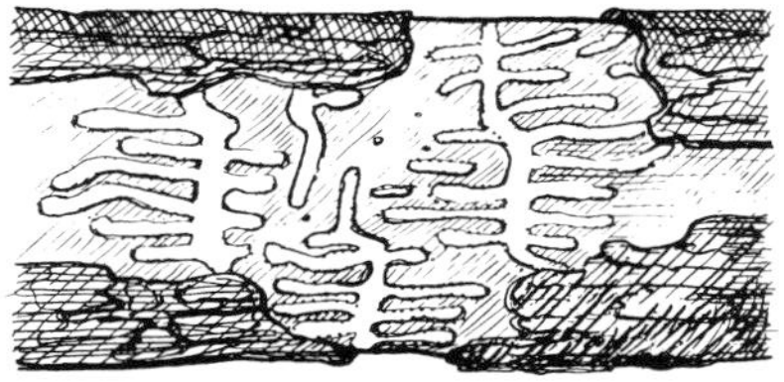

mice, voles

GALLED

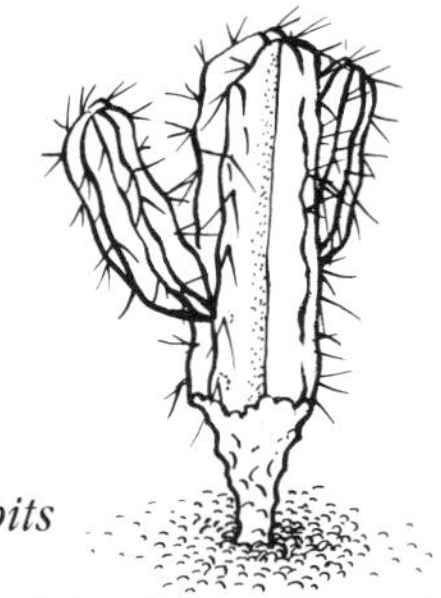

Look for insect larvae inside the gall.

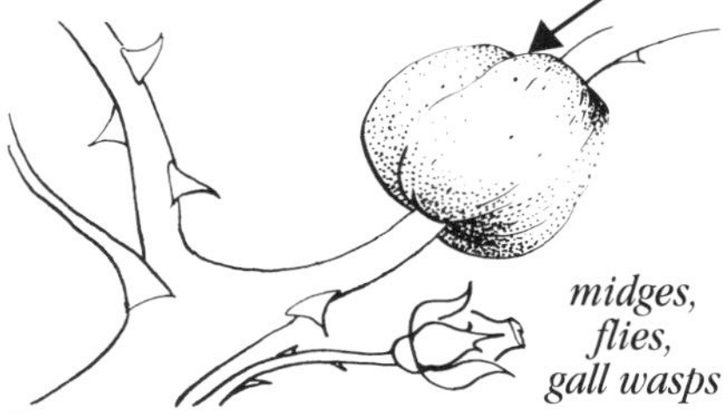

goldenrod gall flies

midges, flies, gall wasps

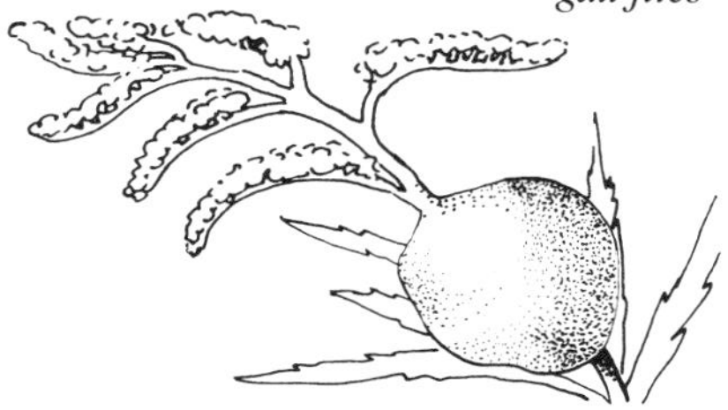

GIRDLED

twig pruner beetles

FROTHED

spittlebugs

HOMES, TRAILS, AND SCRATCHINGS

TRAILS AND TUNNELS

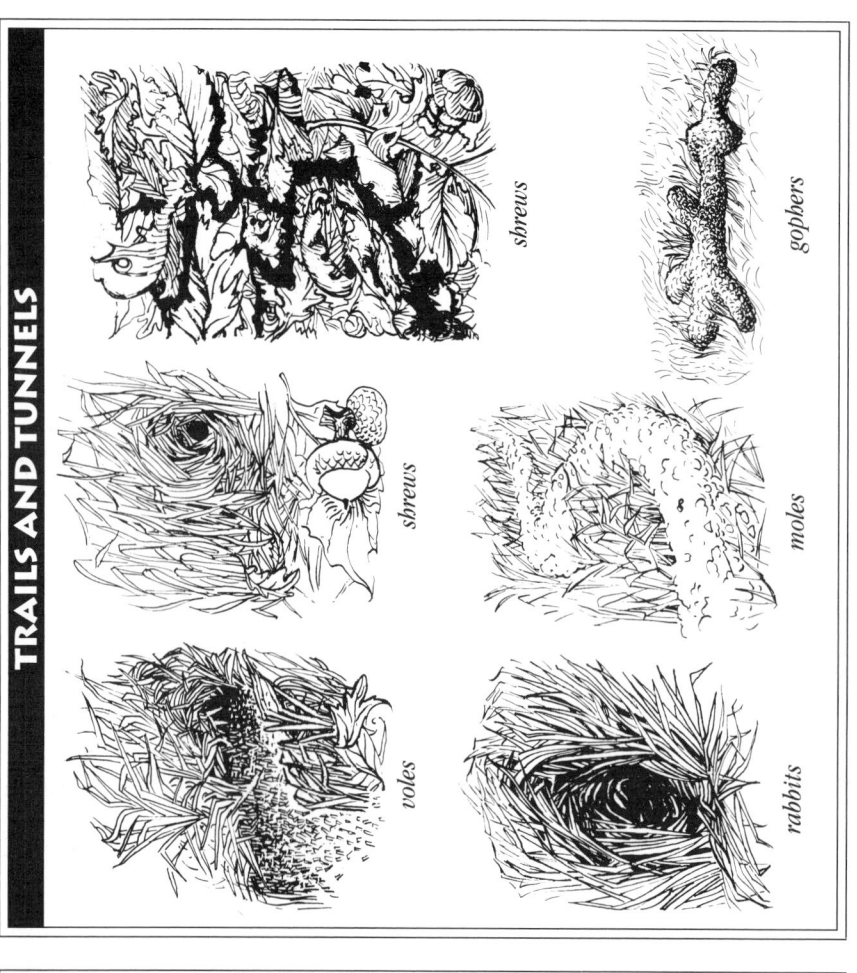

shrews

gophers

shrews

moles

voles

rabbits

DIGGING, SCRATCHING, AND PECKING

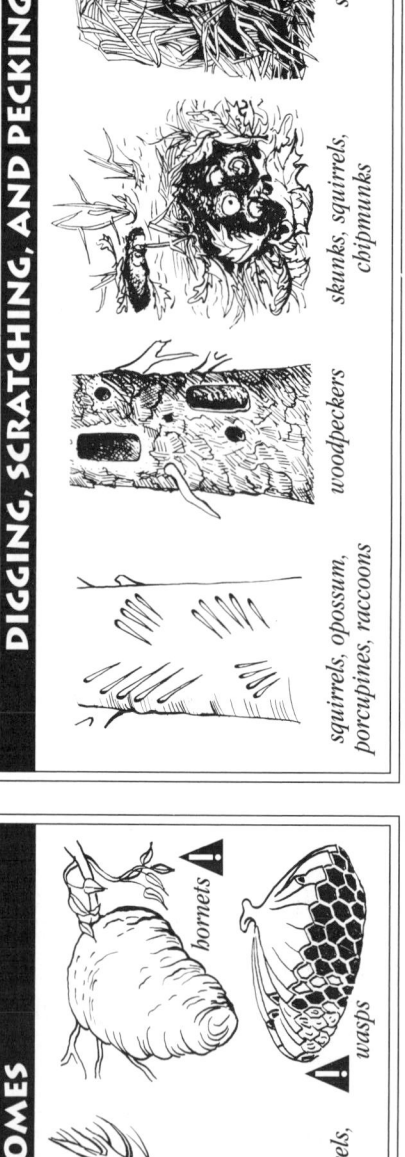

skunks

skunks, squirrels, chipmunks

woodpeckers

squirrels, opossum, porcupines, raccoons

BURROWS AND NESTS

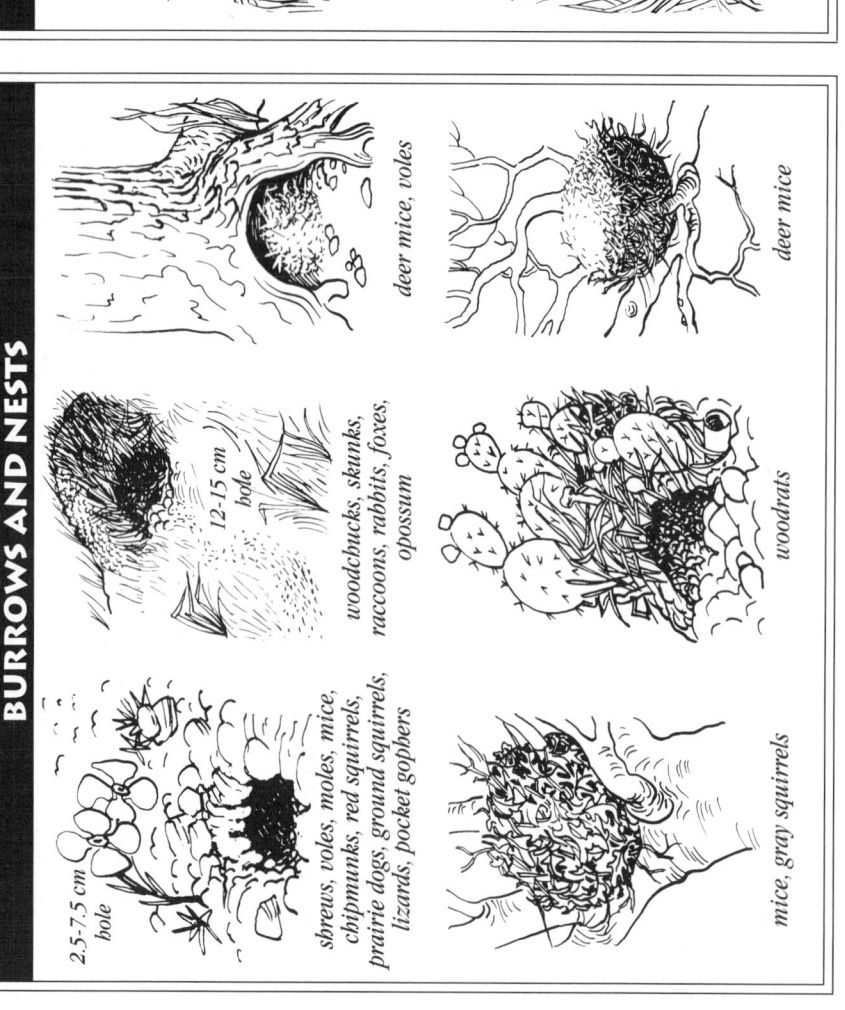

deer mice, voles

deer mice

12-15 cm hole

woodchucks, skunks, raccoons, rabbits, foxes, opossum

woodrats

2.5-7.5 cm hole

shrews, voles, moles, mice, chipmunks, red squirrels, prairie dogs, ground squirrels, lizards, pocket gophers

mice, gray squirrels

OTHER ANIMAL HOMES

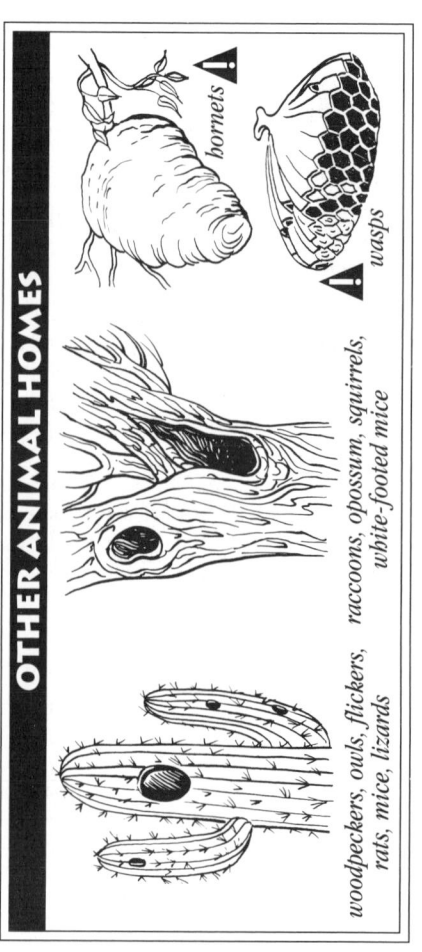

hornets

wasps

raccoons, opossum, squirrels, white-footed mice

woodpeckers, owls, flickers, rats, mice, lizards

Appendix A

WEBS, EGGS, AND COCOONS

COCOONS AND CHRYSALIDES

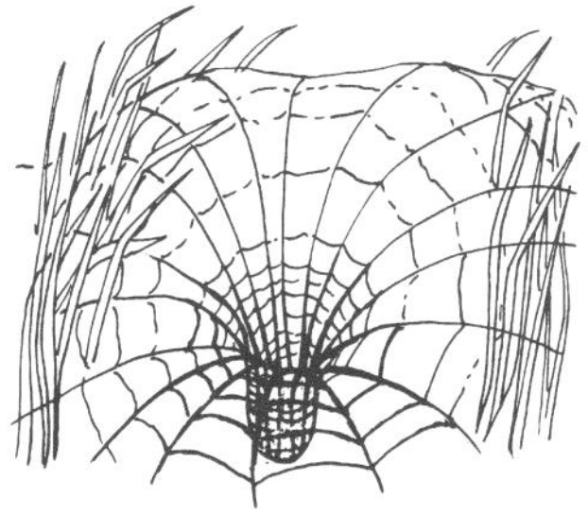

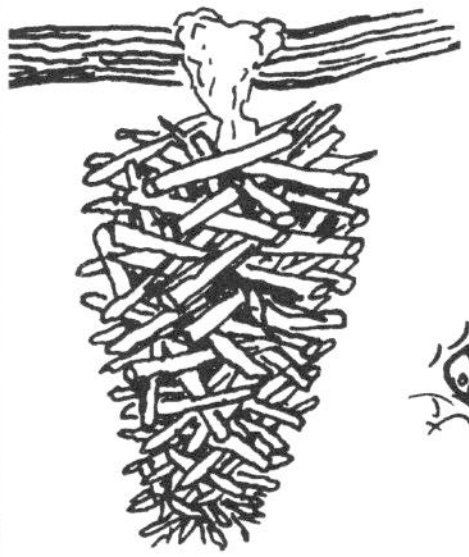

gypsy moths
(wide v-winged moths)

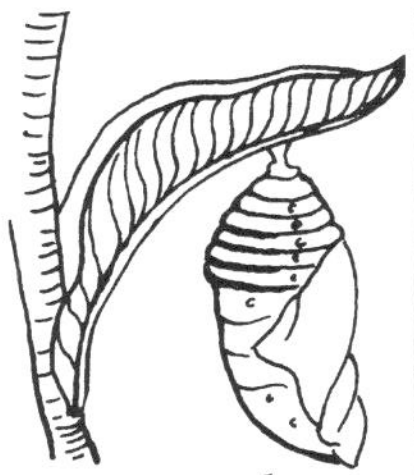

monarch butterfly larvae
(other large butterflies)

hawk moths
(wide v-winged moths)

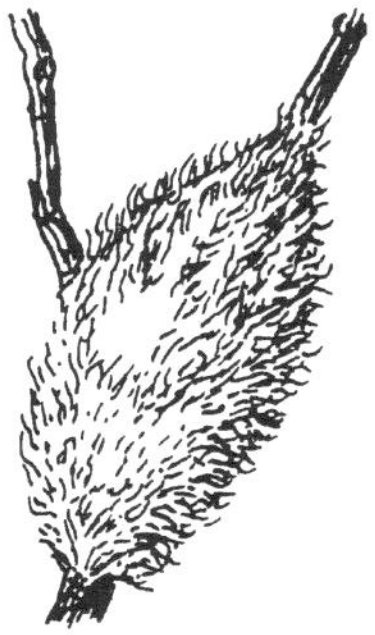

cecropia moths
(large silkworm moths)

bagworm moths
(narrow v-winged moths)

polyphemus moths
(large silkworm moths)

WEBS

orb spiders

comb clawed spiders

hammock spiders

tent caterpillars
(wide v-winged moths)

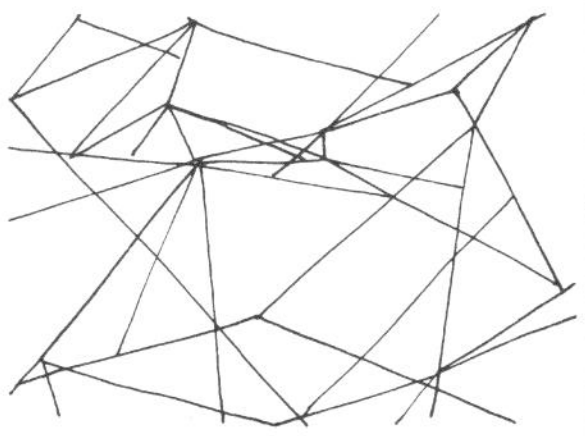

funnel web spiders

webworms
(wide v-winged moths)

MOUNDS AND PITS

ant lions

termites

ants

EGGS

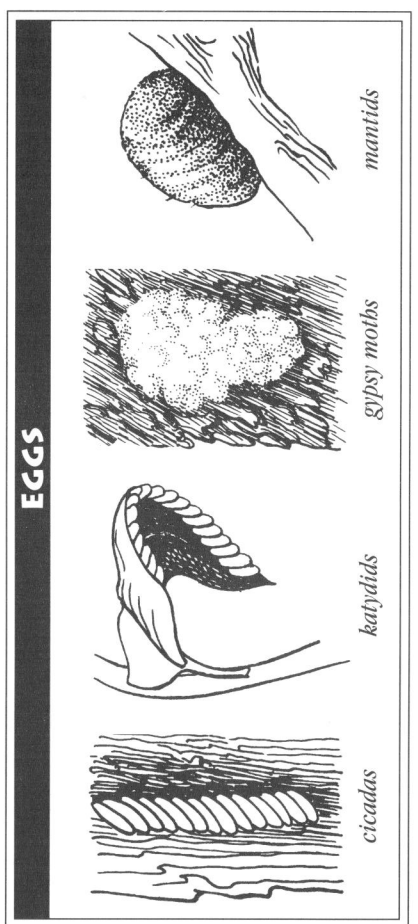

mantids

gypsy moths

katydids

cicadas

TRACKS AND SCAT

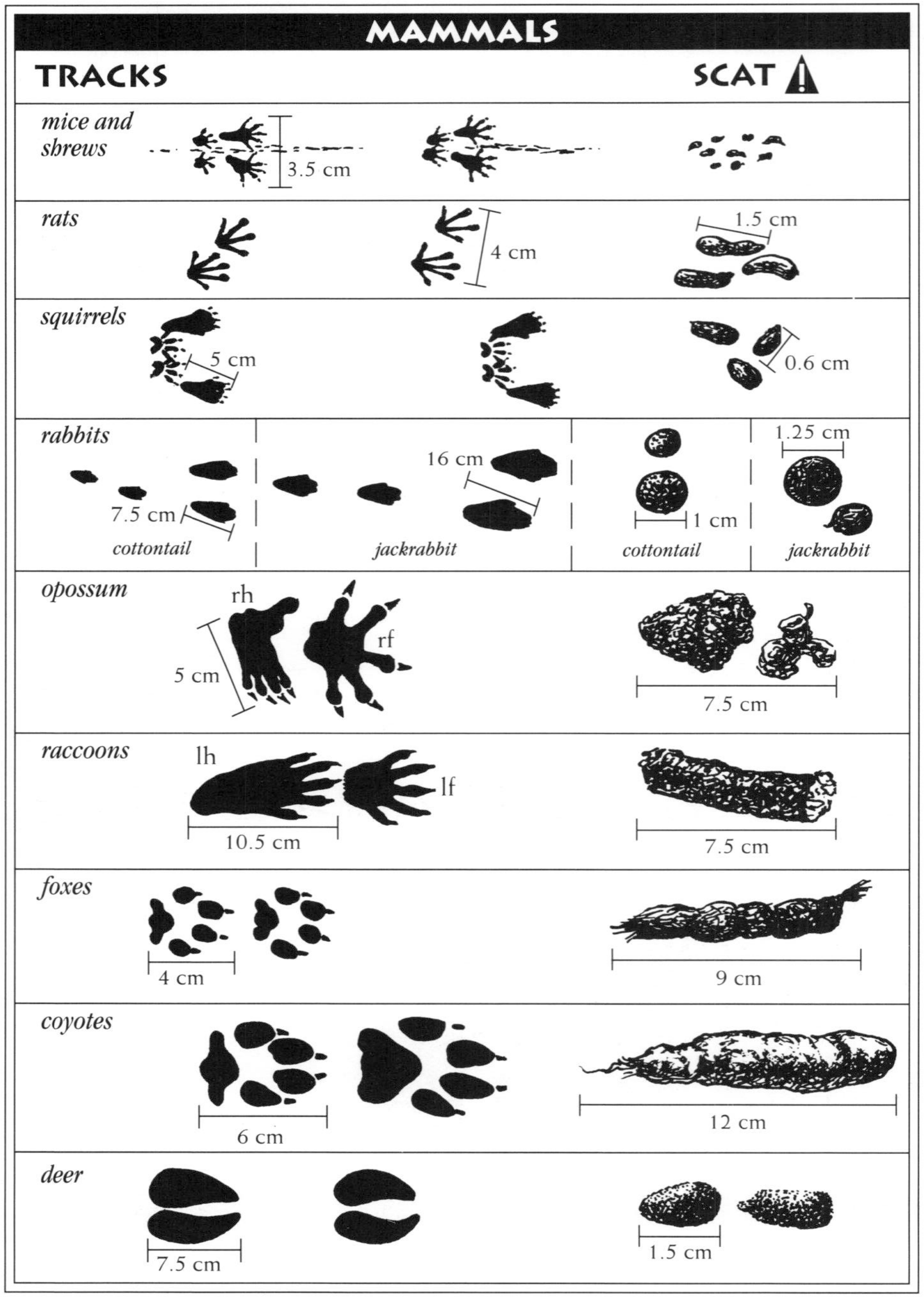

MAMMALS

TRACKS   SCAT

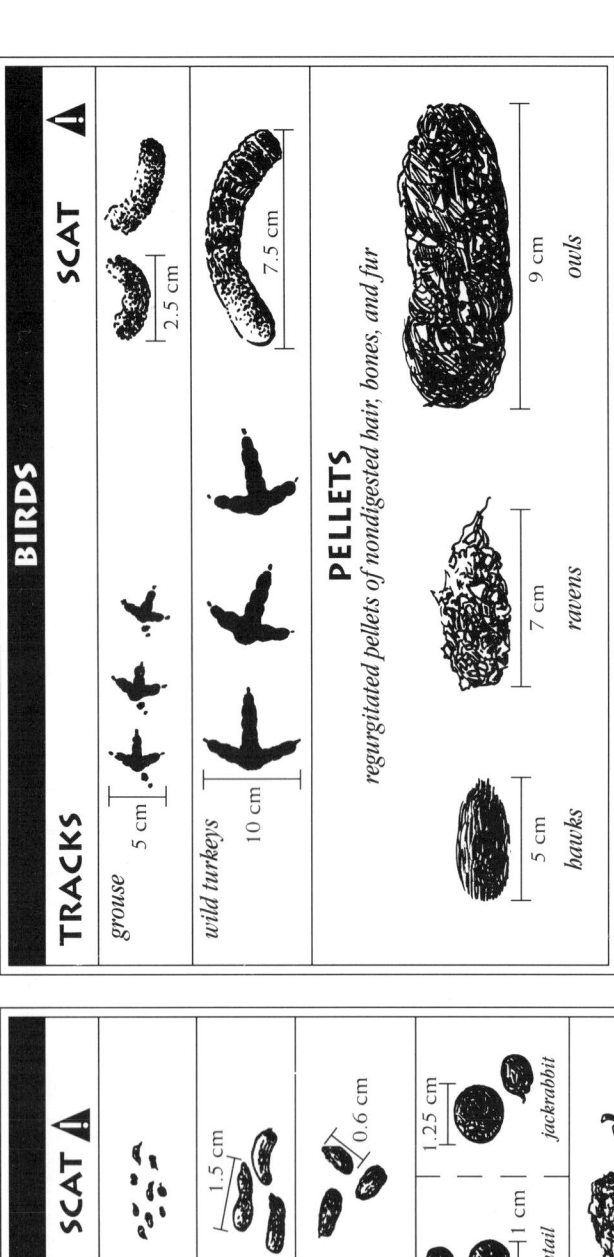

mice and shrews   3.5 cm   2.5 cm

rats   4 cm   1.5 cm

squirrels   5 cm   0.6 cm

rabbits   16 cm   7.5 cm   *jackrabbit*   *cottontail*   1.25 cm   1 cm   *jackrabbit*   *cottontail*

opossum   rf   rh   5 cm   7.5 cm

raccoons   lf   lh   10.5 cm   7.5 cm

foxes   4 cm   9 cm

coyotes   6 cm   12 cm

deer   7.5 cm   1.5 cm

BIRDS

TRACKS   SCAT

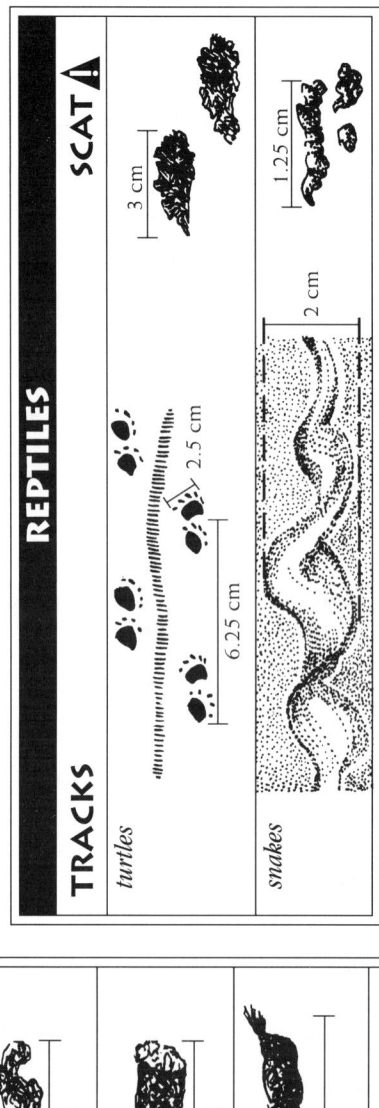

grouse   5 cm   2.5 cm

wild turkeys   10 cm   7.5 cm

PELLETS
regurgitated pellets of nondigested hair, bones, and fur

hawks   5 cm

ravens   7 cm

owls   9 cm

REPTILES

TRACKS   SCAT

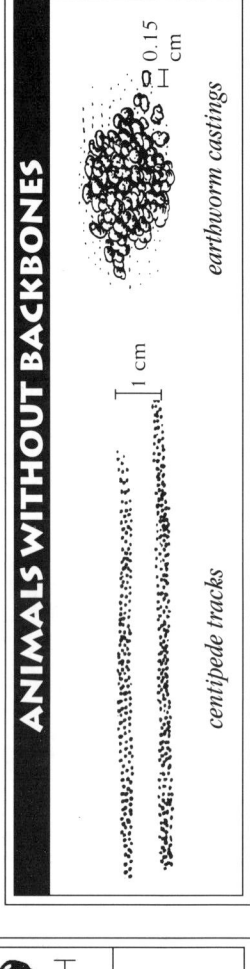

turtles   2.5 cm   6.25 cm   3 cm

snakes   2 cm   1.25 cm

ANIMALS WITHOUT BACKBONES

centipede tracks   1 cm

earthworm castings   0.15 cm

Appendix A

2. ANIMALS AND THEIR FOODS

FINDING THE "WHO" AND FIGURING OUT THE "WHAT"

When students find an animal, they can use the "How to Figure Out What an Animal Eats" page to hone in on clues to the animal's food sources. By observing the animal's behaviors and body parts, students can speculate about the type of food the animal is suited to catch and eat. Since animals spend most of their time near their food sources, students can look around the area where they find an animal to pick out plausible foods.

This section also includes charts of information about six major groups of animals: Insects, Other Animals Without Backbones, Amphibians, Reptiles, Birds, and Mammals. Within each of these major groups, the charts are divided into subgroups of related animals.

When students find an animal, they can consult the charts to try to confirm what type of animal they've found and what it eats. Each chart provides information on the general and specific habitats of each animal, and on the animal's foods.

Habitat. Each chart includes a key to icons for six habitats that occur within or near schoolyards:

- Vacant Lots
- Lawns
- Fields
- Wooded Areas
- Deserts
- Grasslands

Students can tell which habitat(s) each animal is found in by looking at these icons under the "Habitat" column to the right of the animal name. Help your students decide which one or two habitats characterize your study site so that they can scan the charts for these icons. The "Where Found" column provides more detailed habitat information for each animal.

Food Sources. These columns list the plants, animals, and other foods eaten by the entire family or genus of animals within a row. The word "herbs" refers to herbaceous plants, such as wildflowers. Your students' job is to determine which food sources the animal is likely to eat within the habitat they're exploring. Students will also want to take into account the seasonal availability of foods. A jay, for instance, will consume acorns in the fall and insects in the spring and summer. Students should also keep in mind that the food source lists are not always exhaustive. Many animals are opportunists, so although their main diet consists of certain foods, they'll often eat many other things in order to survive.

HOW TO FIGURE OUT WHAT AN ANIMAL EATS

FEEDING BEHAVIOR AND LOCALE

An animal's activities and whereabouts are often related to feeding. Where was the animal and what was it doing when you found it?

pecking for insects, sap, larvae, and seeds

sallying back and forth for flying insects

soaring/circling for small mammals, snakes, flying insects, and dead animals

pecking for seeds

hovering for juices of rotting fruit

hovering for nectar, pollen, and other insects

aphid-stroking to collect honeydew

webmaking to catch insects

dung rolling to collect dung

poking for insects and soil organisms

digging or storing seeds and nuts

BODY PARTS FOR FEEDING

How does the animal get and eat its food? Look carefully at the animal's body parts. What action does the body part look suited for?

MOUTHPARTS

chewing
for grasping, tearing, and crushing parts of other animals, plant roots, stems, wood, leaves, buds, and seeds (*grasshoppers, crickets, katydids, beetles*)
note: some insects have mouthparts for chewing and for lapping flower nectar (*bees, wasps*)

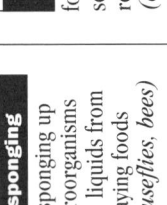
piercing
for piercing leaves, stems, seeds, or the bodies of other animals, to slurp sap or body fluids (*true bugs, leafhoppers, treehoppers, aphids, mosquitoes, some flies*)

sponging
for sponging up microorganisms and liquids from decaying foods (*houseflies, bees*)

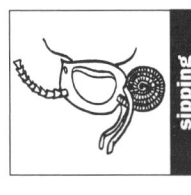
sipping
for sipping nectar from flowers (*butterflies, moths*)

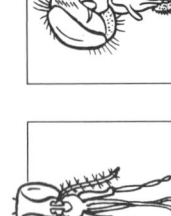
grabbing
for grabbing small, delicate insects and worms (*robins, thrashers, wrens, orioles*)
note: some birds have beaks that can crack seeds and grab insects (*chickadees, blackbirds, jays, doves, bluebirds*)

drilling
for drilling into tree bark for insects (*woodpeckers, nuthatches*)

cracking
for cracking seeds (*grosbeaks, cardinals, sparrows, finches*)

APPENDAGES

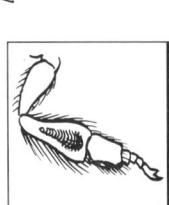
digging (back legs)
for digging into wood for pulp (*beetles, wasps*) or digging into soil for organisms (*spadefoot toads, beetles*)

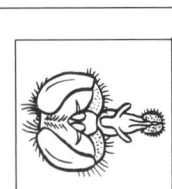
digging (front legs)
for digging into soil to suck plant root juices (*cicadas, mole crickets*)

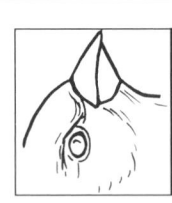
hooking
for attaching onto food plants (*moths, butterflies, beetle larvae*)

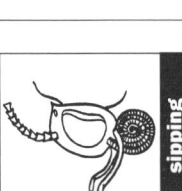
grabbing
for grabbing smaller, weaker or quick-moving prey (*mantids, assassin bugs*)

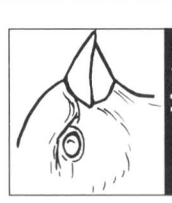
collecting
for collecting pollen (*bees*)

INSECTS

GRASSHOPPERS

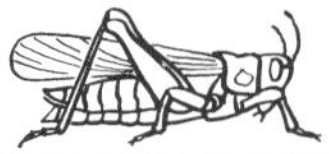

	Habitat	Where Found	Food Sources: Plants: Grasses	Herbs	Shrubs/Vines	Trees	Cacti	Animals	Other
Cockroaches	Vacant Lots, Lawns, Wooded Areas	between or under plant leaves; indoors							moist human food, pet food, organic matter
Crickets	Vacant Lots, Fields, Wooded Areas, Deserts, Grasslands	under moist soil; in high grasses and herbs; on the ground, bushes, and trees		seeds, roots, seedlings, berries, leaves	seeds, roots, seedlings, berries, leaves			other crickets, aphids, caterpillars	dead insects
Grasshoppers *(illustrated above)*	Vacant Lots, Fields, Deserts, Grasslands	in high grass or sparse vegetation; on or below shrubs and trees; on the ground	stems, leaves	stems, leaves	leaves				
Katydids	Lawns, Fields, Wooded Areas, Grasslands	on the ground; in grass; on herb stems and leaves; on leaves of trees and shrubs		flowers, leaves	flowers, leaves	leaves			
Mantids	Fields	on herb leaves, flower heads, and low shrubs						grasshoppers, caterpillars, flies, butterflies, bees, wasps, moths, spiders	

HOPPERS

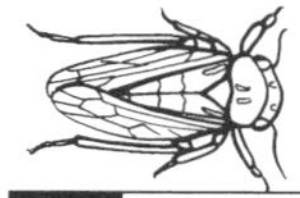

	Habitat	Where Found	Grasses	Herbs	Shrubs/Vines	Trees	Cacti	Animals	Other
Aphids	Vacant Lots, Lawns, Fields, Wooded Areas, Deserts, Grasslands	on plant stems and twigs	stem sap	stem sap	twig sap				
Cicadas	Wooded Areas, Deserts, Grasslands	in tall trees			root juices (l), limb sap, twig sap (a)	root juices (l), limb sap, twig sap (a)			
Leafhoppers *(illustrated above)*	Lawns, Fields, Wooded Areas, Deserts	on leaves	leaf sap	leaf sap	leaf sap	leaf sap			
Scale Insects	Fields, Wooded Areas, Deserts, Grasslands	on bark, twigs, leaves, pads, and stems of plants			stem sap, twig sap, leaf sap	stem sap, twig sap, leaf sap	sap—*cochineal bug only*		
Spittlebugs	Lawns, Fields, Wooded Areas, Grasslands	in a froth of bubbles on herb stems and shrub twigs		stem sap	twig sap				
Treehoppers	Fields, Wooded Areas, Deserts	in trees and shrubs; in grass	leaves (l)	leaf sap (a)	leaf sap (a)	twig sap, fruits (a)			

FLIES

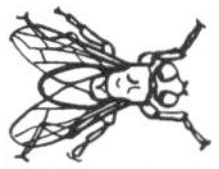

	Habitat	Where Found	Grasses	Herbs	Shrubs/Vines	Trees	Cacti	Animals	Other
Blowflies and Houseflies *(illustrated above)*	Vacant Lots, Lawns, Fields	near flowers, animal carcasses, dead plants, feces, and trash		nectar					feces, decaying animals and plants, fresh food

KEY: Caution · Vacant Lots · Lawns · Fields · Wooded Areas · Deserts · Grasslands · (a) adult · (l) larva / nymph

INSECTS *continued*

FLIES *continued*

	HABITAT	WHERE FOUND	FOOD SOURCES: Plants — Grasses	Herbs	Shrubs/Vines	Trees	Cacti	Animals	Other
Frit Flies	Lawns, Fields, Grasslands	on low herbs; on highest node of grass stems (l)	stems (l)						dead herb and grass leaves
Gall Midges and Gall Flies	Fields, Grasslands	on rotting plant material or fungi (l); in galls on herbs and shrubs (l); in termite or ant nests(l); near herbs and shrubs (a)		stems, leaves	leaves				dead plants, fungi
Hover or Flower Flies	Fields, Grasslands	hovering over flowers		nectar (a)				aphids, larvae of scale insects (l)	
Mosquitoes	Vacant Lots, Lawns, Fields, Wooded Areas, Deserts, Grasslands	near damp places		fruit juices, flower nectar—*males only*				blood of birds and mammals—*females only*	
Robber Flies	Fields, Wooded Areas, Grasslands	resting on leaves and flowers at the edges of woods and fields						leafhoppers, beetle larvae, bees and other flying insects (a), grasshopper eggs (l)	

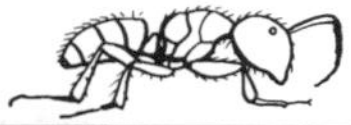

BEES, WASPS, ANTS

	HABITAT	WHERE FOUND	Grasses	Herbs	Shrubs/Vines	Trees	Cacti	Animals	Other
Ants *(illustrated above)*	Vacant Lots, Lawns, Fields, Wooded Areas, Deserts, Grasslands	in mounds and underground nests; under stones; on the ground; on tree twigs and trunks; in dead trees	seeds	nectar, pollen, berries, seeds	nectar, pollen, berries, seeds			termites, liquid from aphids, other small insects, body parts of large insects	fungi
Bees ⚠	Vacant Lots, Lawns, Fields, Wooded Areas, Deserts, Grasslands	in large patches of flowers; near hollow or dead trees; flying low over ground; nesting under cactus arms		nectar, pollen	nectar, pollen	nectar, pollen			
Hornets and Wasps ⚠	Vacant Lots, Lawns, Fields, Wooded Areas, Deserts, Grasslands	around edges of woods; on the ground; on flower clusters; near food, trash, and picnic sites; in underground nests, mud nests, or aerial paper nests; in canopies of dead trees; nesting under cactus arms		nectar (a)	nectar (a)	nectar, juices from crushed or rotting fruits (a)		pre-chewed insect larvae, crickets, grasshoppers (l), insects, juices of beetles (a), spiders	

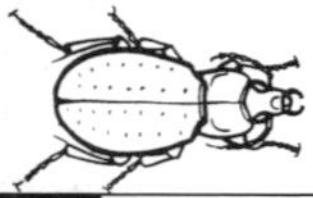

BEETLES

	HABITAT	WHERE FOUND	Grasses	Herbs	Shrubs/Vines	Trees	Cacti	Animals	Other
Bark Beetles	Wooded Areas	in dead trees, seeds, and roots of plants		seeds, roots (l)		inner bark (l), fruits (a)			
Firefly Beetles	Vacant Lots, Fields, Wooded Areas, Grasslands	clinging to leaves; on tree trunks and branches; under bark; in decaying plants; in moist places						insect larvae, slugs, snails	
Ground Beetles *(illustrated above)*	Vacant Lots, Lawns, Fields, Wooded Areas, Deserts, Grasslands	deep in the soil near plant roots (l); at the ground surface; under leaves or rocks; in rotting wood (a)						caterpillars, fly larvae, cutworms, other insects, snails, slugs, earthworms	

KEY: ⚠ Caution   Vacant Lots   Lawns   Fields   Wooded Areas   Deserts   Grasslands   (a) adult   (l) larva / nymph

FOOD SOURCES

BEETLES *continued*

	HABITAT	WHERE FOUND	Grasses	Herbs	Shrubs/Vines	Trees	Cacti	Animals	Other
June Beetles	(symbols)	in soil in grassy fields	roots (l)	roots (l), pollen, leaves (a)	pollen, leaves (a)				
Ladybug Beetles	(symbols)	on plants with insects on them						aphids, scale insects, mealybugs, mites	
Leaf Beetles	(symbols)	in weedy, open areas; in bushes; hiding on the ground; (rarely) on trees		leaves (l), flowers (a)	leaves (l), flowers (a)				
Longhorned Beetles	(symbols)	on flowers; near fallen trees or logs		leaves, fruits, sap, roots, twigs (a)	leaves, fruits, sap, roots, twigs (a)	wood (l)			dead wood (l)
Rove Beetles	(symbols)	on tree leaves, flowers, and mushrooms; under bark; in leaf litter; under stones and logs; around decaying matter						fly larvae, springtails, mites, worms	fungi, dead animals, dung
Tiger Beetles	(symbols)	in sunny spots with dry soil and sparse plants						ants, flies, other small insects, caterpillars	
Weevils	(symbols)	on or in dead branches, stumps, and logs; on tree leaves; on woody fungi; on or in acorns, nuts and other fruits; on all parts of herbs		roots, stems, seeds, flowers, fruits	roots, stems, seeds, flowers, fruits	wood, needles, other leaves			dead wood, fungi

TRUE BUGS

	HABITAT	WHERE FOUND	Grasses	Herbs	Shrubs/Vines	Trees	Cacti	Animals	Other
Ambush Bugs	(symbols)	on blossoms of goldenrod and other herbs						flies, honeybees, butterflies, moths, true bugs	
Assassin Bugs	(symbols)	on leaves						honey bees, caterpillars, beetle larvae, other insects	
Boxelder Bugs	(symbols)	on tree trunks and buildings in sunny locations				leaves, fruits			
Damsel Bugs	(symbols)	near plants with insects on them						aphids, leafhoppers, tree-hoppers, small caterpillars	
Plant Bugs	(symbols)	on herb and shrub leaves; near the edges of woods; on chainlink fences		leaf sap	leaf sap, small fruits				
Seed Bugs *(illustrated above)*	(symbols)	in thickets; on herb leaves; in leaf litter		seeds					
Stink Bugs	(symbols)	on plants	seed juices	seed juices	berries, other fruits	fruits			

KEY: ⚠ Caution   Vacant Lots   Lawns   Fields   Wooded Areas   Deserts   Grasslands   (a) adult   (l) larva / nymph

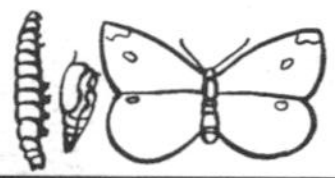

INSECTS *continued*

BUTTERFLIES AND MOTHS

	HABITAT	WHERE FOUND	Grasses	Herbs	Shrubs/Vines	Trees	Cacti	Animals	Other
Gossamer-winged Butterflies		in open sagelands; around trees, shrubs, and flowers		leaves (l), nectar (a)	leaves (l), nectar (a)	leaves (l)			
Hairstreak Butterflies		in open wooded areas; in fields; at the edges of fields; around trees, shrubs and flowers		leaves (l), nectar (a)	leaves (l), nectar (a)	leaves (l),			
Other Large Butterflies		around trees, shrubs, and flowers		leaves (l), nectar (a)		leaves (l), sap (a)			
Satyr Butterflies		flitting about grasses and shrubs; weaving close to the ground	leaves, sap of sedges (l)	nectar (a)		sap, fermenting fruits, leaves (a)		liquid from aphids (a)	
Skippers		visiting flowers; on wet mud	leaves (l)	leaves (l), fermenting fruits (a)	fermenting fruits (a)				
Sulfur and White Butterflies *(White illustrated above)*		in sunny areas; around flowers		leaves (l), nectar (a)					
Swallowtail Butterflies		around damp spots and flowers		leaves (l), nectar (a)	leaves (l)	leaves (l)			
Large Silkworm Moths		on leaves (l); near flowers (a)		leaves	leaves	leaves			
Narrow V-winged Moths		on low herbs and cacti; in trees		leaves (l), nectar (a)		needles, other leaves (l)	pads (l)		
Wide V-winged Moths		camouflaged on tree bark; on lichen-covered rocks	leaves (l)	leaves (l)	leaves (l)	needles, other leaves (l)	pollen (a)		lichens (l)

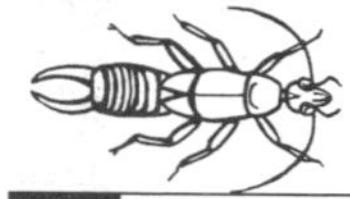

OTHER INSECTS

	HABITAT	WHERE FOUND	Grasses	Herbs	Shrubs/Vines	Trees	Cacti	Animals	Other
Antlions		in pits in dry sandy soil especially under building eaves and bridges						ants, other small insects (l)	
Earwigs *(illustrated above)*		in damp places under bark, logs, and stones; in soil and leaf litter; on plants, shrubs and trees		nectar, leaves				mites, aphids, insect larvae, pupae	trash
Springtails		in leaf litter; in mosses; in rotting wood; in soil; on snow		germinating seeds, roots					fungi, dead herb and grass leaves
Termites		in dead wood or soil; in cactus carcasses and dead yucca stalks	leaves			wood			dead leaves, roots, vines, wood, cacti

KEY: ⚠ Caution   Vacant Lots   Lawns   Fields   Wooded Areas   Deserts   Grasslands   (a) adult   (l) larva / nymph

OTHER ANIMALS WITHOUT BACKBONES

FOOD SOURCES

	WHERE FOUND	Plants: Grasses	Herbs	Shrubs/Vines	Trees	Cacti	Animals	Other
Daddy-longlegs	on open ground; in tree bark cracks; in wood piles; in grass						aphids, leafhoppers, beetle larvae, spiders, snails, centipedes, earthworms	dead insects
Mites and Ticks	in leaf litter and surface soil; in soil under shrubs; on plants and animals						aphids and their eggs, animal fluids	fungi, bacteria
Pseudoscorpions	in dry sand mixed with oak leaf litter; on mosses; under loose bark; in leaf litter; under stones; in tree hollows; in decaying cactus boots						springtails, ants, flies, mites, termites, caterpillars, daddy-longlegs, spiders, sow bugs, pill bugs, earthworms	
Scorpions	in dark crevices; under bark of desert trees and shrubs; under stones and leaf litter; in small, underground burrows						insects, spiders, (occasionally) young lizards and snakes	
Spiders Comb Clawed Spiders	among fallen branches; under trash; in sheltered corners of buildings						insects	
Crab Spiders	on tree bark; among debris on ground; on leaves and stems of low shrubs; in tall grasses; in flower heads						insects	
Hammock Spiders	in shrubby areas; near buildings; in sheet webs spun in the grass; between fence posts or buildings; on lower branches of trees						insects	
Jumping Spiders	in tall grasses and low herbs; on tree trunks; on desert shrubs and flowers						insects	
Orb Spiders	in tall grasses and low shrubs; hanging in or below webs; on stone walls						insects	
Wolf Spiders	on the soil surface between grasses; in burrows; under leaf litter or stones						insects, beetle larvae, earthworms, centipedes, millipedes, sow bugs	

EIGHT-LEGGED

KEY: ⚠ Caution   ⧑ Vacant Lots   ◗ Lawns   ✦ Fields   ◑ Wooded Areas   ◓ Deserts   ❀ Grasslands   (a) adult   (l) larva / nymph

Who Eats What guide

371

OTHER ANIMALS WITHOUT BACKBONES

continued

FOOD SOURCES

	HABITAT WHERE FOUND	Plants — Grasses	Herbs	Shrubs/Vines	Trees	Cacti	Animals	Other
MOLLUSKS								
Slugs	on soil surface; on herbs and grasses	leaves	leaves					dead leaves
Snails	on soil surface; on herbs and grasses	leaves	leaves					fungi, dead leaves
MANY-LEGGED								
Centipedes ⚠	in rotten wood and leaf litter; under stones and logs						insects, sow bugs, earthworms	
Millipedes	in leaf litter at ground surface; in soil; under stones and logs; on and under desert shrubs							dead leaves, bark, cactus pads
Pill Bugs and Sow Bugs	in damp places; under logs, boards and stones; in leaf litter	leaves, stems						dead stems, wood, leaves
WORMS								
Earthworms	in soil and leaf litter			fallen fruits, seeds				soil, dead leaves, dead animals, feces, fungi, bacteria

KEY: ⚠ Caution ▪ Vacant Lots ◗ Lawns ✦ Fields ● Wooded Areas ☀ Deserts ✿ Grasslands (a) adult (l) larva / nymph

Appendix A

AMPHIBIANS

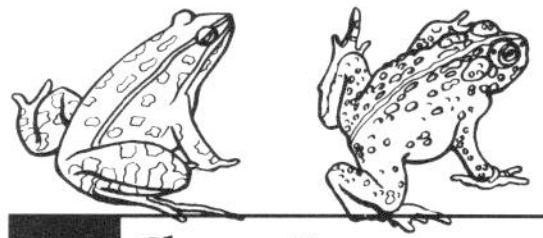

FROGS AND TOADS	HABITAT	WHERE FOUND	FOOD SOURCES: Plants: Grasses	Herbs	Shrubs/Vines	Trees	Cacti	Animals	Other
Chorus Frogs and Peepers	Vacant Lots, Fields, Wooded Areas, Grasslands	on the ground; in damp leaf litter						insects, spiders	
Spadefoot Toads	Fields, Wooded Areas, Deserts, Grasslands	in areas with gravelly or loose, sandy soil						insects, spiders	
Tree Frogs	Wooded Areas	in leaf litter, tree cavities, and underground crevices; on tree limbs						ants, beetles, grasshoppers, katydids, spiders	
True Frogs *(illustrated above left)*	Lawns, Fields, Wooded Areas, Grasslands	in grassy areas; on the forest floor						beetles, caterpillars, grasshoppers, crickets, flies, mosquitoes, spiders, centipedes, millipedes, earthworms	
True Toads *(illustrated above right)*	Vacant Lots, Lawns, Fields, Wooded Areas, Deserts, Grasslands	under logs, boards, and flat stones; in leaf litter						ants, beetles, spiders, centipedes, millipedes, earthworms	

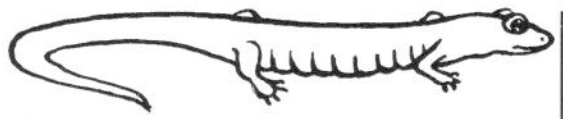

SALAMANDERS	HABITAT	WHERE FOUND	Grasses	Herbs	Shrubs/Vines	Trees	Cacti	Animals	Other
Lungless Salamanders *(illustrated above)*	Vacant Lots, Wooded Areas, Grasslands	under trash, logs, bark, stones; in leaf litter; on moss						ants and other small insects with stingers and odors, beetles, earthworms	
Mole Salamanders	Fields, Wooded Areas, Grasslands	in leaf litter; in underground burrows in loose soil; in logs; under logs, boards, and flat rocks						large insects, insect larvae, sow bugs, earthworms, small mice, other amphibians	
Newts	Wooded Areas, Grasslands	under logs, boards, rocks, and leaf litter; along trails						springtails, aphids, earthworms	

KEY: Caution   Vacant Lots   Lawns   Fields   Wooded Areas   Deserts   Grasslands   (a) adult   (l) larva / nymph

REPTILES

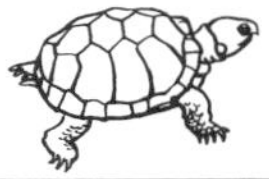

FOOD SOURCES

TURTLES

	HABITAT	WHERE FOUND	Plants: Grasses	Herbs	Shrubs/Vines	Trees	Cacti	*Animals*	*Other*
Tortoises	Wooded Areas, Deserts	on rocky hillsides and dry sandy areas; in open wooded areas with an understory; in dens	leaves	flowers, berries	leaves, berries		pads		
Box & Water Turtles Box Turtles *(illustrated above)*	Fields, Wooded Areas, Deserts, Grasslands	at the edges of woods; in dens	leaves	fruits	berries	fallen berries		grasshoppers, cicadas, beetles, caterpillars, slugs—*grassland and desert species only*	dead animals, mushrooms

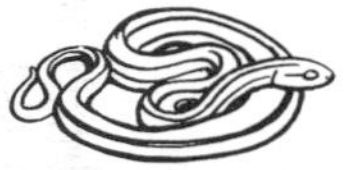

SNAKES

	HABITAT	WHERE FOUND	Grasses	Herbs	Shrubs/Vines	Trees	Cacti	*Animals*	*Other*
Brown Snakes	Vacant Lots, Wooded Areas, Deserts	in moist places; in areas with sparse plant growth; under trash; under debris on hillsides						soft-bodied insects, slugs, snails, earthworms	
Garter Snakes *(illustrated above)*	Lawns, Fields, Wooded Areas, Deserts, Grasslands	under logs, boards, or plants; in leaf litter and on the ground; sunning on grassy slopes.						insects, spiders, slugs, centipedes, earthworms, frogs, toads, fish, mice, moles, shrews	
Gopher Snakes (Caution)	Wooded Areas, Deserts, Grasslands	in dry areas; in mammal burrows; under rocks, logs, or boards; in areas with grasses and shrubs; in trees						lizards, baby birds, bird eggs, rats, gophers, ground squirrels, rabbits	
Hognose Snakes	Fields, Wooded Areas, Grasslands	in sandy areas						other snakes, lizards, toads, salamanders, birds	
King Snakes (Caution)	Wooded Areas, Deserts	in shrubs; on rocky hillsides; under rocks						other snakes, lizards, birds, eggs, mice	
Milk Snakes	Fields, Wooded Areas, Grasslands	under logs, boards, and leaf litter in sunny places; in crevices						beetles, insects, slugs, other snakes, lizards, eggs, chipmunks, mice	
Racer Snakes	Fields, Wooded Areas, Deserts, Grasslands	in open, brushy areas, or sparsely wooded areas; hibernating on rocky hillsides						grasshoppers, crickets, moths, other snakes, toads, tree frogs, lizards, birds, eggs, rodents	
Ringneck Snakes	Wooded Areas, Grasslands	in moist places beneath boards, rotting logs, stumps, rocks; (occasionally) out in the open						insects, earthworms, other snakes, skinks, tree frogs, salamanders	

KEY: Caution · Vacant Lots · Lawns · Fields · Wooded Areas · Deserts · Grasslands (a) adult (l) larva / nymph

REPTILES *continued*

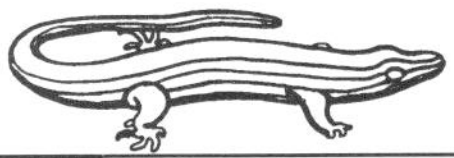

LIZARDS	HABITAT	WHERE FOUND	Grasses	Herbs	Shrubs/ Vines	Trees	Cacti	Animals	Other
			Plants (FOOD SOURCES)						
Skinks *(illustrated above)*	Vacant Lots, Fields, Wooded Areas, Grasslands	in rocky areas with low shrubs; in grassy areas; in moist areas with loose soil and trees; under rocks, leaf litter, logs, and trash						beetles, grasshoppers, crickets, leafhoppers, adult and larval moths, wasp pupae, spiders, sow bugs, earthworms, small lizards	
Geckos	Deserts	in rock crevices, sand dunes and flats; under bark, dead cactus pads, logs, rubbish, and yucca stems; near buildings and trash						insects, spiders	
Whiptails	Vacant Lots, Fields, Deserts, Grasslands	in dry, disturbed, open areas with sparse plants; in leaf litter; in ditches; near gravelly soil; under shrubs; near trash; on fences						termites, ant lions, wasps, mantids, beetles, grasshoppers, daddy-longlegs, scorpions, spiders	
Iguanids									
Anoles	Vacant Lots, Lawns, Wooded Areas	on trees, fence posts, walls, and shrubs; in tall grasses and palm fronds; in shady areas						flies, beetles, moths, spiders	
Collared Lizards (Caution)	Wooded Areas, Deserts	basking on large rocks; in rock crevices; in hilly areas; near small rock piles						other lizards, small snakes, grasshoppers, locusts, crickets, beetles, moths, spiders	
Fence Lizards	Vacant Lots, Wooded Areas, Deserts, Grasslands	in sunny, brushy, rocky areas; near old buildings; on woodpiles and fences; in old woodrat nests; in banks with rodent burrows; in burrows under brush						ladybug beetles, ants, wasps, leafhoppers, aphids, caterpillars, spiders, snails, sow bugs, millipedes	
Horned Lizards	Vacant Lots, Deserts, Grasslands	basking on rocks; in dry, open areas with shrubs and loose soil; in sandy, gravelly drainage areas; on open patches of hard-packed sand; near sunny anthills						ants, beetle larvae, butterflies, spiders, snails, sow bugs	
Spiny Lizards	Deserts	on rocks in sandy areas; in burrows under bushes; on tree trunks and sides of buildings			buds, leaves			ants, bees, wasps, flies, grasshoppers, caterpillars, true bugs, lizards	

KEY: Caution · Vacant Lots · Lawns · Fields · Wooded Areas · Deserts · Grasslands (a) adult (l) larva / nymph

BIRDS

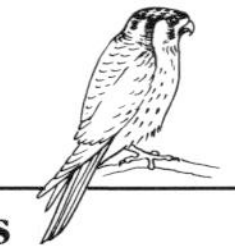

RAPTORS

	HABITAT	WHERE FOUND	FOOD SOURCES: Plants: Grasses	Herbs	Shrubs/Vines	Trees	Cacti	Animals	Other
Falcons *(illustrated above)*	Vacant Lots, Lawns, Fields, Wooded Areas, Deserts, Grasslands	in open areas; on exposed poles and trees; soaring along large cliffs						grasshoppers and other insects, birds, rodents	
Hawks	Fields, Wooded Areas, Deserts, Grasslands	in trees near roadsides; on telephone poles and fence posts; flying low over trees or desert shrubs; near edges of woods; nesting in cacti						grasshoppers, snakes, frogs, lizards, birds, mice, prairie dogs, squirrels, rabbits	
Vultures	Vacant Lots, Fields, Deserts, Grasslands	circling high above open areas; nesting in caves, hollow logs, and under abandoned buildings; roosting on cacti							dead animals

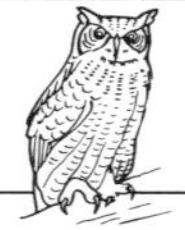

OWLS

	HABITAT	WHERE FOUND	Grasses	Herbs	Shrubs/Vines	Trees	Cacti	Animals	Other
Owls *(illustrated above)*	Vacant Lots, Wooded Areas, Deserts, Grasslands	on living and dead trees, or telephone poles; on the ground near abandoned gopher or prairie dog burrows; nesting in cactus arms						large insects, scorpions, centipedes, birds, mice, moles, shrews, squirrels, skunks	

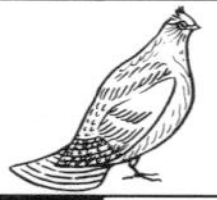

GROUND BIRDS

	HABITAT	WHERE FOUND	Grasses	Herbs	Shrubs/Vines	Trees	Cacti	Animals	Other
Grouse *(illustrated above)*	Wooded Areas, Deserts, Grasslands	in small depressions in the ground beneath shrubs; near thickets and trees; at the edges of woods; nesting in brush	leaves	seeds, leaves	blossoms, leaves, buds, twigs, berries, fruits	acorns, nuts, seeds		grasshoppers, crickets [ants, ladybug beetles—*sage grouse only*]	
Prairie Chickens	Grasslands	in tall grass	seeds	seeds	fruits, buds, leaves	fruits, buds, leaves		grasshoppers, beetles, caterpillars, ants	
Quail	Wooded Areas, Deserts, Grasslands	along grassy roadsides; near thickets; under trees		seeds	seeds	acorns		ground beetles, leaf beetles, weevils, caterpillars, grasshoppers, crickets, spiders, snails, centipedes, sow bugs, [true bugs, leafhoppers, ants—*gambel's quail only*]	
Wild Turkeys	Wooded Areas	in wooded areas with scattered clearings; at the edges of woods	seeds	seeds	seeds, fruits	seeds, cones, acorns		beetles, grasshoppers, crickets, ants, wasps, bees, flies, true bugs, caterpillars, spiders, snails, millipedes, centipedes, salamanders	

KEY: Caution · Vacant Lots · Lawns · Fields · Wooded Areas · Deserts · Grasslands · (a) adult · (l) larva / nymph

BIRDS *continued*

DOVES

	HABITAT	WHERE FOUND	Grasses	Herbs	Shrubs/Vines	Trees	Cacti	Animals	Other
Doves *(illustrated above)*	(Lawns, Fields, Vacant Lots, Wooded Areas, Grasslands icons)	in places with trees and shrubs; searching on ground for seeds; nesting on cactus arms, or low in shrubs	seeds	seeds, [berries —Inca doves only]	berries, [nectar—Inca doves only]		nectar—Inca doves only		
Rock Doves (pigeons)	(Vacant Lots, Lawns icons)	near food trash; nesting on rock ledges, window ledges, and overhangs	grain in bird feed	seeds, berries				insects, earthworms	

OTHER BIRDS

	HABITAT	WHERE FOUND	Grasses	Herbs	Shrubs/Vines	Trees	Cacti	Animals	Other
Roadrunners	(Deserts icon)	on the ground near shrubs; nesting in cactus arms						grasshoppers, large crawling insects, scorpions, spiders, small snakes, lizards, young ground-nesting birds, bird eggs, mice, rodents	
Woodpeckers *(illustrated above)*	(Vacant Lots, Fields, Wooded Areas, Grasslands icons)	on living or dead tree trunks and branches; in areas with low shrubs; in, on, or near cacti; on the ground near anthills—*flickers only*			berries	acorns, nuts, seeds, berries, [sap—*sapsuckers only*]	fruits	ants, adult and larval beetles, termites, crickets	

PERCHING BIRDS

	HABITAT	WHERE FOUND	Grasses	Herbs	Shrubs/Vines	Trees	Cacti	Animals	Other
Blackbirds, Orioles, and Meadowlarks	(Vacant Lots, Fields, Lawns, Wooded Areas, Grasslands icons)	in thick brushy areas, open areas with sparse shrubs, wet areas, and parking lots; moving through tall trees; feeding on the ground; near buildings and trash—*grackles only*	seeds		berries— *orioles only*	berries— *orioles only;* cones— *meadowlark only*		bees, grasshoppers, crickets, caterpillars, sow bugs, snails, earthworms, bird eggs, [ants, grubs, weevils, cankerworms—*red-winged blackbirds only*]	
Chickadees, Titmice, and Verdin	(Vacant Lots, Wooded Areas, Grasslands icons)	in edges and interiors of wooded areas; on low branches; nesting in rotting tree stumps; nesting in cacti—*verdin only*			berries, seeds	seeds, cones, nuts		moth and butterfly adults, larvae, and eggs, katydids, weevils, flies, wasps, scale insects, leafhoppers, treehoppers, aphids	
Grosbeaks, Sparrows, Finches, and Cardinals *(sparrow illustrated above)*	(Vacant Lots, Fields, Wooded Areas, Grasslands icons)	near edges of deciduous woods; in brushy undergrowth of wooded areas; in weedy, brushy, or grassy fields; perched on tips of herb stalks or tree branches; among small saplings; near buildings and orchards; in desert shrubs and thickets	seeds	seeds	fruits, berries	seeds, cones, fruits, berries		beetles, ants, bees, wasps, grasshoppers, caterpillars, flies, [aphids—finches only]	

KEY: ⚠ Caution ⬗ Vacant Lots ◐ Lawns ✪ Fields ✿ Deserts ✾ Wooded Areas ✤ Grasslands (a) adult (l) larva / nymph

Who Eats What guide

FOOD SOURCES

PERCHING BIRDS *continued*

	HABITAT	WHERE FOUND	Plants — Grasses	Herbs	Shrubs/ Vines	Trees	Cacti	Animals	Other
Jays, Crows, Ravens, and Magpies									
Jays	(icons)	in dense thickets; pine and oak woods; perched high in trees; on the ground			berries	acorns, cones		caterpillars, grasshoppers; wasps, beetles, bird eggs; young birds	
Crows and Ravens	(icons)	near roadsides and orchards; in open wooded areas; feeding in grass; near trash; nesting in trees or cacti			seeds, berries	acorns, berries, fruits		cutworms, beetles, grasshoppers, caterpillars, cicadas, scorpions, spiders, lizards, amphibians, bird eggs, young birds, small mammals	dead animals, garbage
Magpies	(icons)	in open country and pine woods; near heavy brush and brush piles; nesting in trees; on telephone wires			berries	berries, fruits		weevils, ground beetles, wasps, bees, grasshoppers, rodents	dead animals
Larks	(icons)	in open areas with brushy borders; nesting in grass or open patches of bare soil between desert shrubs		seeds				adult and larval beetles, caterpillars, grasshoppers	
Mockingbirds and Thrashers	(icons)	in brushy areas; on dry hillsides; nesting in desert shrubs; flying between bushes; on ground picking through leaf litter		berries	berries, fruits	berries, fruits		beetles, ants, bees, wasps, grasshoppers, crickets, lizards, salamanders, [frogs—*thrashers only*]	
Nuthatches	(icons)	on tree trunks and branches; nesting in tree cavities				acorns, cones		beetles, weevils, ants, wasps, moth and butterfly adults, larvae, and eggs, caterpillars, scale insects, spiders	
Robins and Bluebirds	(icons)	near abandoned orchards and roadsides; in open woods, clearings, and lawns; on fence posts; nesting in tree cavities—*bluebird only*			berries	berries, fruits		ground beetles, weevils, caterpillars, ants, snails, millipedes, sow bugs; [earthworms—*robins only*]	
Starlings	(icons)	near orchards; on building ledges; nesting in cactus cavities			berries	berries, fruits		ground beetles, grasshoppers, caterpillars, cicadas, millipedes	
Swallows	(icons)	in cacti; near buildings and cliffs; flying overhead						flies, bees, wasps, moths, ground and other beetles, weevils, ants, grasshoppers, spiders	
Wrens	(icons)	on or near ground with leaf litter; in partly brush-covered areas; in rocky, brushy ravines; nesting in tree cavities; nesting in cactus arms—*cactus wren only*			seeds, berries	acorns, cones, seeds	fruits	beetles, grasshoppers, crickets, caterpillars, ants, wasps, flies, millipedes	

KEY: ⚠ Caution   Vacant Lots   Lawns   Fields   Wooded Areas   Grasslands   Deserts   (a) adult   (l) larva / nymph

Appendix A

MAMMALS

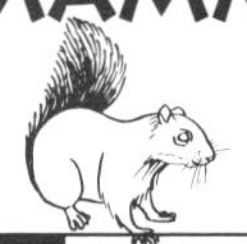

GNAWING MAMMALS

	HABITAT	WHERE FOUND	FOOD SOURCES: Plants — Grasses	Herbs	Shrubs/Vines	Trees	Cacti	Animals	Other
Jumping Mice	Lawns, Fields, Wooded Areas, Grasslands	in shrubs; under grasses; near wooded, rocky areas	seeds	seeds, fruits	berries			caterpillars, beetles	mushrooms
Mice and Rats — Deer Mice	Fields, Wooded Areas, Deserts, Grasslands	in open or dense areas; in abandoned bird nests in trees; in hollow logs; under tree stumps; in rock piles; under low bushes		seeds		seeds, nuts, cones, acorns, seedlings		crickets, grasshoppers, beetles	
Rats (Caution)	Vacant Lots, Fields	in burrows along foundations of buildings; in rubbish piles and ravines; (occasionally) in fields near buildings							garbage, household grains
Voles	Lawns, Fields, Deserts, Grasslands	in matted grass; in burrows; underneath shrubs	leaves, seeds	leaves, seeds		bark, leaves, seeds, acorns		insects	mushrooms
White-footed Mice	Fields, Wooded Areas	in thick, brushy, wooded and rocky areas; in trees; in hollow logs; under tree stumps; in rock piles				seeds, acorns, nuts, cones, fruits, roots, seedlings		grasshoppers, beetles, moths, craneflies, caterpillars, pupae, cocoons, snails, centipedes, millipedes	
Woodrats	Wooded Areas, Deserts, Grasslands	in cone-shaped nests near cacti; in stick nests on the forest floor; in crevices in cliffs and rocky areas			seeds	acorns, cones, nuts, berries	pads	ants, beetles, termites	
Pocket Gophers	Deserts, Grasslands	in underground burrows in loose, slightly moist soil	roots	tubers		roots of seedlings			
Pocket Mice, Kangaroo Mice, and Kangaroo Rats	Wooded Areas, Deserts, Grasslands	in sandy areas with sparse vegetation; in hardpacked soil; in wooded or grassy foothills; in tiny burrows with entrances under shrubs and cacti	seeds, [leaves—*kangaroo rats only]*	seeds, [leaves—*kangaroo rats only]*	seeds, [leaves—*kangaroo rats only]*			insects—*pocket mice only*	
Squirrels — Chipmunks	Lawns, Wooded Areas, Deserts	in brushy and wooded areas; on stone walls; near trash cans		berries, bulbs	berries	cones, acorns, nuts, seedlings		beetles, slugs, cankerworms, earthworms	mushrooms
Squirrels *(illustrated above)*	Vacant Lots, Lawns, Fields, Wooded Areas, Deserts, Grasslands	on branches of trees; on the ground; sitting on boulders			berries	acorns, seeds, nuts, cones, buds, inner bark, galls		beetles, caterpillars, bird eggs, young birds	mushrooms
Ground Squirrels	Wooded Areas, Deserts, Grasslands	on sandy flats near plants; on partly wooded slopes; in open grassland; on fence posts	leaves, seeds	leaves, berries, seeds, bulbs	seeds, leaves	fruits, seedlings	fruits, flowers	insects, eggs, birds	mushrooms
Woodchucks	Lawns, Fields, Wooded Areas	near plants; in open woods and fields; in ravines; along roadsides	leaves, roots	stems, flowers, leaves, roots	twigs	fruits			

KEY: Caution · Vacant Lots · Lawns · Fields · Wooded Areas · Deserts · Grasslands · (a) adult · (l) larva / nymph

FOOD SOURCES

GNAWING

	HABITAT	WHERE FOUND	Grasses	Herbs	Shrubs/Vines	Trees	Cacti	Animals	Other
					Plants				
Porcupines	(icons)	on or in trees; in rocky dens; near desert shrubs		leaves, stems, fruits		roots, leaves, seeds, acorns, twigs, inner bark, buds, berries, fruits, cones			

INSECT-EATING

	HABITAT	WHERE FOUND	Grasses	Herbs	Shrubs/Vines	Trees	Cacti	Animals	Other
Moles	(icons)	underground in loose soil		bulbs				insect larvae, spiders, worms, centipedes, millipedes	
Shrews *(illustrated above)*	(icons)	in other animals' nests; in large masses of plants; at the base of desert plants; under logs; near rocky places; on dry hillsides; in brushy areas		seeds, fruits		fruits, seeds, cones, nuts, roots		springtails, gypsy moths, moth and beetle larvae, grasshoppers, crickets, spiders, snails, slugs, centipedes, sow bugs, worms, mice, voles, salamanders, birds, small snakes, young rabbits	

RABBITS, HARES

	HABITAT	WHERE FOUND	Grasses	Herbs	Shrubs/Vines	Trees	Cacti	Animals	Other
Rabbits and Hares									
Cottontails *(illustrated above)*	(icons)	in forests and dense thickets; sitting in small, scratched-out areas among clumps of grass; in desert trees	leaves	stems, leaves	twigs, bark, buds	twigs, sapling buds, bark	pads		
Jackrabbits	(icons)	sitting in small, scratched-out places in shrubby areas; under desert shrubs	leaves	leaves, stems	leaves, twigs		pads		
Snowshoe Hares	(icons)	in small, scratched-out areas in thickets; near logs under trees; in hollow logs	leaves	leaves	leaves, buds, twigs, fruits	leaves, sapling twigs, bark			

HOOVED

	HABITAT	WHERE FOUND	Grasses	Herbs	Shrubs/Vines	Trees	Cacti	Animals	Other
Deer *(illustrated above)*	(icons)	near brushy edges of woods; in fields	leaves	leaves	leaves, twigs, buds	leaves, twigs, buds, bark, fallen fruits			mushrooms

KEY: ⚠ Caution Vacant Lots Lawns Fields Wooded Areas Deserts Grasslands (a) adult (l) larva / nymph

   Appendix A

FOOD SOURCES

MAMMALS *continued*

FLESH-EATING MAMMALS

	HABITAT	WHERE FOUND	Grasses	Herbs	Shrubs/Vines	Trees	Cacti	Animals	Other
Doglike Mammals									
Coyotes		in dens; along brushy edges of woods			berries	fallen fruits	fruits	snakes, frogs, grouse, mice, squirrels, rabbits, livestock	dead animals
Foxes		in brushy fields and dense, rocky woods; in dens; in trees			berries, fruits	fallen fruits		insects, scorpions, snakes, lizards, frogs, toads, ground birds and their eggs, mice, voles, shrews, skunks, rabbits, squirrels, porcupines, deer	
Raccoons *(illustrated above)* !		in trees; near trash; near streams, rivers, and lakes			berries, fruits	fruits		insects, slugs, snails, turtles, toads, frogs, salamanders, crayfish, eggs, muskrats, moles, mice, shrews, young rabbits	garbage
Skunks									
Spotted Skunks ⚠		in brushy or rocky areas; eating in trees; in hollow logs; in woodpiles		berries	berries, fruits	berries		beetles and their larvae, spiders, centipedes, millipedes, small snakes, lizards, birds, salamanders, eggs, crayfish, mice, rats, young rabbits	dead animals
Striped Skunks ⚠		in dens; on rock and brush piles; in hollow logs on sunny slopes; near trash; in grassy areas		berries	berries, fruits		fruits	crickets, grasshoppers, beetle larvae, moth larvae, spiders, centipedes, millipedes, turtles, eggs, snakes, frogs, toads, voles, mice, rats, chipmunks, moles	garbage

OTHER MAMMALS

	HABITAT	WHERE FOUND	Grasses	Herbs	Shrubs/Vines	Trees	Cacti	Animals	Other
Opossum *(illustrated above)*		in wooded areas; near city trash and brush piles		berries	fruits	acorns, fruits		insects, lizards, bird eggs, mice	garbage
Armadillos		in shrubby, open woods; in underground burrows					fruits	beetles, spiders, centipedes, millipedes, snakes, lizards, toads, salamanders, birds and their eggs	dead animals
Bats		in rocky outcrops; on building ledges; in hollow trees; hanging from tree branches		nectar, pollen	nectar, pollen	nectar, pollen	nectar, pollen	moths, crickets, ants, other insects	

KEY: Wooded Areas · Vacant Lots · Lawns · Fields · Deserts · Grasslands · ⚠ Caution · (a) adult · (l) larva / nymph

REFERENCES

Information presented within the *Who Eats What* guide was drawn from the following sources:

Benyus, J. 1989. *The Field Guide to Wildlife Habitats of the Eastern United States.* New York: Fireside/Simon & Schuster.

Benyus, J. 1989. *The Field Guide to Wildlife Habitats of the Western United States.* New York: Fireside/Simon & Schuster.

Brown, L. 1985. *The Audubon Society Nature Guide to Grasslands.* New York: Knopf.

Burt, W. 1964. *A Peterson Field Guide to the Mammals.* Boston: Houghton Mifflin.

Conant, R. 1958. *A Peterson Field Guide to Reptiles and Amphibians of Eastern and Central North America.* Boston: Houghton Mifflin.

Macmahon, J. 1992. *The Audubon Society Nature Guide to Deserts.* New York: Knopf.

Martin, A., Zim, H., & Nelson, A. 1989. *American Wildlife and Plants: A Guide to Wildlife Food Habits.* New York: Dover.

Murie, O. 1954. *A Peterson Field Guide to Animal Tracks.* Boston: Houghton Mifflin.

Stebbins, R. 1954. *Amphibians and Reptiles of Western North America.* New York: McGraw Hill.

Swan, L. & Papp, C. 1972. *The Common Insects of North America.* New York: Harper & Row.

MATERIALS

Materials

MATERIALS FOR ALL MODULES

Item (★ = consumable materials)	Quantity (for class of 30)	Distribution (group = 3-4 students)	Notes	Source
hand lenses	30	1 per student		SS
rulers, standard size	30	1 per student		OS
rulers, 15 cm size	10 - 12	1-2 per group		SS
cleanup supplies: broom, whisk broom, dustpan, paper towels, sponges, bucket for water				D, G
★ newsprint paper	1 pad		for making class lists	OS
blank photocopier transparencies			for making overheads	OS
assorted school materials: permanent and non-permanent markers, scissors, glue, masking tape, clear tape, graph paper, oak tag, art supplies				D, OS
resource books			see Resource Lists in module introductions	SS, library

KEY: D = Department Store   G = Grocery Store   GS = Garden Supply Store   H = Hardware Store   SS = Science Supply Catalog   O = Outdoors   OS = Office Supply Store

Appendix B

MATERIALS FOR MODULE 1

Item (★ = consumable materials)	Quantity (for class of 30)	Distribution (group = 3-4 students)	Notes	Source
tweezers	1 pair		for teacher demonstration	D, SS
★ match or lighter	1		for teacher demonstration	D, G
small cup	1		for teacher demonstration	D, G
pointed metal or wooden stakes	10	1 per group	each stake about 60 cm long	GS, H
metal rings	10	1 per group	should be large enough to slip over the stakes	H
laundry cord	25 meters	2.5meters per group		D, H
★ white flour	5 lb. bag	1 cup per group	distribute in a sandwich bag	G
shopping bags	10	1 per group	paper or plastic; used as carrying containers for field equipment	G
assorted habitat chambers: plastic salad takeout containers, wide-mouthed glass jars (20-30 cm high) with lids, glass or plastic terrariums, styrofoam coolers, plastic soda bottles	10	1 per group	type of chamber depends on type of animal to be contained	D, SS, restaurant supply store
spoons or trowels	10	1 per group		D, GS, H
assorted food items: peanuts, sugar, flour, beef jerky, potato chips, candy, vegetables, fruit, bread, oatmeal, apple juice, grass or leaves, an insect or other small critter	small amounts of each			G, O
assorted non-food items: salt, water, potting soil, sand, rock, metal, sugar-free vitamin pills, fertilizer	small amounts of each			D, GS, O
★ assorted animal foods: peanut butter, honey, seeds, nuts and grains (e.g., sunflower, millet, bulgur, shelled and unshelled peanuts, popcorn), tuna fish, jelly, sugar, molasses, fruit juice, mint and vanilla flavoring, liver, cheese, hot dogs, raisins, bread, suet	selection and amounts depend on which studies students do; see Lesson 1.4			G
★ assorted items for setting up feeding habits investigations: boxes, jars, funnels, cotton strips, jar lids, white cloth, index cards, aluminum foil, talcum powder, mineral oil, white vegetable shortening	materials needed depend on studies students do; see Lesson 1.4			D, G
★ 5" x 7" index cards	40	3-4 per group	or pieces of oak tag	D, OS
★ string or yarn	20 meters	2 meters per group	used to hang cards	D, H

KEY: D=Department Store   G=Grocery Store   GS=Garden Supply Store   H=Hardware Store   SS=Science Supply Catalog   O=Outdoors   OS=Office Supply Store

MATERIALS FOR MODULE 1 (continued)

Item (★ = consumable materials)	Quantity (for class of 30)	Distribution (group = 3-4 students)	Notes	Source
safety goggles	1 pair		for teacher demonstration	H, SS
9-oz. clear plastic cups	30	1 per student	plastic should be flexible, not rigid	D, G
plastic spoons	30	1 per student		D, G
★ cotton swabs	30	1 per student		D, G
3" x 5" index cards	30	1 per student		D, OS
items to observe: small stones, dead leaves, pine cones, twigs, or pieces of fruit	15	1 per pair		G, O

OPTIONAL MATERIALS FOR MODULE 1

Item (★ = consumable materials)	Quantity (for class of 30)	Distribution (group = 3-4 students)	Notes	Source
trays lined with white paper	10	1 per group		D, G
whistle	1		for teacher	D
metal soupspoons	10	1 per group		D
compass	1		for teacher	D, SS
sweep nets	5-10	1 per group	commercial or homemade (broom handle, coat hanger, and nylon stocking)	SS
buttons or beans	20-30		two colors	D, G
★ self-stick removable notes	20 packs	2 packs per group	in two colors, for food webs	D, OS
video or Polaroid camera	1		to document study site	D

KEY: D=Department Store   G=Grocery Store   GS=Garden Supply Store   H=Hardware Store   SS=Science Supply Store   O=Outdoors   OS=Office Supply Store

Materials

MATERIALS FOR MODULE 2

Item (★ = consumable materials)	Quantity (for class of 30)	Distribution (group = 3-4 students)	Notes	Source
★ Jello	1-2 3-oz. boxes		lemon, lime, or orange flavors work well	G
bowl	1			D
spoon	1			D
measuring cup	1			D, G
paper grocery bag of dead leaves	1		fill bag about one third to half full with leaves, grass clippings, twigs	O
plastic animal cage with cover	1 2.5 gallon (30 x 15 x 17cm)		or a similar clear plastic container to use as a decomposition chamber	SS, pet store
★ clear plastic bag	1		should be large enough to line the decomposition chamber	D, G, H
★ alfalfa hay	1 24-oz. mini-bale	6 cups per chamber		GS, pet store
★ hardwood shavings	1 24-oz. bag	6 cups per chamber	hardwood animal bedding can be used	SS, carpentry shop, pet store
★ materials to vary conditions for growing microbes: soil, decomposing leaves, water, mushrooms, freezer packs, non-electric heating pads, black construction paper, compost starter	types and amounts depend on studies students do			D, GS, O, OS
miscellaneous containers: plastic cups, trays			used for carrying water and compost	D, G
★ plastic bags	3-4		to compare with biodegradeable plastic bags	G
★ biodegradable plastic bags	3-4	1 13 x 20 cm piece per group	do not use photodegradeable bags	G, H
pushpin	1		for teacher	OS
★ soil	1 large bag	3-5 cups per group	outdoor soil or potting soil plus small amount of outdoor soil	GS, O
watering device	1		watering can with sprinkler head, spray bottle, or homemade (punch holes in soda bottle cap)	D, GS, H
2-liter plastic soda bottles	11	1 per group	use one for demonstration	collect from students

KEY: D=Department Store   G=Grocery Store   GS=Garden Supply Store   H=Hardware Store   SS=Science Supply Catalog   O=Outdoors   OS=Office Supply Store

MATERIALS FOR MODULE 2 *(continued)*

Item (★ = consumable materials)	Quantity *(for class of 30)*	Distribution *(group = 3-4 students)*	Notes	Source
cup	10	1 per group	for scooping soil	D, G, H
★ sandwich-size ziplock baggies of moldy squash or pumpkin	15	1 per pair		G
★ sandwich-size ziplock baggies	90	6 per pair		G
plastic petri dishes	45	3 per pair	or other clear containers with flat bottoms and covers	D, SS
assorted measuring tools: a balance, dropping pipettes, measuring cups, thermometers, microscope				H, SS

OPTIONAL MATERIALS FOR MODULE 2

Item (★ = consumable materials)	Quantity *(for class of 30)*	Distribution *(group = 3-4 students)*	Notes	Source
plastic gloves	1 pair		for teacher	D, G

KEY: D=Department Store   G=Grocery Store   GS=Garden Supply Store   H=Hardware Store   SS=Science Supply Catalog   O=Outdoors   OS=Office Supply Store

MATERIALS FOR MODULE 3

Item (★ = consumable materials)	Quantity (for class of 30)	Distribution (group = 3-4 students)	Notes	Source
large bucket or dishpan	1			D, H
measuring cups	3		or 8-oz. plastic cups	D, G
★ compost	4 cups		prepared in decomposition chamber during Module 2	
★ cheesecloth	1 package		use culinary grade	G
rubber band	1			D, OS
6-oz. clear plastic cups	240	24 per group	plastic should be flexible, not rigid	D, G
pushpins	10	1 per group		OS
★ vermiculite	2.5 cubic feet	9 cups per group	use face mask when measuring	GS, H
1-gallon plastic bag	10	1 per group		G, H
★ radish seeds	240	24 per group		GS, SS
mini paper cups	10	1 per group		D, G
pot labels	120	12 per group	or use craft (popsicle) sticks	GS, school art supply
plastic dropping pipettes	20	2 per group		SS
8- or 9-oz. plastic cups	20	2 per group		D, G
trays lined with white paper	10	1 per group	use cookie sheet, foil pan, dishpan	D, G
trowels	10	1 per group	or large metal spoons	D, GS
assorted materials for making advertisements: magazines, stencils, tape recorder, costumes			also use art supplies	D, school art supply, collect from students
★ large beans	60	2 per student		G
small clear bags or containers of poor soil	10	1 per group	use sand or clay	GS, H
small clear bags or containers of good soil	10	1 per group	use potting or garden soil	GS, H, O
houseplant	1			

KEY: D=Department Store   G=Grocery Store   GS=Garden Supply Store   H=Hardware Store   SS=Science Supply Catalog   O=Outdoors   OS=Office Supply Store

OPTIONAL MATERIALS FOR MODULE 3

Item (★ = consumable materials)	Quantity (for class of 30)	Distribution (group = 3-4 students)	Notes	Source
water dispenser	1		or use a bucket	G, SS
★ distilled water	3-4 gallons		use only if tapwater is high in nitrogen	D, G
★ assorted containers: paper cups, milk cartons, margarine tubs	10	1 per group	for planting thinned seedlings	D, G
★ potting soil	30 lb. bag	6 cups per group	for planting thinned seedlings	GS
★ 8-oz. paper cups	120	3-4 per student	for taking plants home	D, G
sample cards of paint chips in shades of green	10	1 per group		paint supply store
rigid plastic ½" pipe	10 50-cm pieces	1 per group		H

KEY: D=Department Store   G=Grocery Store   GS=Garden Supply Store   H=Hardware Store   SS=Science Supply Catalog   O=Outdoors   OS=Office Supply Store

Vocabulary

ABIOTIC—Something that was never alive (water, rocks); the physical environment.

BACTERIA—Living things that have only one cell, and are so small that they can be seen only with a microscope.

BIODEGRADABLE—The ability to be broken down by being consumed by living things.

BIODIVERSITY—The variety of different kinds of living things in an area.

BIOTIC—Something that is alive, or used to be alive.

CALORIE—A unit for measuring the amount of energy that food supplies to the body.

CARNIVORE—An animal that eats meat.

COMPETITION—The interaction of two or more organisms seeking a limited resource that they both need.

COMPOST—Decayed plants, usually used for improving garden soil.

CONSUMER—An animal or microbe that gets food by eating things.

CONTROL—The unchanged item or group in an experiment.

COTYLEDONS—Seed leaves; the leaves of the embryo in a seed.

CULTURE—To grow living things in a prepared substance.

DECOMPOSER—An animal or microbe that uses dead plants and animals as food.

DECOMPOSITION—The breaking down of dead things into their basic materials by decomposers that use them as food.

ECOLOGIST—A scientist who studies how living things interact with each other and their physical environment.

ECOSYSTEM—An area where living things interact with each other and their physical environment.

EMBRYO—The early stage of development of an organism.

ENERGY—The ability to make things move or change.

ENGINEER—A person who uses scientific knowledge to make products and solve problems for people.

ENVIRONMENTAL IMPACT STATEMENT—A scientific report predicting how proposed changes to a site will affect its ecosystem.

FAIR TEST—An experiment in which everything is kept the same except for the one condition being tested.

FIBROUS ROOTS—Fine roots that branch out in all directions with no central main root.

FIELD—Scientists' name for the outdoors.

FOOD—A substance that gives both nutrients and energy to a living thing.

FOOD CHAIN—A diagram that shows the flow of food from producers to all types of consumers. The original food source for all organisms in a food chain can be traced to plants.

FOOD WEB—The connections among everything organisms in a location eat and are eaten by.

FUNGUS—An organism that uses other living or dead organisms as food by secreting chemicals that break it down, and then absorbing the substances into its cells.

GERMINATE—To sprout; to begin to grow.

HABITAT—The place where an organism lives that provides all of its needs for survival.

HERBIVORE—An animal that eats plants.

HYPHAE—Threadlike, food-absorbing strands of a fungus.

HYPOTHESIS—A statement that can be tested. It often states an action as well as a predicted result (e.g., "If I do such-and-such, then such-and-such will happen").

LEAF LITTER—A layer of dead leaves on the ground.

MEDIUM—A substance in which an organism lives.

MICROBE—A living thing (or "microorganism") whose individuals are too small to see with the naked eye. Fungi and bacteria are two kinds of microbes.

MOLD—A fungus that produces a fuzzy growth.

NUTRIENT—A substance that does not provide energy, but supplies minerals that living things need to stay healthy.

NUTRIENT CYCLE—The transfer of nutrients back and forth between living things and the non-living environment (soil, water, and air).

OMNIVORE—An animal that eats both plants and animals.

ORGANISM—A living thing (plant, animal, or microbe).

PEER REVIEW—Scientists' process of reviewing each other's work to make sure their methods and conclusions are as valid as possible.

PHOTOSYNTHESIS—The process by which plants make sugars in their leaves.

PHYSICAL ENVIRONMENT—The non-living surroundings (air, water, rocks, soil) and conditions (light, heat, wind) that something lives in.

PLANT COMMUNITY—The group of different kinds of plants growing in the same area.

POPULATION—A group of the same kind of organism living in the same place.

PREDATOR—An animal that kills and eats other animals.

PREY—An animal that is eaten by other animals.

PRODUCER—A green plant that makes sugar for food using the process of photosynthesis.

REPLICATES—Identical copies of an experiment.

SEED COAT—Tough outer layer of a seed that protects the embryo.

SEEDLING—A plant in its first stages of growth.

SHRUB—A low-growing woody plant that usually has many stems.

SPECS—Short for "specifications" that provide design details.

SPORES—Structures that can grow into new individuals, and can often survive harsh conditions.

STUDY PLOT—A small piece of land used for observations.

TAPROOT—A central root that grows downward and has smaller roots extending outward from it.

TREATMENT—The item or group that has been manipulated in an experiment.

VARIABLE—Something that is changed in a fair test (controlled experiment).